Say I Love You.

8

P9-AFD-593

by
Kanae
Hazuki

Kanae Hazuki
presents

Chapter 29

Chapter 30

Chapter 31

Chapter 32

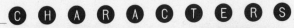

CHARACTERS

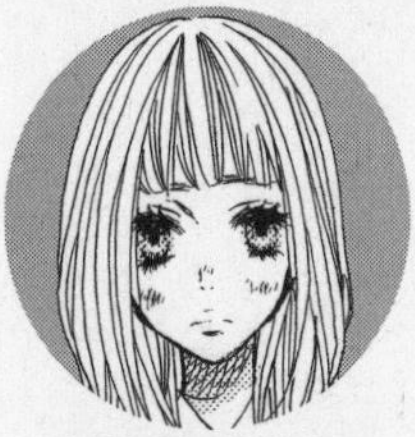

Mei Tachibana

A girl who hasn't had a single friend, let alone a boyfriend, in sixteen years, and has lived her life trusting no one. She finds herself attracted to Yamato, who, for some reason, just won't leave her alone, and they start dating.

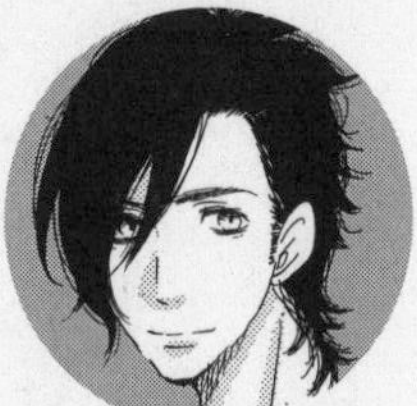

Yamato Kurosawa

The most popular boy at Mei's school. He has the love of many girls, yet for some reason, he is obsessed with Mei, the brooding weirdo girl from another class.

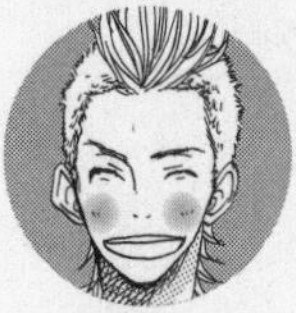

Kai

Yamato's classmate from middle school who had been the victim of bullying. For his own reasons, he started high school a year late. He likes Mei and told her so, but...?

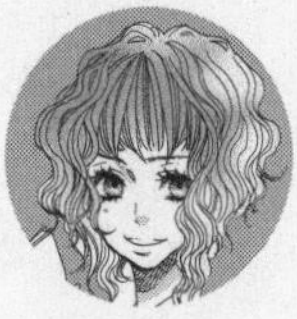

Megumi

An amateur model who has her sights set on Yamato. She transferred to his school and got him a modeling job, and the two gradually grew closer. She was plotting to pull Mei and Yamato apart, but...?

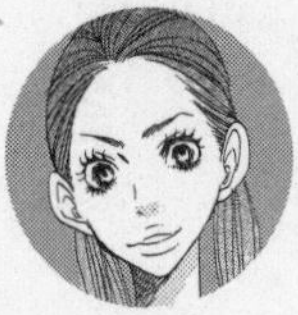

Aiko

She likes Yamato and was jealous of Mei, but now that she has seen Mei trying so hard to confront her own insecurities, she has decided to cheer her on. They were put in the same class in their second year of high school.

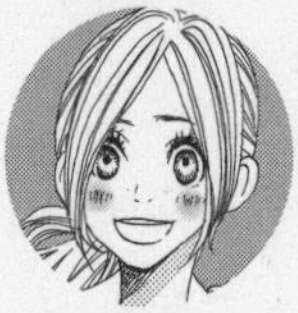

Asami

A girl who treats Mei as a real friend. She had a thing for Yamato, but now she is dating his friend Nakanishi. She and Mei were put in different classes in their second year of high school.

STORY

Mei Tachibana spent sixteen years without a single friend or boyfriend, but then, for some reason, Yamato Kurosawa, the most popular boy in school, took a liking to her. Mei was drawn in by Yamato's kindness and sincerity, and they started dating. Gradually, she realized that she was in love. After dating for a year, they celebrated their anniversary by going on an overnight trip during summer break. They didn't do what most people might expect that night, but the bond between them grew deeper. Meanwhile, Megumi, the amateur model who had her sights set on Yamato, was facing ostracism at school and work, but with some help from Yamato and her best friend, she bade farewell to her past self. She has started to walk a new path, but...?

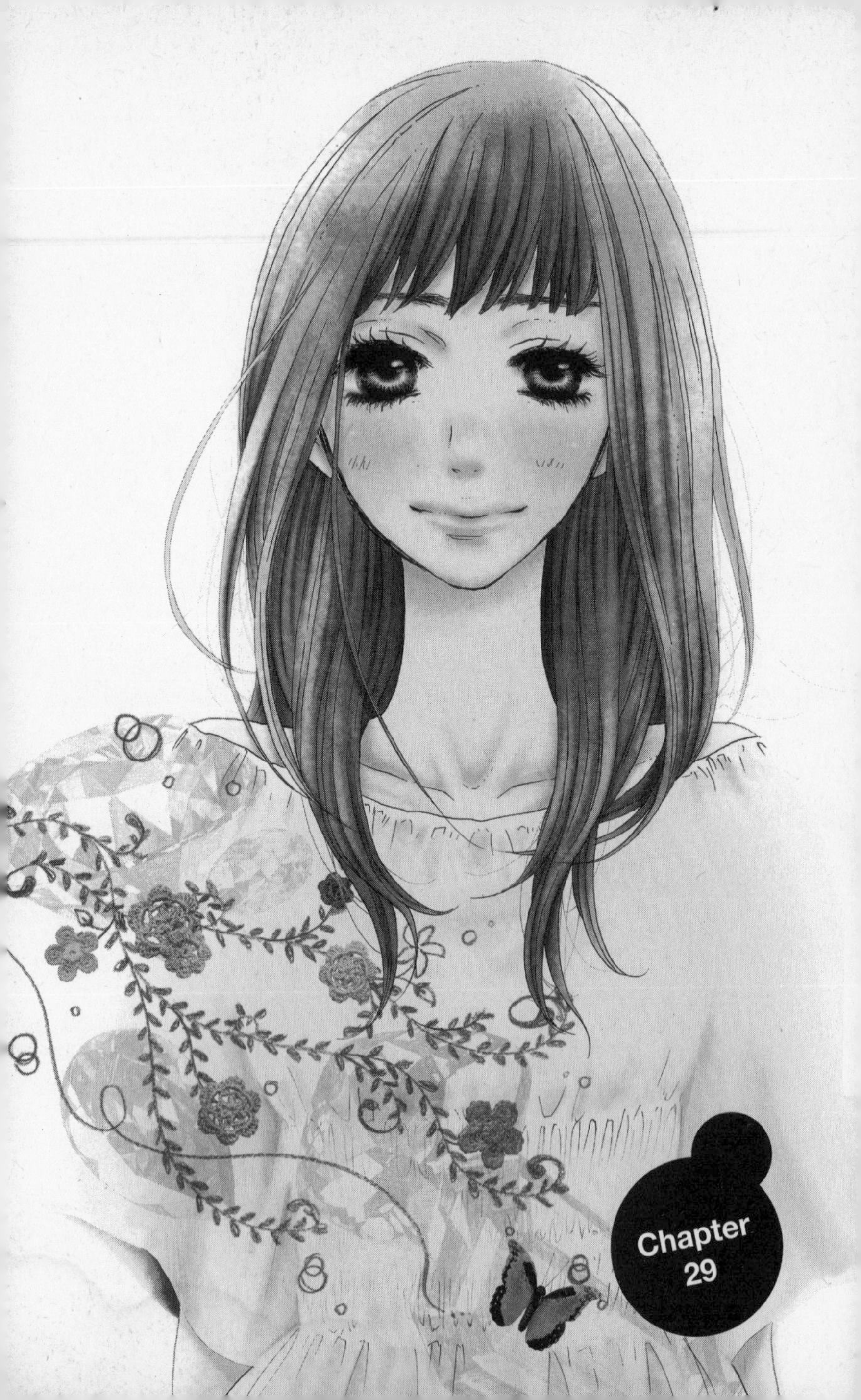
Chapter
29

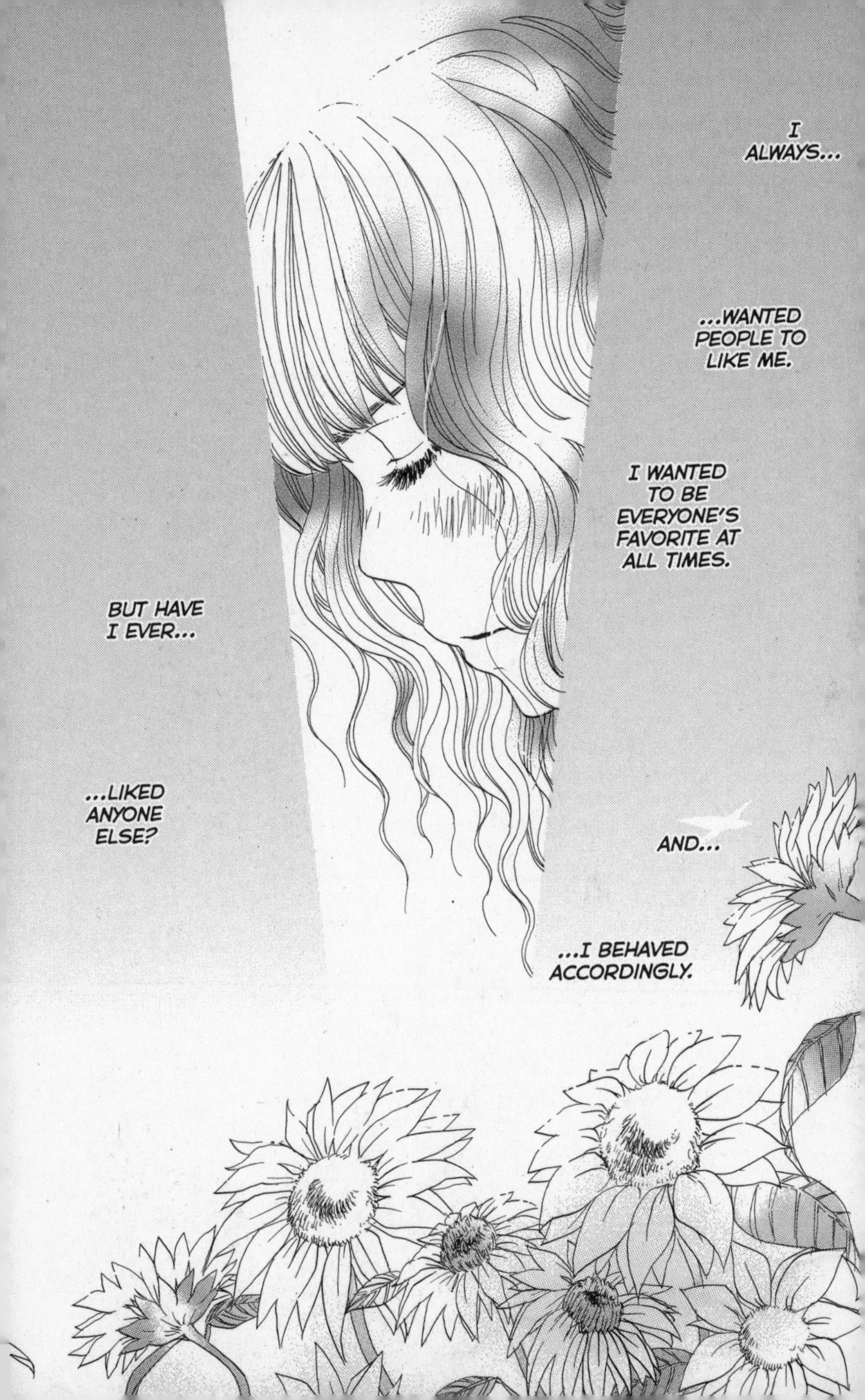
I ALWAYS...
...WANTED PEOPLE TO LIKE ME.
I WANTED TO BE EVERYONE'S FAVORITE AT ALL TIMES.
AND...
...I BEHAVED ACCORDINGLY.
BUT HAVE I EVER...
...LIKED ANYONE ELSE?

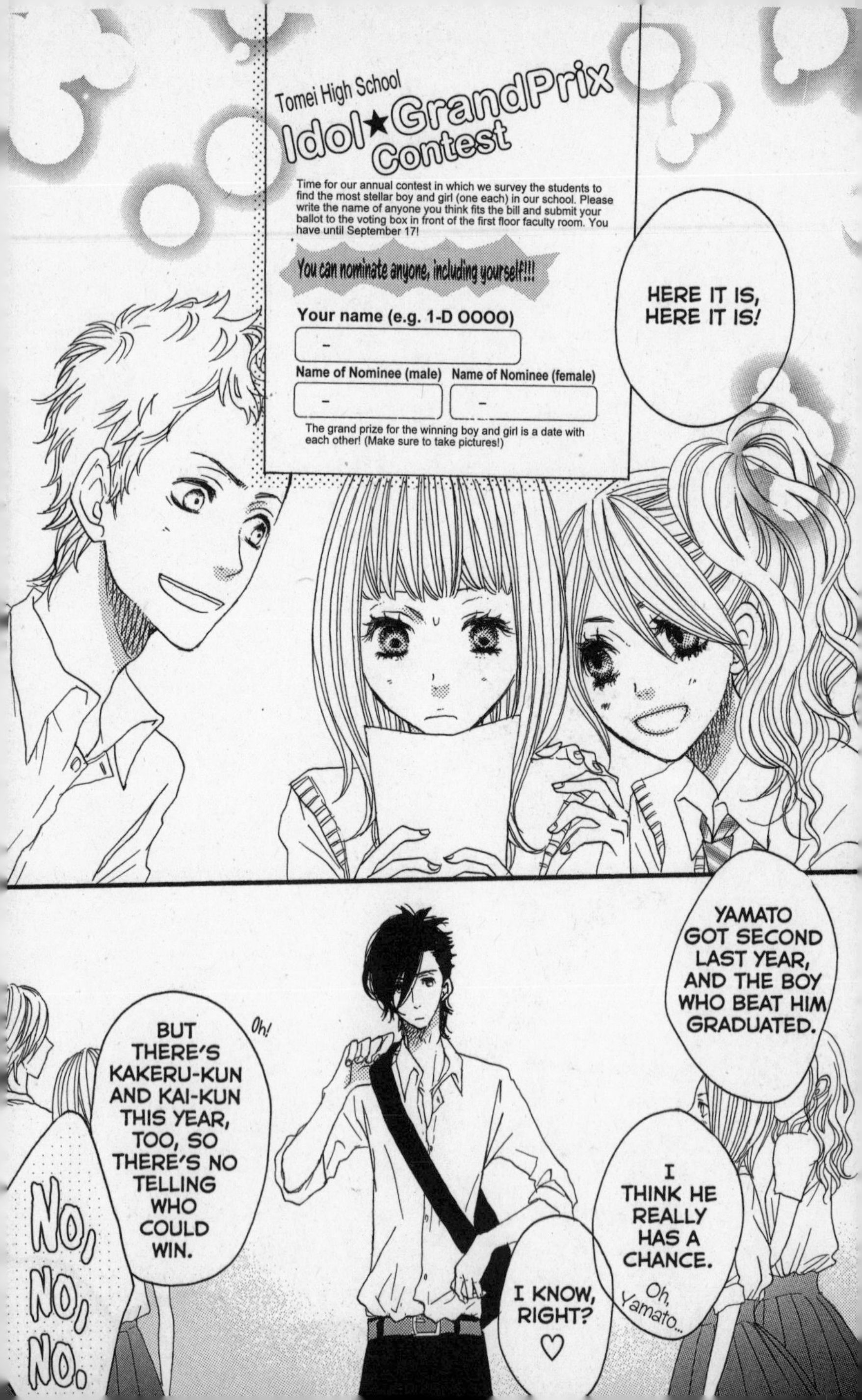
Tomei High School
Idol★GrandPrix Contest
Time for our annual contest in which we survey the students to find the most stellar boy and girl (one each) in our school. Please write the name of anyone you think fits the bill and submit your ballot to the voting box in front of the first floor faculty room. You have until September 17!
You can nominate anyone, including yourself!!!
Your name (e.g. 1-D OOOO)
Name of Nominee (male)
Name of Nominee (female)
The grand prize for the winning boy and girl is a date with each other! (Make sure to take pictures!)
HERE IT IS, HERE IT IS!
YAMATO GOT SECOND LAST YEAR, AND THE BOY WHO BEAT HIM GRADUATED.
I THINK HE REALLY HAS A CHANCE.
Oh, Yamato...
I KNOW, RIGHT? ♡
Oh!
BUT THERE'S KAKERU-KUN AND KAI-KUN THIS YEAR, TOO, SO THERE'S NO TELLING WHO COULD WIN.
NO, NO, NO.

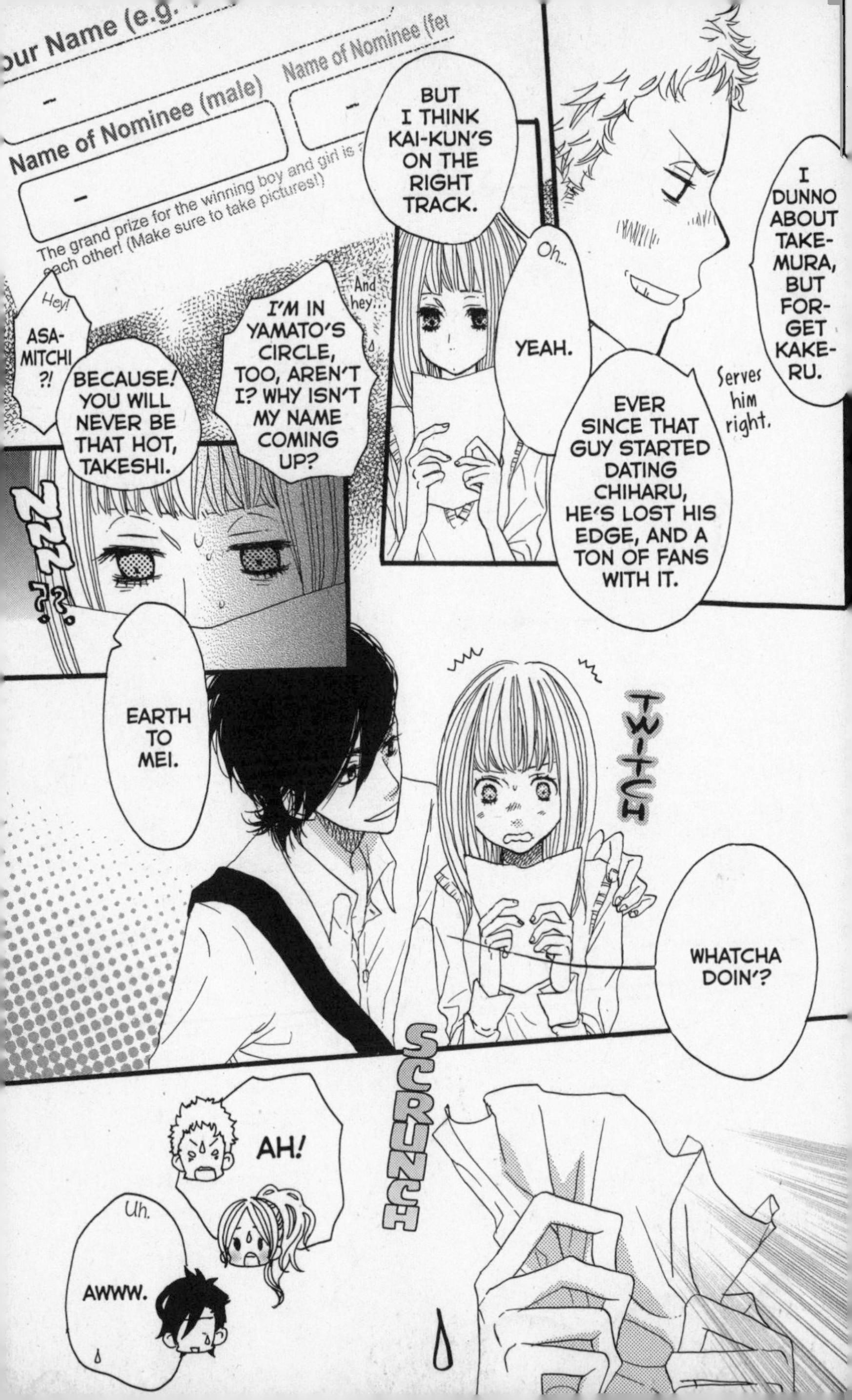
I DUNNO ABOUT TAKE-MURA, BUT FOR-GET KAKE-RU.
Serves him right.
EVER SINCE THAT GUY STARTED DATING CHIHARU, HE'S LOST HIS EDGE, AND A TON OF FANS WITH IT.
Oh...
YEAH.
BUT I THINK KAI-KUN'S ON THE RIGHT TRACK.
our Name (e.g.
Name of Nominee (fe
Name of Nominee (male)
The grand prize for the winning boy and girl is a
each other! (Make sure to take pictures!)
And hey...
I'M IN YAMATO'S CIRCLE, TOO, AREN'T I? WHY ISN'T MY NAME COMING UP?
Hey!
ASA-MITCHI?!
BECAUSE! YOU WILL NEVER BE THAT HOT, TAKESHI.
ZZZ ??
WHATCHA DOIN'?
TWITCH
EARTH TO MEI.
SCRUNCH
AH!
Uh.
AWWW.

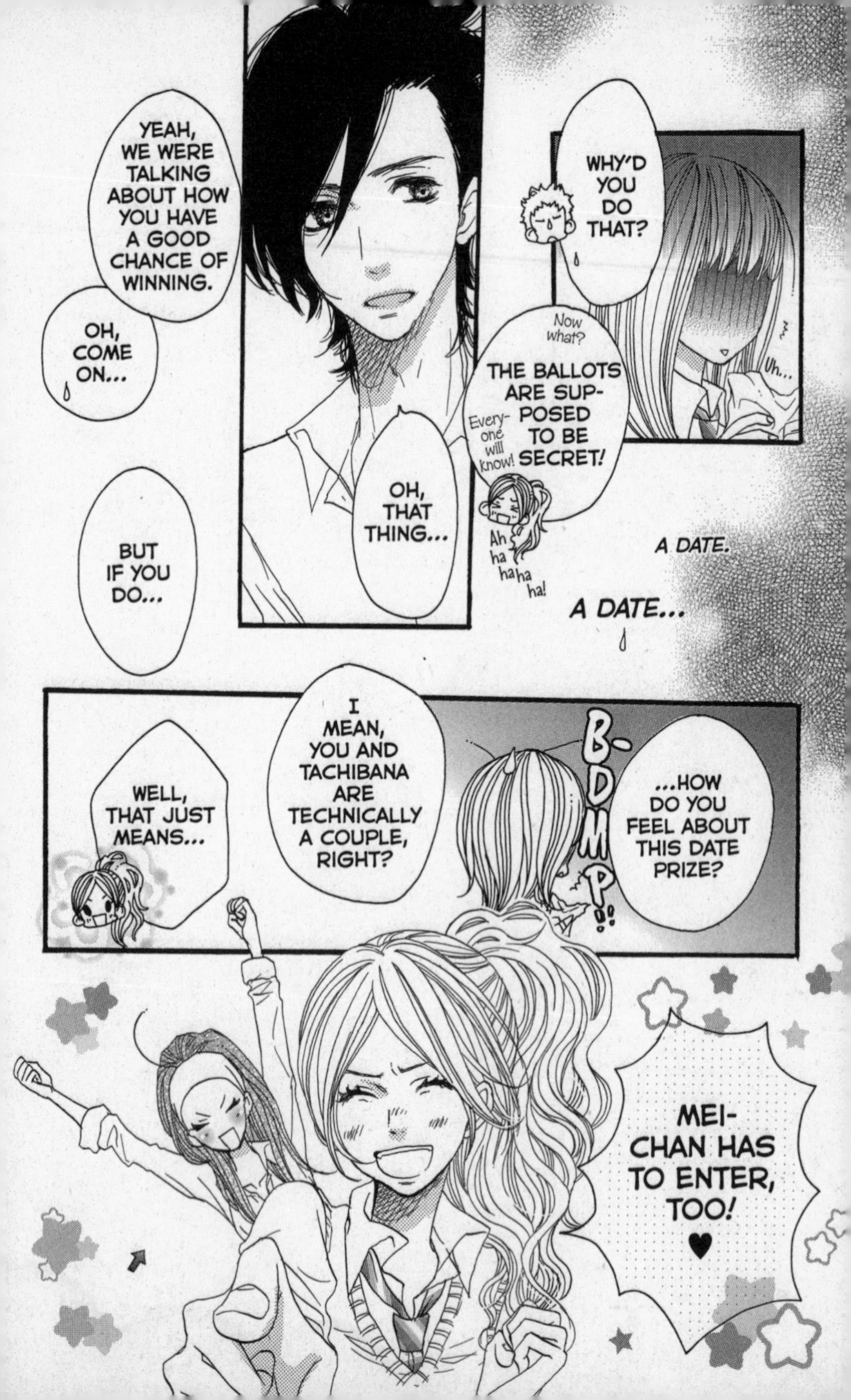
WHY'D YOU DO THAT?
Uh...
Now what?
THE BALLOTS ARE SUP-POSED TO BE SECRET!
Every-one will know!
Ah ha ha ha ha!
A DATE.
A DATE...
OH, THAT THING...
YEAH, WE WERE TALKING ABOUT HOW YOU HAVE A GOOD CHANCE OF WINNING.
OH, COME ON...
BUT IF YOU DO...
...HOW DO YOU FEEL ABOUT THIS DATE PRIZE?
B-DMP!!
I MEAN, YOU AND TACHIBANA ARE TECHNICALLY A COUPLE, RIGHT?
WELL, THAT JUST MEANS...
MEI-CHAN HAS TO ENTER, TOO! ♥

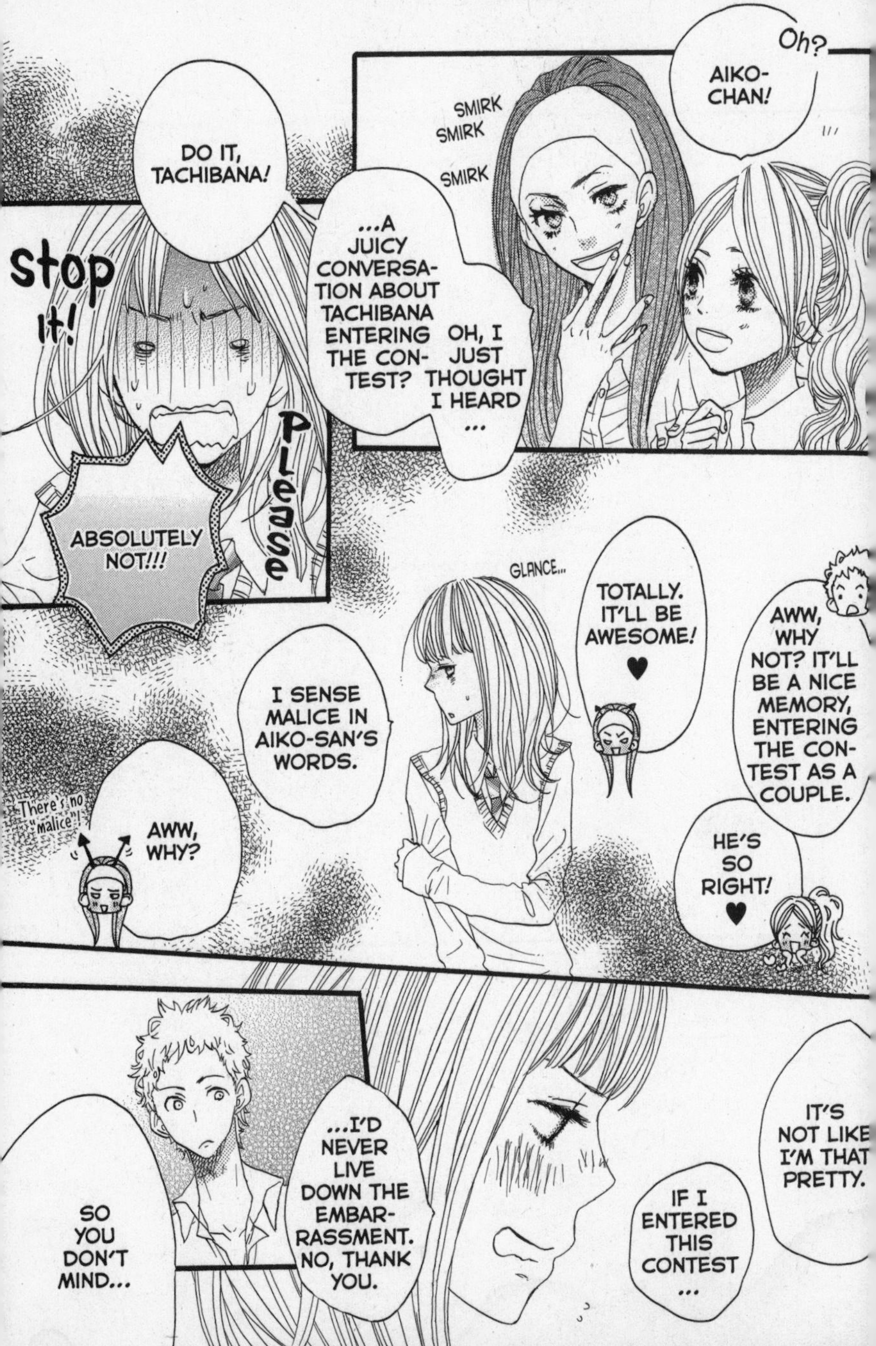
Oh?
AIKO-CHAN!
SMIRK SMIRK SMIRK
OH, I JUST THOUGHT I HEARD ...
...A JUICY CONVERSATION ABOUT TACHIBANA ENTERING THE CONTEST?
DO IT, TACHIBANA!
Stop it!
Please
ABSOLUTELY NOT!!!
AWW, WHY NOT? IT'LL BE A NICE MEMORY, ENTERING THE CONTEST AS A COUPLE.
HE'S SO RIGHT! ♥
TOTALLY. IT'LL BE AWESOME! ♥
GLANCE...
I SENSE MALICE IN AIKO-SAN'S WORDS.
AWW, WHY?
There's no malice!
IT'S NOT LIKE I'M THAT PRETTY.
IF I ENTERED THIS CONTEST ...
...I'D NEVER LIVE DOWN THE EMBARRASSMENT. NO, THANK YOU.
SO YOU DON'T MIND...

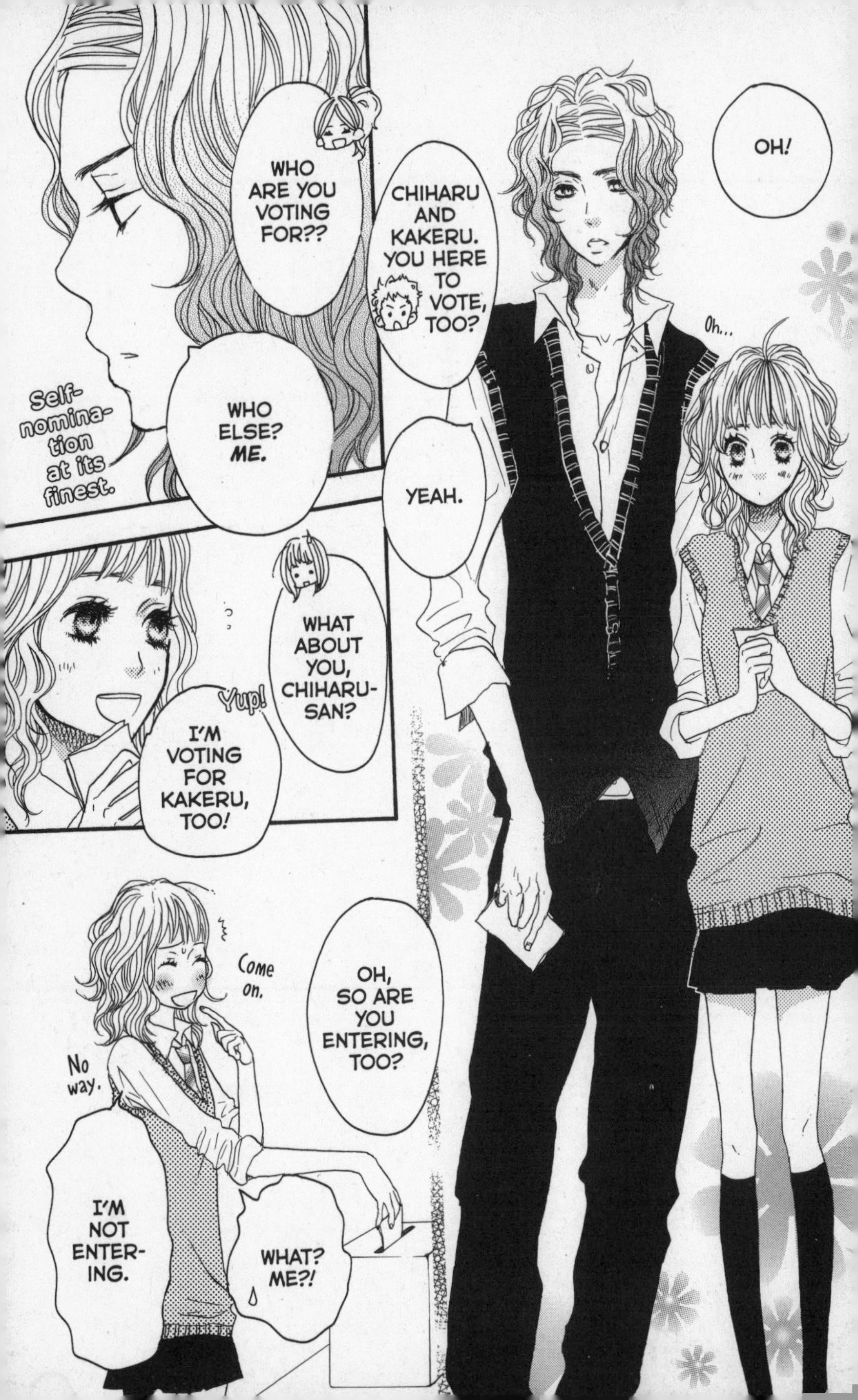
OH!
Oh...
CHIHARU AND KAKERU. YOU HERE TO VOTE, TOO?
YEAH.
OH, SO ARE YOU ENTERING, TOO?
WHO ARE YOU VOTING FOR??
WHO ELSE? ME.
Self-nomination at its finest.
WHAT ABOUT YOU, CHIHARU-SAN?
Yup!
I'M VOTING FOR KAKERU, TOO!
Come on.
WHAT? ME?!
No way.
I'M NOT ENTERING.

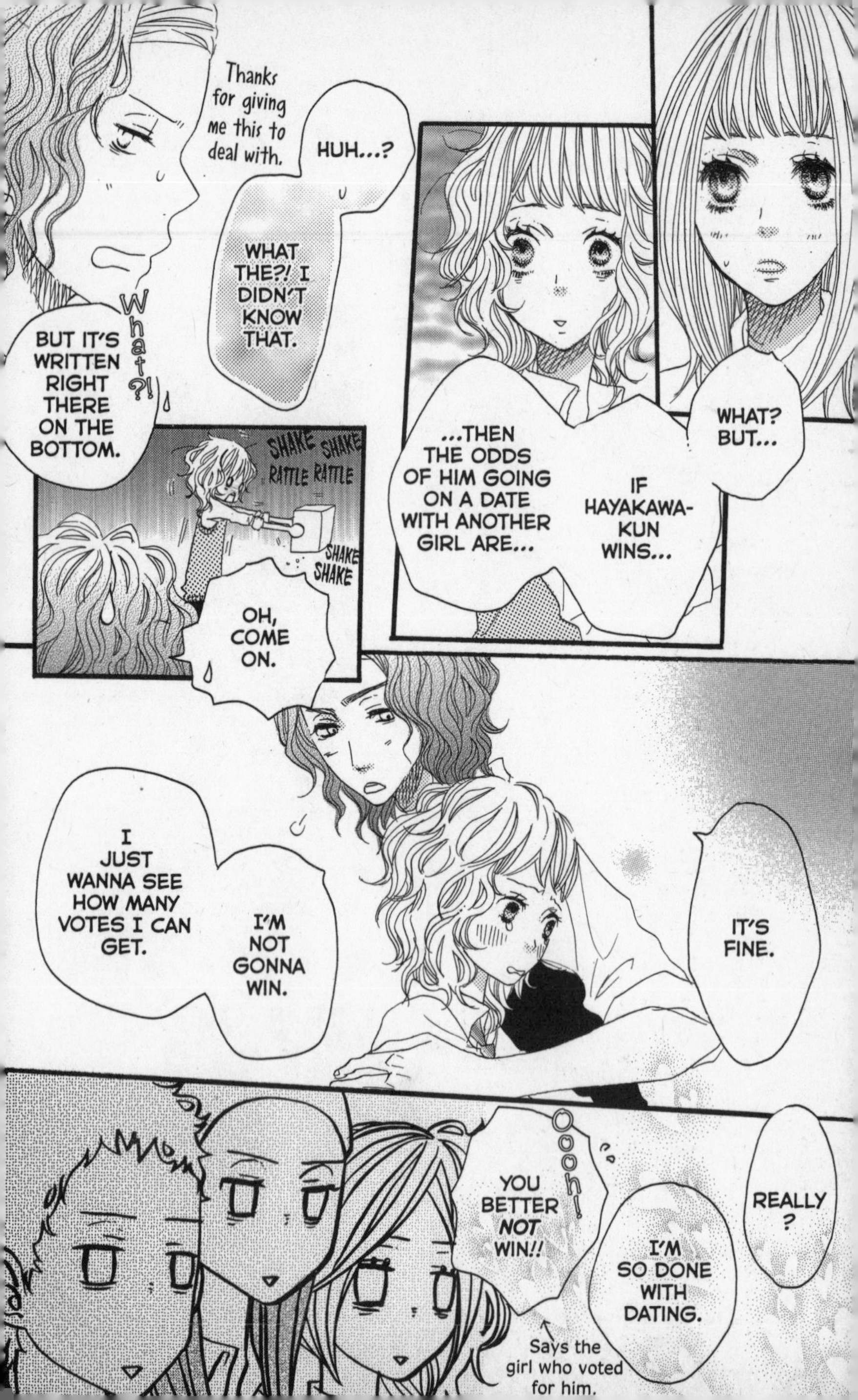
WHAT? BUT...
IF HAYAKAWA-KUN WINS...
...THEN THE ODDS OF HIM GOING ON A DATE WITH ANOTHER GIRL ARE...
Thanks for giving me this to deal with.
HUH...?
WHAT THE?! I DIDN'T KNOW THAT.
What?!
BUT IT'S WRITTEN RIGHT THERE ON THE BOTTOM.
SHAKE SHAKE
RATTLE RATTLE
SHAKE SHAKE
OH, COME ON.
IT'S FINE.
I'M NOT GONNA WIN.
I JUST WANNA SEE HOW MANY VOTES I CAN GET.
REALLY?
I'M SO DONE WITH DATING.
Oooh!
YOU BETTER NOT WIN!!
Says the girl who voted for him.

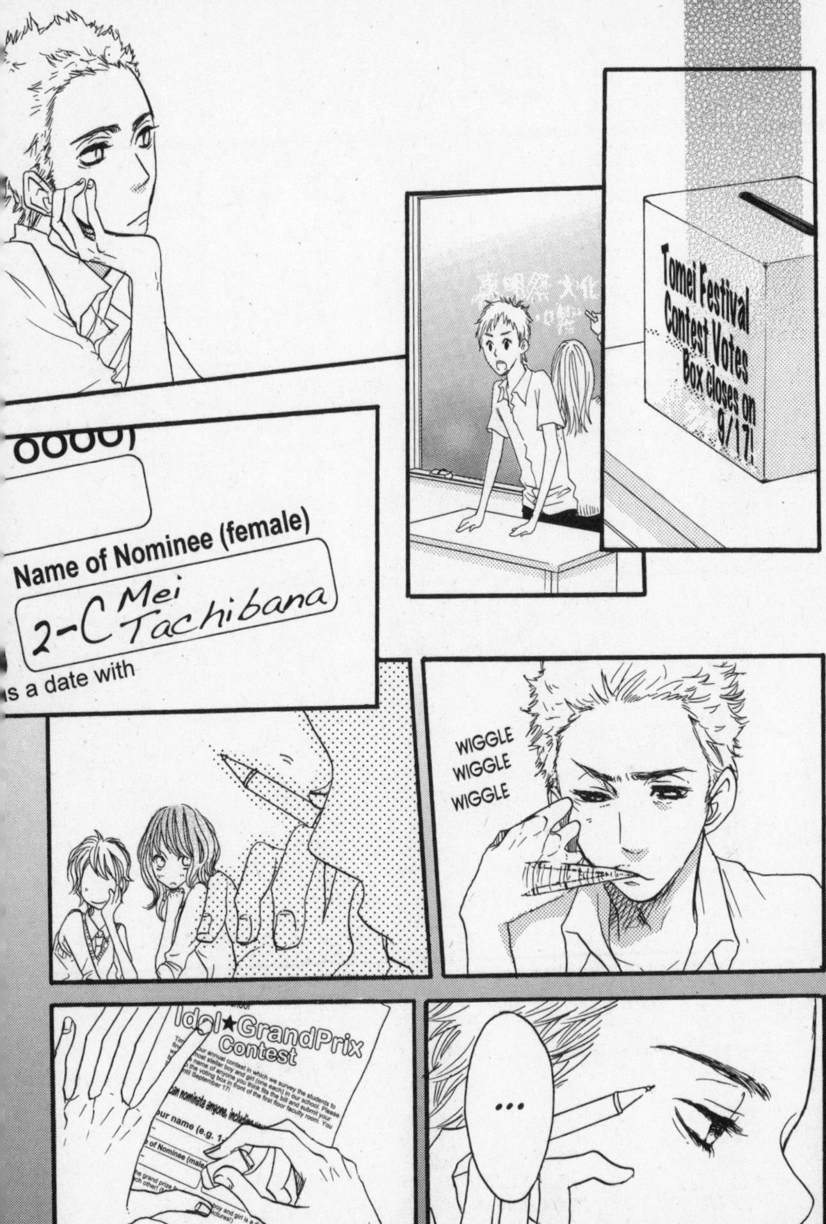
Tomei Festival Contest Votes
Box closes on 9/17!
Name of Nominee (female)
2-C Mei Tachibana
s a date with
WIGGLE WIGGLE WIGGLE
...
Idol★GrandPrix Contest
of Nominee (male)

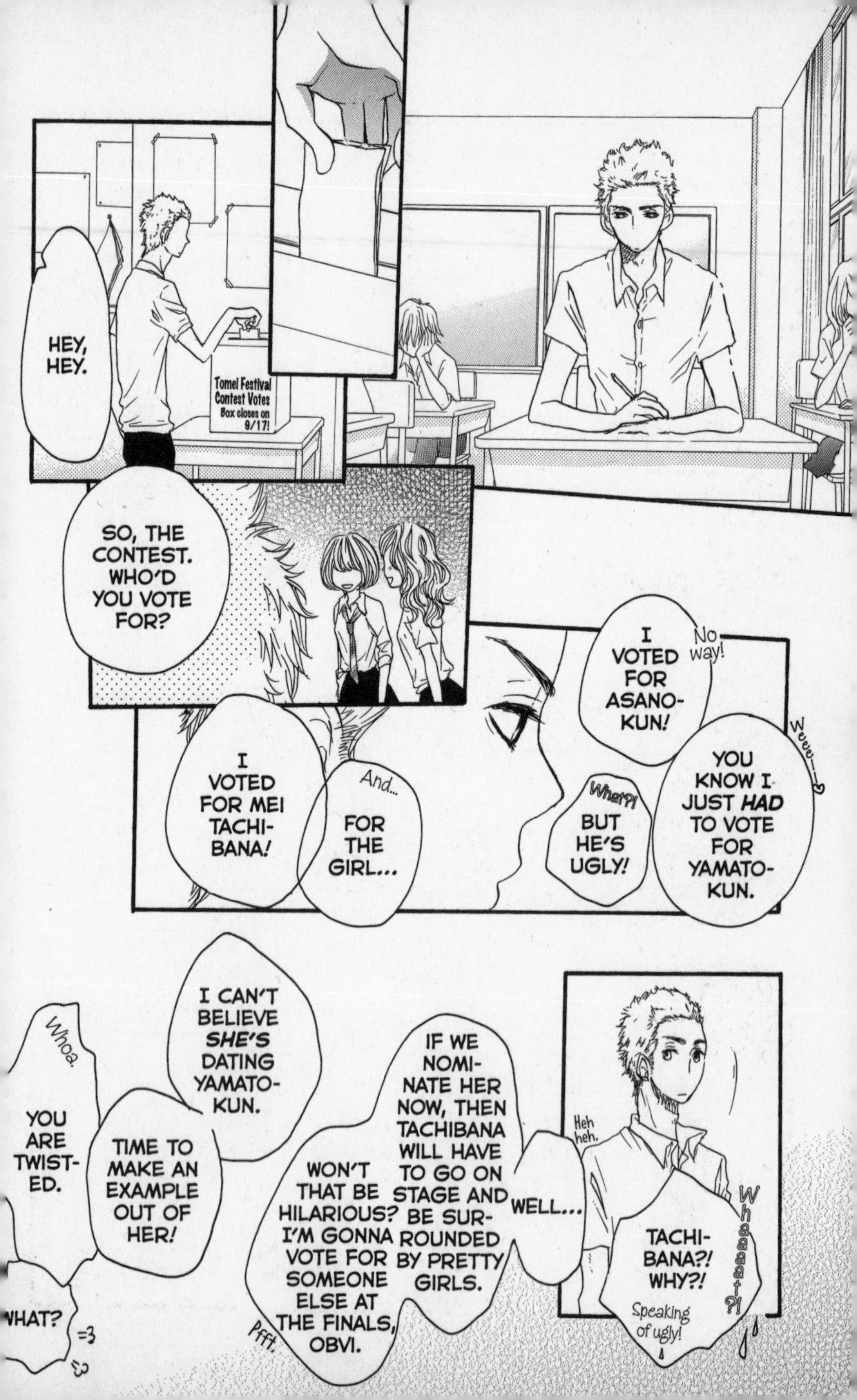

Tomei Festival Contest Votes Box closes on 9/17!
HEY, HEY.
SO, THE CONTEST. WHO'D YOU VOTE FOR?
I VOTED FOR ASANO-KUN!
No way!
YOU KNOW I JUST *HAD* TO VOTE FOR YAMATO-KUN.
Weee—♥
What?!
BUT HE'S UGLY!
And...
FOR THE GIRL...
I VOTED FOR MEI TACHIBANA!
TACHIBANA?! WHY?!
Whaaaat?!
Speaking of ugly!
Heh heh.
WELL...
IF WE NOMINATE HER NOW, THEN TACHIBANA WILL HAVE TO GO ON STAGE AND BE SURROUNDED BY PRETTY GIRLS.
WON'T THAT BE HILARIOUS? I'M GONNA VOTE FOR SOMEONE ELSE AT THE FINALS, OBVI.
Pfft.
I CAN'T BELIEVE *SHE'S* DATING YAMATO-KUN.
TIME TO MAKE AN EXAMPLE OUT OF HER!
YOU ARE TWISTED.
Whoa.
WHAT?
=3

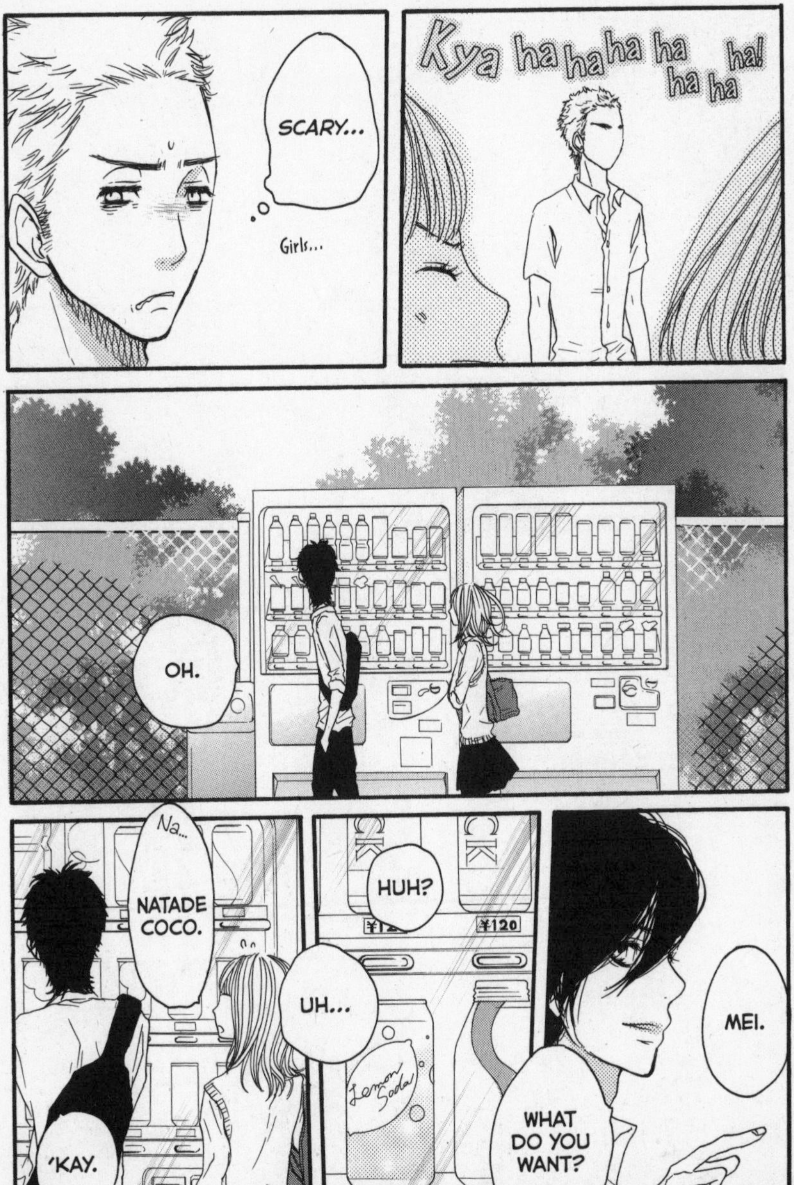

Kya ha ha ha ha ha ha ha!
SCARY...
Girls...
OH.
MEI.
WHAT DO YOU WANT?
HUH?
UH...
Lemon Soda
¥120
Na...
NATADE COCO.
'KAY.

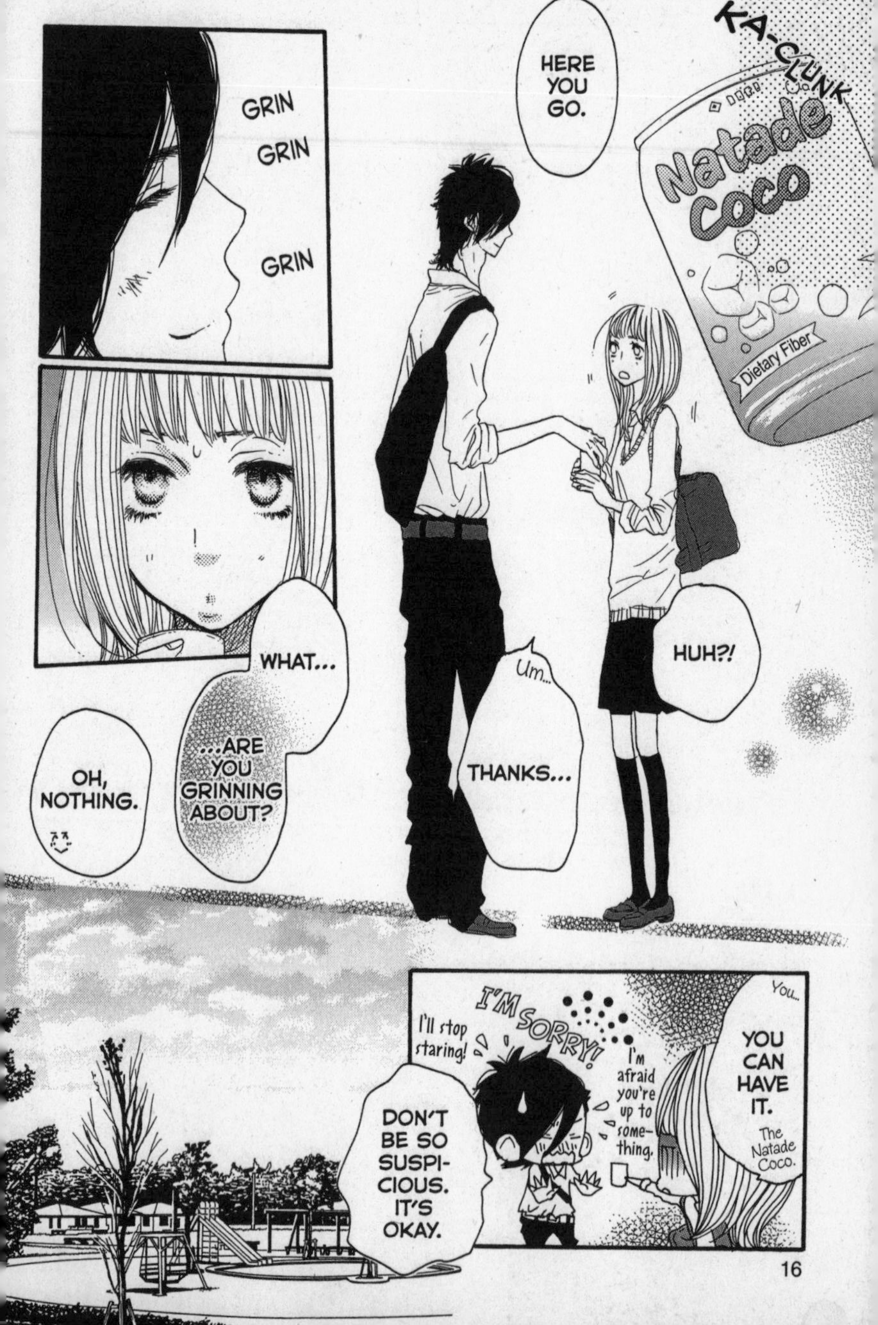
KA-CLUNK
Natade Coco
Dietary Fiber
HERE YOU GO.
HUH?!
Um...
THANKS...
GRIN
GRIN
GRIN
WHAT...
...ARE YOU GRINNING ABOUT?
OH, NOTHING.
You...
YOU CAN HAVE IT.
The Natade Coco.
I'm afraid you're up to some-thing.
I'M SORRY!
I'll stop staring!
DON'T BE SO SUSPICIOUS. IT'S OKAY.

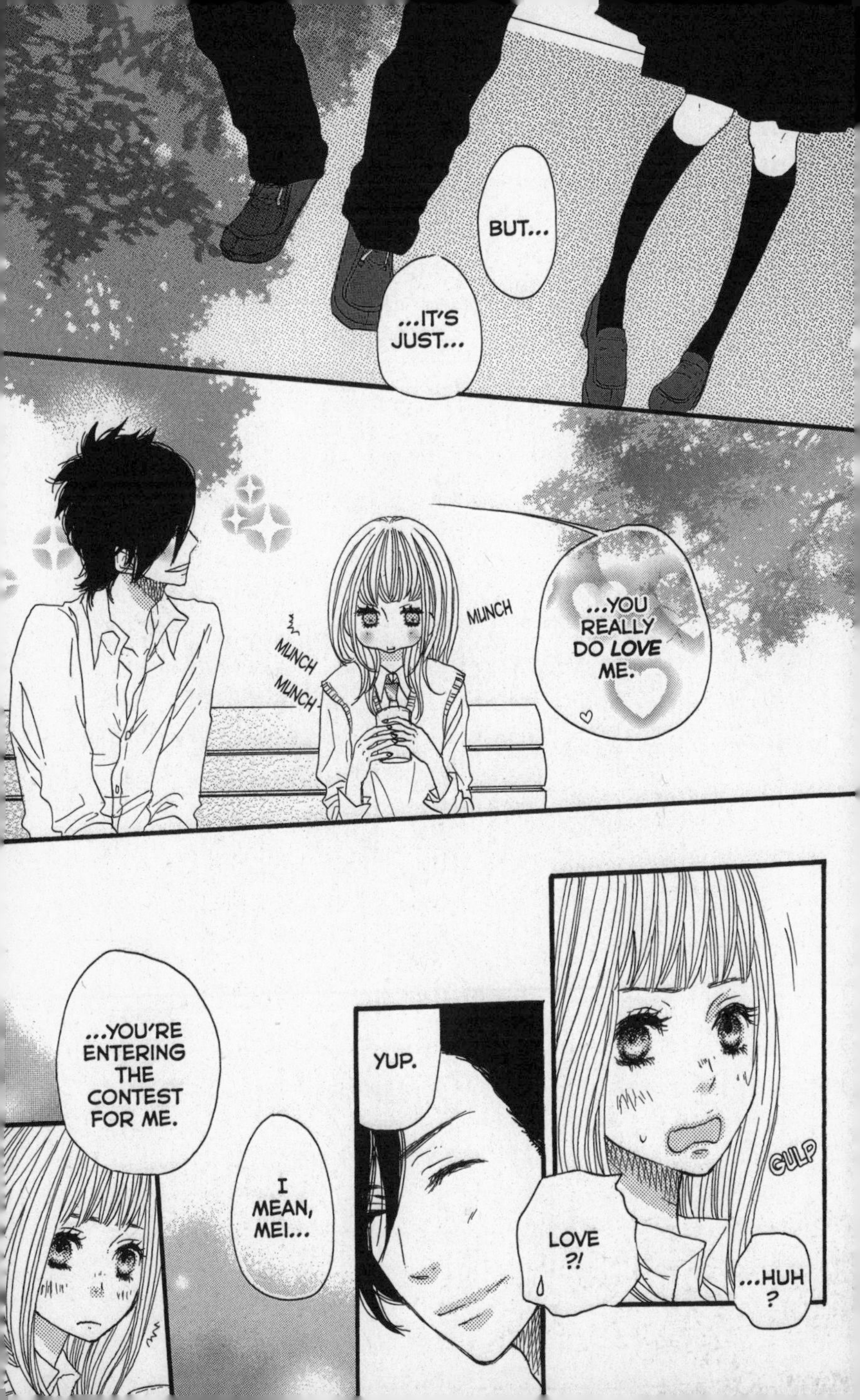
BUT...
...IT'S JUST...
...YOU REALLY DO LOVE ME.
MUNCH
MUNCH
MUNCH
...HUH ?
GULP
LOVE ?!
YUP.
...YOU'RE ENTERING THE CONTEST FOR ME.
I MEAN, MEI...

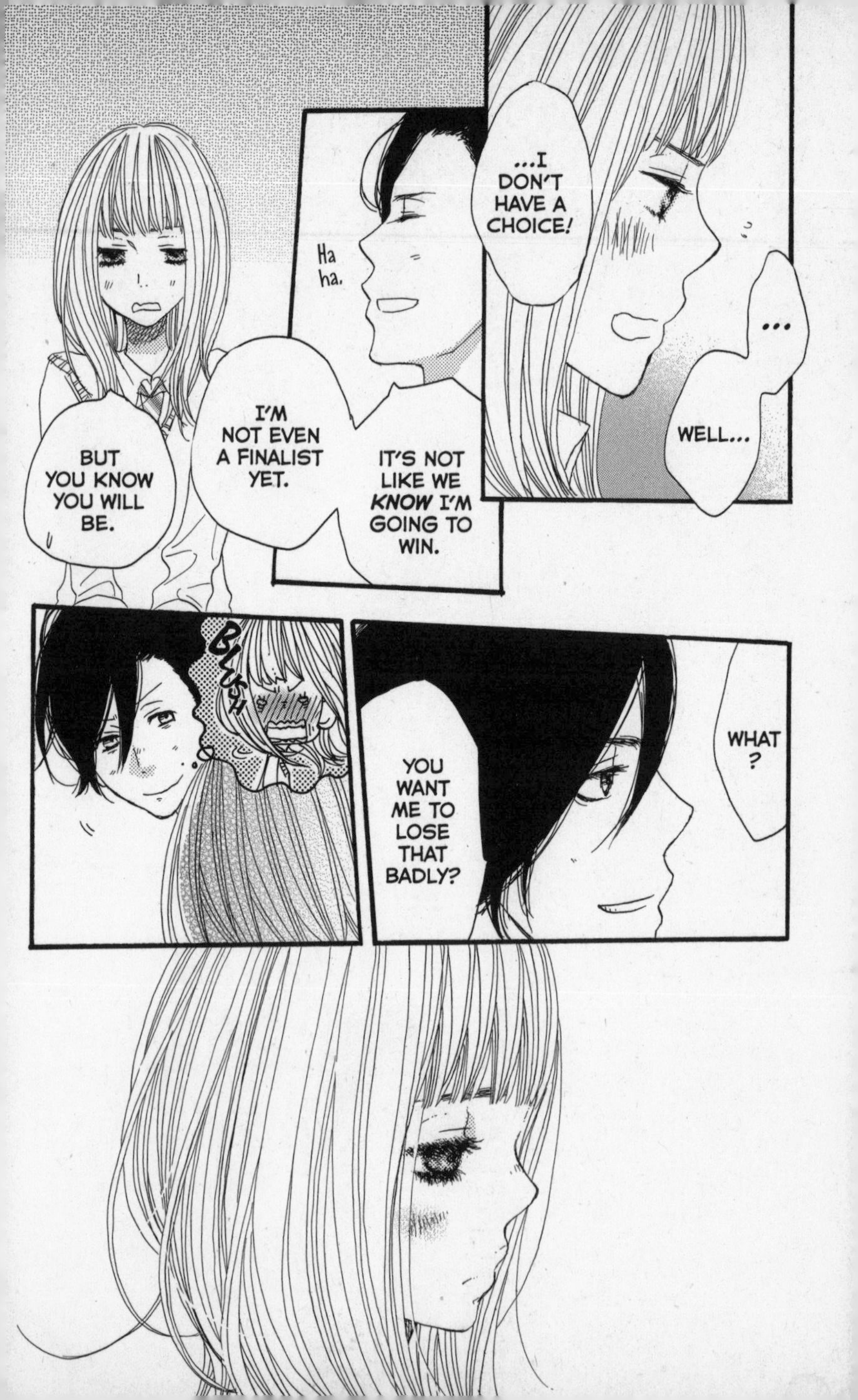
...
WELL...
...I DON'T HAVE A CHOICE!
Ha ha.
IT'S NOT LIKE WE *KNOW* I'M GOING TO WIN.
I'M NOT EVEN A FINALIST YET.
BUT YOU KNOW YOU WILL BE.
WHAT?
YOU WANT ME TO LOSE THAT BADLY?
BLUSH

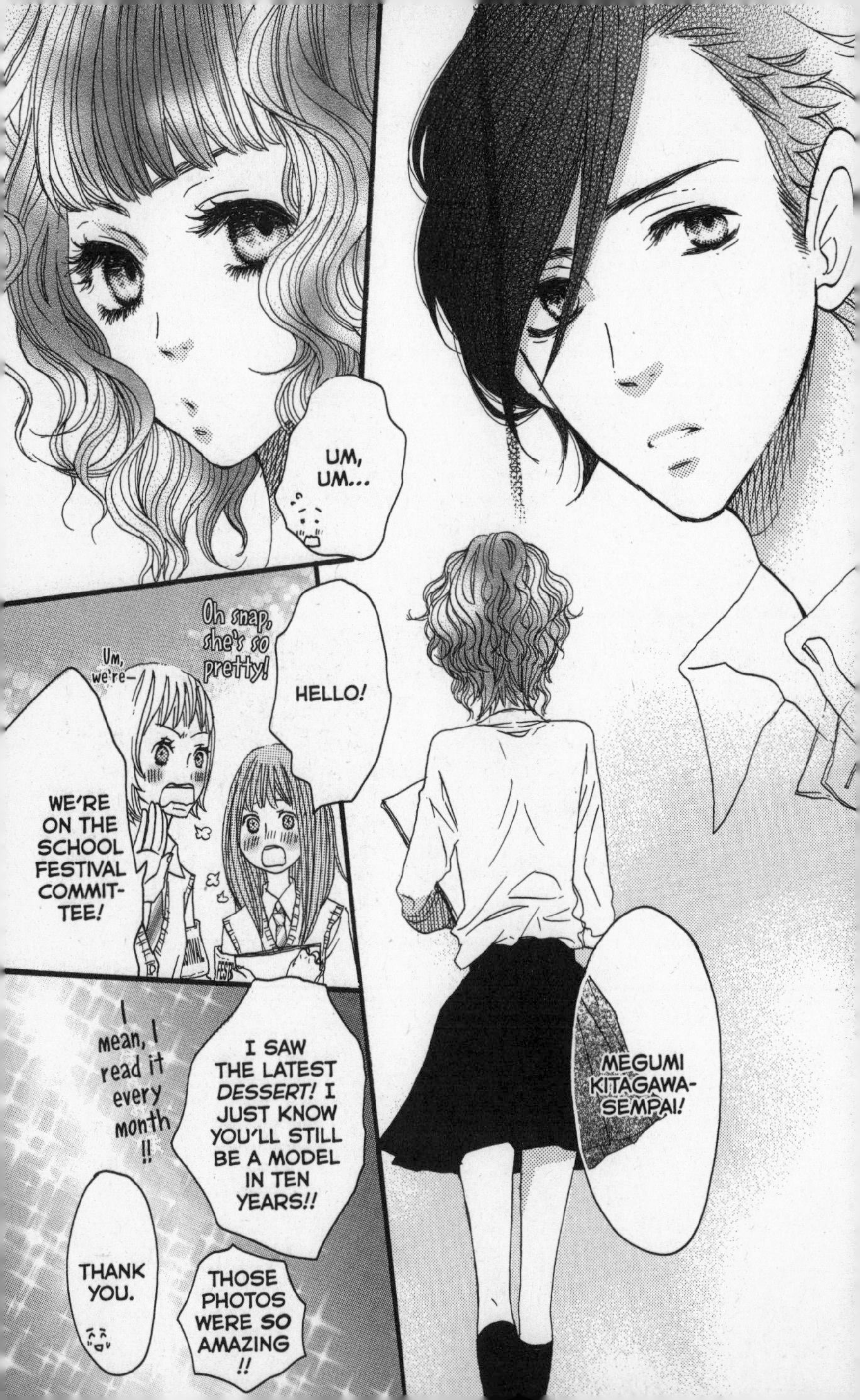
MEGUMI KITAGAWA-SEMPAI!
UM, UM...
HELLO!
Oh snap, she's so pretty!
Um, we're—
WE'RE ON THE SCHOOL FESTIVAL COMMIT-TEE!
I SAW THE LATEST *DESSERT*! I JUST KNOW YOU'LL STILL BE A MODEL IN TEN YEARS!!
I mean, I read it every month!!
THOSE PHOTOS WERE SO AMAZING!!
THANK YOU.

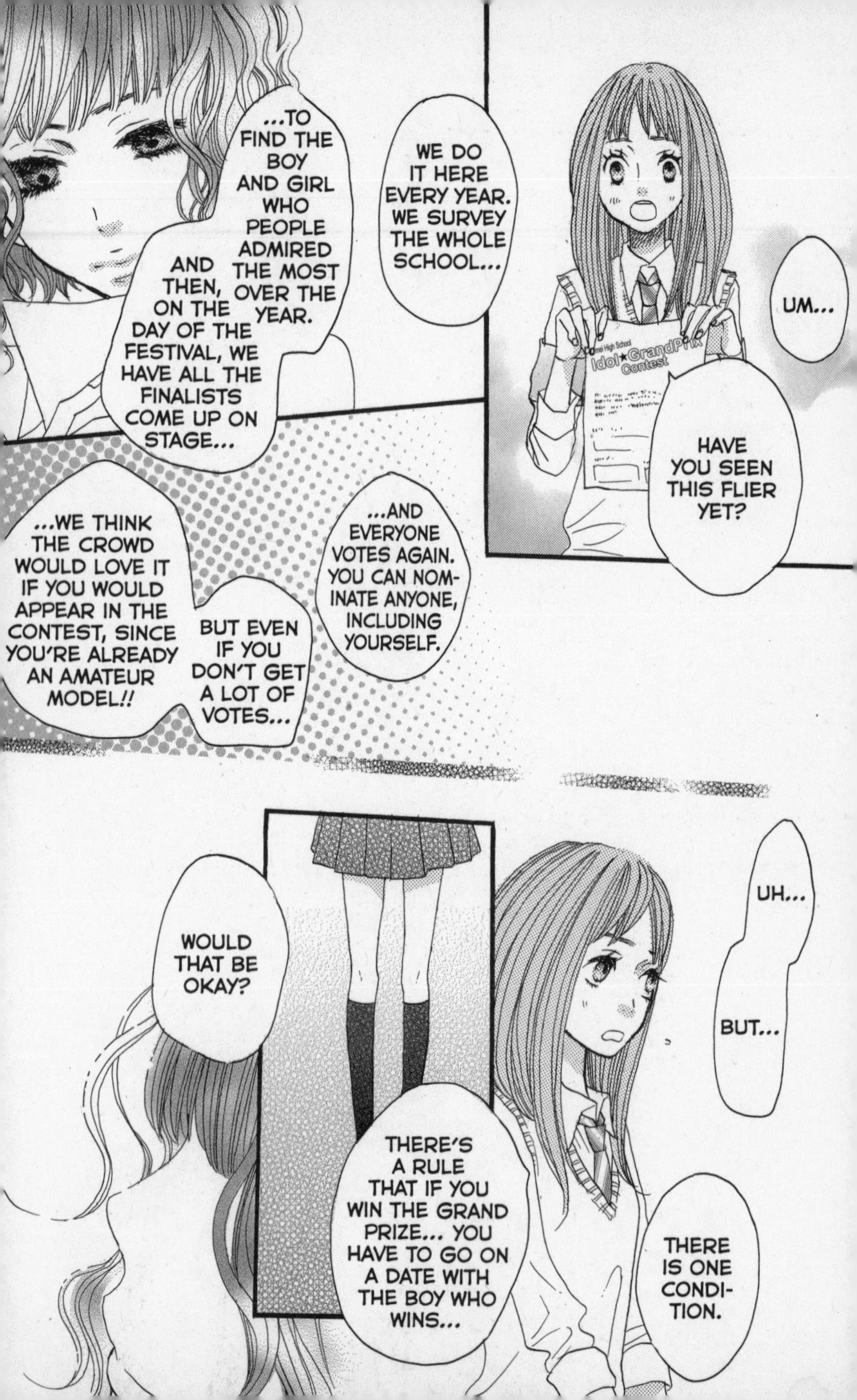
UM...
HAVE YOU SEEN THIS FLIER YET?
Idol★GrandPrix Contest
WE DO IT HERE EVERY YEAR. WE SURVEY THE WHOLE SCHOOL...
...TO FIND THE BOY AND GIRL WHO PEOPLE ADMIRED THE MOST OVER THE YEAR.
AND THEN, ON THE DAY OF THE FESTIVAL, WE HAVE ALL THE FINALISTS COME UP ON STAGE...
...AND EVERYONE VOTES AGAIN. YOU CAN NOMINATE ANYONE, INCLUDING YOURSELF.
BUT EVEN IF YOU DON'T GET A LOT OF VOTES...
...WE THINK THE CROWD WOULD LOVE IT IF YOU WOULD APPEAR IN THE CONTEST, SINCE YOU'RE ALREADY AN AMATEUR MODEL!!
UH...
BUT...
THERE IS ONE CONDITION.
THERE'S A RULE THAT IF YOU WIN THE GRAND PRIZE... YOU HAVE TO GO ON A DATE WITH THE BOY WHO WINS...
WOULD THAT BE OKAY?

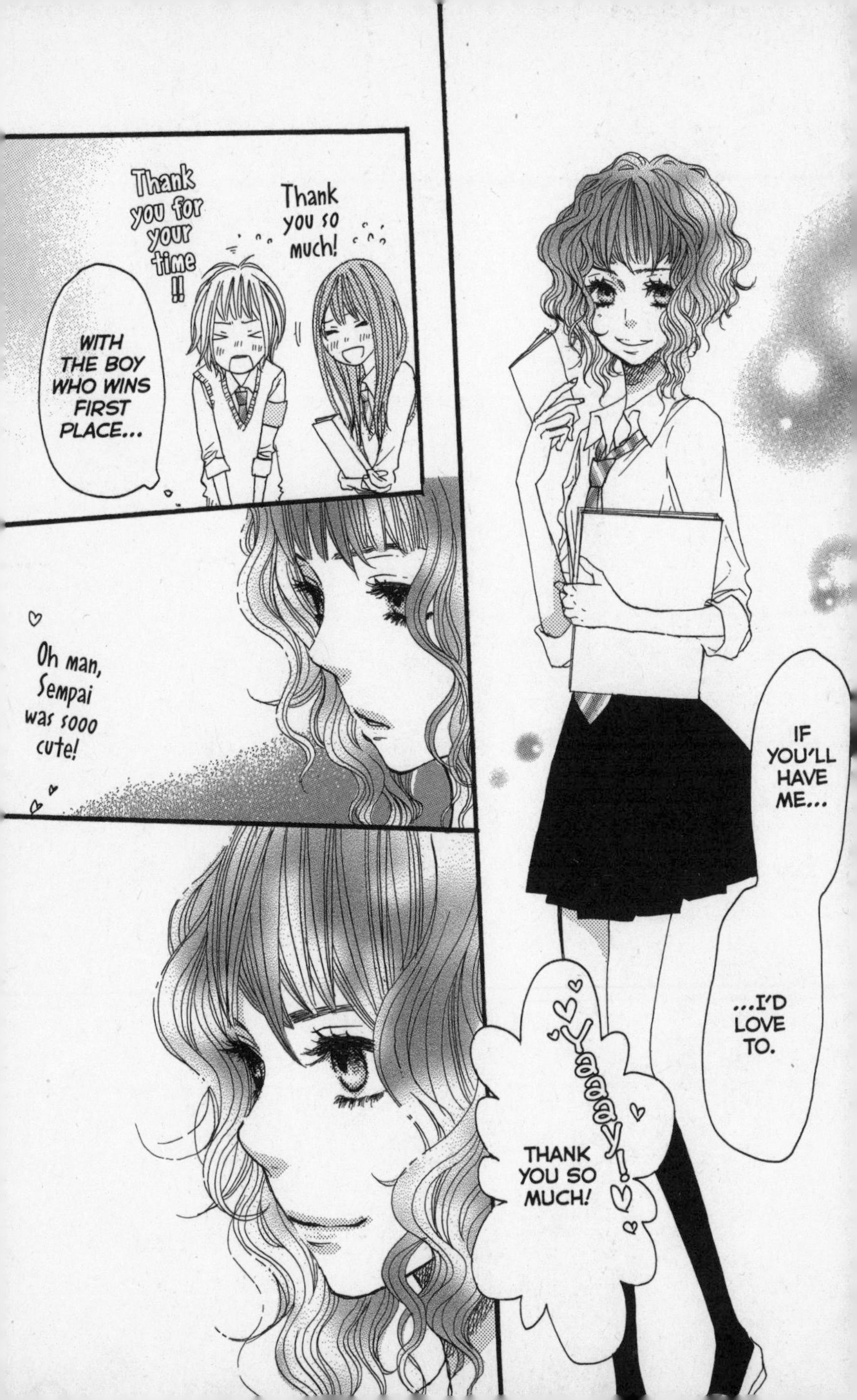
IF YOU'LL HAVE ME...
...I'D LOVE TO.
Thank you so much!
Thank you for your time !!
WITH THE BOY WHO WINS FIRST PLACE...
Oh man, Sempai was sooo cute!
Yaaay!
THANK YOU SO MUCH!

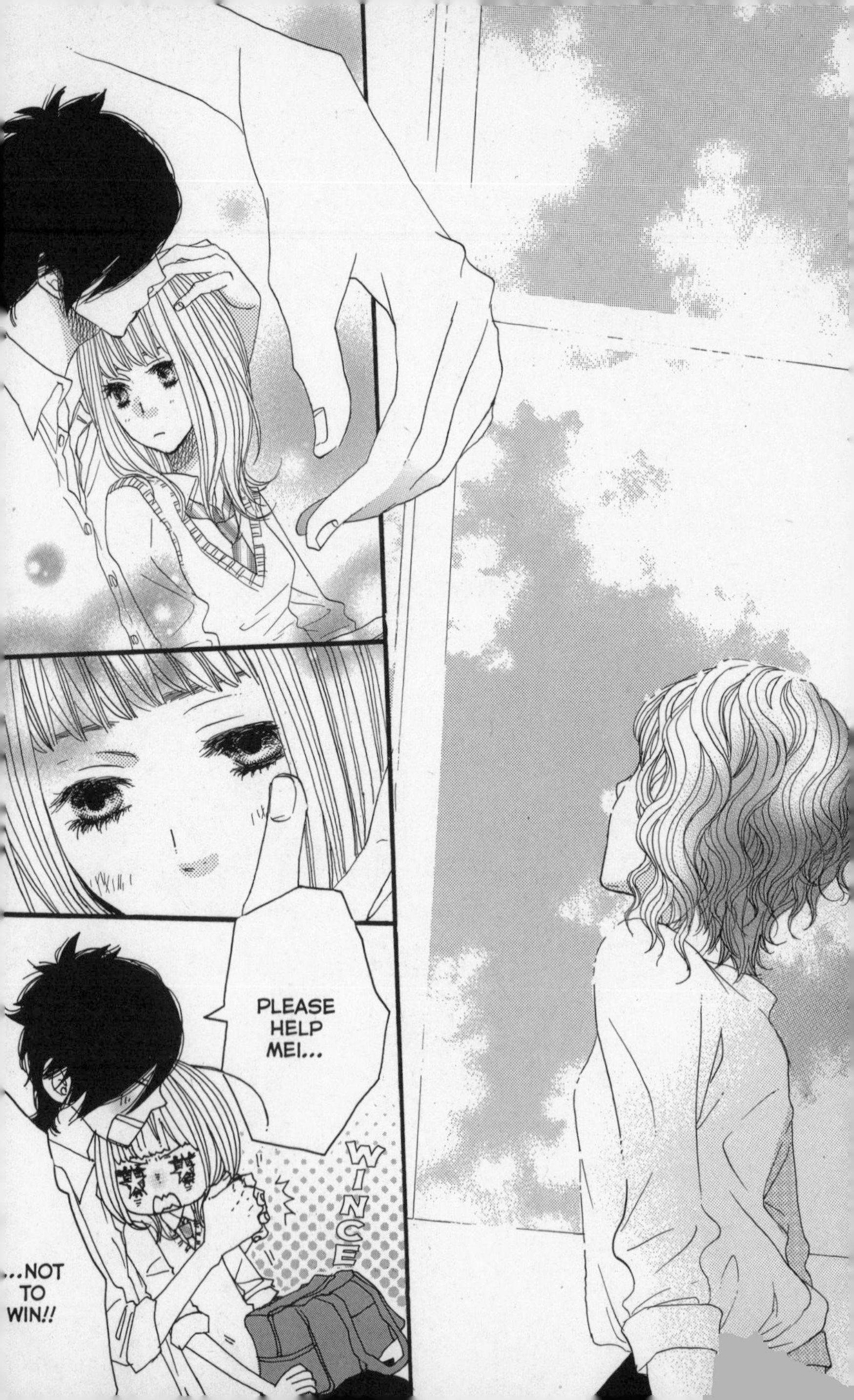
PLEASE HELP MEI...
WINCE
...NOT TO WIN!!

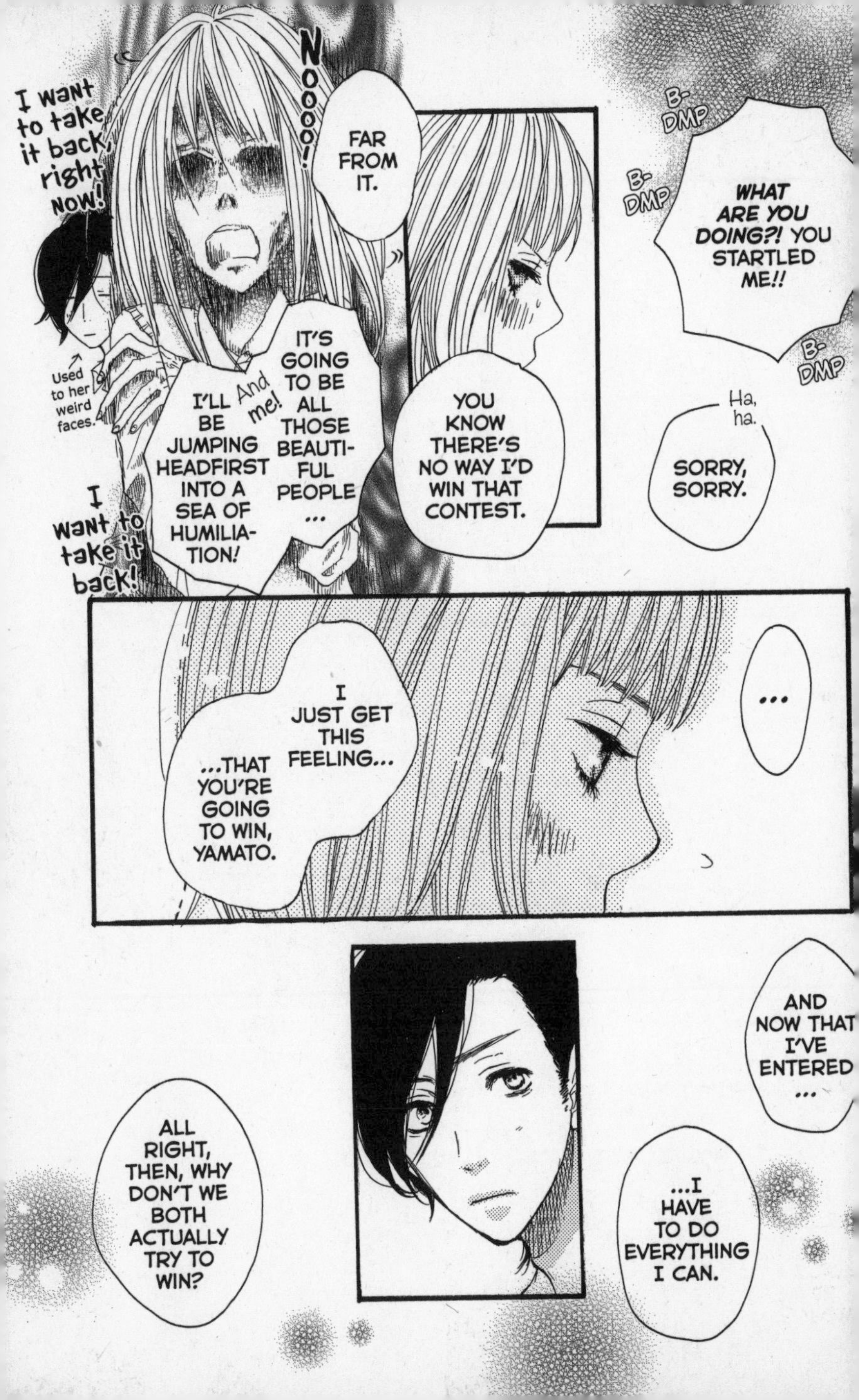
B-DMP
B-DMP
WHAT ARE YOU DOING?! YOU STARTLED ME!!
B-DMP
Ha, ha.
SORRY, SORRY.
YOU KNOW THERE'S NO WAY I'D WIN THAT CONTEST.
FAR FROM IT.
NOOOO!
IT'S GOING TO BE ALL THOSE BEAUTIFUL PEOPLE...
I'LL BE JUMPING HEADFIRST INTO A SEA OF HUMILIATION!
And me!
I want to take it back, right now!
I want to take it back!
Used to her weird faces.
...
I JUST GET THIS FEELING...
...THAT YOU'RE GOING TO WIN, YAMATO.
AND NOW THAT I'VE ENTERED...
...I HAVE TO DO EVERYTHING I CAN.
ALL RIGHT, THEN, WHY DON'T WE BOTH ACTUALLY TRY TO WIN?

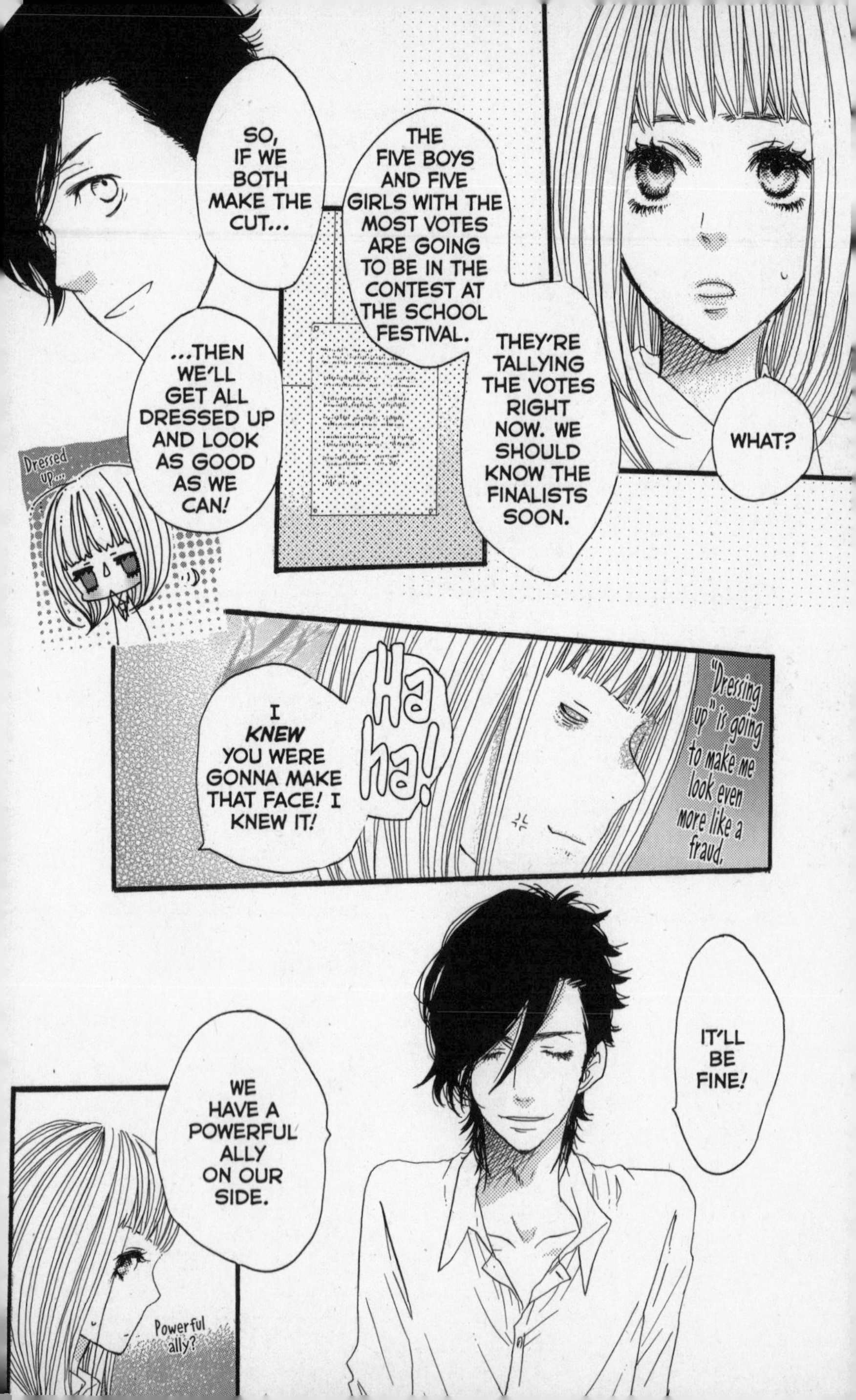

WHAT?
THE FIVE BOYS AND FIVE GIRLS WITH THE MOST VOTES ARE GOING TO BE IN THE CONTEST AT THE SCHOOL FESTIVAL.
THEY'RE TALLYING THE VOTES RIGHT NOW. WE SHOULD KNOW THE FINALISTS SOON.
SO, IF WE BOTH MAKE THE CUT...
...THEN WE'LL GET ALL DRESSED UP AND LOOK AS GOOD AS WE CAN!
Dressed up...
"Dressing up" is going to make me look even more like a fraud.
Ha ha!
I *KNEW* YOU WERE GONNA MAKE THAT FACE! I KNEW IT!
IT'LL BE FINE!
WE HAVE A POWERFUL ALLY ON OUR SIDE.
Powerful ally?

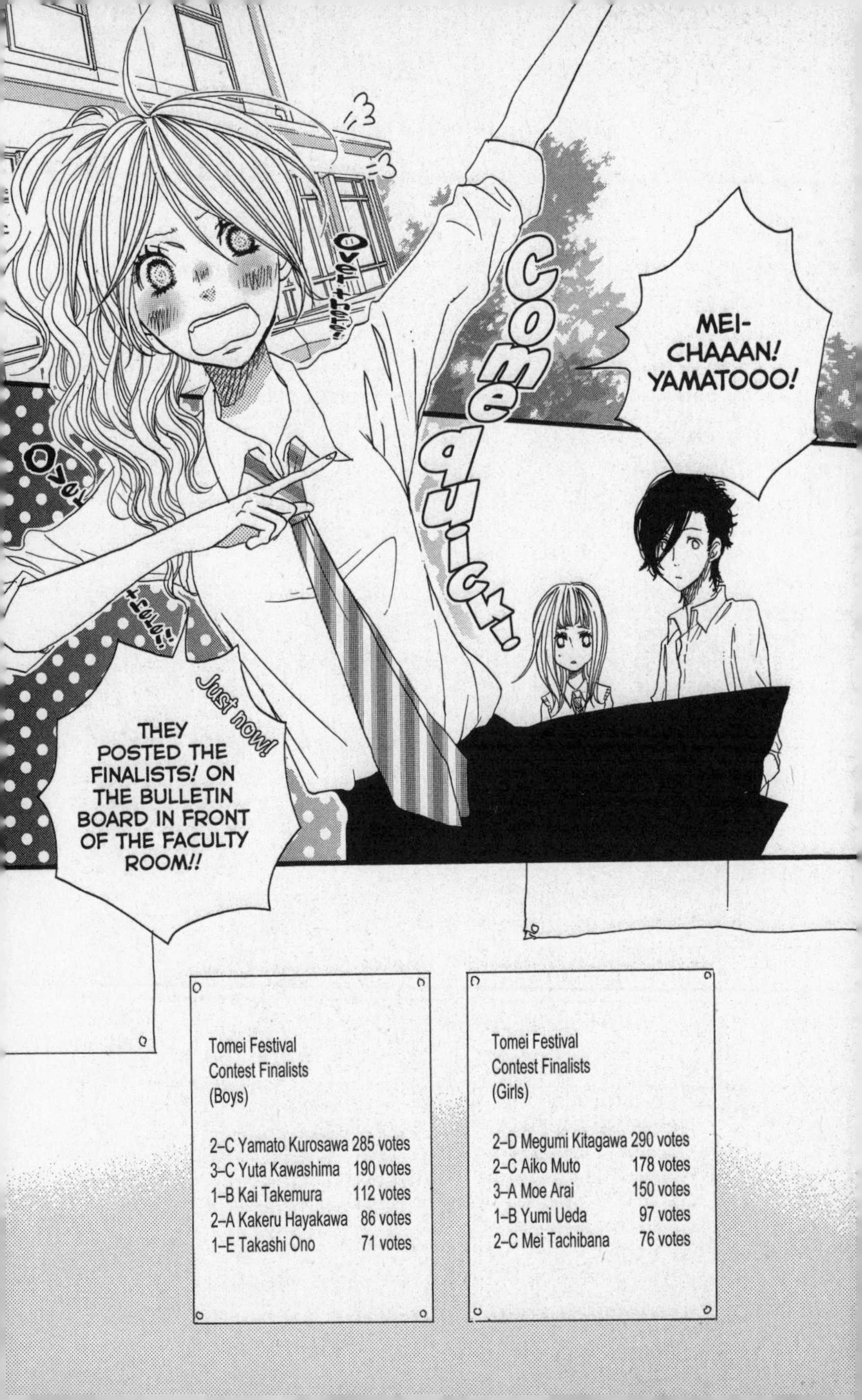
MEI-CHAAAN! YAMATOOO!
Come quick!
Over there!
Over there!
Just now!
THEY POSTED THE FINALISTS! ON THE BULLETIN BOARD IN FRONT OF THE FACULTY ROOM!!
Tomei Festival
Contest Finalists
(Girls)
2–D Megumi Kitagawa 290 votes
2–C Aiko Muto 178 votes
3–A Moe Arai 150 votes
1–B Yumi Ueda 97 votes
2–C Mei Tachibana 76 votes
Tomei Festival
Contest Finalists
(Boys)
2–C Yamato Kurosawa 285 votes
3–C Yuta Kawashima 190 votes
1–B Kai Takemura 112 votes
2–A Kakeru Hayakawa 86 votes
1–E Takashi Ono 71 votes

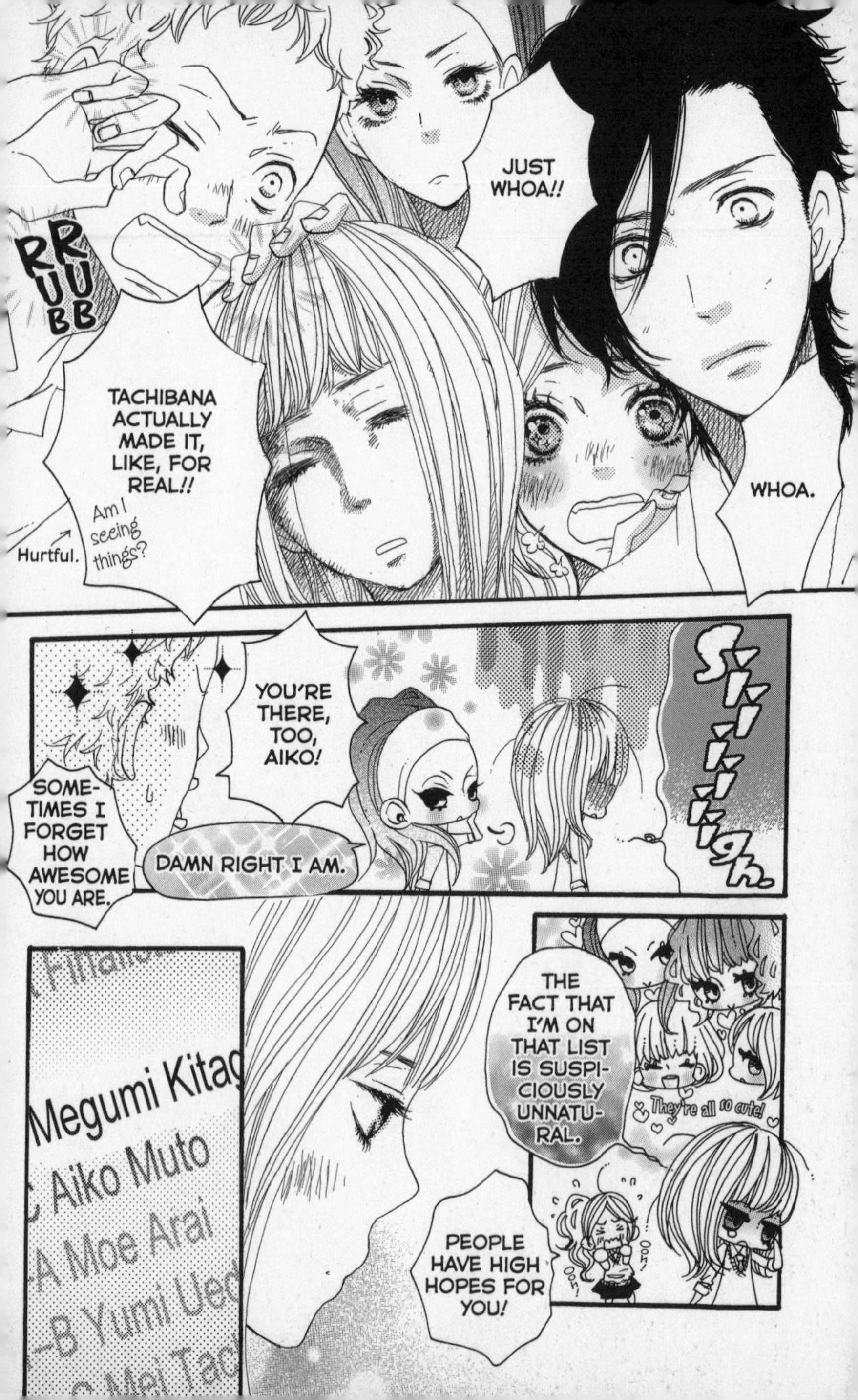
JUST WHOA!!
WHOA.
RRUUBB
TACHIBANA ACTUALLY MADE IT, LIKE, FOR REAL!!
Am I seeing things?
Hurtful.
Siiiiiigh.
YOU'RE THERE, TOO, AIKO!
DAMN RIGHT I AM.
SOME-TIMES I FORGET HOW AWESOME YOU ARE.
THE FACT THAT I'M ON THAT LIST IS SUSPICIOUSLY UNNATURAL.
They're all so cute!
Ooh!
Ooh!
PEOPLE HAVE HIGH HOPES FOR YOU!
Megumi Kitag
Aiko Muto
Moe Arai
Yumi Ued

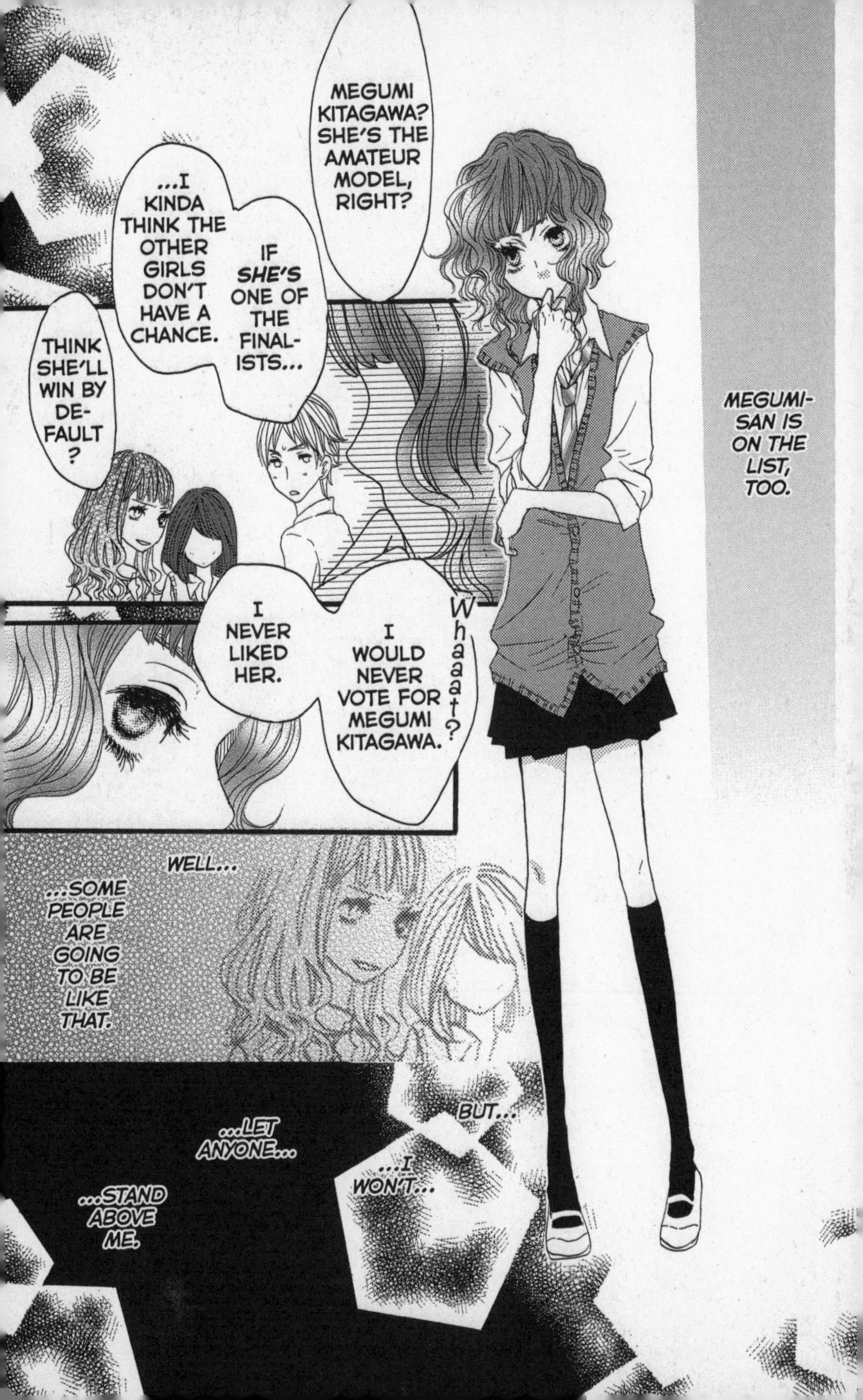
MEGUMI-SAN IS ON THE LIST, TOO.
MEGUMI KITAGAWA? SHE'S THE AMATEUR MODEL, RIGHT?
IF *SHE'S* ONE OF THE FINALISTS...
...I KINDA THINK THE OTHER GIRLS DON'T HAVE A CHANCE.
THINK SHE'LL WIN BY DEFAULT?
Whaaat?
I WOULD NEVER VOTE FOR MEGUMI KITAGAWA.
I NEVER LIKED HER.
WELL...
...SOME PEOPLE ARE GOING TO BE LIKE THAT.
BUT...
...I WON'T...
...LET ANYONE...
...STAND ABOVE ME.

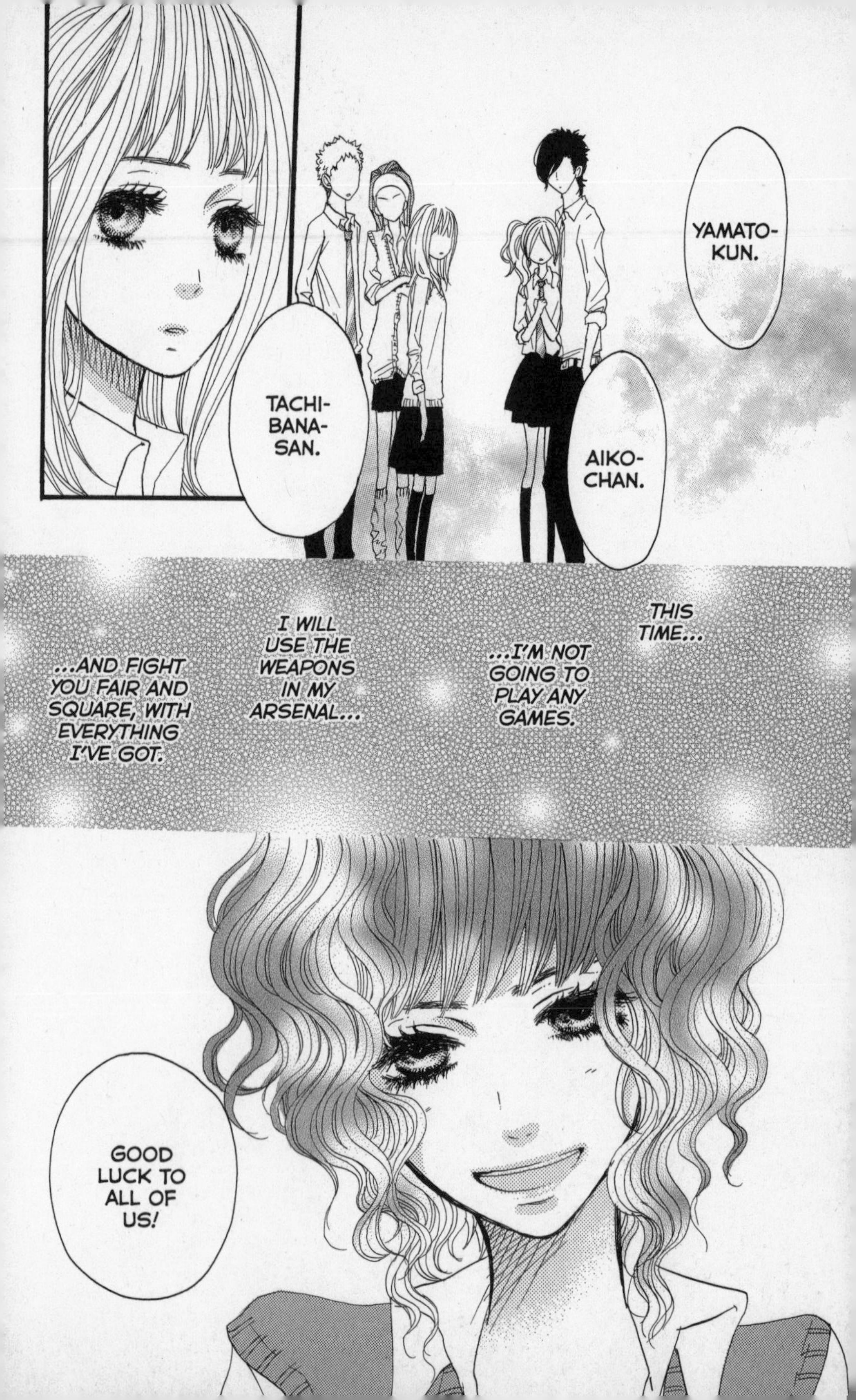
YAMATO-KUN.
AIKO-CHAN.
TACHI-BANA-SAN.
THIS TIME...
...I'M NOT GOING TO PLAY ANY GAMES.
I WILL USE THE WEAPONS IN MY ARSENAL...
...AND FIGHT YOU FAIR AND SQUARE, WITH EVERYTHING I'VE GOT.
GOOD LUCK TO ALL OF US!

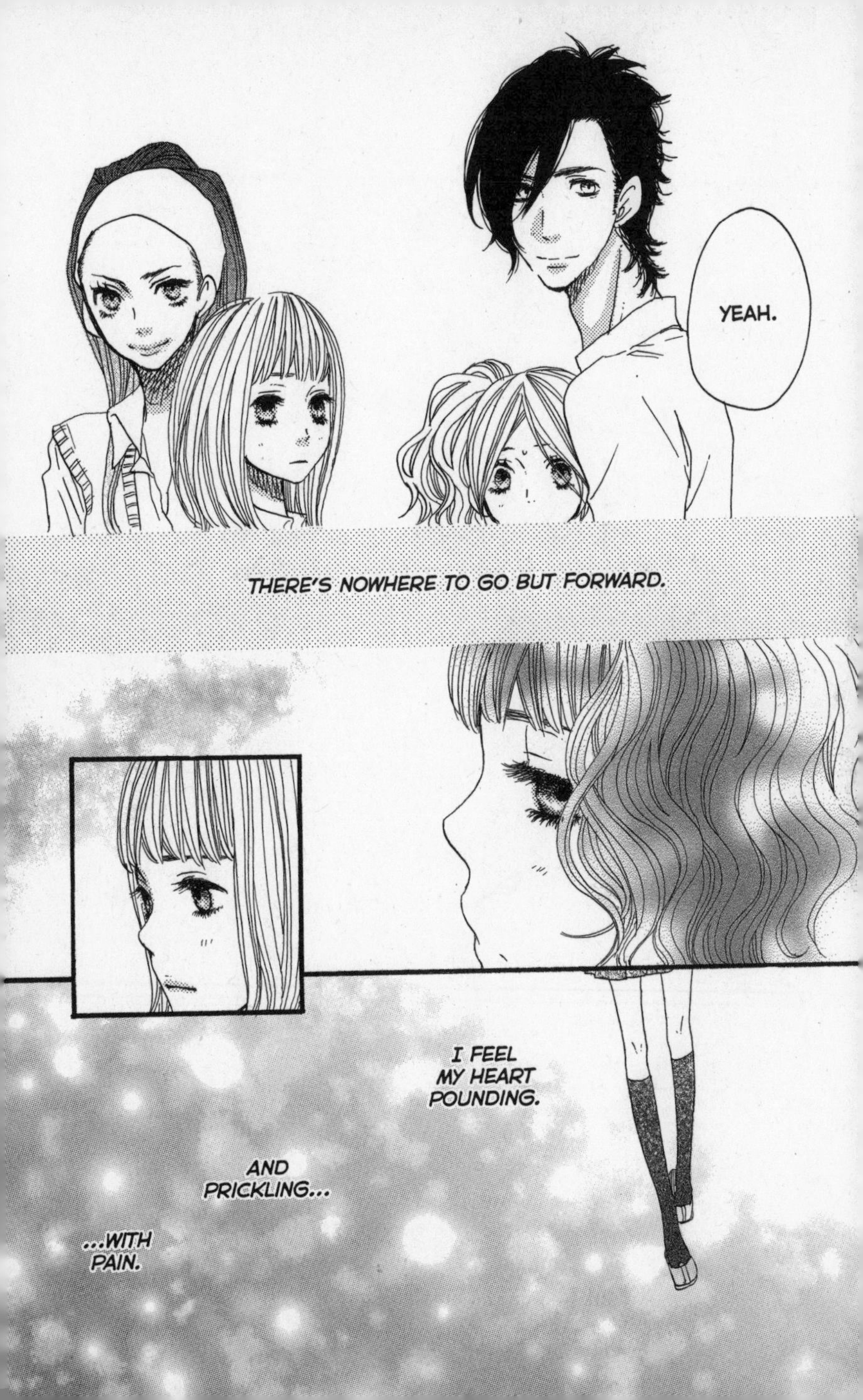
YEAH.
THERE'S NOWHERE TO GO BUT FORWARD.
I FEEL MY HEART POUNDING.
AND PRICKLING...
...WITH PAIN.

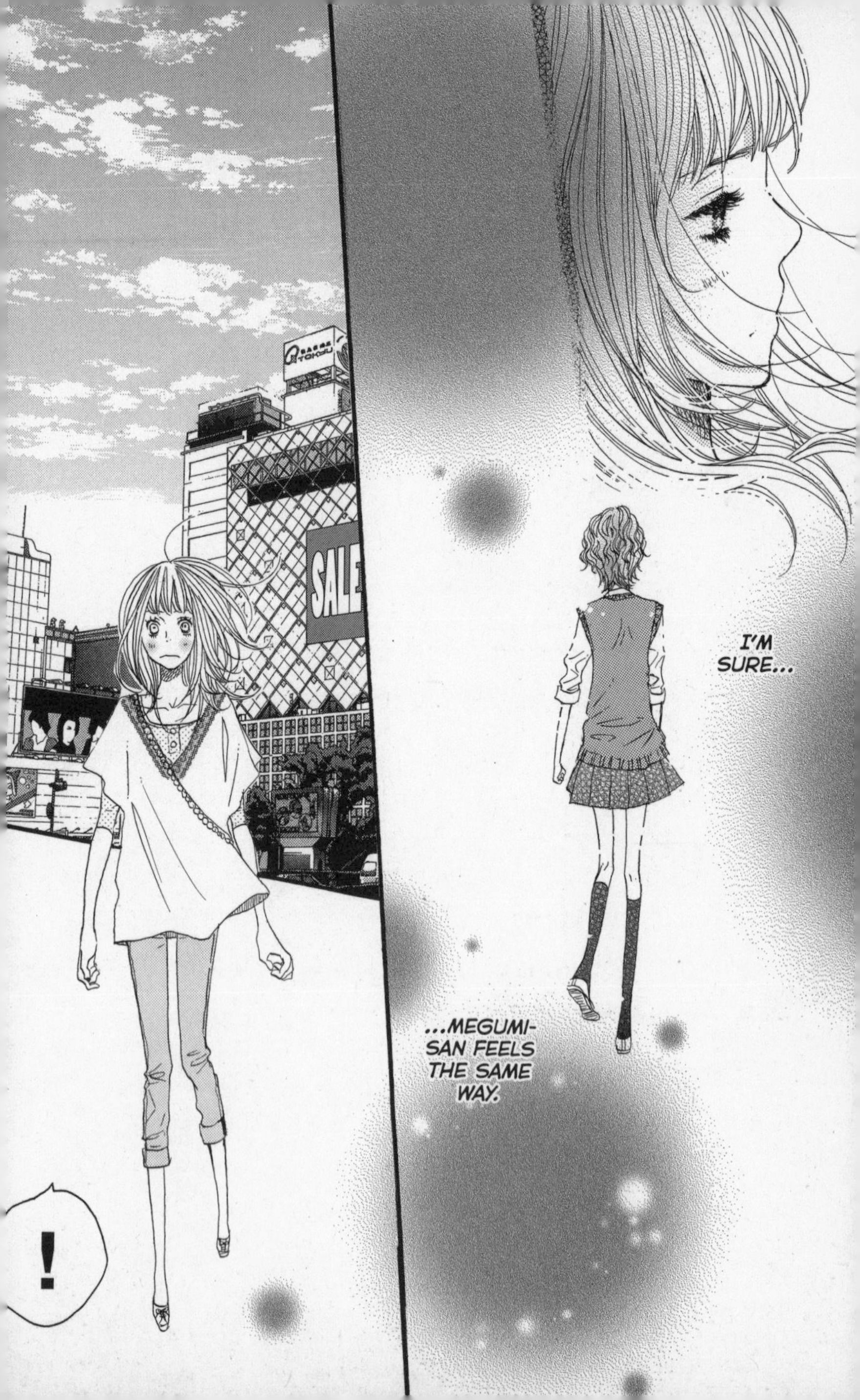
I'M SURE...
...MEGUMI-SAN FEELS THE SAME WAY.
SALE
!

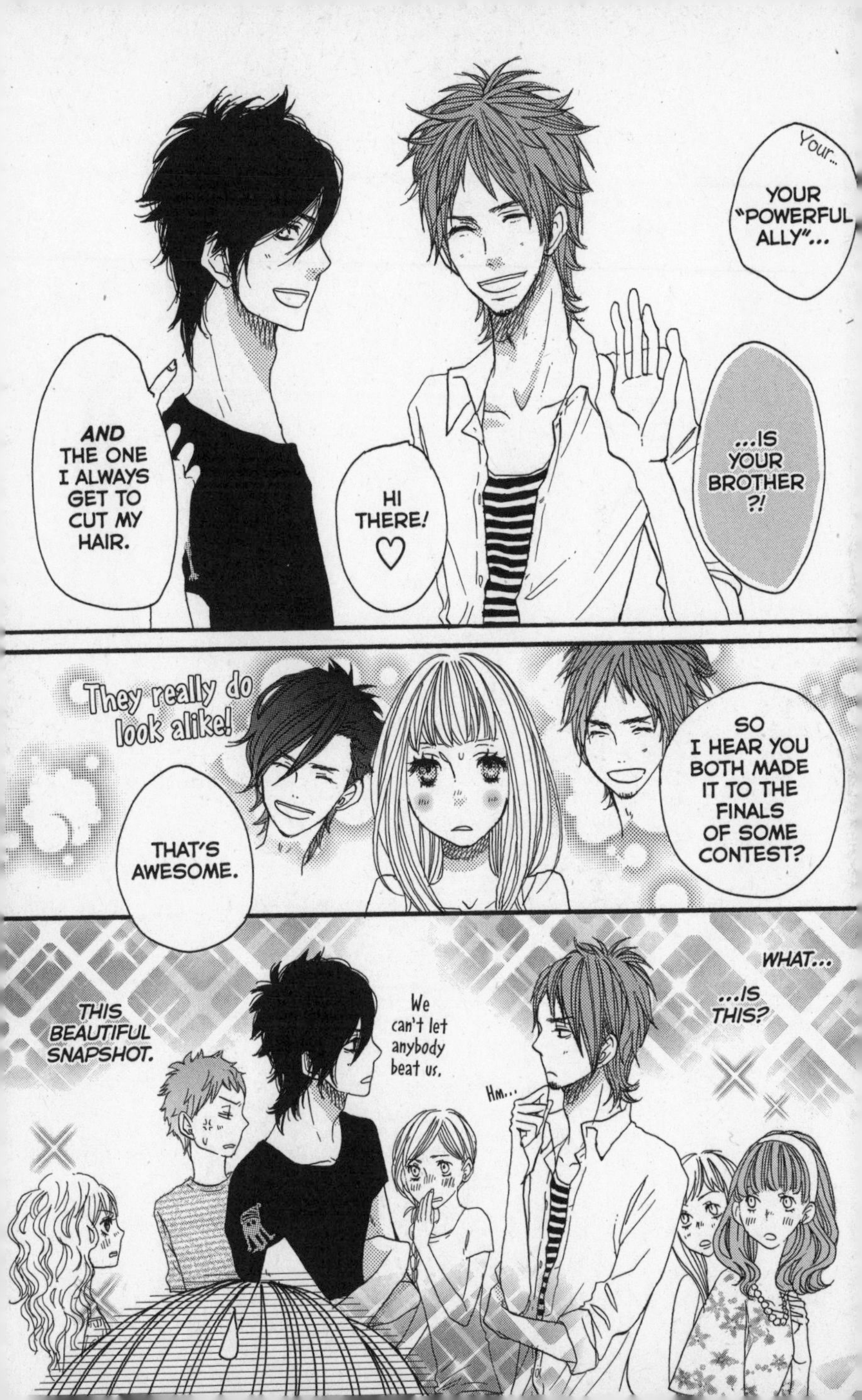
Your...
YOUR "POWERFUL ALLY"...
...IS YOUR BROTHER ?!
HI THERE! ♡
AND THE ONE I ALWAYS GET TO CUT MY HAIR.
SO I HEAR YOU BOTH MADE IT TO THE FINALS OF SOME CONTEST?
They really do look alike!
THAT'S AWESOME.
WHAT...
...IS THIS?
Hm...
We can't let anybody beat us.
THIS BEAUTIFUL SNAPSHOT.

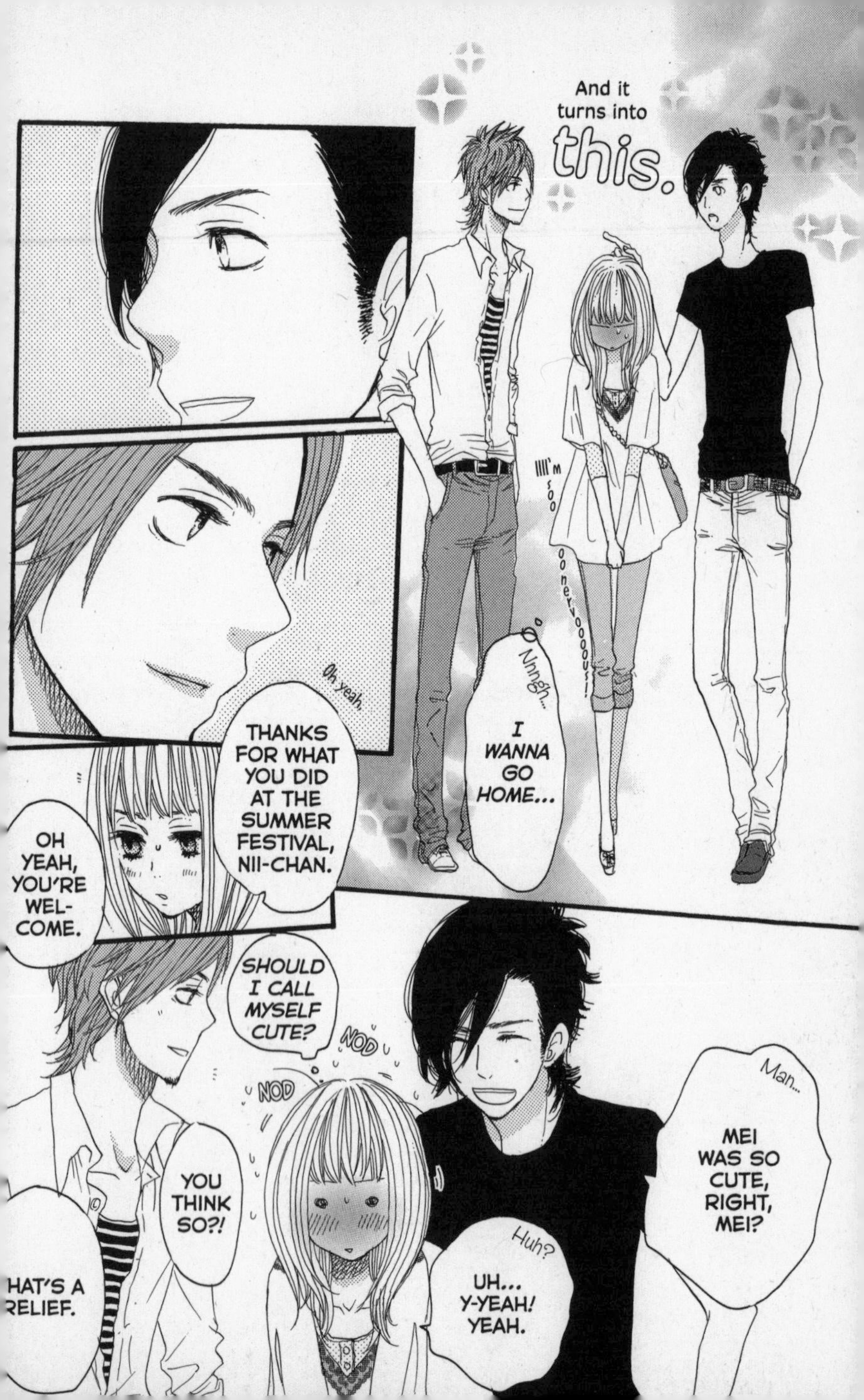
And it turns into this.
I'm soooo nervoooous!!
Nnngh...
I WANNA GO HOME...
Oh yeah.
THANKS FOR WHAT YOU DID AT THE SUMMER FESTIVAL, NII-CHAN.
OH YEAH, YOU'RE WEL-COME.
Man...
MEI WAS SO CUTE, RIGHT, MEI?
Huh?
UH... Y-YEAH! YEAH.
NOD
NOD
SHOULD I CALL MYSELF CUTE?
YOU THINK SO?!
HAT'S A RELIEF.

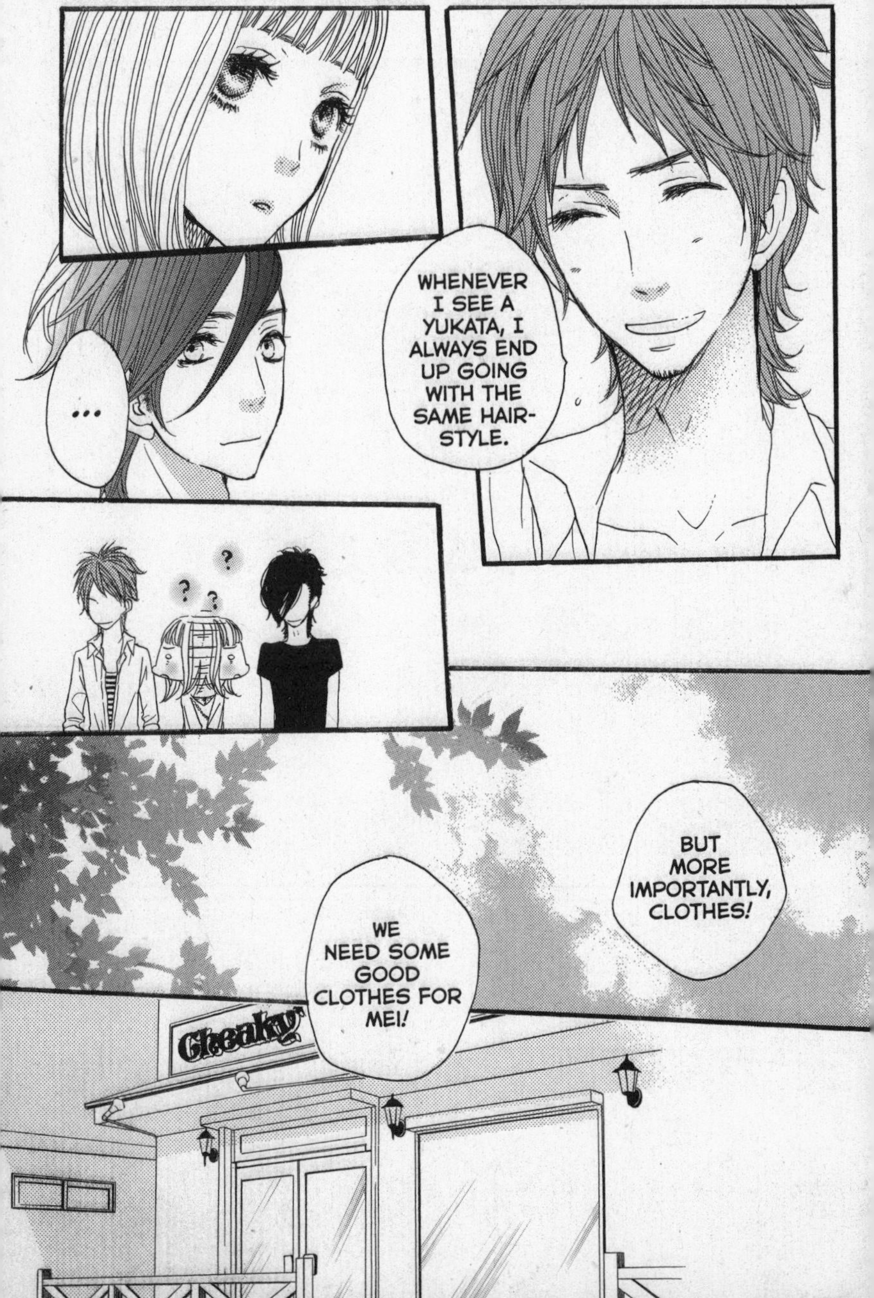
WHENEVER I SEE A YUKATA, I ALWAYS END UP GOING WITH THE SAME HAIR-STYLE.
...
?
?
?
BUT MORE IMPORTANTLY, CLOTHES!
WE NEED SOME GOOD CLOTHES FOR MEI!
Cheaky

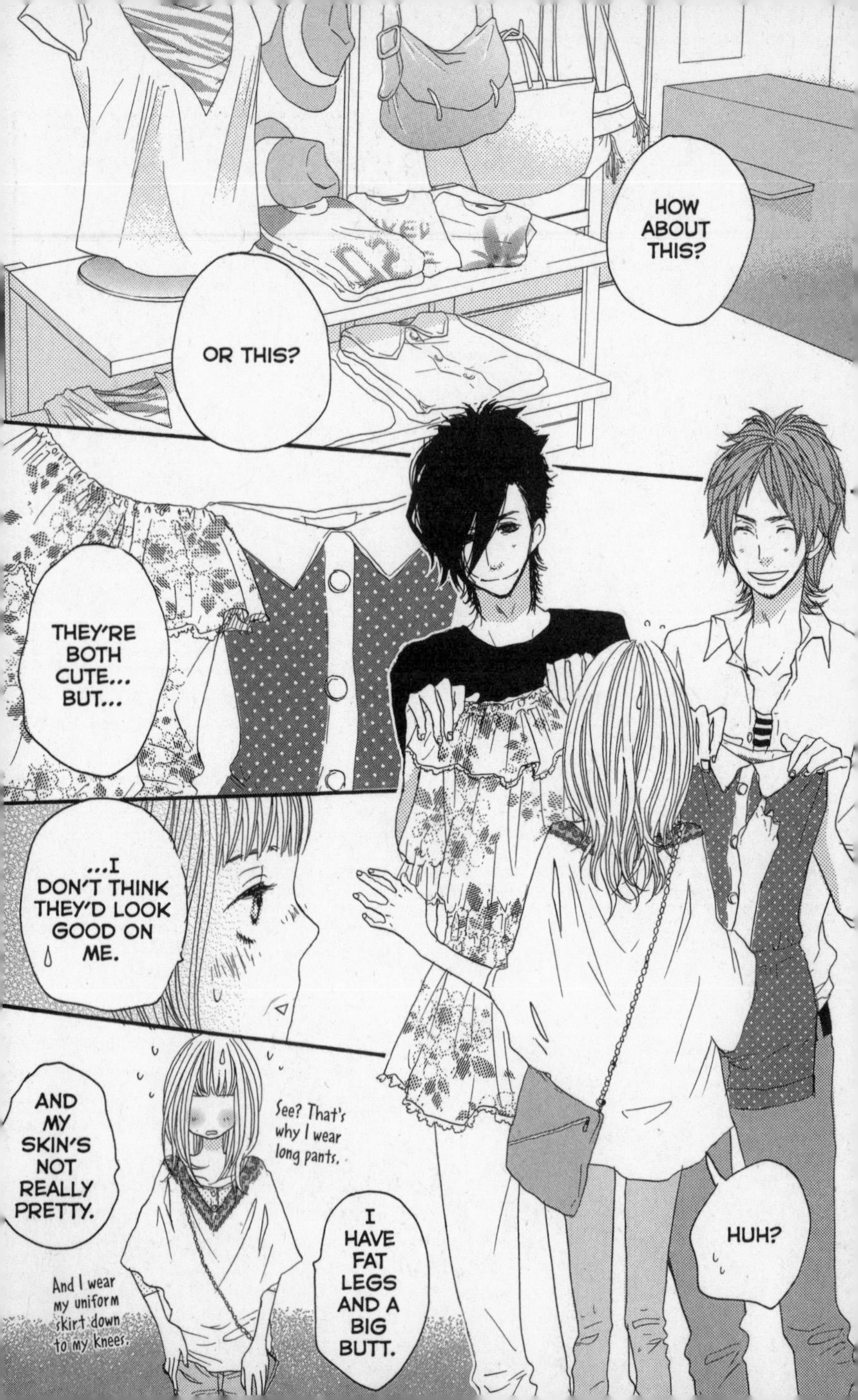
HOW ABOUT THIS?
OR THIS?
HUH?
THEY'RE BOTH CUTE... BUT...
...I DON'T THINK THEY'D LOOK GOOD ON ME.
AND MY SKIN'S NOT REALLY PRETTY.
I HAVE FAT LEGS AND A BIG BUTT.
See? That's why I wear long pants.
And I wear my uniform skirt down to my knees.

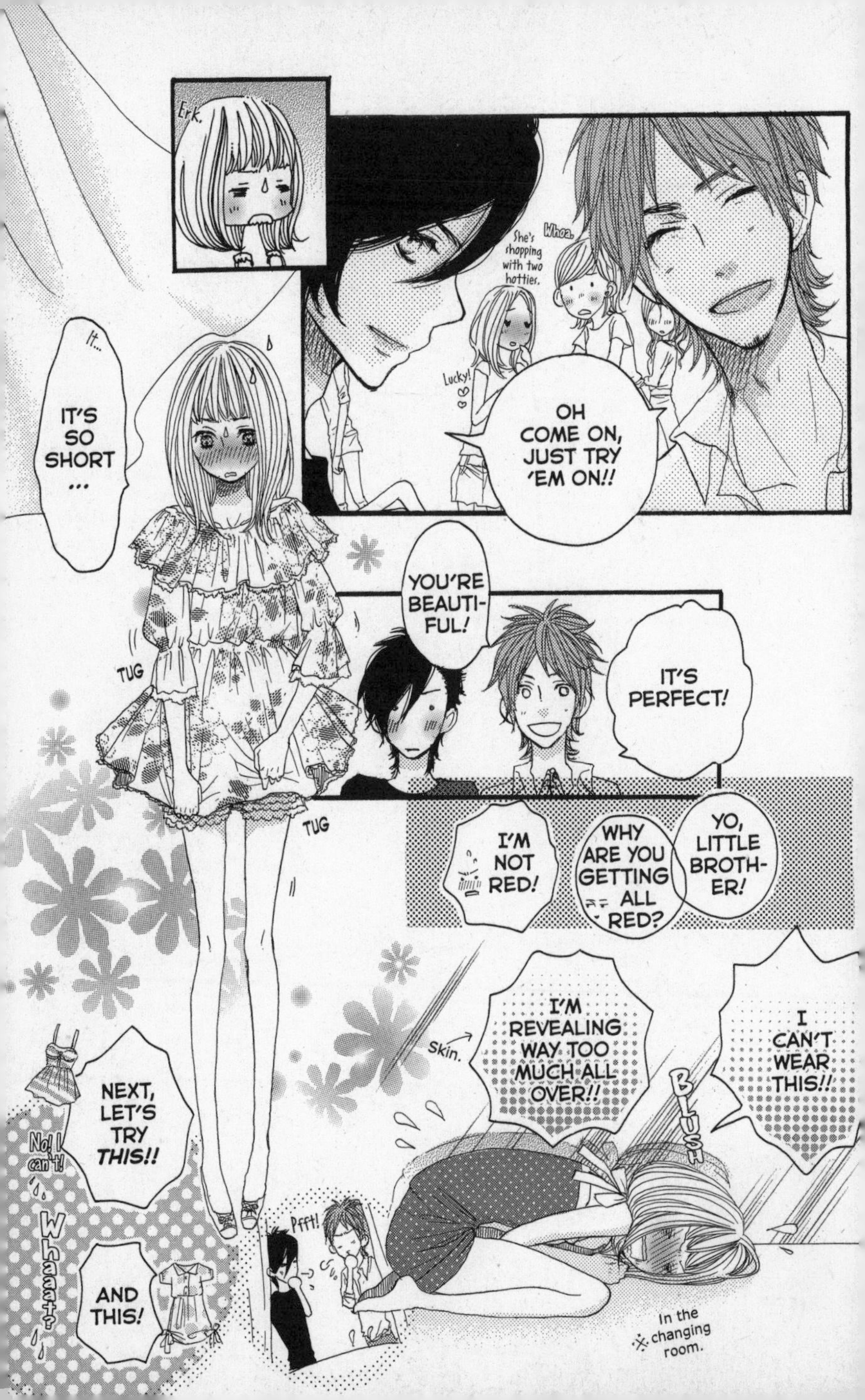

Whoa.
She's shopping with two hotties.
Lucky!
OH COME ON, JUST TRY 'EM ON!!
Erk.
It...
IT'S SO SHORT ...
IT'S PERFECT!
YOU'RE BEAUTI-FUL!
YO, LITTLE BROTH-ER!
WHY ARE YOU GETTING ALL RED?
I'M NOT RED!
TUG
TUG
I CAN'T WEAR THIS!!
BLUSH
I'M REVEALING WAY TOO MUCH ALL OVER!!
Skin.
In the changing room.
Pfft!
NEXT, LET'S TRY THIS!!
AND THIS!
No! I can't!
Whaaaat?

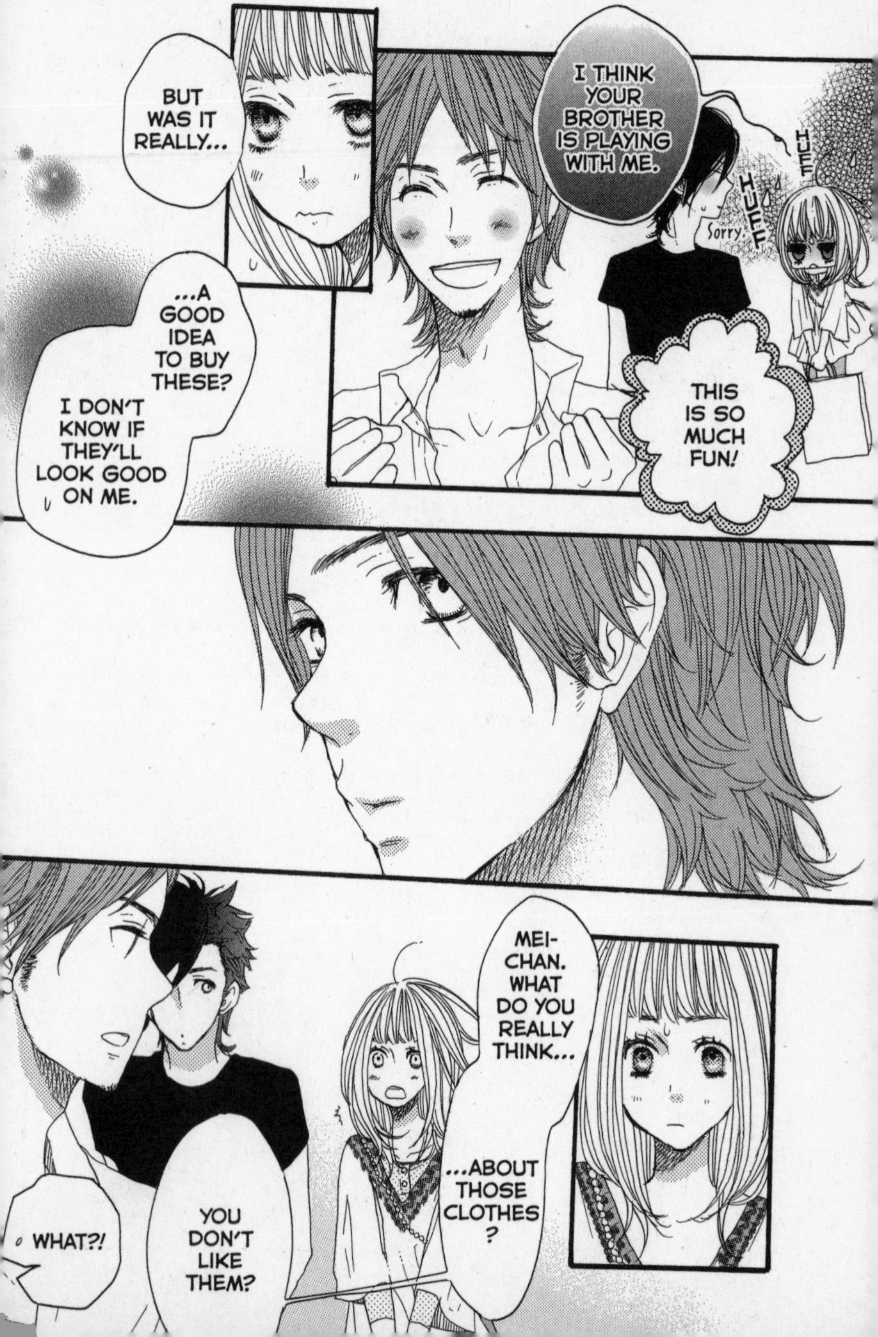
HUFF
HUFF
Sorry.
I THINK YOUR BROTHER IS PLAYING WITH ME.
THIS IS SO MUCH FUN!
BUT WAS IT REALLY...
...A GOOD IDEA TO BUY THESE?
I DON'T KNOW IF THEY'LL LOOK GOOD ON ME.
MEI-CHAN. WHAT DO YOU REALLY THINK...
...ABOUT THOSE CLOTHES?
YOU DON'T LIKE THEM?
WHAT?!

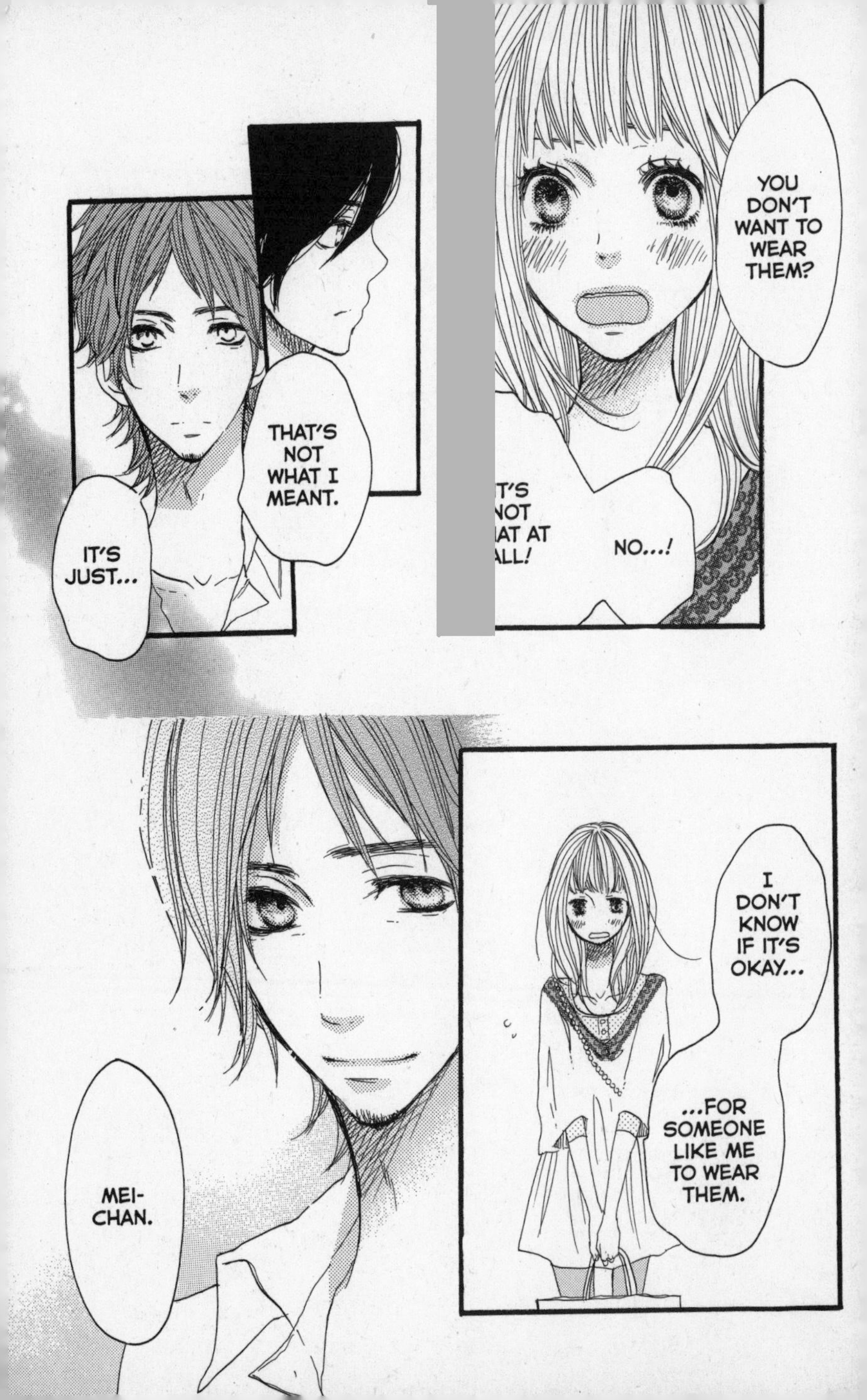

YOU DON'T WANT TO WEAR THEM?
NO...!
T'S NOT AT AT LL!
THAT'S NOT WHAT I MEANT.
IT'S JUST...
I DON'T KNOW IF IT'S OKAY...
...FOR SOMEONE LIKE ME TO WEAR THEM.
MEI-CHAN.

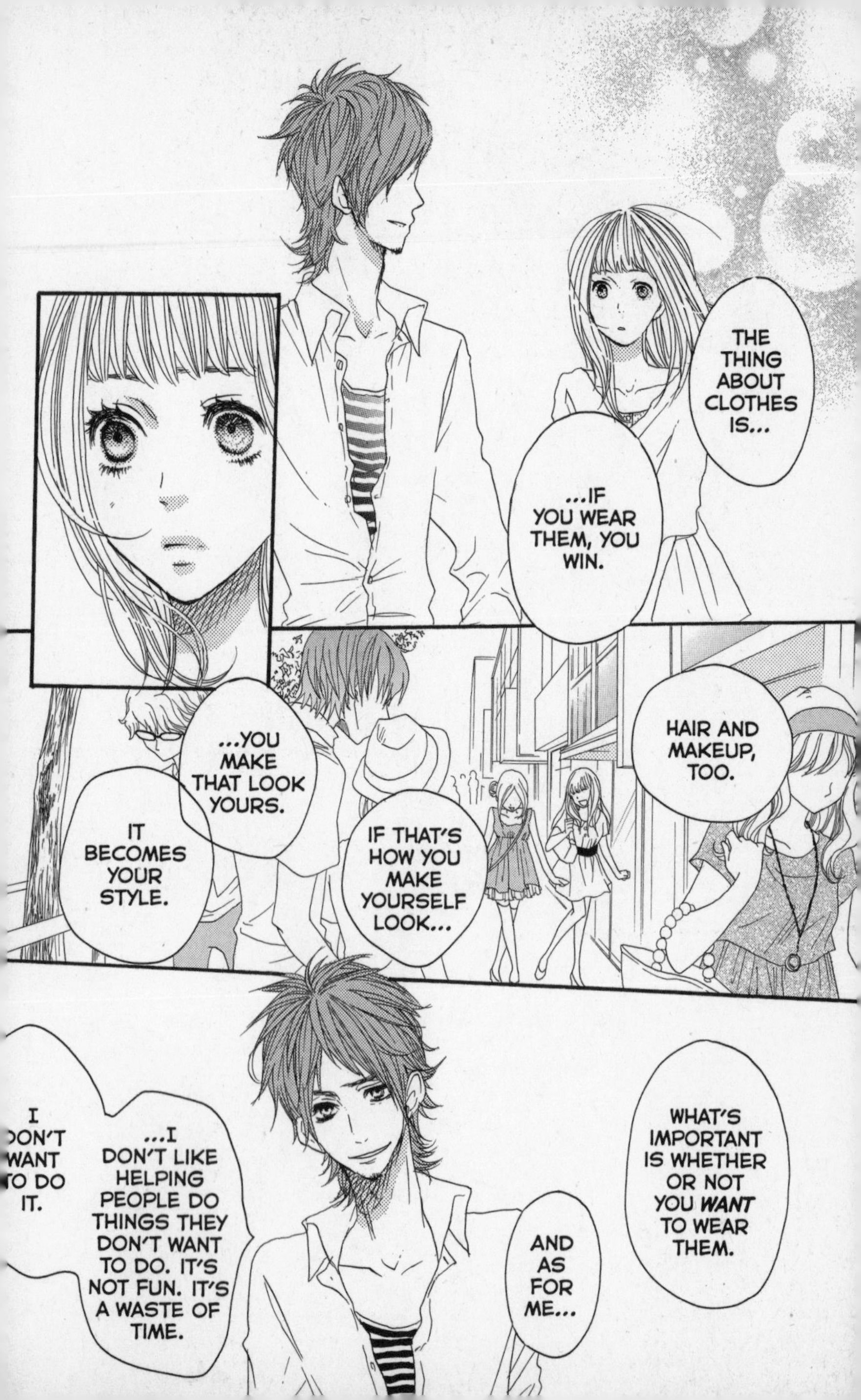
THE THING ABOUT CLOTHES IS...
...IF YOU WEAR THEM, YOU WIN.
HAIR AND MAKEUP, TOO.
IF THAT'S HOW YOU MAKE YOURSELF LOOK...
...YOU MAKE THAT LOOK YOURS.
IT BECOMES YOUR STYLE.
WHAT'S IMPORTANT IS WHETHER OR NOT YOU *WANT* TO WEAR THEM.
AND AS FOR ME...
...I DON'T LIKE HELPING PEOPLE DO THINGS THEY DON'T WANT TO DO. IT'S NOT FUN. IT'S A WASTE OF TIME.
I DON'T WANT TO DO IT.

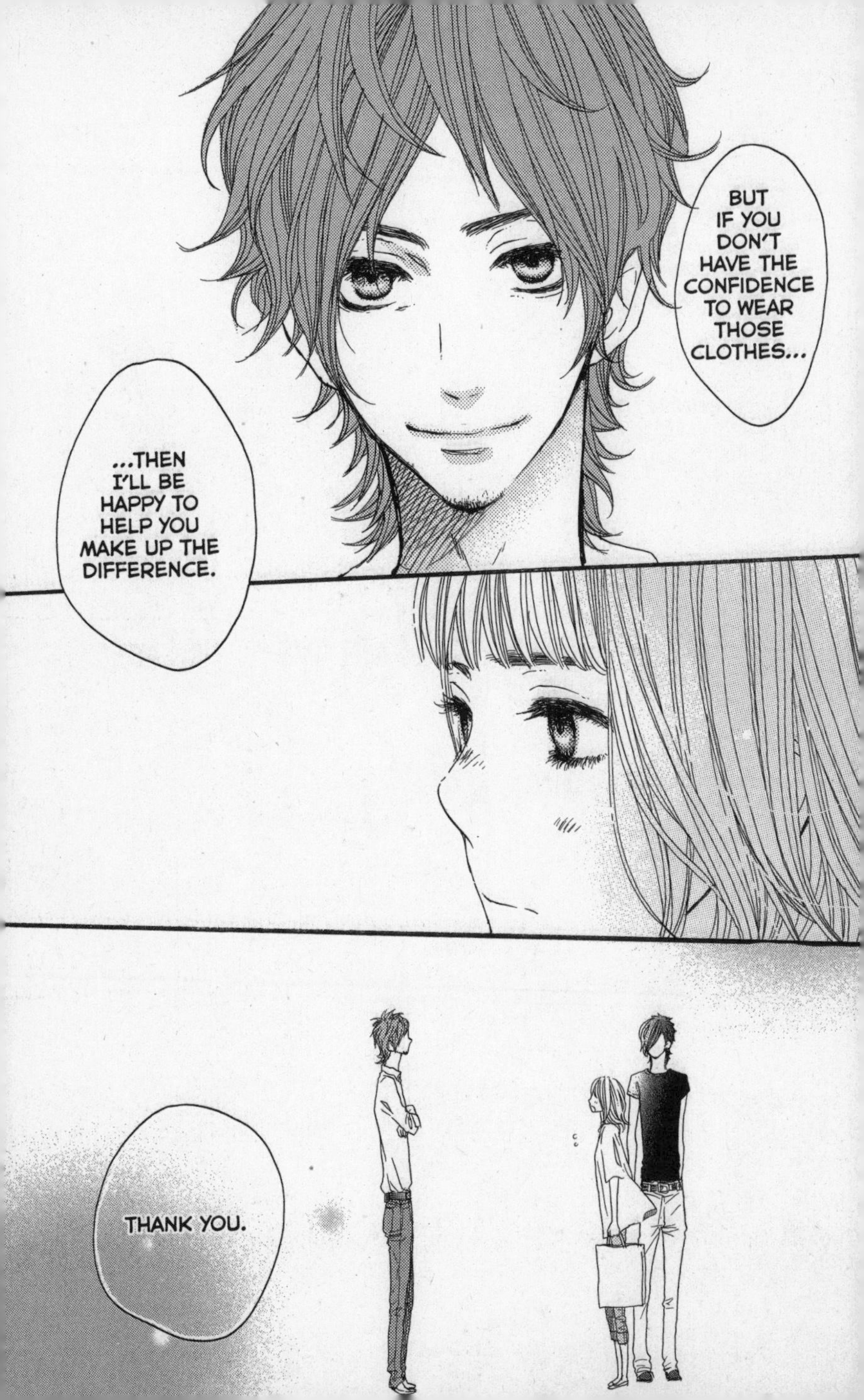
BUT IF YOU DON'T HAVE THE CONFIDENCE TO WEAR THOSE CLOTHES...
...THEN I'LL BE HAPPY TO HELP YOU MAKE UP THE DIFFERENCE.
THANK YOU.

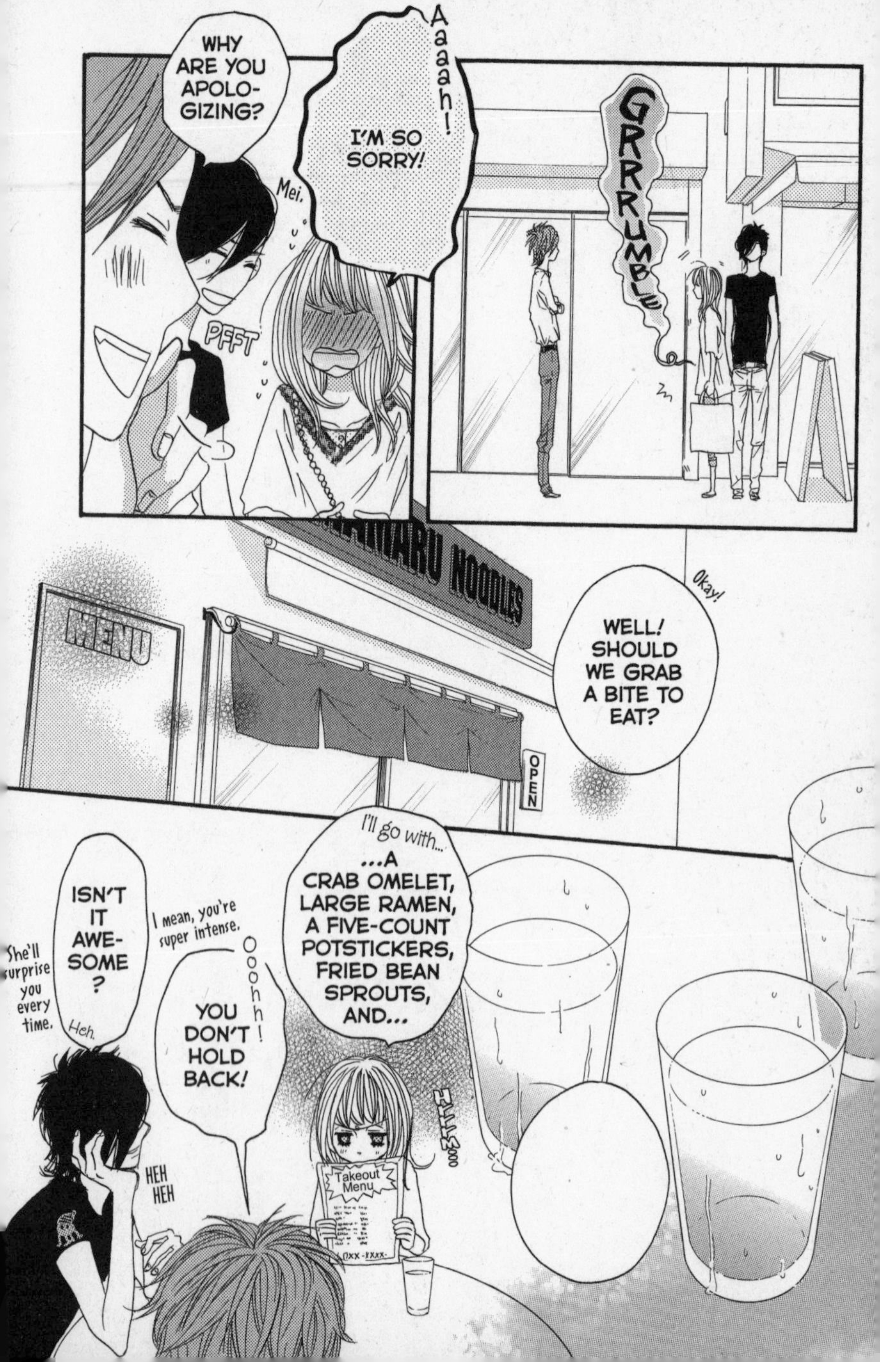

GRRRUMBLE
Aaaah!
I'M SO SORRY!
Mei.
WHY ARE YOU APOLOGIZING?
PFFT
NOODLES
Okay!
WELL! SHOULD WE GRAB A BITE TO EAT?
MENU
OPEN
I'll go with...
...A CRAB OMELET, LARGE RAMEN, A FIVE-COUNT POTSTICKERS, FRIED BEAN SPROUTS, AND...
Takeout Menu
Ooohh!
YOU DON'T HOLD BACK!
I mean, you're super intense.
ISN'T IT AWESOME?
Heh.
She'll surprise you every time.
HEH HEH

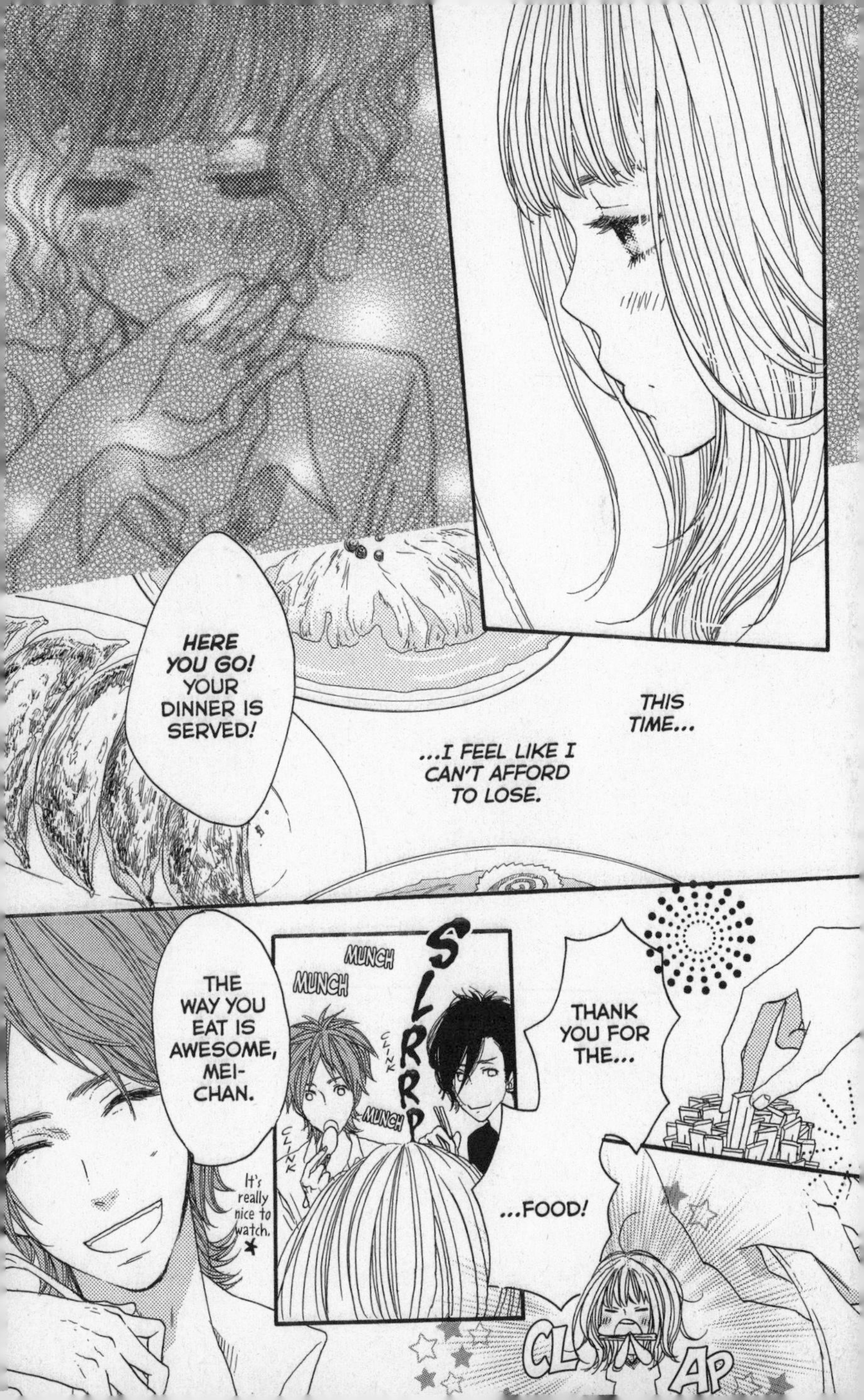
THIS TIME...
...I FEEL LIKE I CAN'T AFFORD TO LOSE.
HERE YOU GO! YOUR DINNER IS SERVED!
THANK YOU FOR THE...
...FOOD!
CLAP
MUNCH
MUNCH
SLRRP
CLINK
MUNCH
CLINK
THE WAY YOU EAT IS AWESOME, MEI-CHAN.
It's really nice to watch. ★

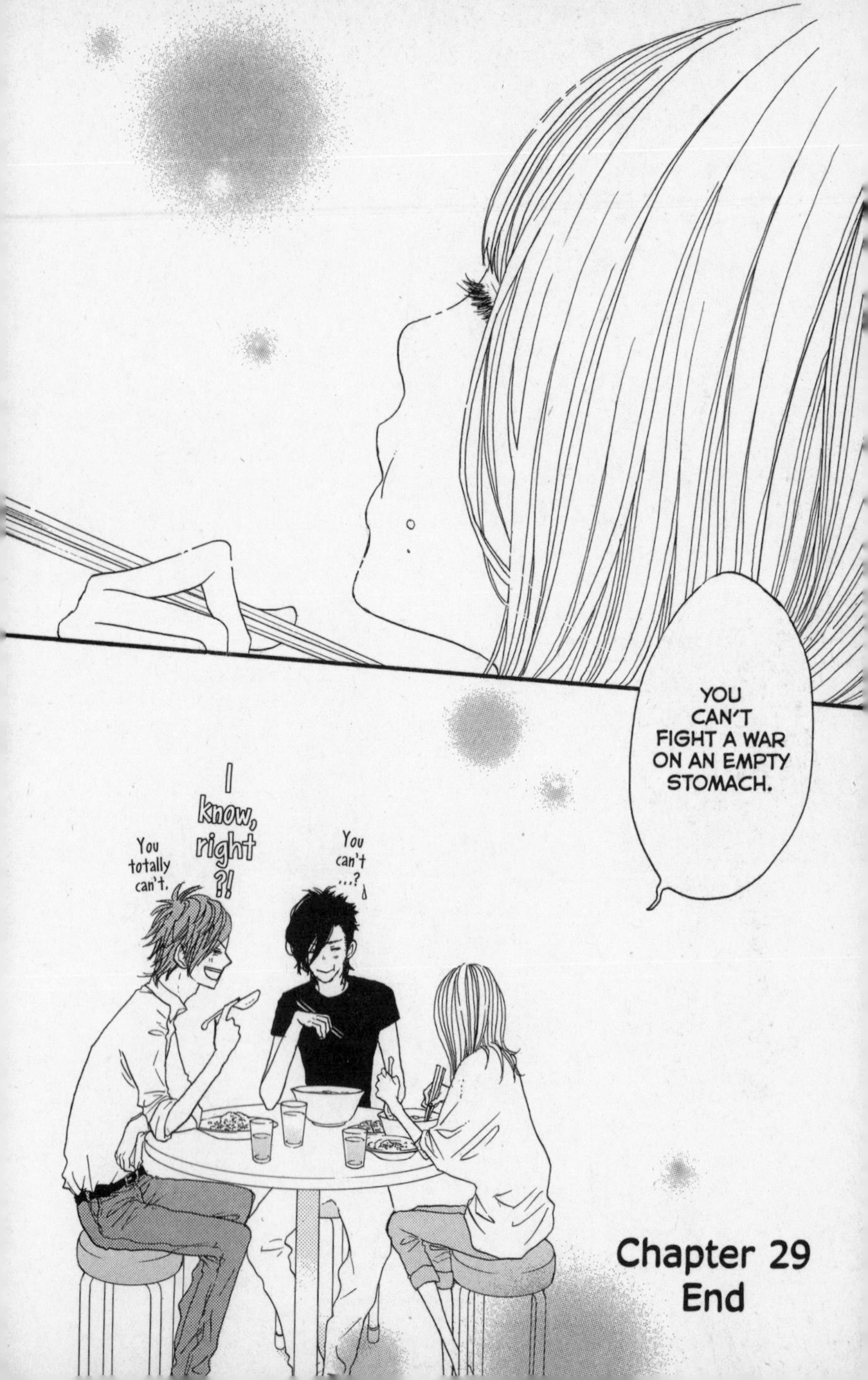
YOU CAN'T FIGHT A WAR ON AN EMPTY STOMACH.
You can't ...?
I know, right?!
You totally can't.
Chapter 29 End

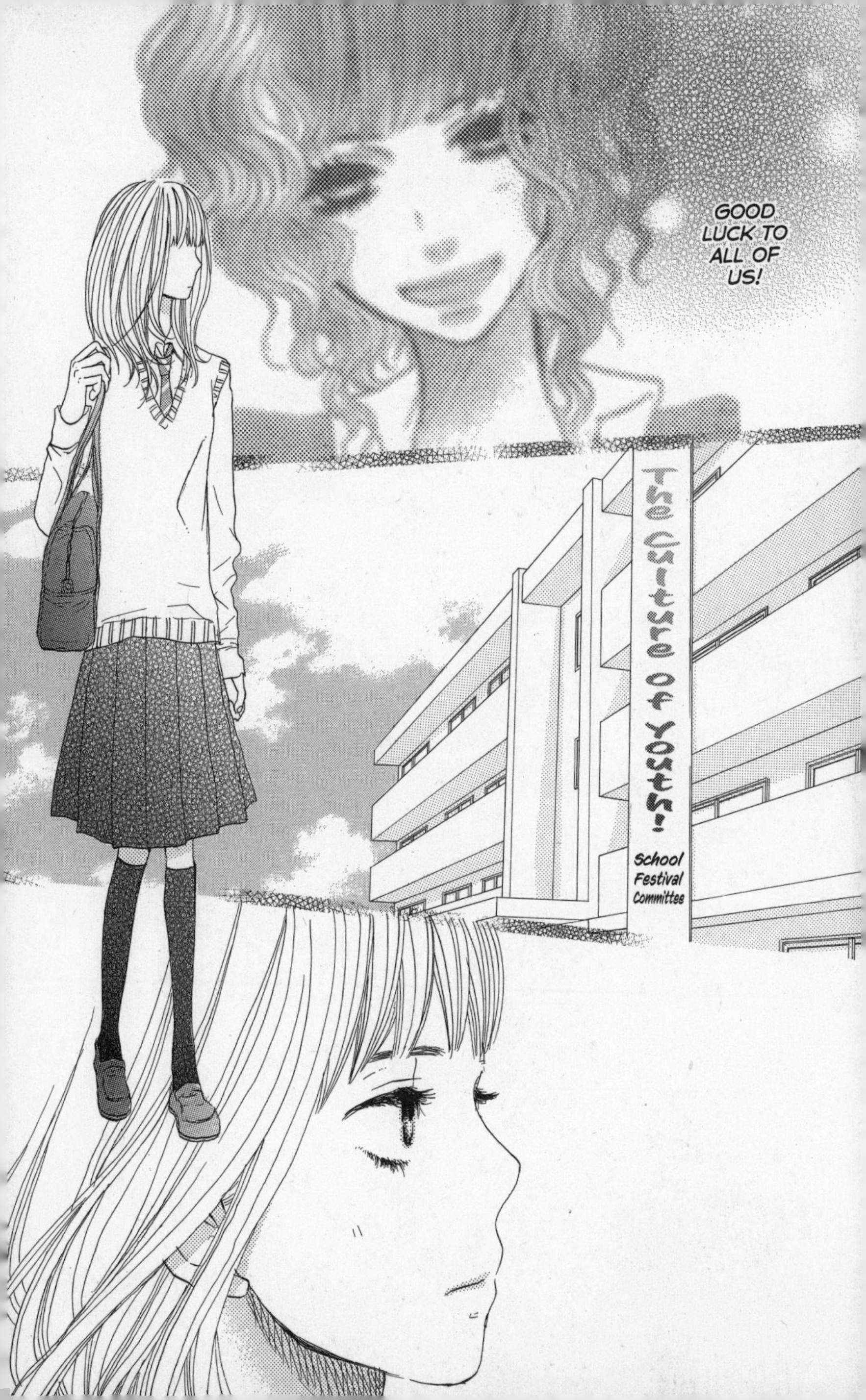
GOOD LUCK TO ALL OF US!
The Culture of Youth!
School Festival Committee

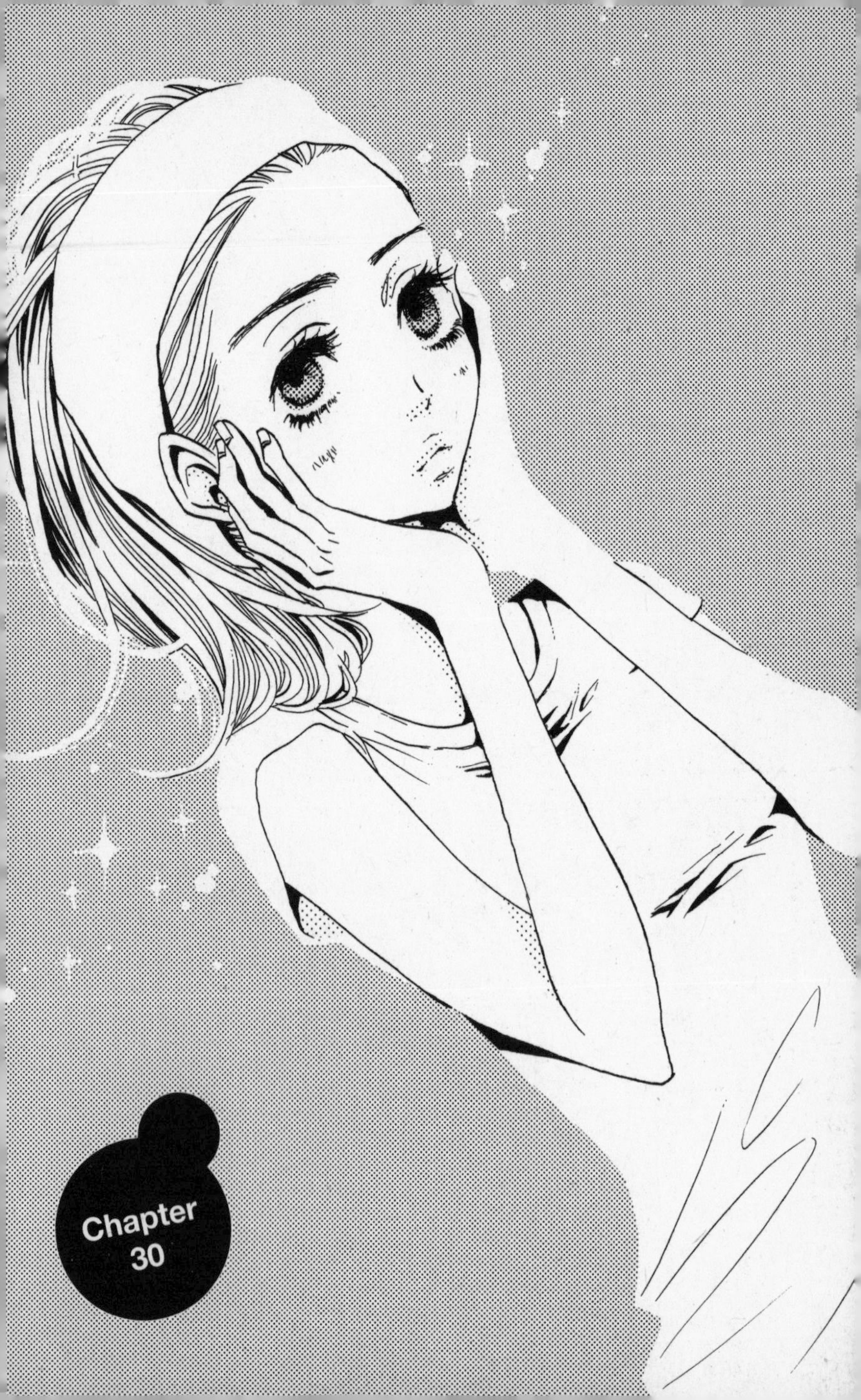
Chapter
30

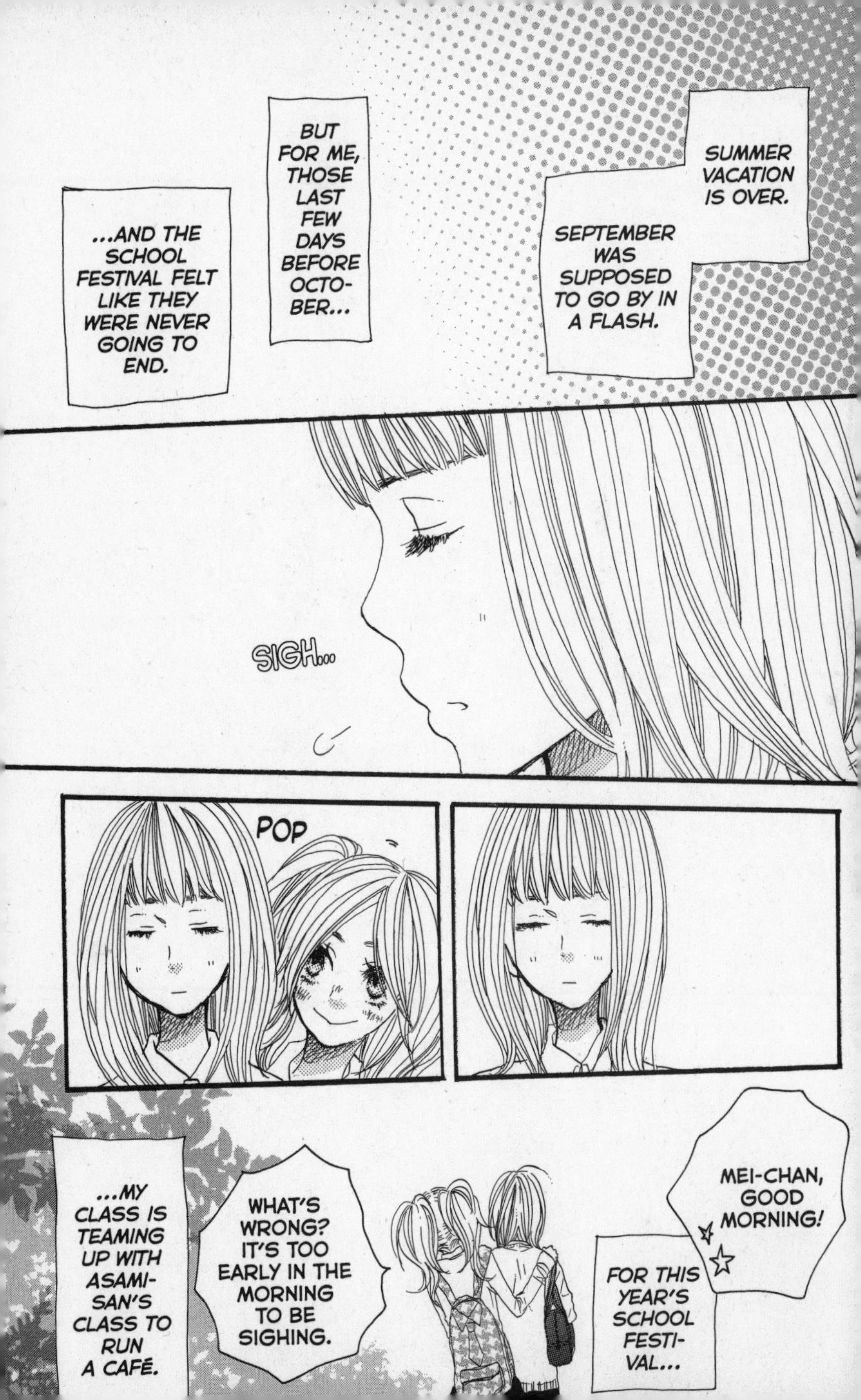
SUMMER VACATION IS OVER.
SEPTEMBER WAS SUPPOSED TO GO BY IN A FLASH.
BUT FOR ME, THOSE LAST FEW DAYS BEFORE OCTOBER...
...AND THE SCHOOL FESTIVAL FELT LIKE THEY WERE NEVER GOING TO END.
SIGH...
POP
MEI-CHAN, GOOD MORNING!
FOR THIS YEAR'S SCHOOL FESTIVAL...
WHAT'S WRONG? IT'S TOO EARLY IN THE MORNING TO BE SIGHING.
...MY CLASS IS TEAMING UP WITH ASAMI-SAN'S CLASS TO RUN A CAFÉ.

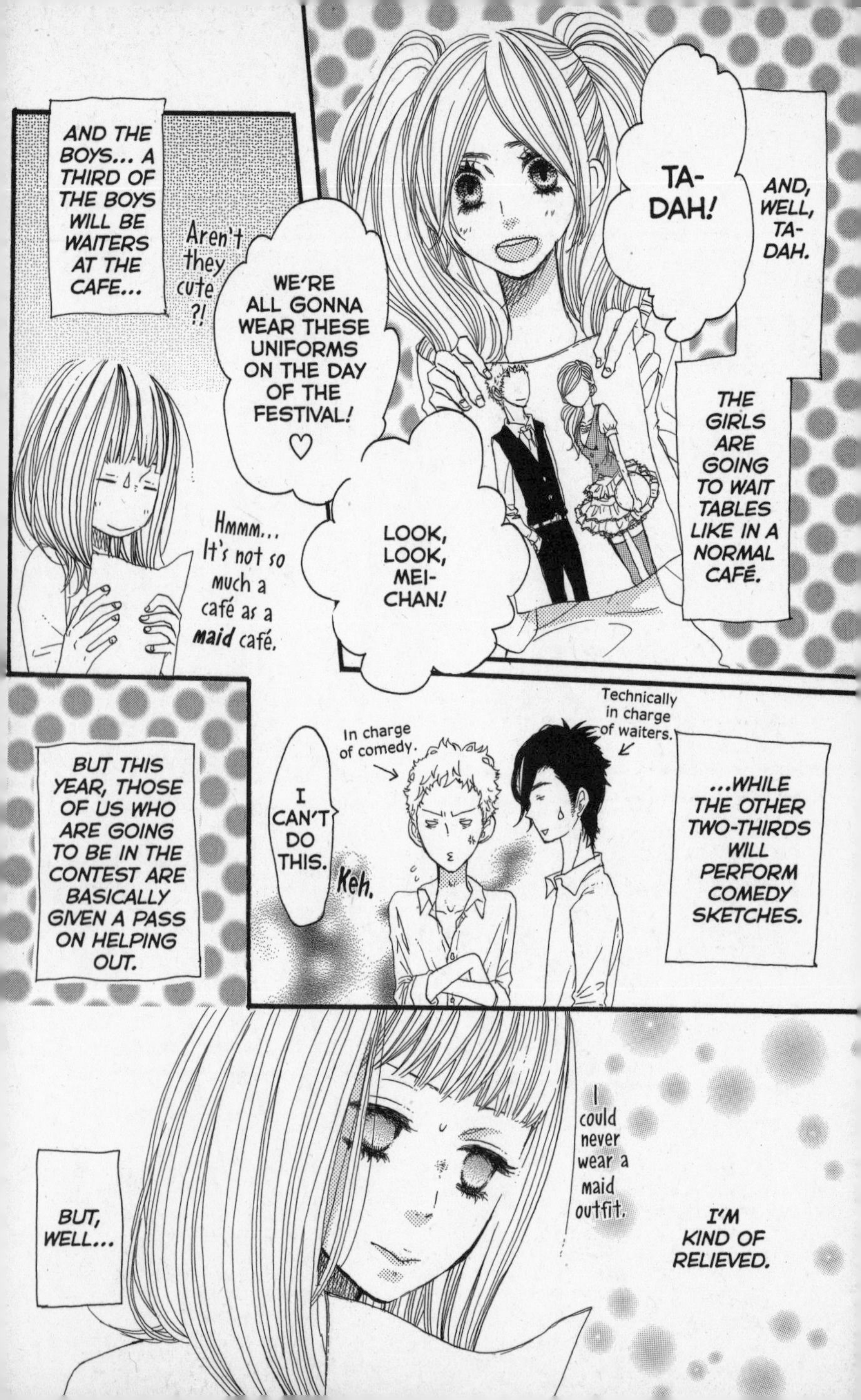
TA-DAH!
AND, WELL, TA-DAH.
THE GIRLS ARE GOING TO WAIT TABLES LIKE IN A NORMAL CAFÉ.
WE'RE ALL GONNA WEAR THESE UNIFORMS ON THE DAY OF THE FESTIVAL! ♡
LOOK, LOOK, MEI-CHAN!
AND THE BOYS... A THIRD OF THE BOYS WILL BE WAITERS AT THE CAFE...
Aren't they cute?!
Hmmm... It's not so much a café as a maid café.
...WHILE THE OTHER TWO-THIRDS WILL PERFORM COMEDY SKETCHES.
Technically in charge of waiters.
In charge of comedy.
I CAN'T DO THIS.
Keh.
BUT THIS YEAR, THOSE OF US WHO ARE GOING TO BE IN THE CONTEST ARE BASICALLY GIVEN A PASS ON HELPING OUT.
I'M KIND OF RELIEVED.
I could never wear a maid outfit.
BUT, WELL...

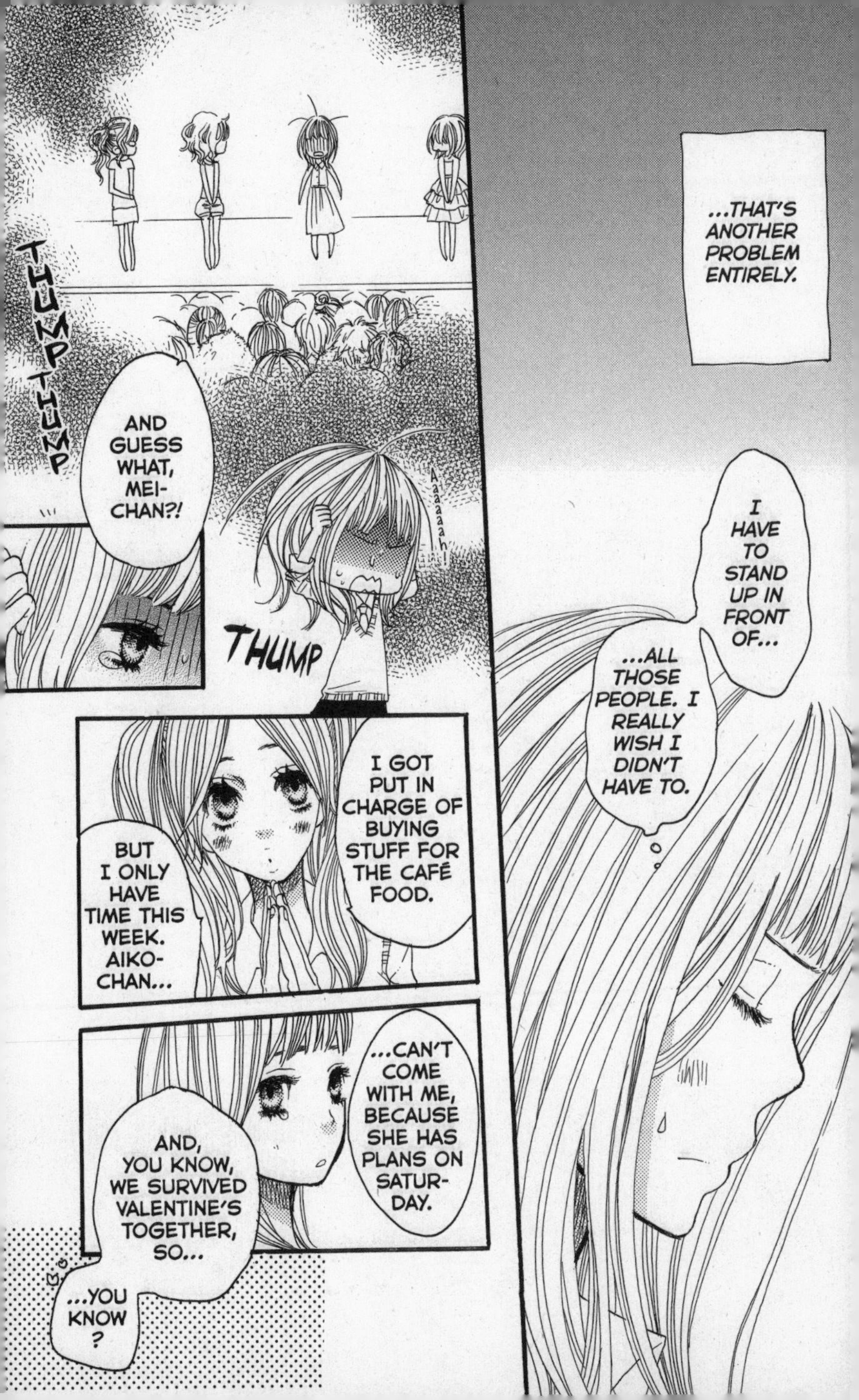
...THAT'S ANOTHER PROBLEM ENTIRELY.
I HAVE TO STAND UP IN FRONT OF...
...ALL THOSE PEOPLE. I REALLY WISH I DIDN'T HAVE TO.
THUMP THUMP
Aaaaaaah!
THUMP
AND GUESS WHAT, MEI-CHAN?!
I GOT PUT IN CHARGE OF BUYING STUFF FOR THE CAFÉ FOOD.
BUT I ONLY HAVE TIME THIS WEEK. AIKO-CHAN...
...CAN'T COME WITH ME, BECAUSE SHE HAS PLANS ON SATUR-DAY.
AND, YOU KNOW, WE SURVIVED VALENTINE'S TOGETHER, SO...
...YOU KNOW?

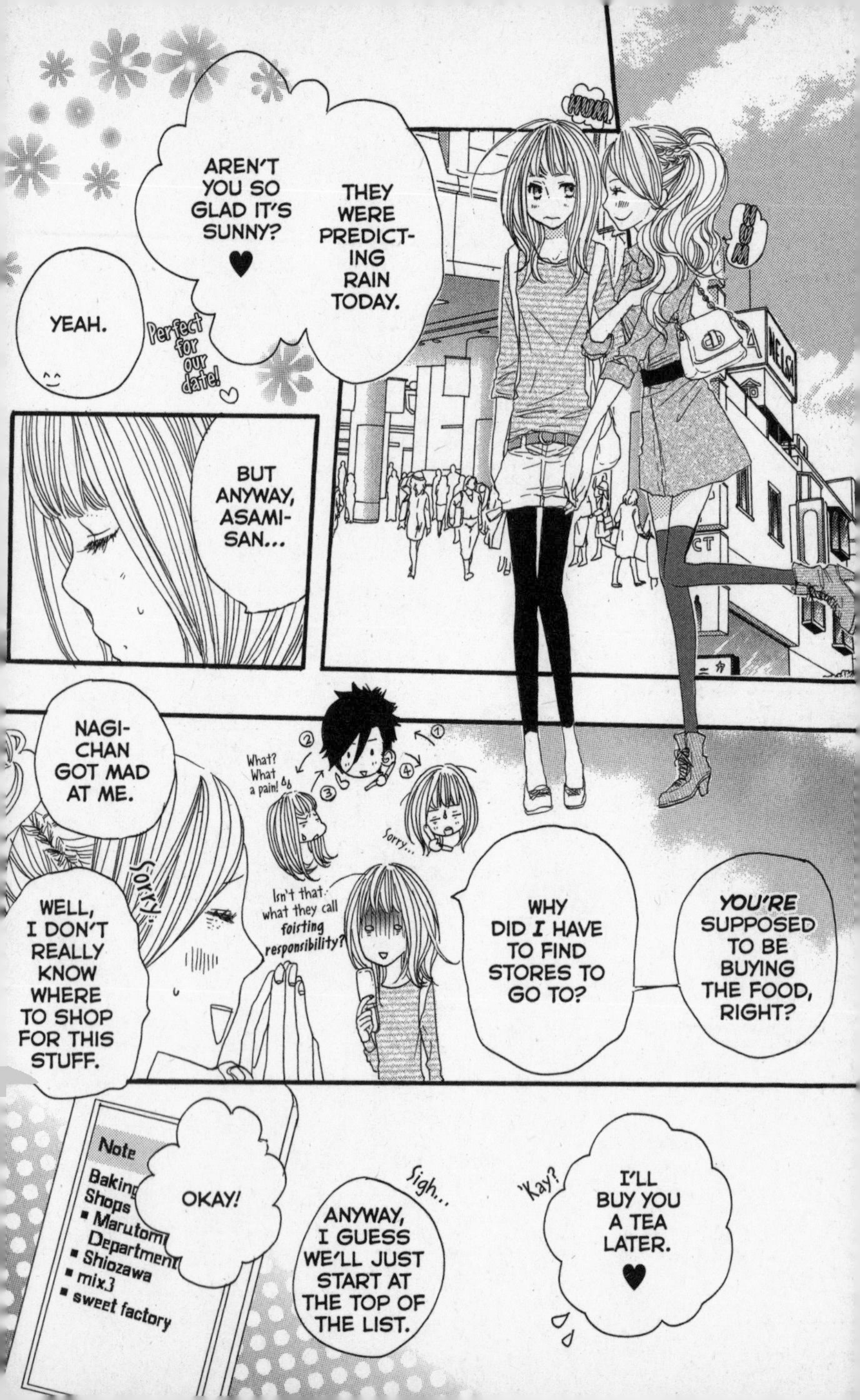
THEY WERE PREDICT-ING RAIN TODAY.
AREN'T YOU SO GLAD IT'S SUNNY? ♥
Perfect for our date!
YEAH.
BUT ANYWAY, ASAMI-SAN...
YOU'RE SUPPOSED TO BE BUYING THE FOOD, RIGHT?
WHY DID I HAVE TO FIND STORES TO GO TO?
Isn't that what they call foisting responsibility?
Sorry...
What? What a pain!
NAGI-CHAN GOT MAD AT ME.
Sorry
WELL, I DON'T REALLY KNOW WHERE TO SHOP FOR THIS STUFF.
I'LL BUY YOU A TEA LATER. ♥
'Kay?
Sigh...
ANYWAY, I GUESS WE'LL JUST START AT THE TOP OF THE LIST.
OKAY!
Note
Baking Shops
■ Marutomi Department
■ Shiozawa
■ mix.3
■ sweet factory

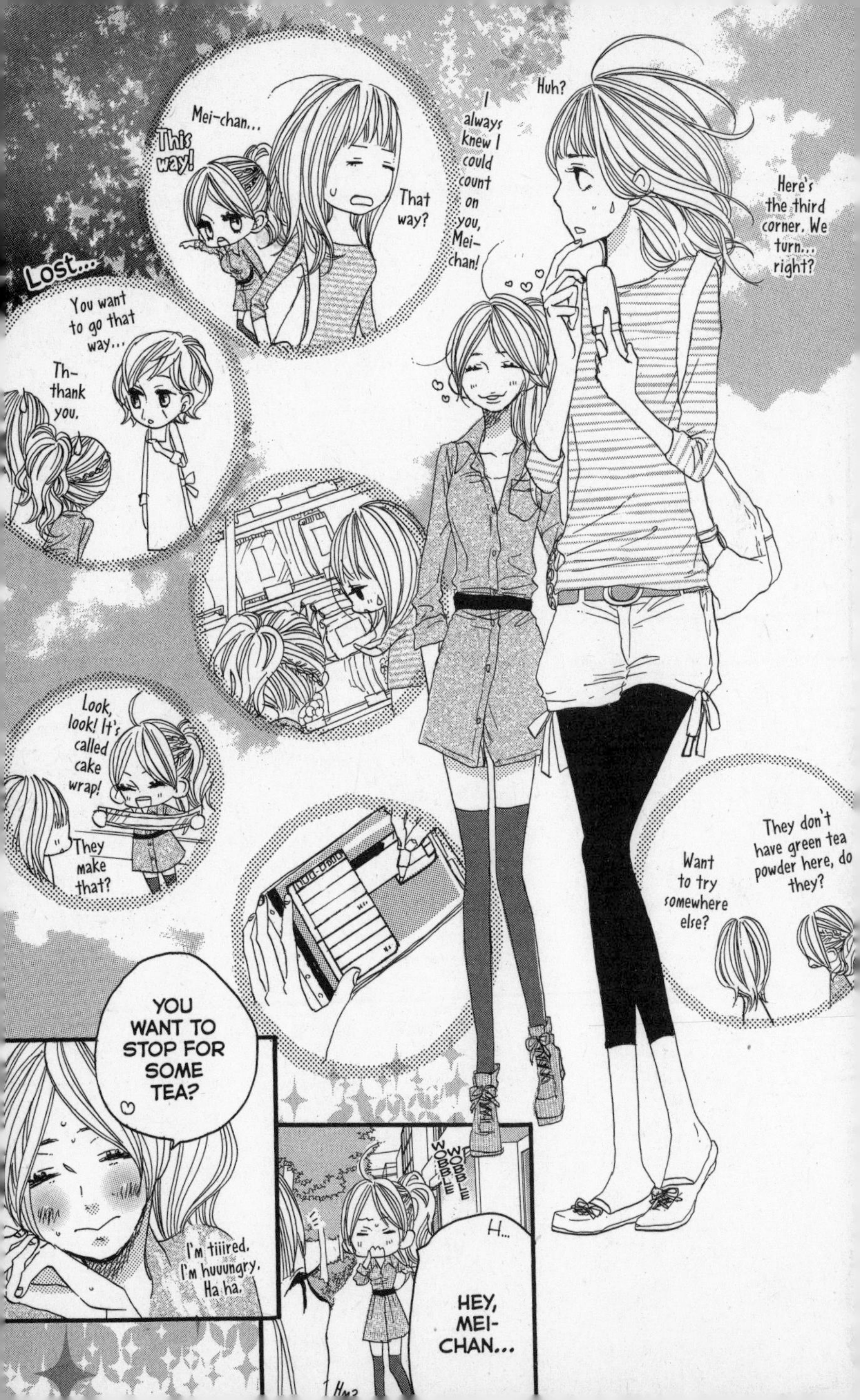

Here's the third corner. We turn... right?
Huh?
I always knew I could count on you, Mei-chan!
Mei-chan...
This way!
That way?
Lost...
You want to go that way...
Th-thank you.
They don't have green tea powder here, do they?
Want to try somewhere else?
Look, look! It's called cake wrap!
They make that?
H...
HEY, MEI-CHAN...
Hm?
WOBBLE WOBBLE
I'm tiiired. I'm huuungry. Ha ha.
YOU WANT TO STOP FOR SOME TEA?

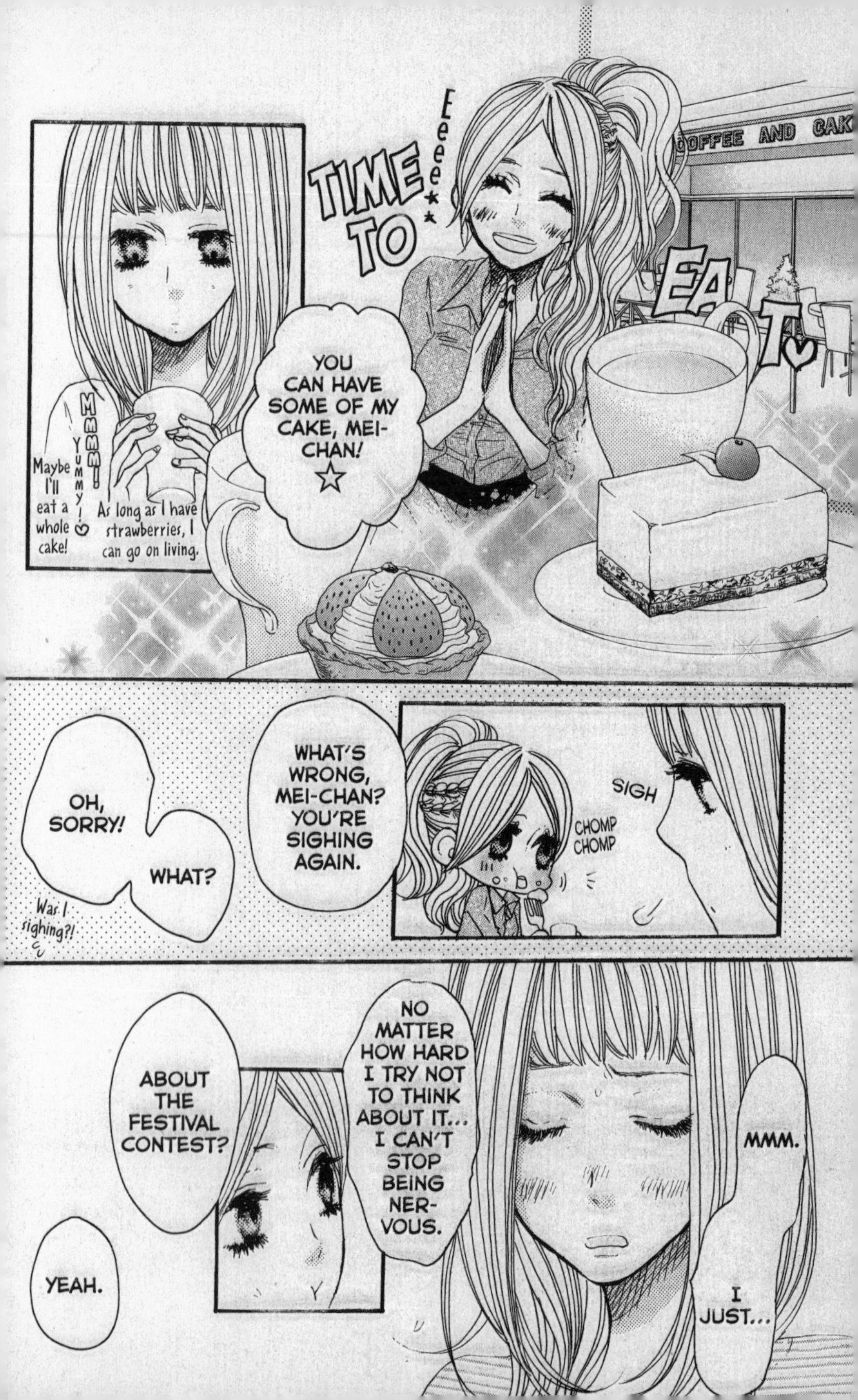
Eeeee★★
TIME TO EAT♥
YOU CAN HAVE SOME OF MY CAKE, MEI-CHAN! ☆
MMMM!
Yummy!
As long as I have strawberries, I can go on living.
Maybe I'll eat a whole cake!
SIGH
CHOMP CHOMP
WHAT'S WRONG, MEI-CHAN? YOU'RE SIGHING AGAIN.
WHAT?
OH, SORRY!
Was I sighing?!
MMM.
I JUST...
NO MATTER HOW HARD I TRY NOT TO THINK ABOUT IT... I CAN'T STOP BEING NERVOUS.
ABOUT THE FESTIVAL CONTEST?
YEAH.

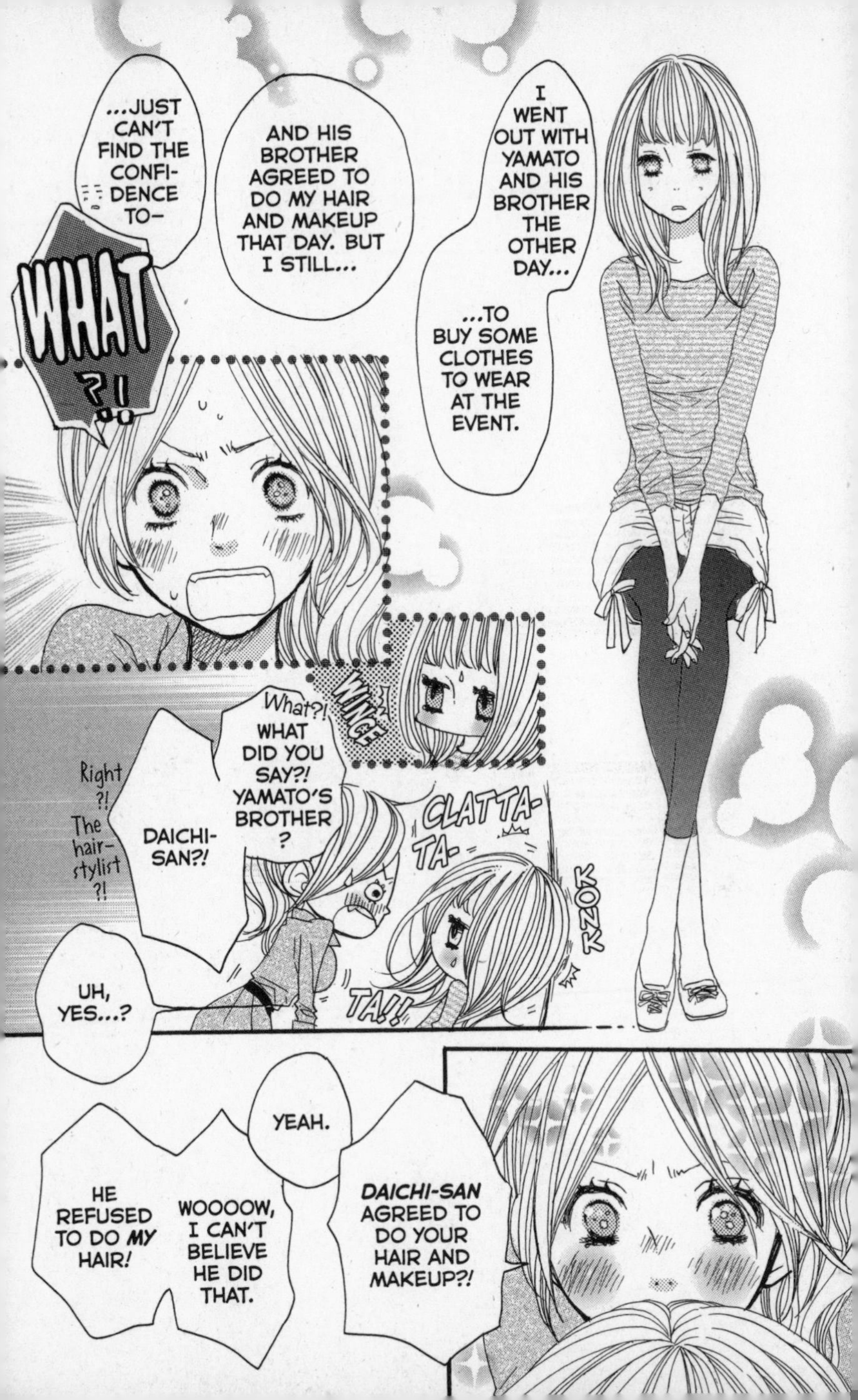
I WENT OUT WITH YAMATO AND HIS BROTHER THE OTHER DAY...
...TO BUY SOME CLOTHES TO WEAR AT THE EVENT.
AND HIS BROTHER AGREED TO DO MY HAIR AND MAKEUP THAT DAY. BUT I STILL...
...JUST CAN'T FIND THE CONFI-DENCE TO—
WHAT ?!
WINCE
What?! WHAT DID YOU SAY?! YAMATO'S BROTHER?
CLATTA-TA-TA!!
KONK
DAICHI-SAN?!
Right?! The hair-stylist?!
UH, YES...?
DAICHI-SAN AGREED TO DO YOUR HAIR AND MAKEUP?!
YEAH.
WOOOOW, I CAN'T BELIEVE HE DID THAT.
HE REFUSED TO DO *MY* HAIR!

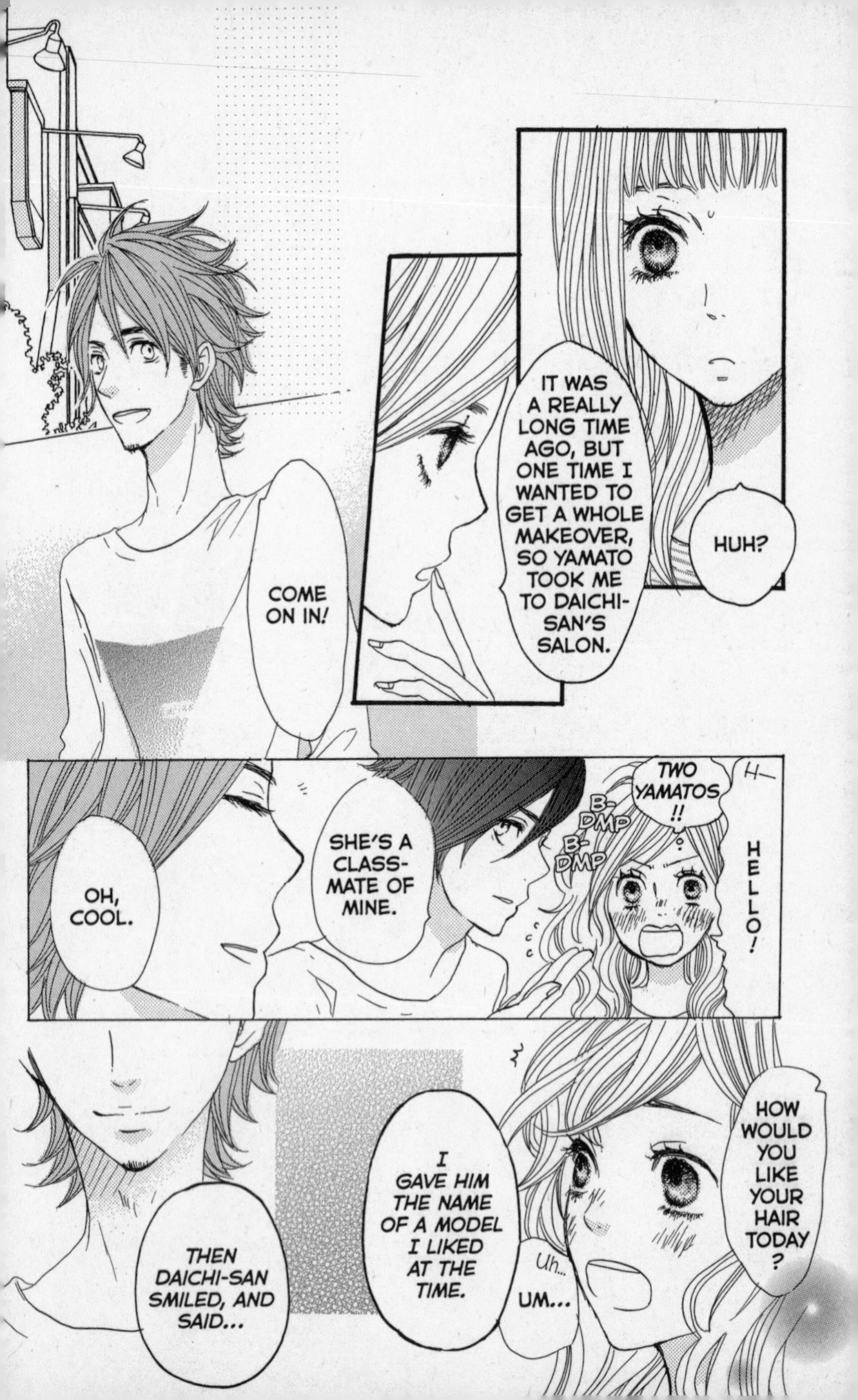
HUH?
IT WAS A REALLY LONG TIME AGO, BUT ONE TIME I WANTED TO GET A WHOLE MAKEOVER, SO YAMATO TOOK ME TO DAICHI-SAN'S SALON.
COME ON IN!
H—
HELLO!
TWO YAMATOS!!
B-DMP
B-DMP
SHE'S A CLASSMATE OF MINE.
OH, COOL.
HOW WOULD YOU LIKE YOUR HAIR TODAY?
Uh...
UM...
I GAVE HIM THE NAME OF A MODEL I LIKED AT THE TIME.
THEN DAICHI-SAN SMILED, AND SAID...

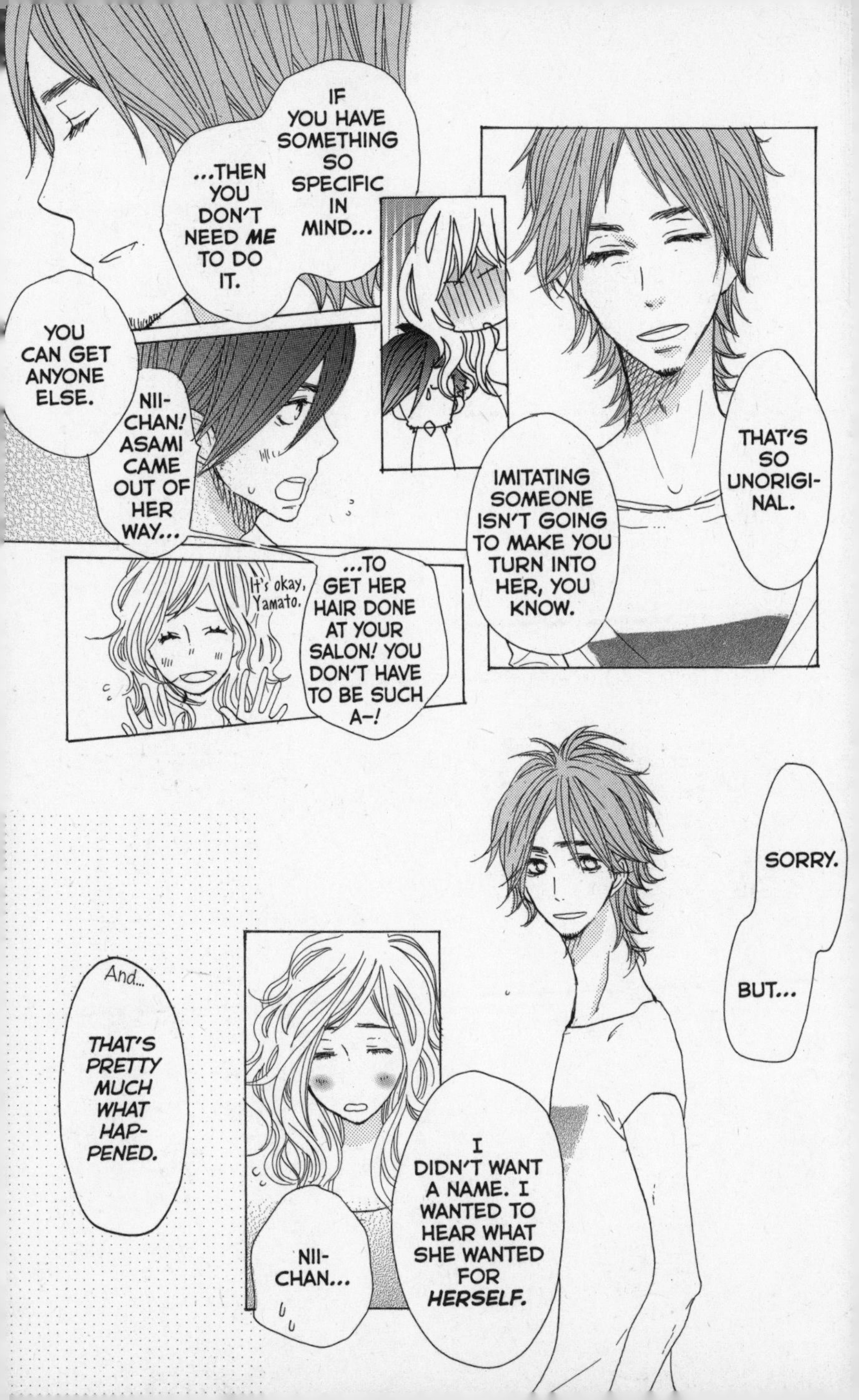
THAT'S SO UNORIGINAL.
IMITATING SOMEONE ISN'T GOING TO MAKE YOU TURN INTO HER, YOU KNOW.
IF YOU HAVE SOMETHING SO SPECIFIC IN MIND...
...THEN YOU DON'T NEED *ME* TO DO IT.
YOU CAN GET ANYONE ELSE.
NII-CHAN! ASAMI CAME OUT OF HER WAY...
...TO GET HER HAIR DONE AT YOUR SALON! YOU DON'T HAVE TO BE SUCH A-!
It's okay, Yamato.
SORRY.
BUT...
I DIDN'T WANT A NAME. I WANTED TO HEAR WHAT SHE WANTED FOR *HERSELF*.
NII-CHAN...
And...
THAT'S PRETTY MUCH WHAT HAPPENED.

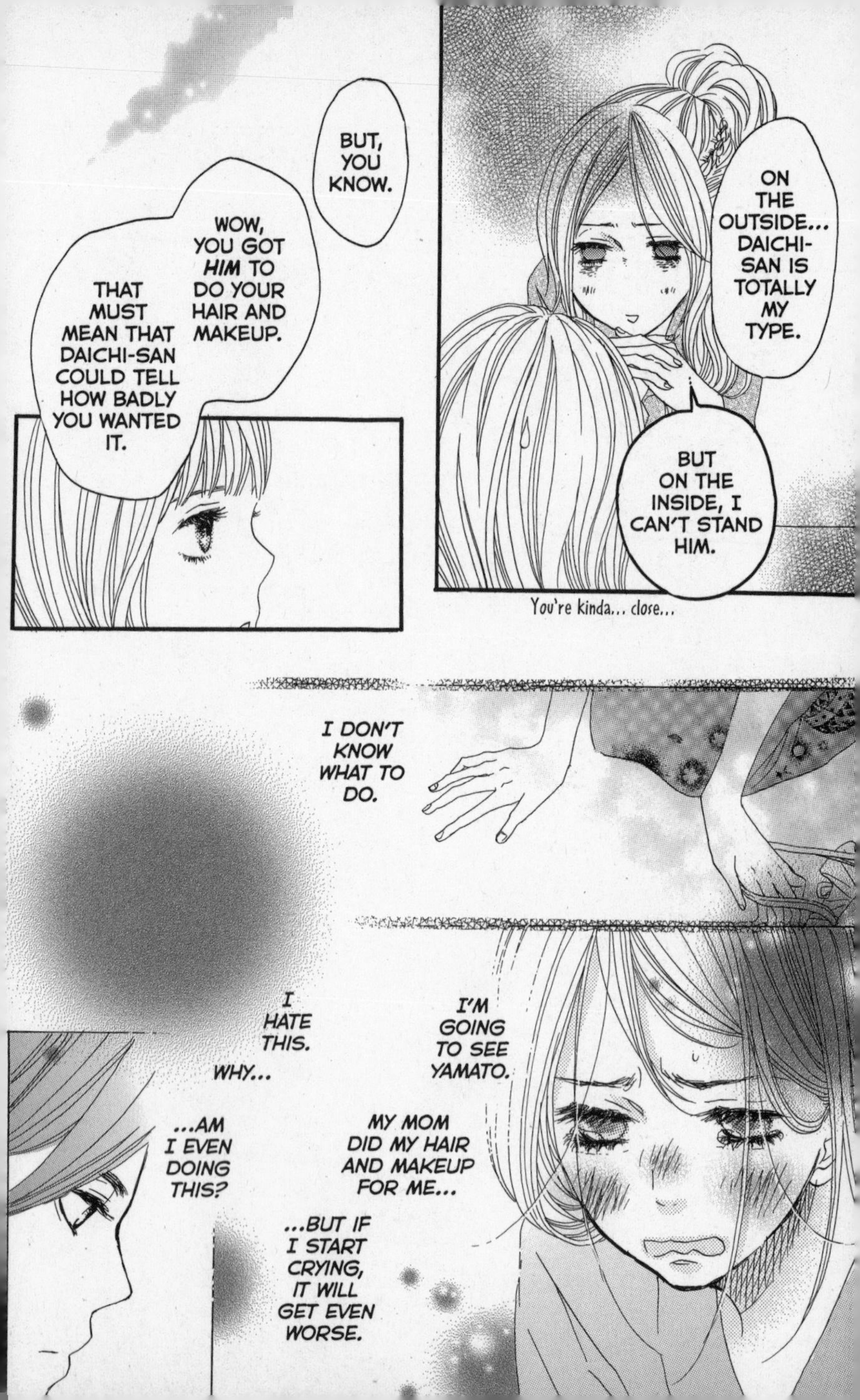

ON THE OUTSIDE... DAICHI-SAN IS TOTALLY MY TYPE.
BUT ON THE INSIDE, I CAN'T STAND HIM.
You're kinda... close...
BUT, YOU KNOW.
WOW, YOU GOT *HIM* TO DO YOUR HAIR AND MAKEUP.
THAT MUST MEAN THAT DAICHI-SAN COULD TELL HOW BADLY YOU WANTED IT.
I DON'T KNOW WHAT TO DO.
I'M GOING TO SEE YAMATO.
MY MOM DID MY HAIR AND MAKEUP FOR ME...
...BUT IF I START CRYING, IT WILL GET EVEN WORSE.
I HATE THIS.
WHY...
...AM I EVEN DOING THIS?

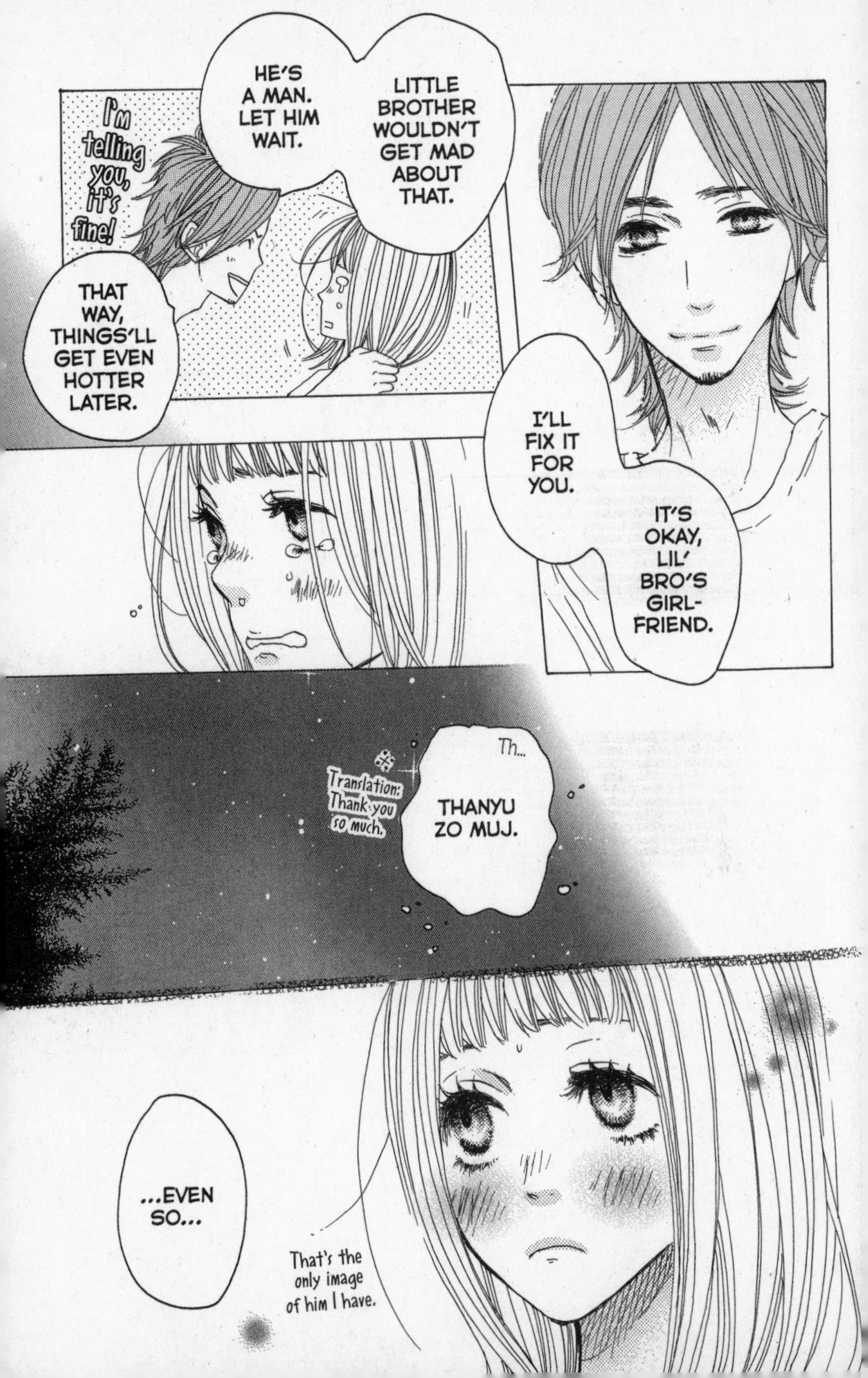
I'LL FIX IT FOR YOU.
IT'S OKAY, LIL' BRO'S GIRL-FRIEND.
LITTLE BROTHER WOULDN'T GET MAD ABOUT THAT.
HE'S A MAN. LET HIM WAIT.
I'm telling you, it's fine!
THAT WAY, THINGS'LL GET EVEN HOTTER LATER.
Th...
THANYU ZO MUJ.
Translation: Thank you so much.
...EVEN SO...
That's the only image of him I have.

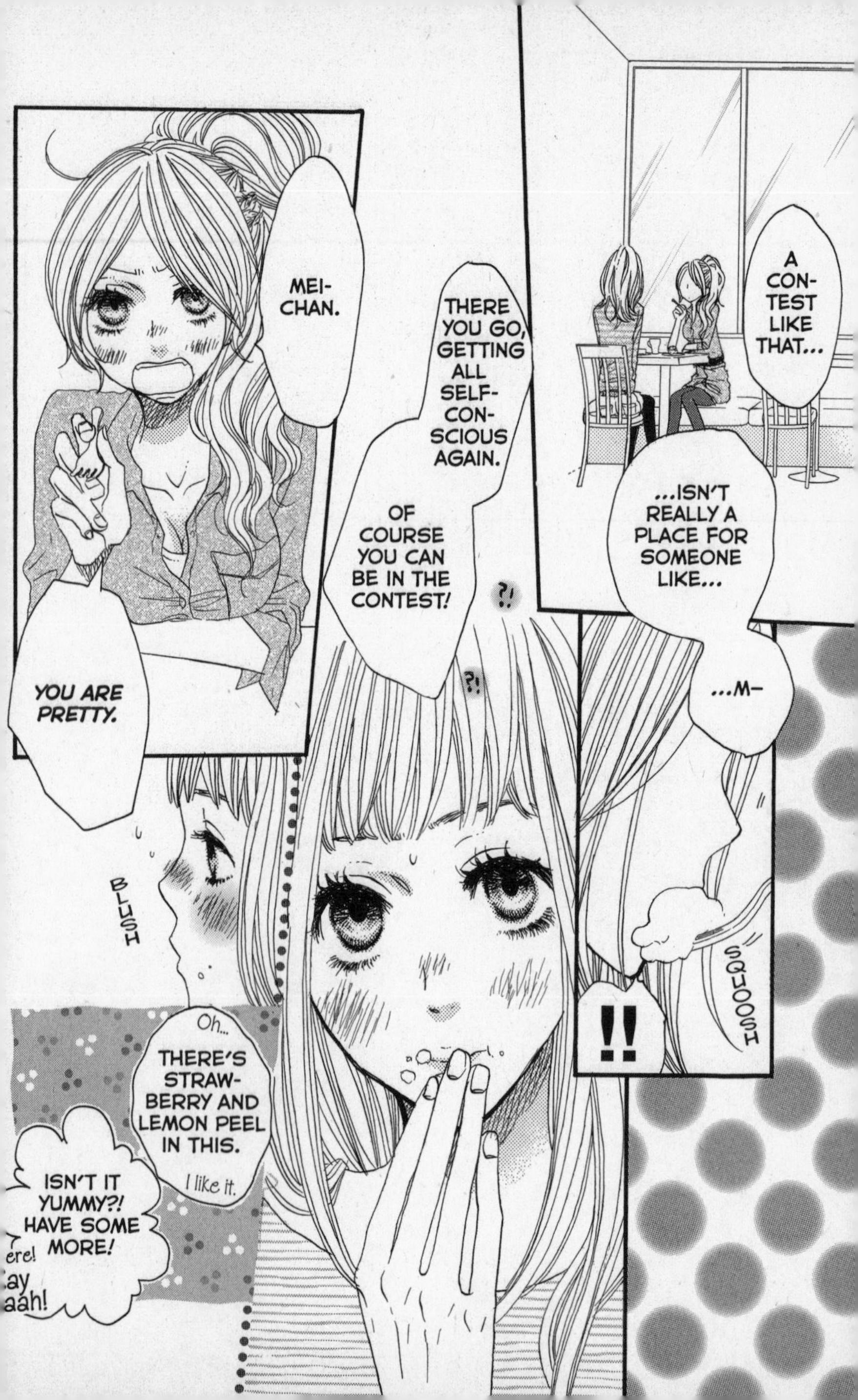
A CONTEST LIKE THAT...
...ISN'T REALLY A PLACE FOR SOMEONE LIKE...
MEI-CHAN.
THERE YOU GO, GETTING ALL SELF-CONSCIOUS AGAIN.
OF COURSE YOU CAN BE IN THE CONTEST!
YOU ARE PRETTY.
?!
?!
...M-
SQUOOSH
!!
BLUSH
Oh...
THERE'S STRAWBERRY AND LEMON PEEL IN THIS.
I like it.
ISN'T IT YUMMY?! HAVE SOME MORE!

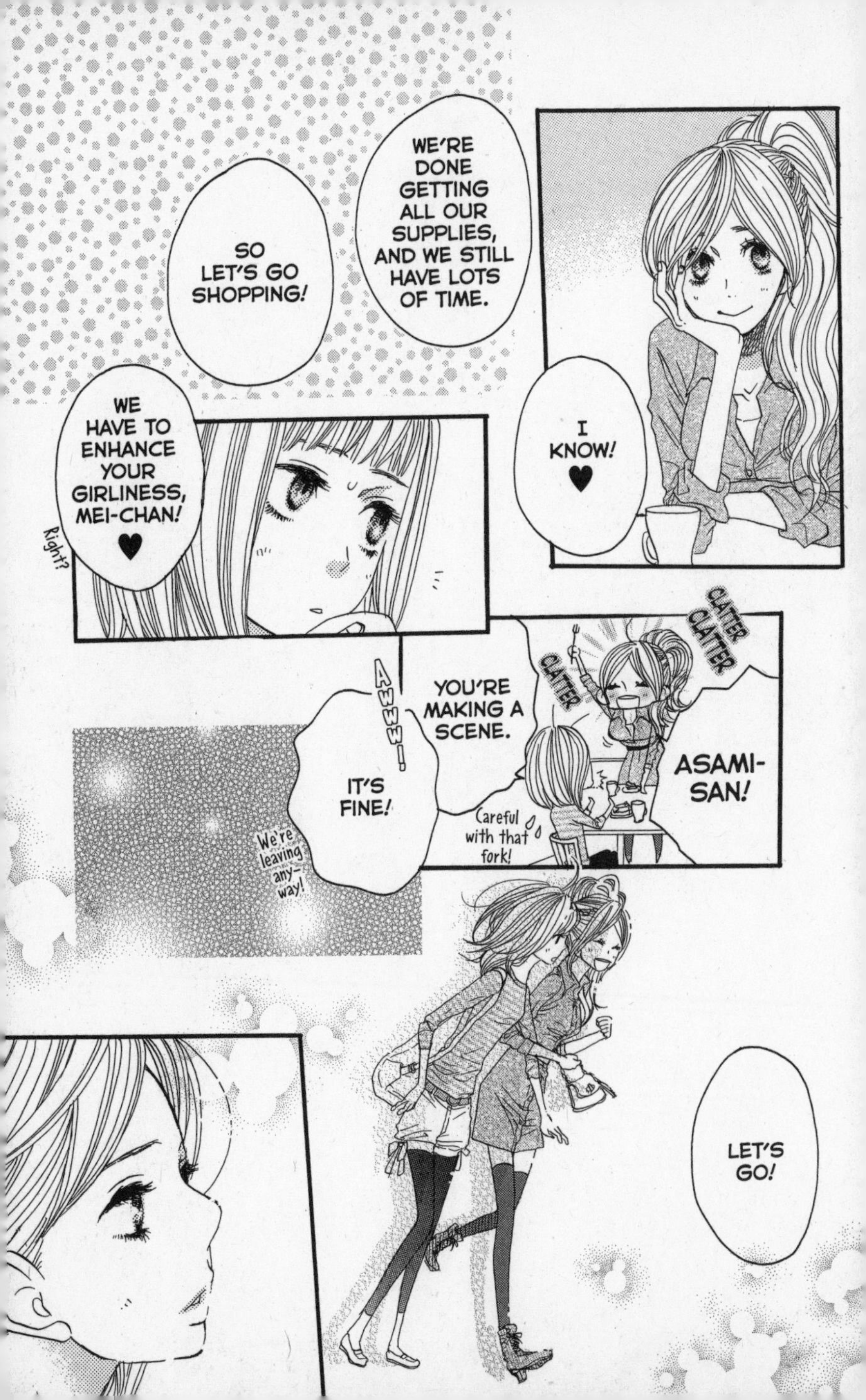
I KNOW! ♥
WE'RE DONE GETTING ALL OUR SUPPLIES, AND WE STILL HAVE LOTS OF TIME.
SO LET'S GO SHOPPING!
WE HAVE TO ENHANCE YOUR GIRLINESS, MEI-CHAN! ♥
Right?
CLATTER CLATTER
CLATTER
ASAMI-SAN!
YOU'RE MAKING A SCENE.
Careful with that fork!
AWWWW!
IT'S FINE!
We're leaving any-way!
LET'S GO!

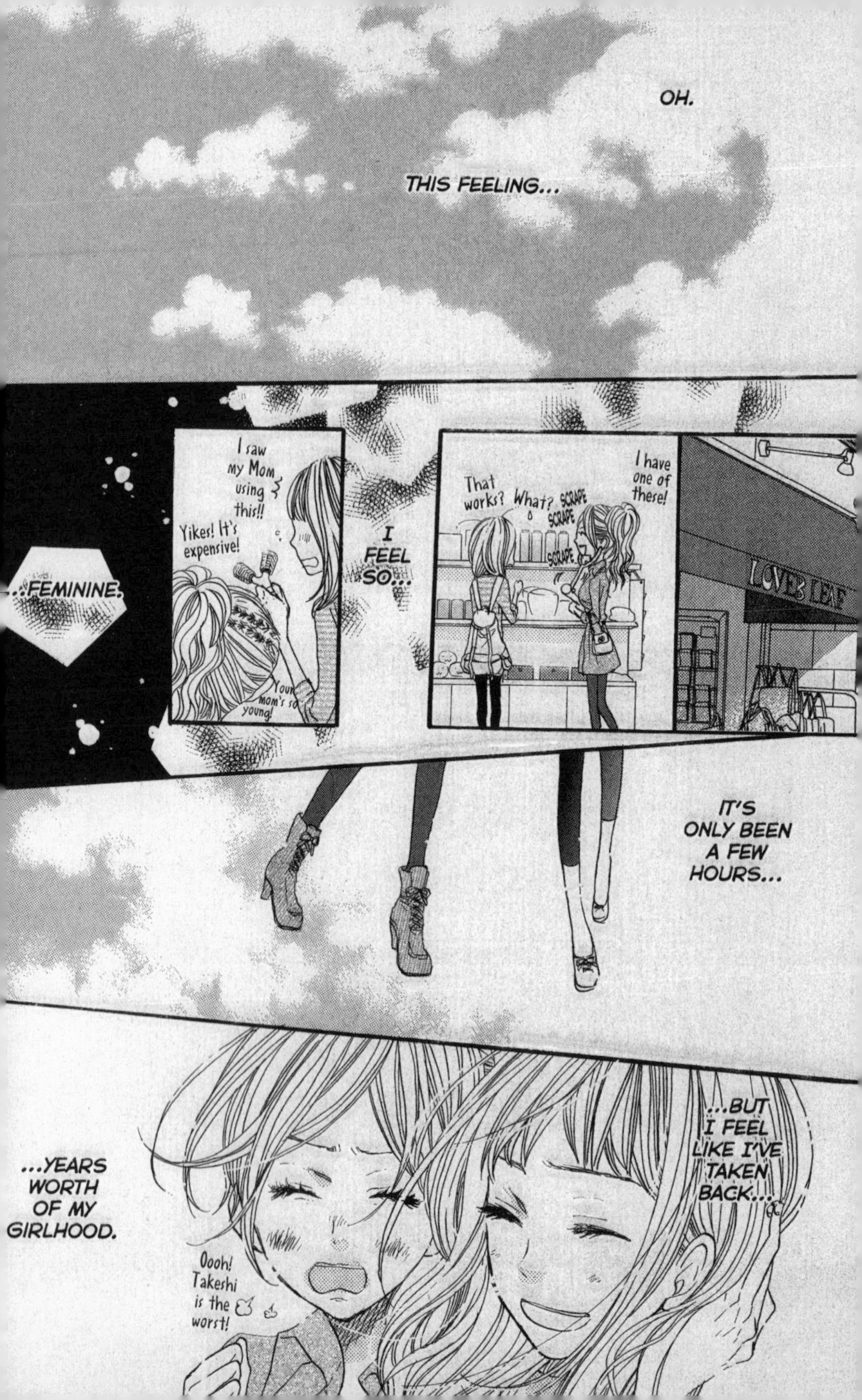
OH.
THIS FEELING...
I have one of these!
SCRAPE SCRAPE
SCRAPE
What?
That works?
I FEEL SO...
I saw my Mom using this!!
Yikes! It's expensive!
Your mom's so young!
...FEMININE.
IT'S ONLY BEEN A FEW HOURS...
...BUT I FEEL LIKE I'VE TAKEN BACK...
...YEARS WORTH OF MY GIRLHOOD.
Oooh! Takeshi is the worst!

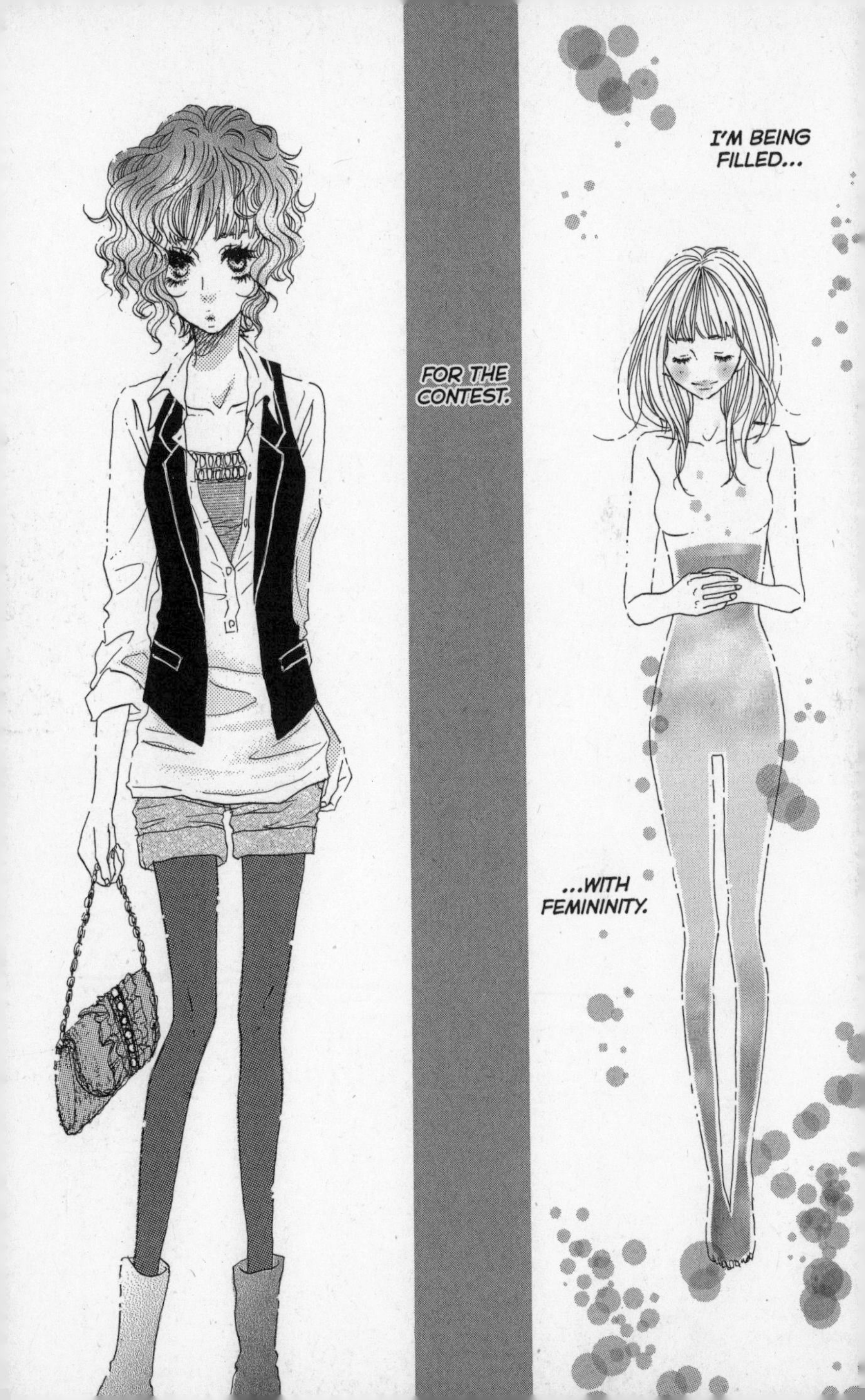
I'M BEING FILLED...
...WITH FEMININITY.
FOR THE CONTEST.

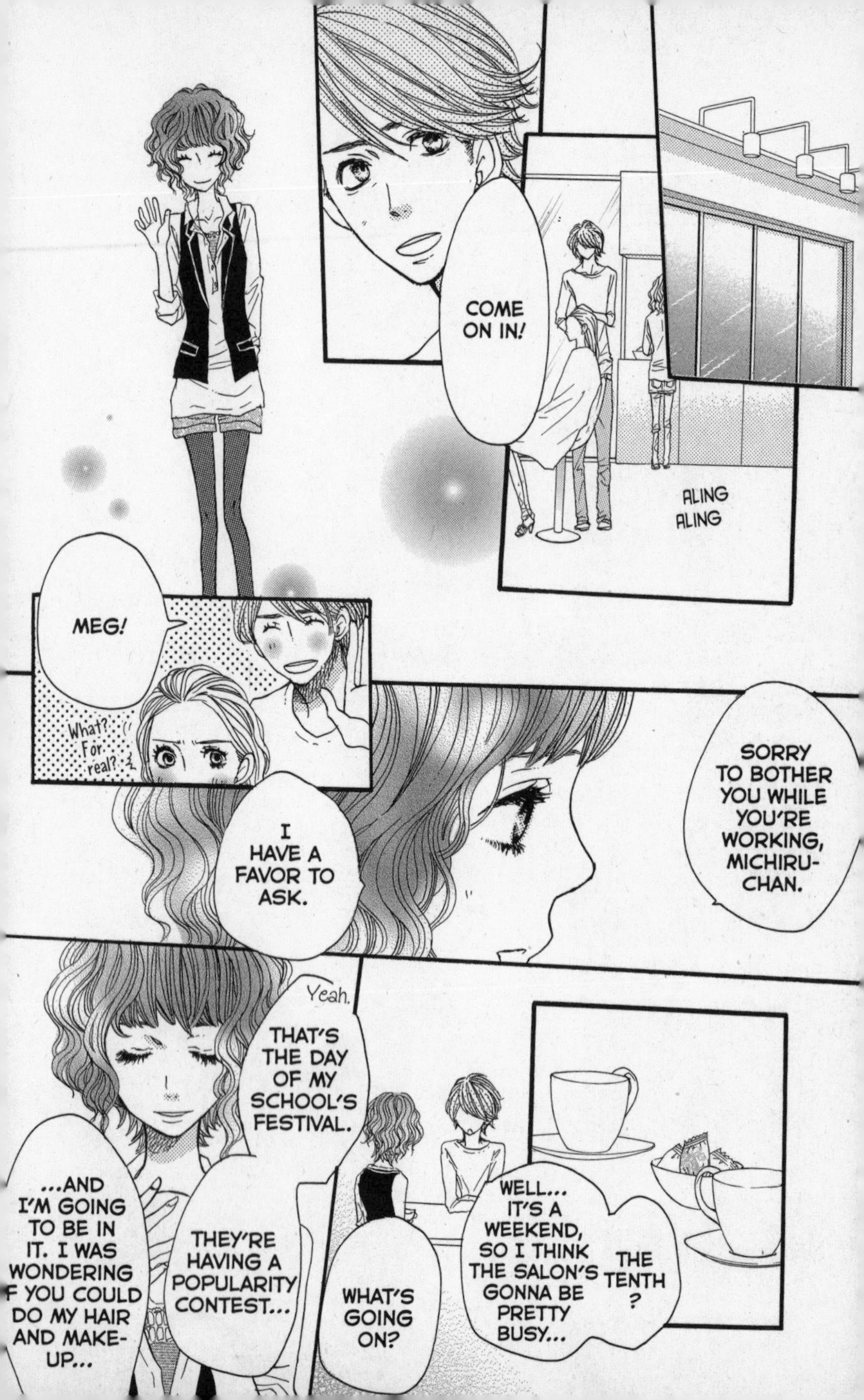
ALING ALING
COME ON IN!
MEG!
What? For real?
SORRY TO BOTHER YOU WHILE YOU'RE WORKING, MICHIRU-CHAN.
I HAVE A FAVOR TO ASK.
THE TENTH?
WELL... IT'S A WEEKEND, SO I THINK THE SALON'S GONNA BE PRETTY BUSY...
Yeah.
THAT'S THE DAY OF MY SCHOOL'S FESTIVAL.
WHAT'S GOING ON?
THEY'RE HAVING A POPULARITY CONTEST...
...AND I'M GOING TO BE IN IT. I WAS WONDERING F YOU COULD DO MY HAIR AND MAKE-UP...

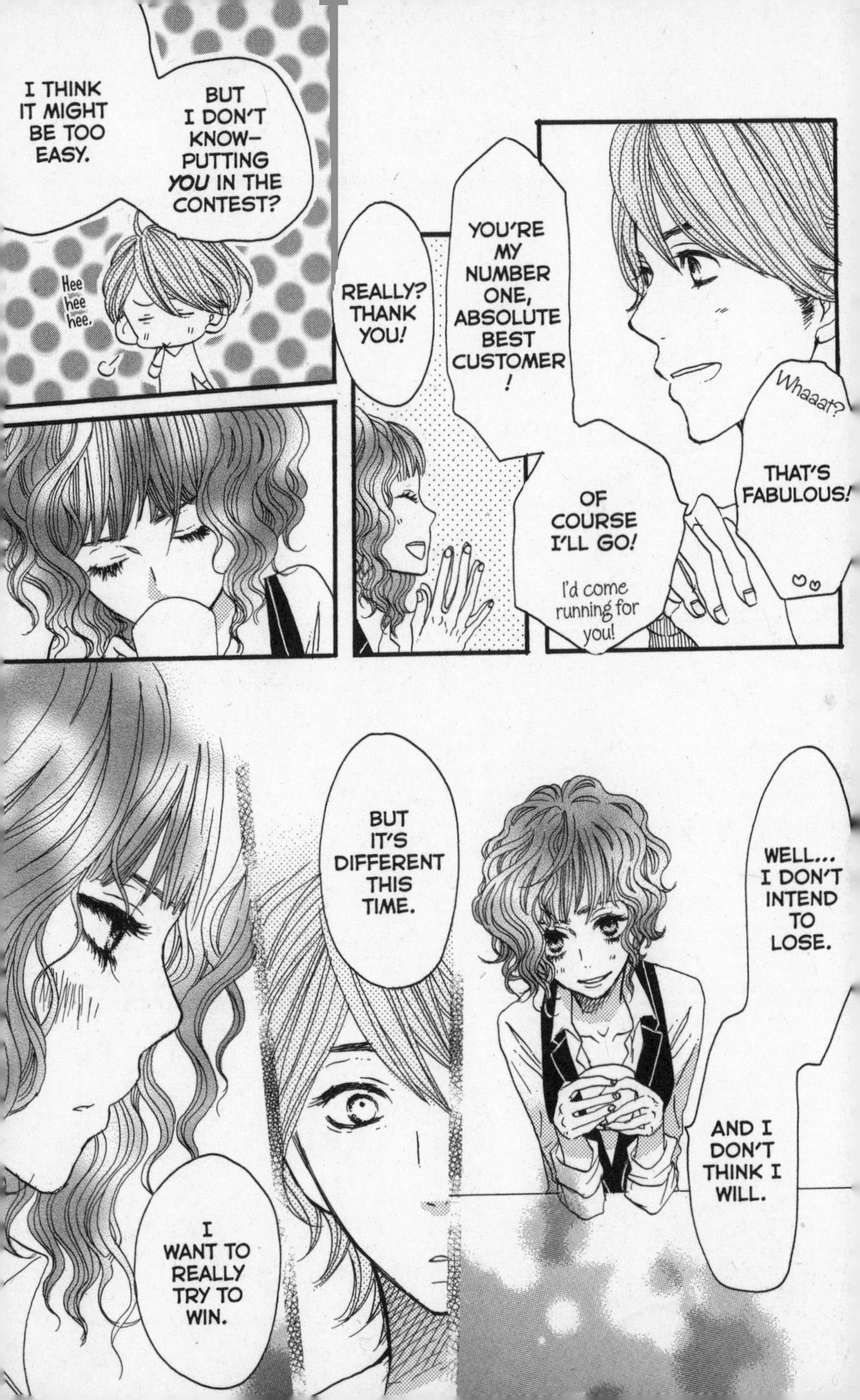
YOU'RE MY NUMBER ONE, ABSOLUTE BEST CUSTOMER!
Whaaat?
THAT'S FABULOUS!
OF COURSE I'LL GO!
I'd come running for you!
REALLY? THANK YOU!
BUT I DON'T KNOW— PUTTING *YOU* IN THE CONTEST?
I THINK IT MIGHT BE TOO EASY.
Hee hee hee.
WELL... I DON'T INTEND TO LOSE.
AND I DON'T THINK I WILL.
BUT IT'S DIFFERENT THIS TIME.
I WANT TO REALLY TRY TO WIN.

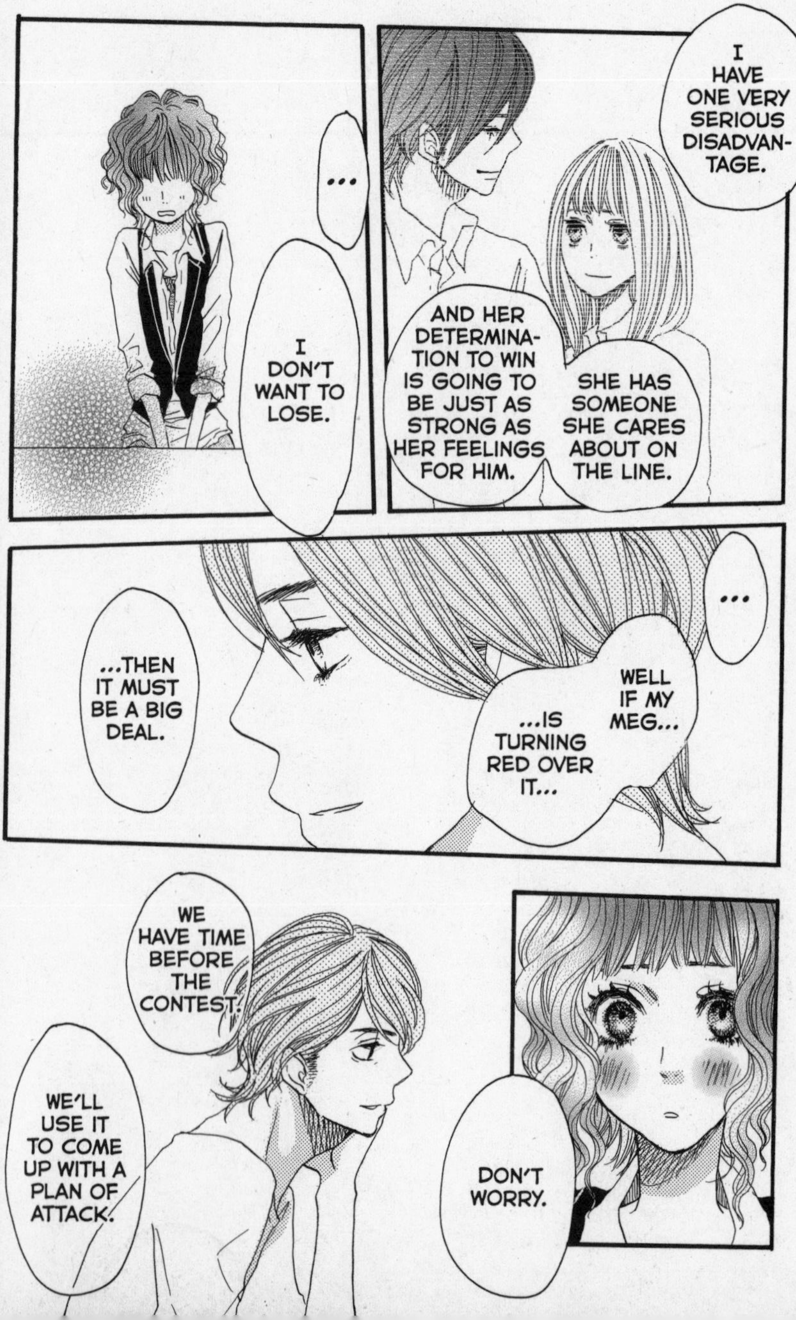
I HAVE ONE VERY SERIOUS DISADVANTAGE.
SHE HAS SOMEONE SHE CARES ABOUT ON THE LINE.
AND HER DETERMINATION TO WIN IS GOING TO BE JUST AS STRONG AS HER FEELINGS FOR HIM.
...
I DON'T WANT TO LOSE.
...
WELL IF MY MEG...
...IS TURNING RED OVER IT...
...THEN IT MUST BE A BIG DEAL.
DON'T WORRY.
WE HAVE TIME BEFORE THE CONTEST.
WE'LL USE IT TO COME UP WITH A PLAN OF ATTACK.

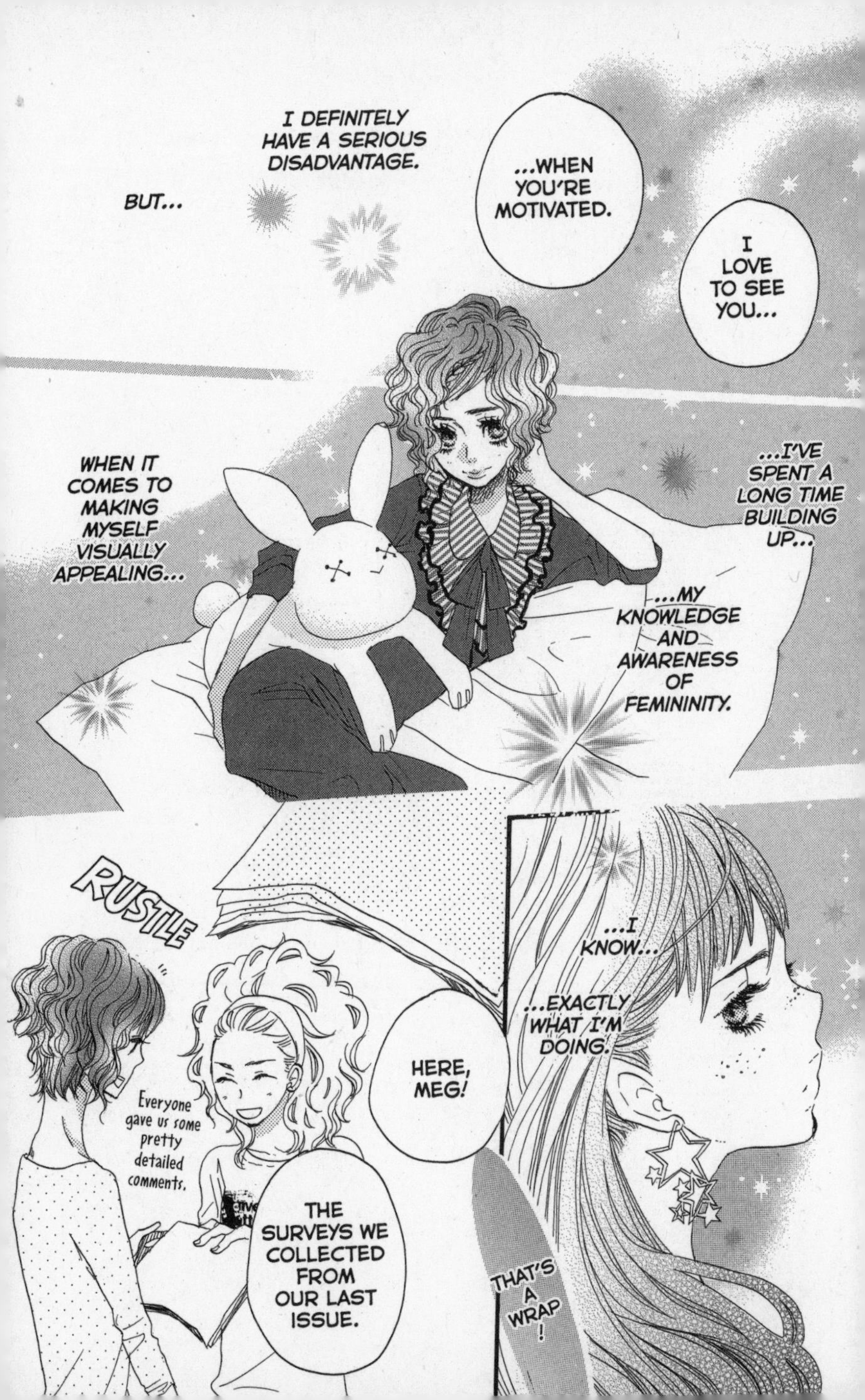
I LOVE TO SEE YOU...
...WHEN YOU'RE MOTIVATED.
I DEFINITELY HAVE A SERIOUS DISADVANTAGE.
BUT...
WHEN IT COMES TO MAKING MYSELF VISUALLY APPEALING...
...I'VE SPENT A LONG TIME BUILDING UP...
...MY KNOWLEDGE AND AWARENESS OF FEMININITY.
...I KNOW...
...EXACTLY WHAT I'M DOING.
THAT'S A WRAP!
RUSTLE
HERE, MEG!
THE SURVEYS WE COLLECTED FROM OUR LAST ISSUE.
Everyone gave us some pretty detailed comments.

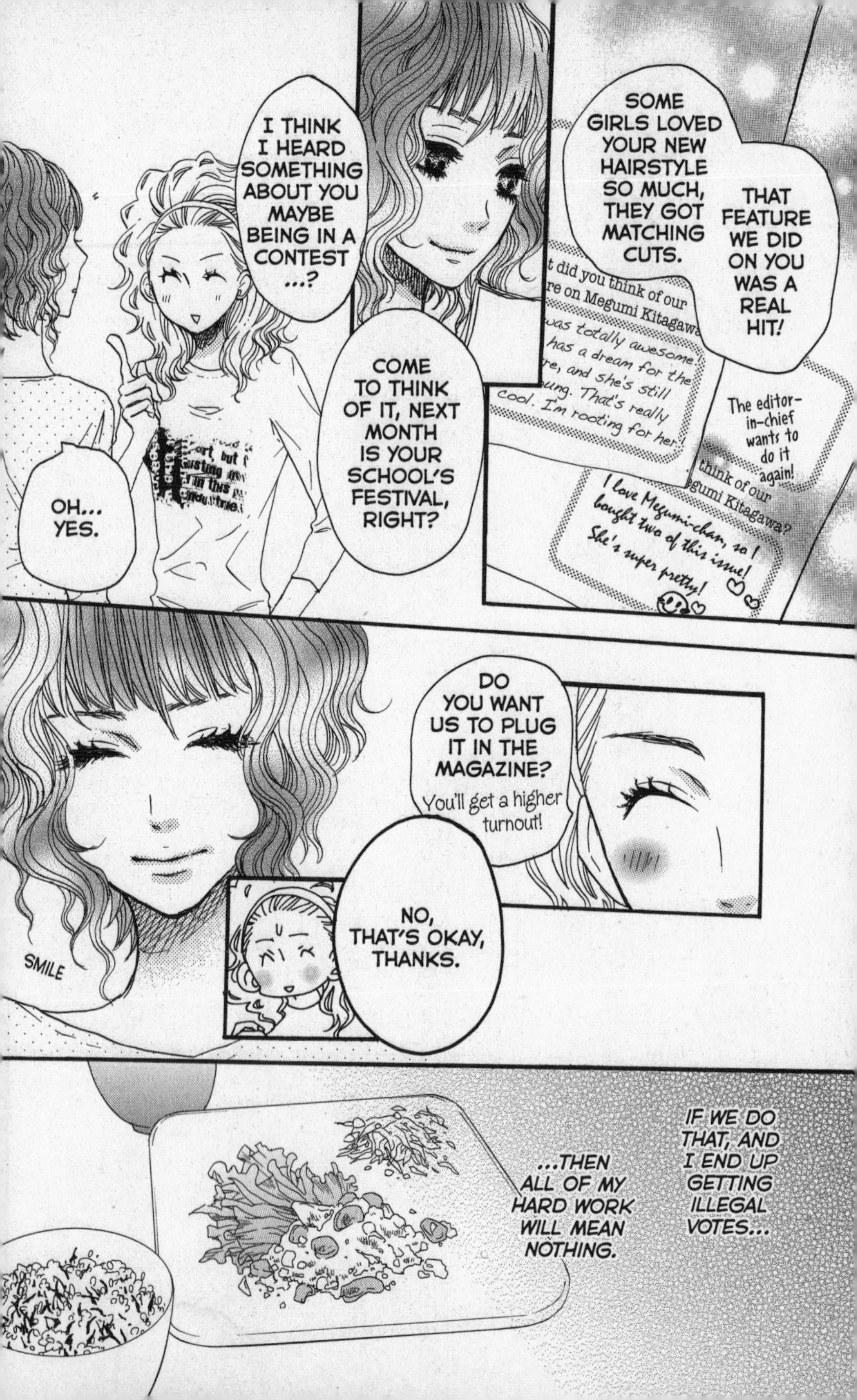
THAT FEATURE WE DID ON YOU WAS A REAL HIT!
SOME GIRLS LOVED YOUR NEW HAIRSTYLE SO MUCH, THEY GOT MATCHING CUTS.
did you think of our
on Megumi Kitagawa
was totally awesome!
has a dream for the
and she's still
That's really cool. I'm rooting for her!
The editor-in-chief wants to do it again!
think of our
I love Megumi-chan, so I bought two of this issue! She's super pretty!
COME TO THINK OF IT, NEXT MONTH IS YOUR SCHOOL'S FESTIVAL, RIGHT?
OH... YES.
I THINK I HEARD SOMETHING ABOUT YOU MAYBE BEING IN A CONTEST ...?
DO YOU WANT US TO PLUG IT IN THE MAGAZINE?
You'll get a higher turnout!
NO, THAT'S OKAY, THANKS.
SMILE
IF WE DO THAT, AND I END UP GETTING ILLEGAL VOTES...
...THEN ALL OF MY HARD WORK WILL MEAN NOTHING.

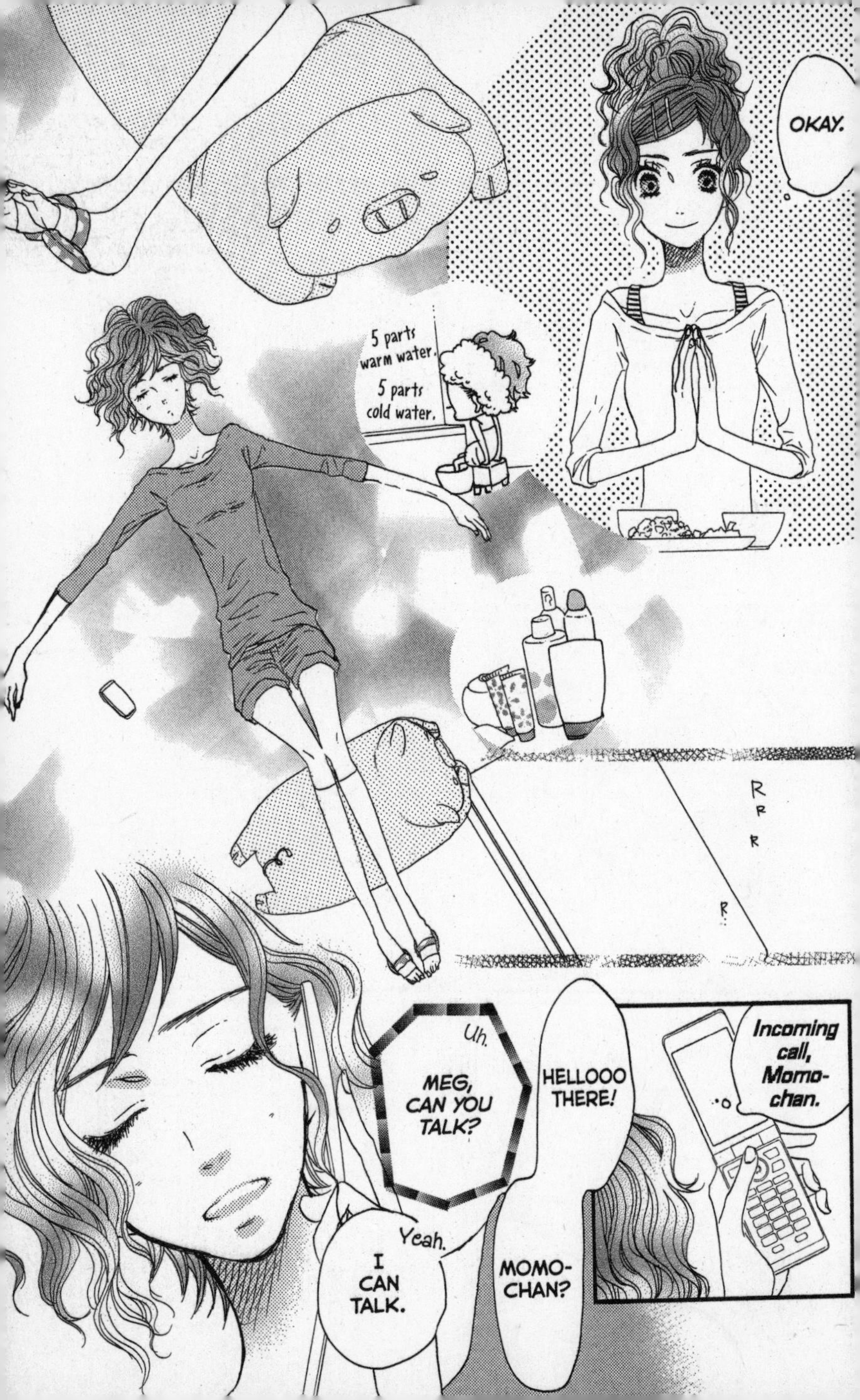
OKAY.
5 parts warm water.
5 parts cold water.
RRRR
Incoming call, Momo-chan.
HELLOOO THERE!
MOMO-CHAN?
Uh.
MEG, CAN YOU TALK?
Yeah.
I CAN TALK.

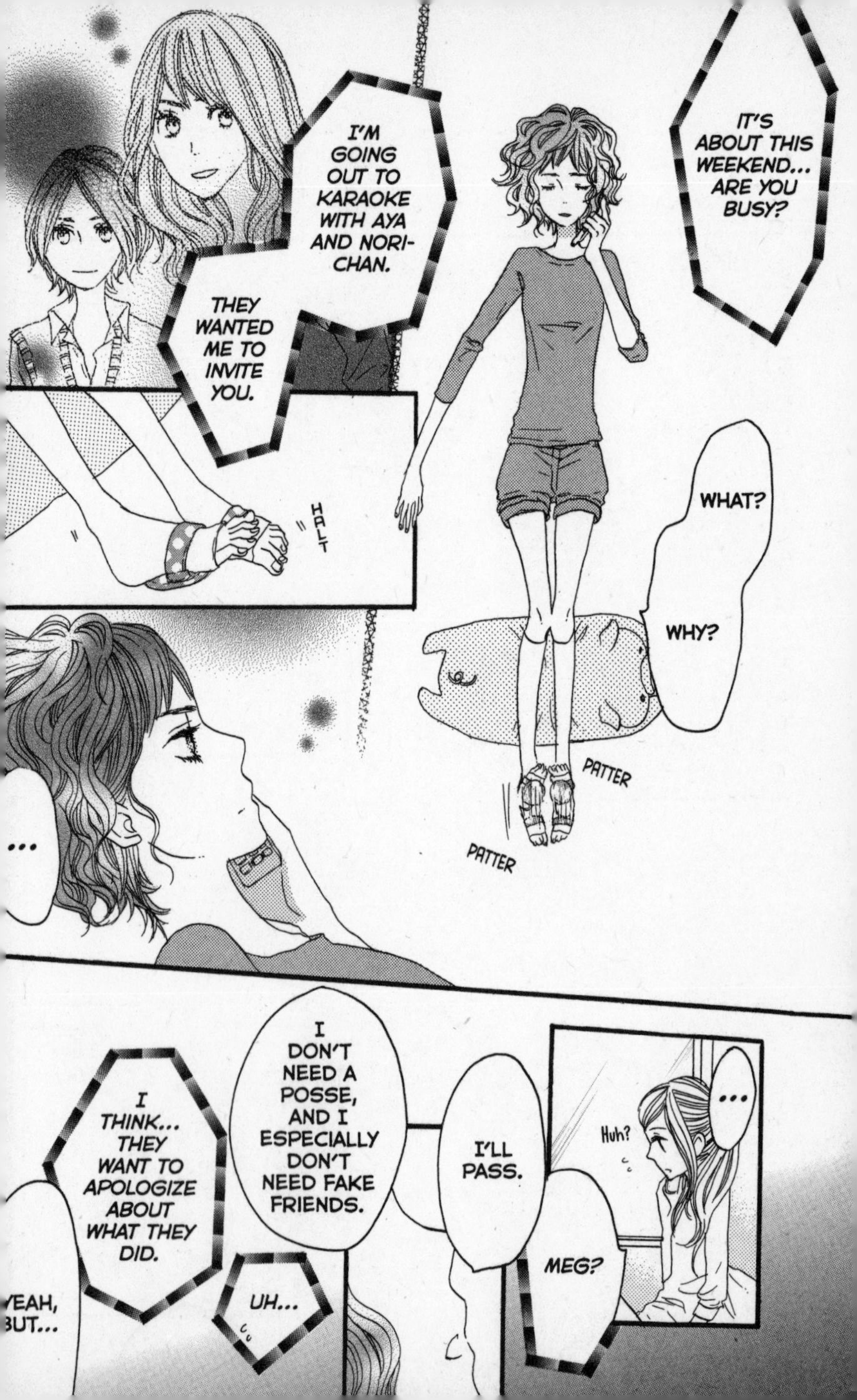
IT'S ABOUT THIS WEEKEND... ARE YOU BUSY?
WHAT?
WHY?
PATTER
PATTER
I'M GOING OUT TO KARAOKE WITH AYA AND NORI-CHAN.
THEY WANTED ME TO INVITE YOU.
HALT
...
...
Huh?
MEG?
I'LL PASS.
I DON'T NEED A POSSE, AND I ESPECIALLY DON'T NEED FAKE FRIENDS.
I THINK... THEY WANT TO APOLOGIZE ABOUT WHAT THEY DID.
UH...
YEAH, BUT...

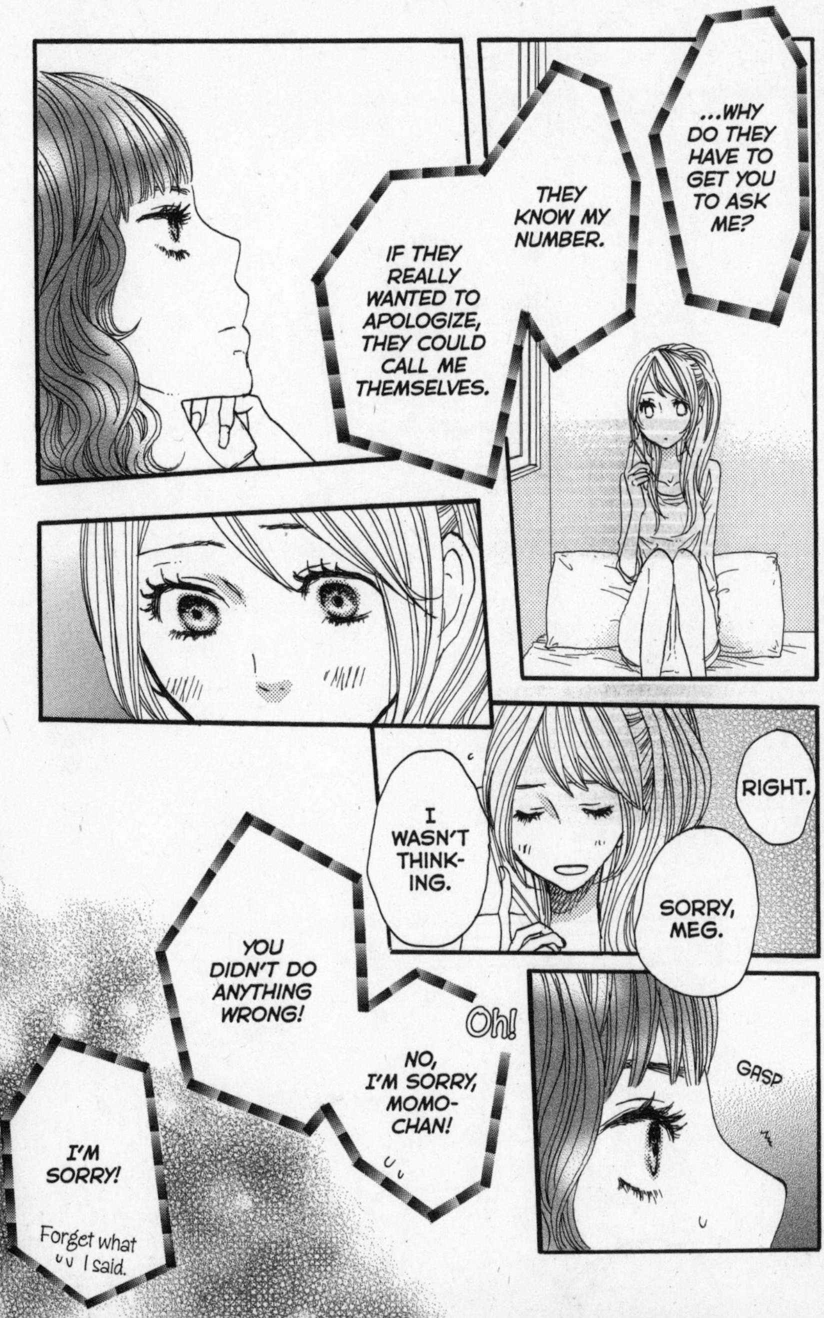
...WHY DO THEY HAVE TO GET YOU TO ASK ME?
THEY KNOW MY NUMBER.
IF THEY REALLY WANTED TO APOLOGIZE, THEY COULD CALL ME THEMSELVES.
RIGHT.
SORRY, MEG.
I WASN'T THINK-ING.
Oh!
YOU DIDN'T DO ANYTHING WRONG!
NO, I'M SORRY, MOMO-CHAN!
GASP
I'M SORRY!
Forget what I said.

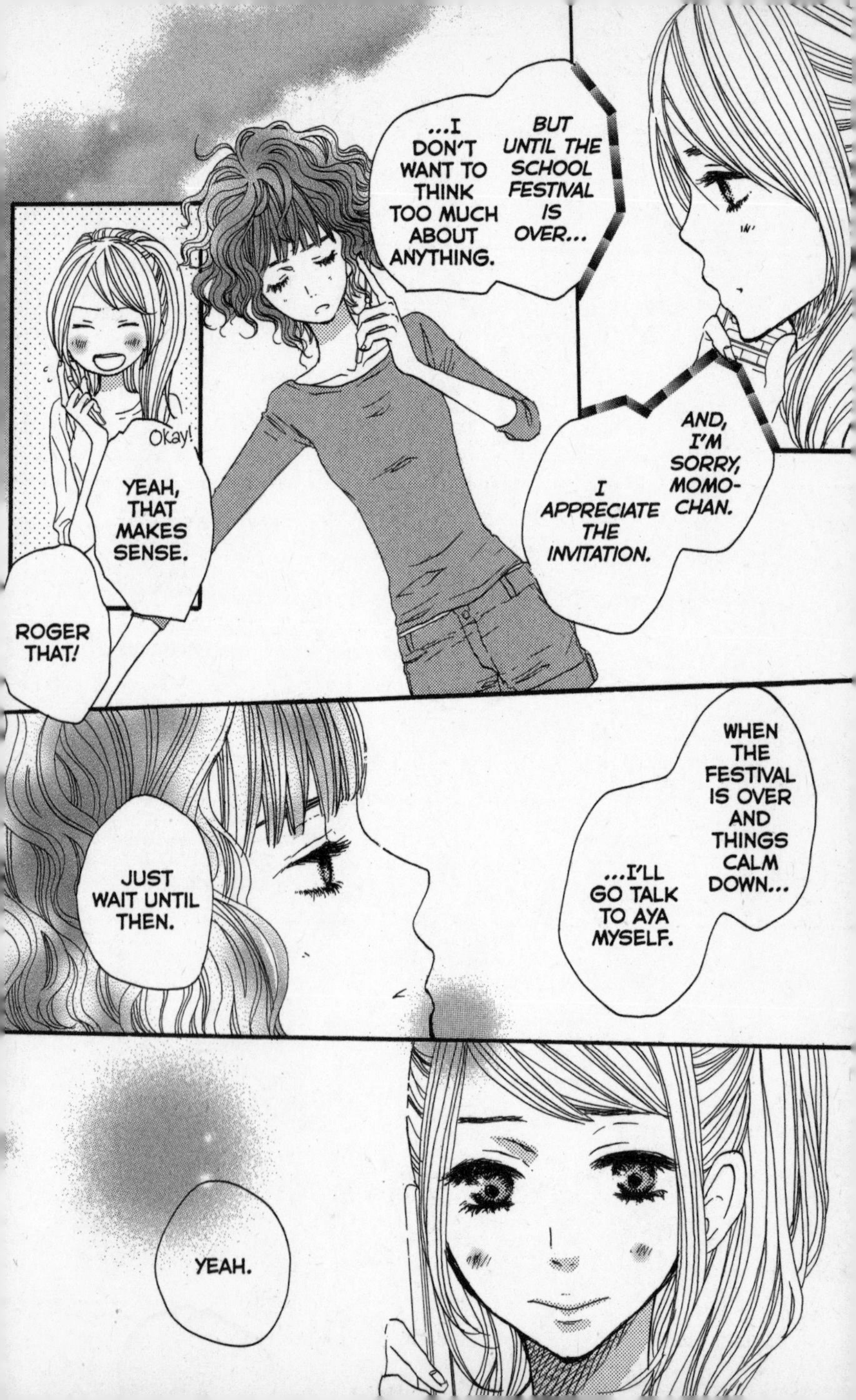
BUT UNTIL THE SCHOOL FESTIVAL IS OVER...
...I DON'T WANT TO THINK TOO MUCH ABOUT ANYTHING.
AND, I'M SORRY, MOMO-CHAN.
I APPRECIATE THE INVITATION.
Okay!
YEAH, THAT MAKES SENSE.
ROGER THAT!
WHEN THE FESTIVAL IS OVER AND THINGS CALM DOWN...
...I'LL GO TALK TO AYA MYSELF.
JUST WAIT UNTIL THEN.
YEAH.

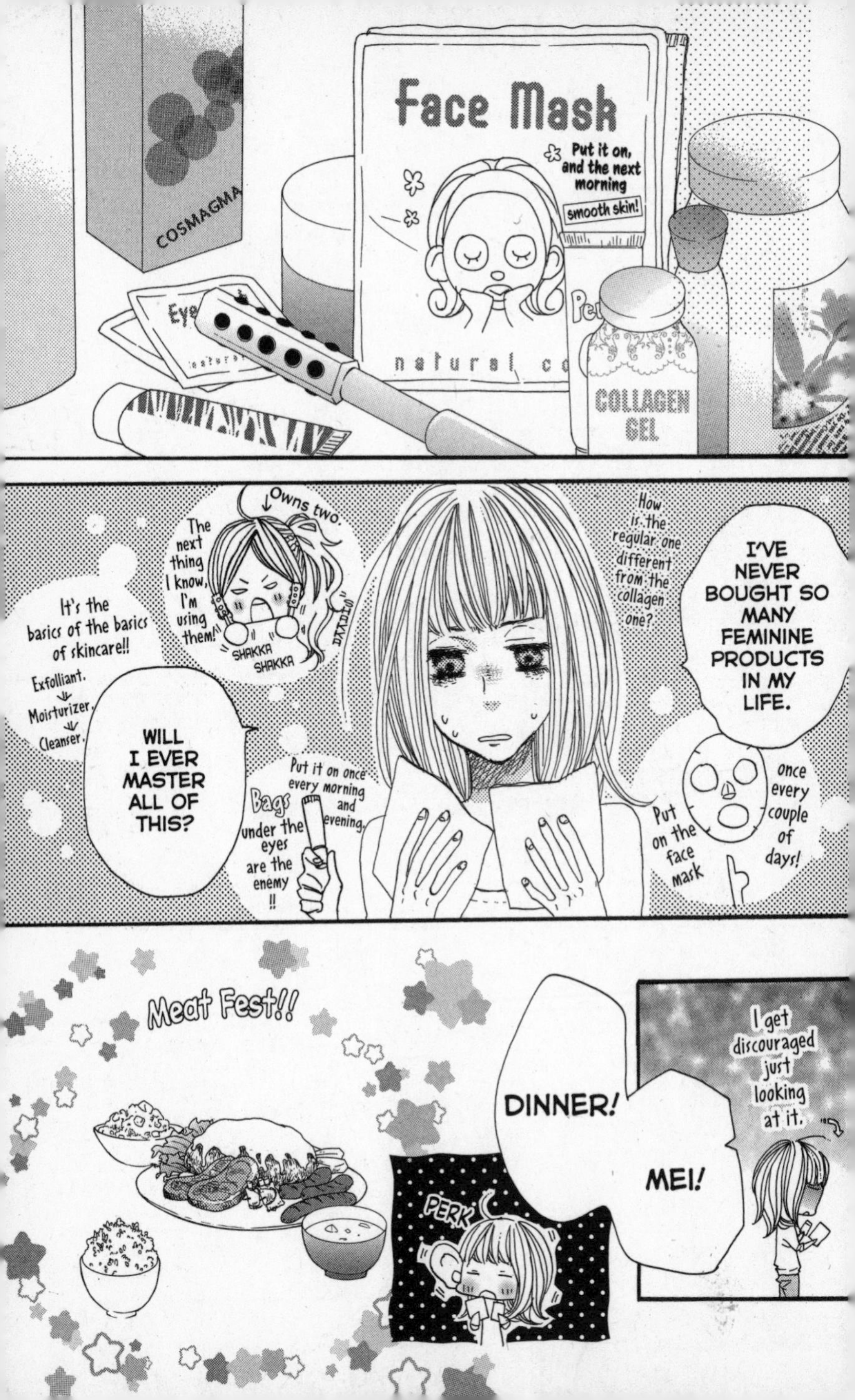
Face Mask
Put it on, and the next morning
smooth skin!
COSMAGMA
COLLAGEN GEL
I'VE NEVER BOUGHT SO MANY FEMININE PRODUCTS IN MY LIFE.
How is the regular one different from the collagen one?
Put on the face mask once every couple of days!
Bags under the eyes are the enemy!!
Put it on once every morning and evening.
Owns two.
The next thing I know, I'm using them!
SHAKKA SHAKKA
WILL I EVER MASTER ALL OF THIS?
It's the basics of the basics of skincare!!
Exfolliant.
Moisturizer.
Cleanser.
I get discouraged just looking at it.
MEI!
DINNER!
PERK
Meat Fest!!

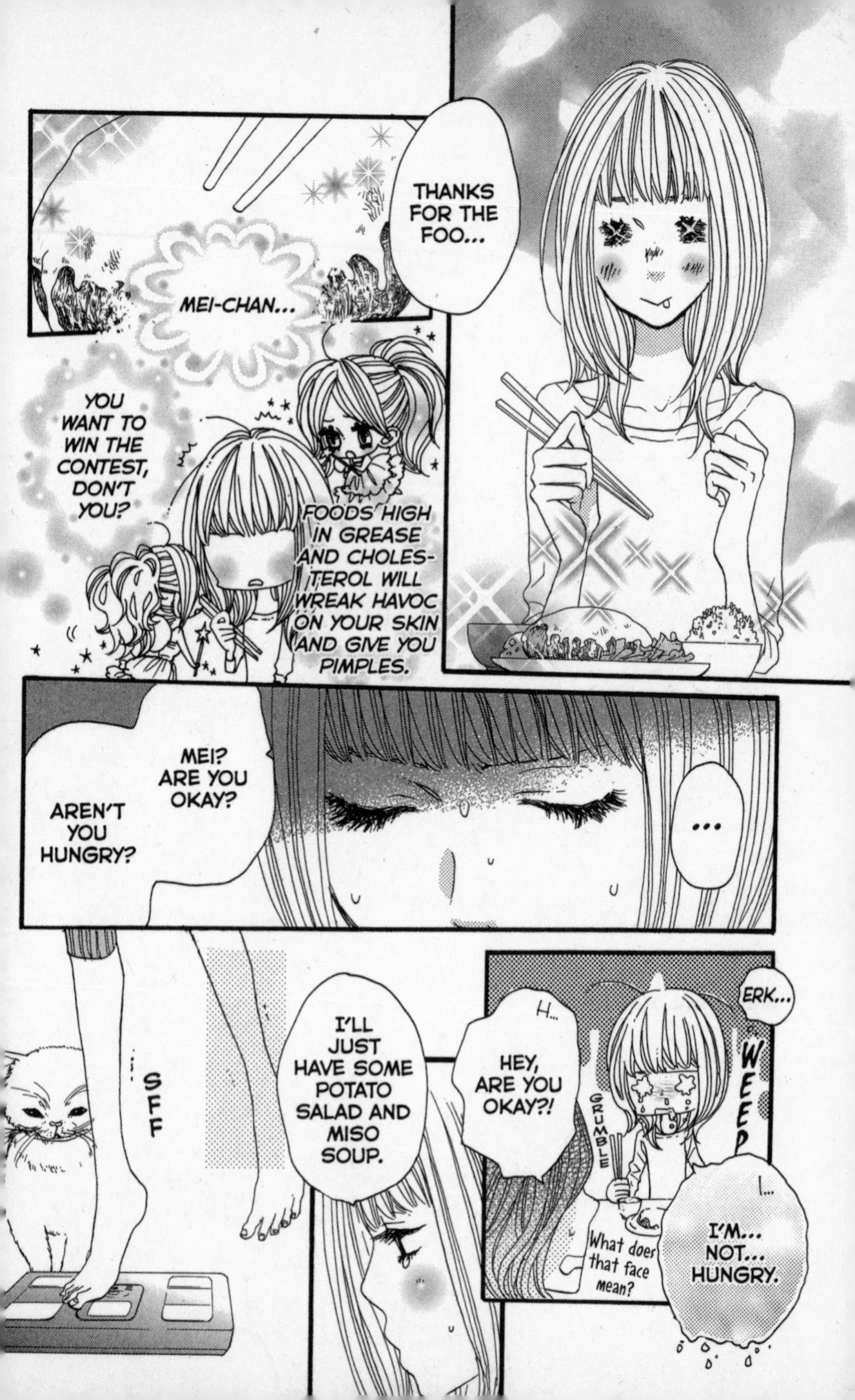
THANKS FOR THE FOO...
MEI-CHAN...
YOU WANT TO WIN THE CONTEST, DON'T YOU?
FOODS HIGH IN GREASE AND CHOLES-TEROL WILL WREAK HAVOC ON YOUR SKIN AND GIVE YOU PIMPLES.
...
MEI? ARE YOU OKAY?
AREN'T YOU HUNGRY?
ERK...
WEEP
H...
HEY, ARE YOU OKAY?!
GRUMBLE
I...
I'M... NOT... HUNGRY.
What does that face mean?
I'LL JUST HAVE SOME POTATO SALAD AND MISO SOUP.
SFF

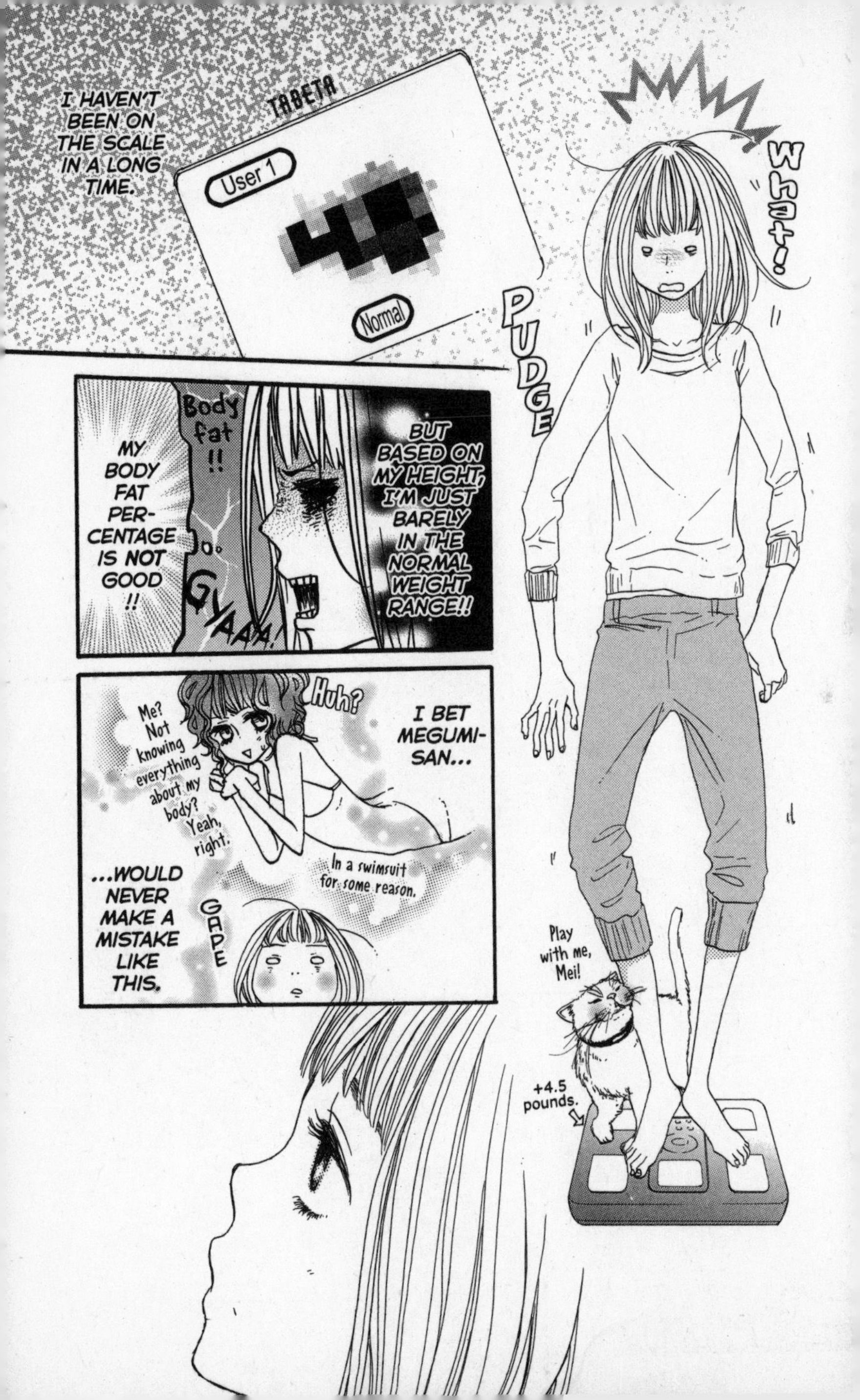
What!
PUDGE
Play with me, Mei!
+4.5 pounds.
I HAVEN'T BEEN ON THE SCALE IN A LONG TIME.
TABETA
User 1
Normal
BUT BASED ON MY HEIGHT, I'M JUST BARELY IN THE NORMAL WEIGHT RANGE!!
Body fat !!
MY BODY FAT PER-CENTAGE IS NOT GOOD !!
GYAAA
Huh?
I BET MEGUMI-SAN...
Me? Not knowing everything about my body? Yeah, right.
In a swimsuit for some reason.
GAPE
...WOULD NEVER MAKE A MISTAKE LIKE THIS.

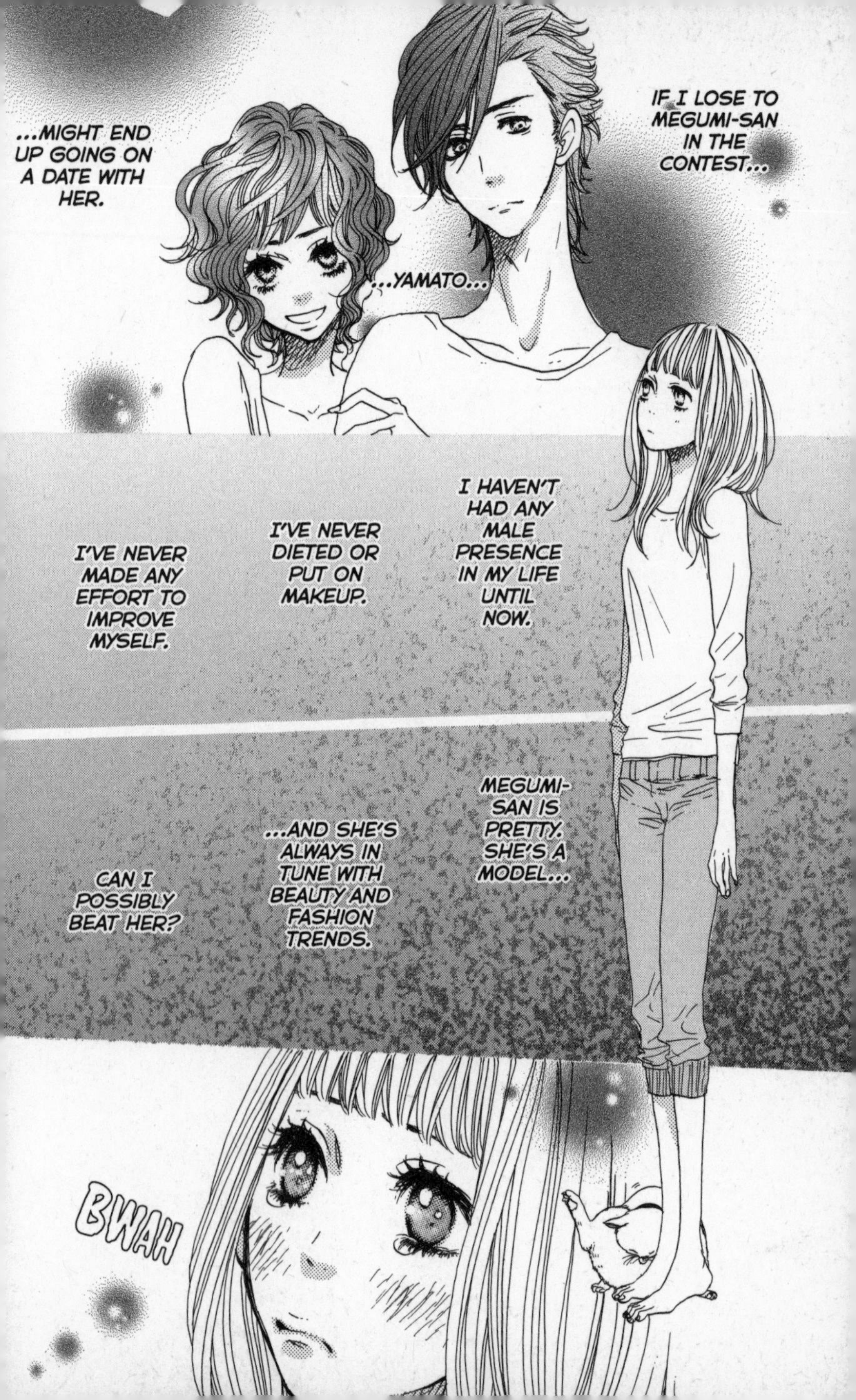
IF I LOSE TO MEGUMI-SAN IN THE CONTEST...
...YAMATO...
...MIGHT END UP GOING ON A DATE WITH HER.
I HAVEN'T HAD ANY MALE PRESENCE IN MY LIFE UNTIL NOW.
I'VE NEVER DIETED OR PUT ON MAKEUP.
I'VE NEVER MADE ANY EFFORT TO IMPROVE MYSELF.
MEGUMI-SAN IS PRETTY. SHE'S A MODEL...
...AND SHE'S ALWAYS IN TUNE WITH BEAUTY AND FASHION TRENDS.
CAN I POSSIBLY BEAT HER?
BWAH

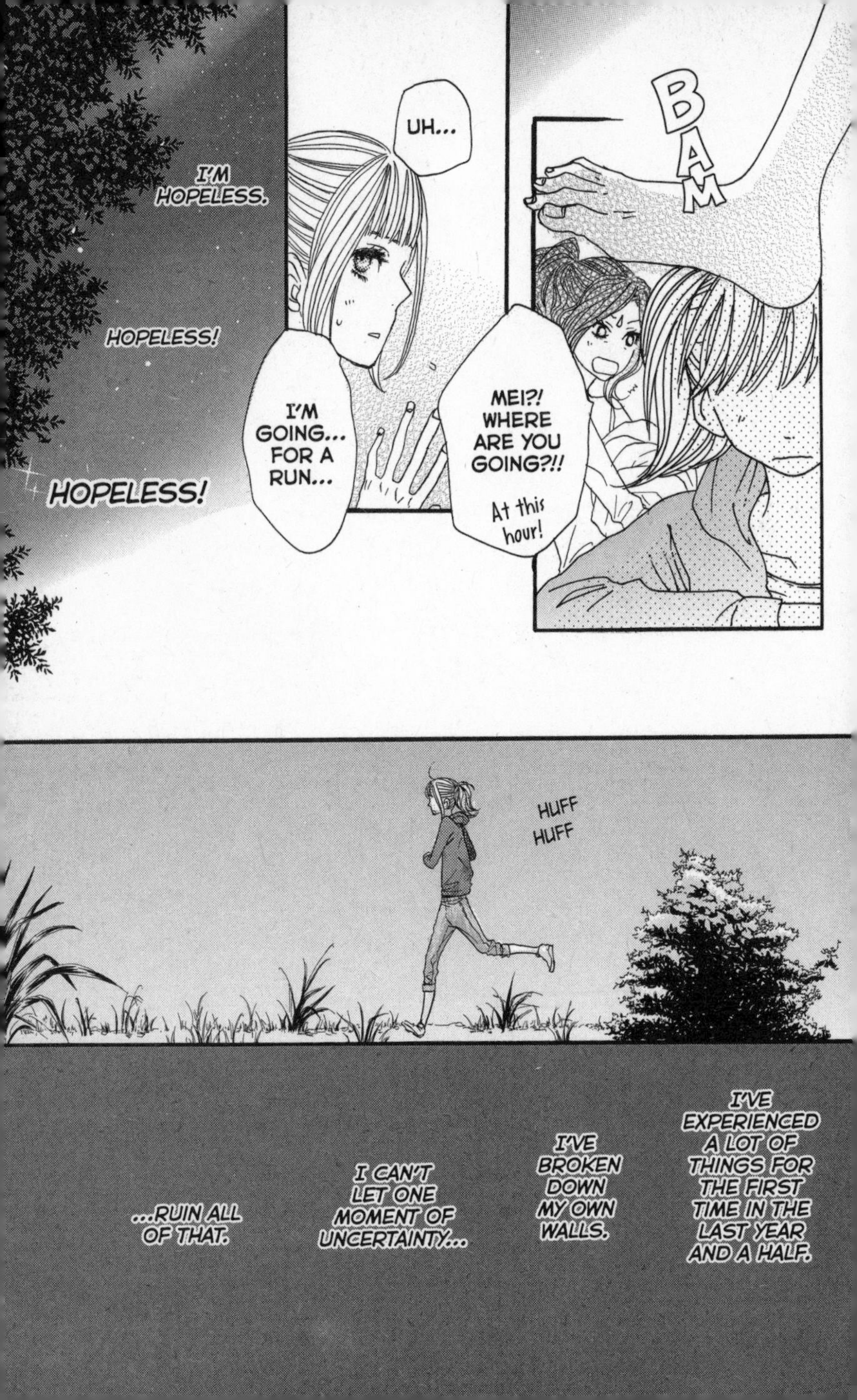
BAM
MEI?! WHERE ARE YOU GOING?!!
At this hour!
UH...
I'M GOING... FOR A RUN...
I'M HOPELESS.
HOPELESS!
HOPELESS!
HUFF HUFF
I'VE EXPERIENCED A LOT OF THINGS FOR THE FIRST TIME IN THE LAST YEAR AND A HALF.
I'VE BROKEN DOWN MY OWN WALLS.
I CAN'T LET ONE MOMENT OF UNCERTAINTY...
...RUIN ALL OF THAT.

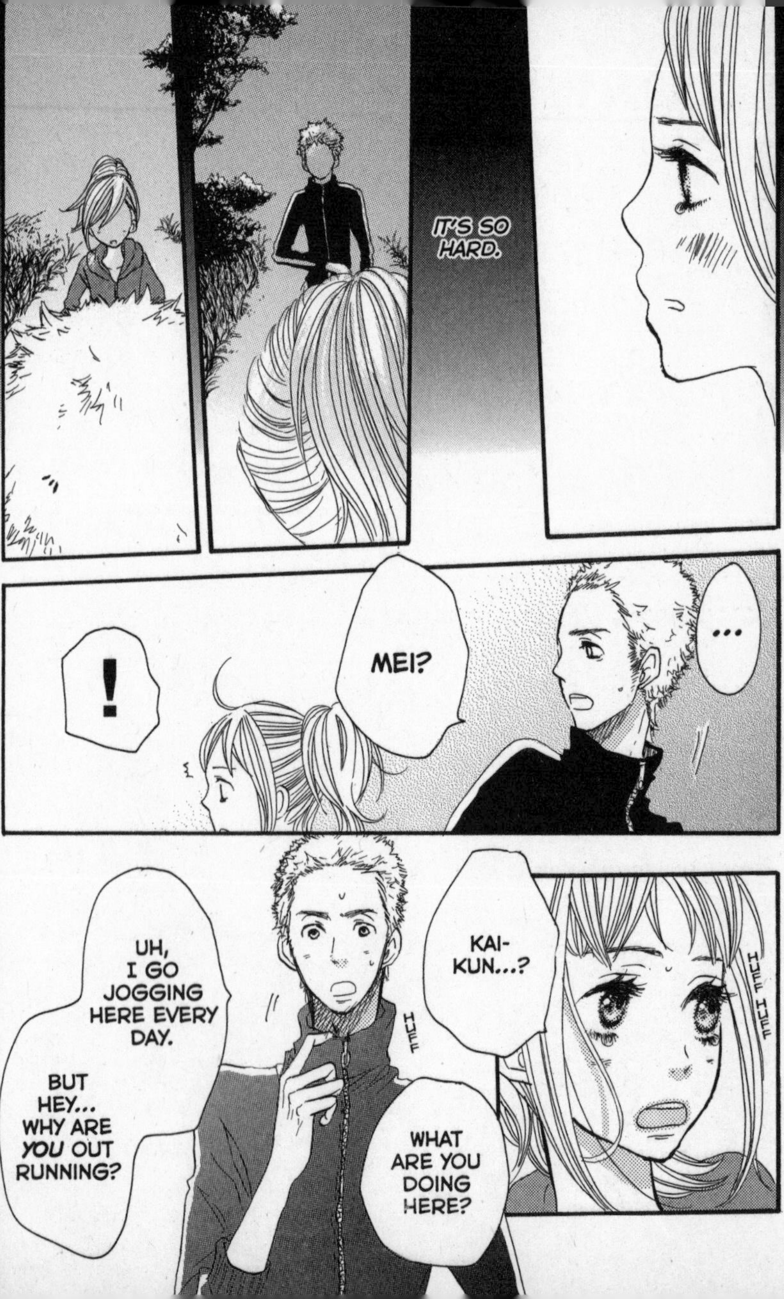
IT'S SO HARD.
...
MEI?
!
KAI-KUN...?
HUFF HUFF
WHAT ARE YOU DOING HERE?
HUFF
UH, I GO JOGGING HERE EVERY DAY.
BUT HEY... WHY ARE *YOU* OUT RUNNING?

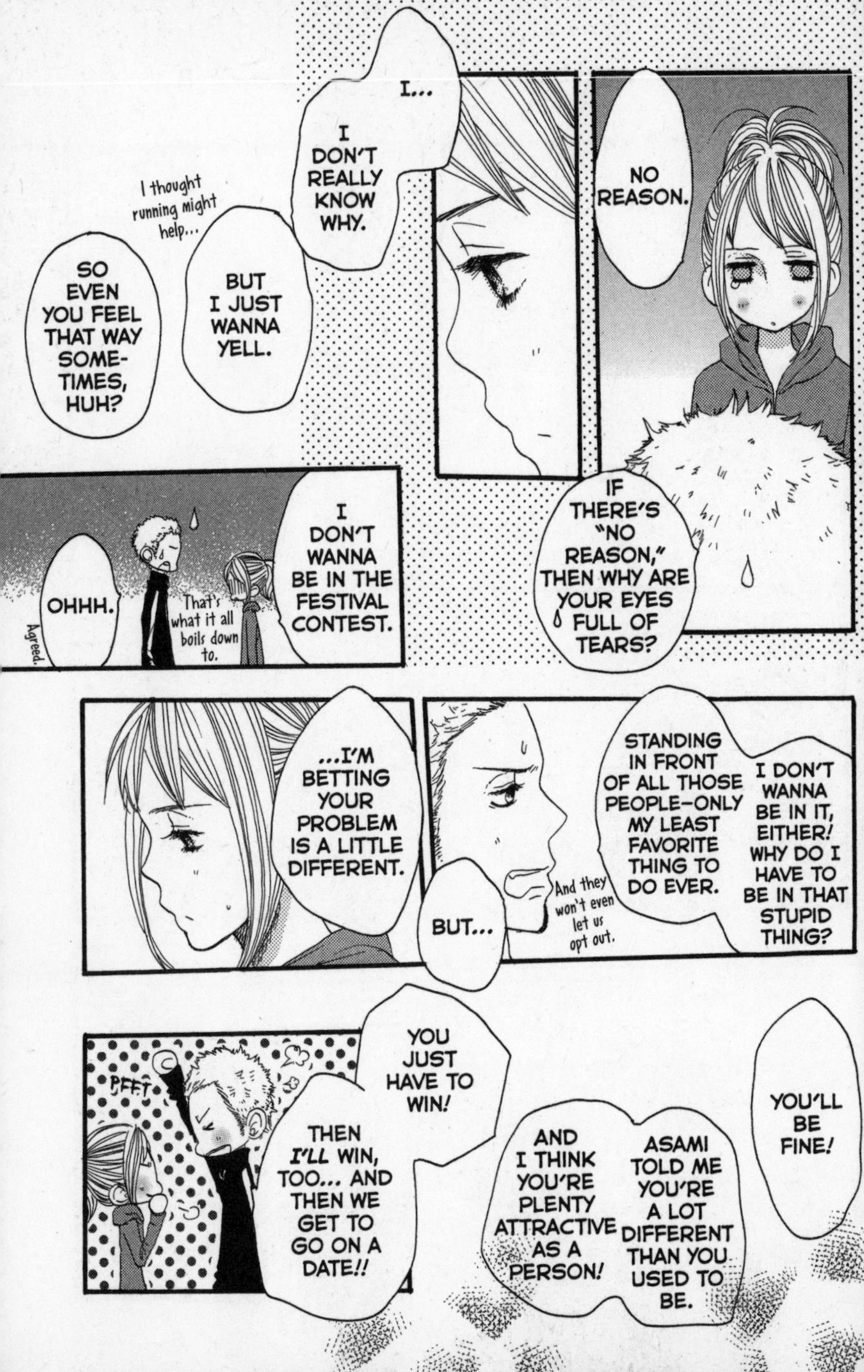
NO REASON.
IF THERE'S "NO REASON," THEN WHY ARE YOUR EYES FULL OF TEARS?
I...
I DON'T REALLY KNOW WHY.
BUT I JUST WANNA YELL.
I thought running might help...
SO EVEN YOU FEEL THAT WAY SOMETIMES, HUH?
I DON'T WANNA BE IN THE FESTIVAL CONTEST.
That's what it all boils down to.
OHHH.
Agreed.
I DON'T WANNA BE IN IT, EITHER! WHY DO I HAVE TO BE IN THAT STUPID THING?
STANDING IN FRONT OF ALL THOSE PEOPLE—ONLY MY LEAST FAVORITE THING TO DO EVER.
And they won't even let us opt out.
BUT...
...I'M BETTING YOUR PROBLEM IS A LITTLE DIFFERENT.
YOU'LL BE FINE!
ASAMI TOLD ME YOU'RE A LOT DIFFERENT THAN YOU USED TO BE.
AND I THINK YOU'RE PLENTY ATTRACTIVE AS A PERSON!
YOU JUST HAVE TO WIN!
THEN I'LL WIN, TOO... AND THEN WE GET TO GO ON A DATE!!
PFFT

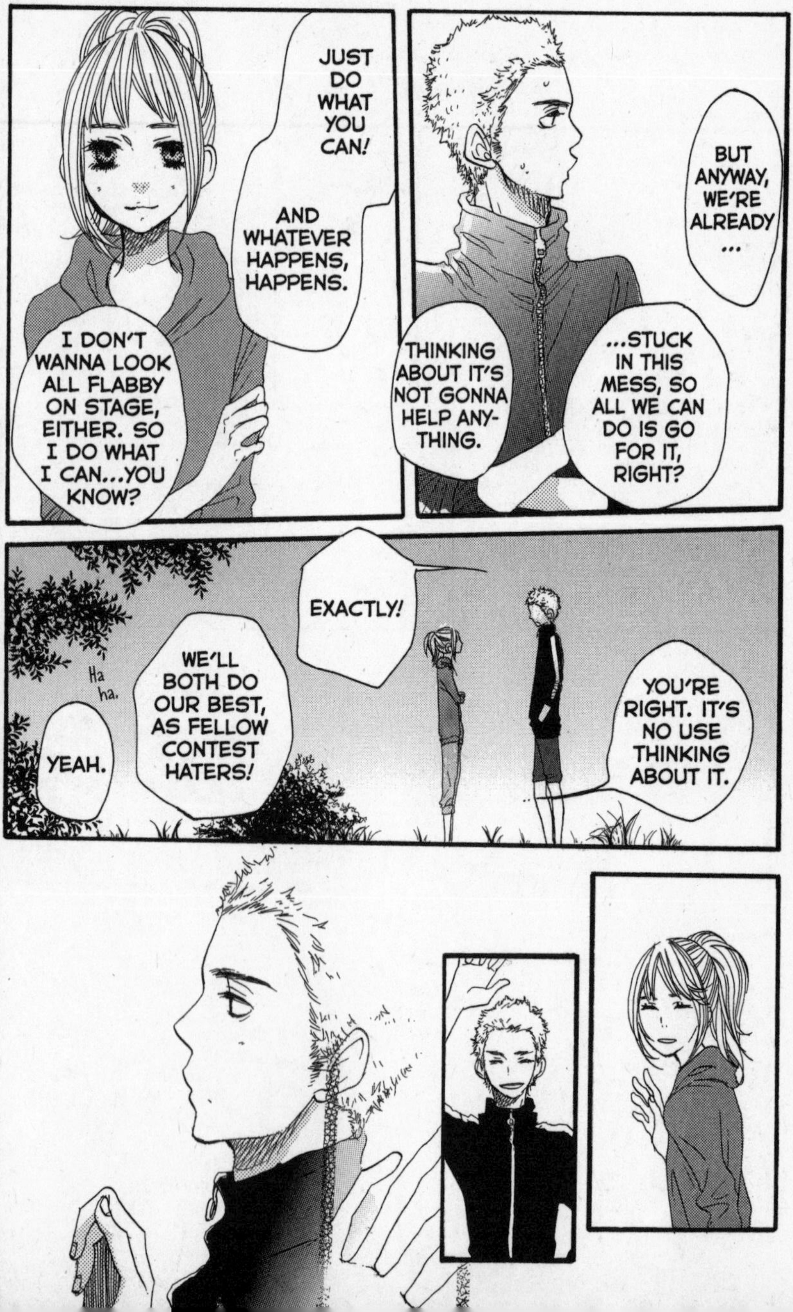
BUT ANYWAY, WE'RE ALREADY ...
...STUCK IN THIS MESS, SO ALL WE CAN DO IS GO FOR IT, RIGHT?
THINKING ABOUT IT'S NOT GONNA HELP ANY-THING.
JUST DO WHAT YOU CAN!
AND WHATEVER HAPPENS, HAPPENS.
I DON'T WANNA LOOK ALL FLABBY ON STAGE, EITHER. SO I DO WHAT I CAN...YOU KNOW?
YOU'RE RIGHT. IT'S NO USE THINKING ABOUT IT.
EXACTLY!
WE'LL BOTH DO OUR BEST, AS FELLOW CONTEST HATERS!
Ha ha.
YEAH.

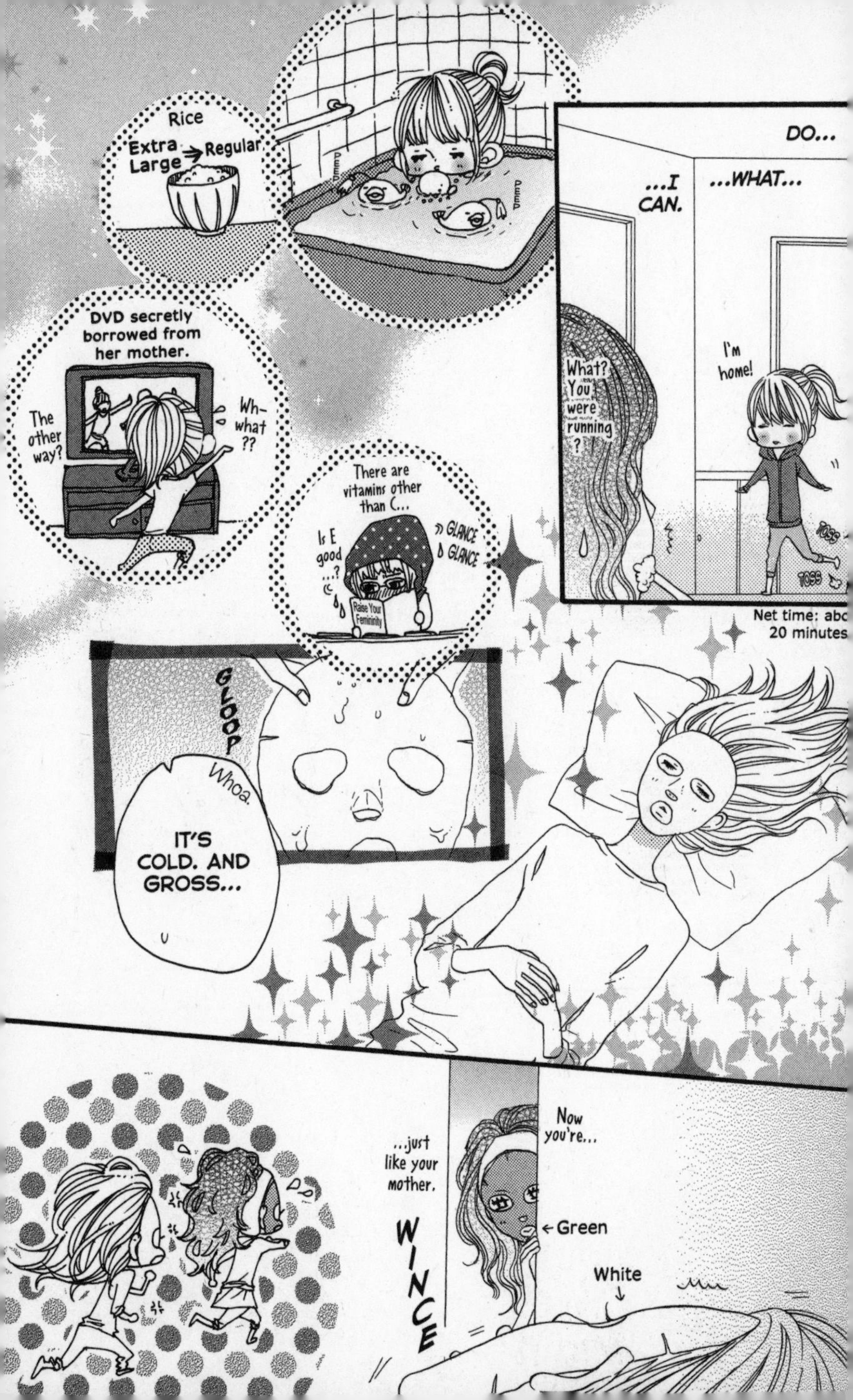
DO...
...WHAT...
...I CAN.
I'm home!
TOSS TOSS
What? You were running?
Net time: ab
20 minutes
PEEP
PEEP
Rice
Extra Large → Regular
DVD secretly borrowed from her mother.
Wh-what??
The other way?
There are vitamins other than C...
GLANCE GLANCE
Is E good...?
Raise Your Femininity
GLOOP
Whoa.
IT'S COLD. AND GROSS...
Now you're...
...just like your mother.
WINCE
← Green
White ↓

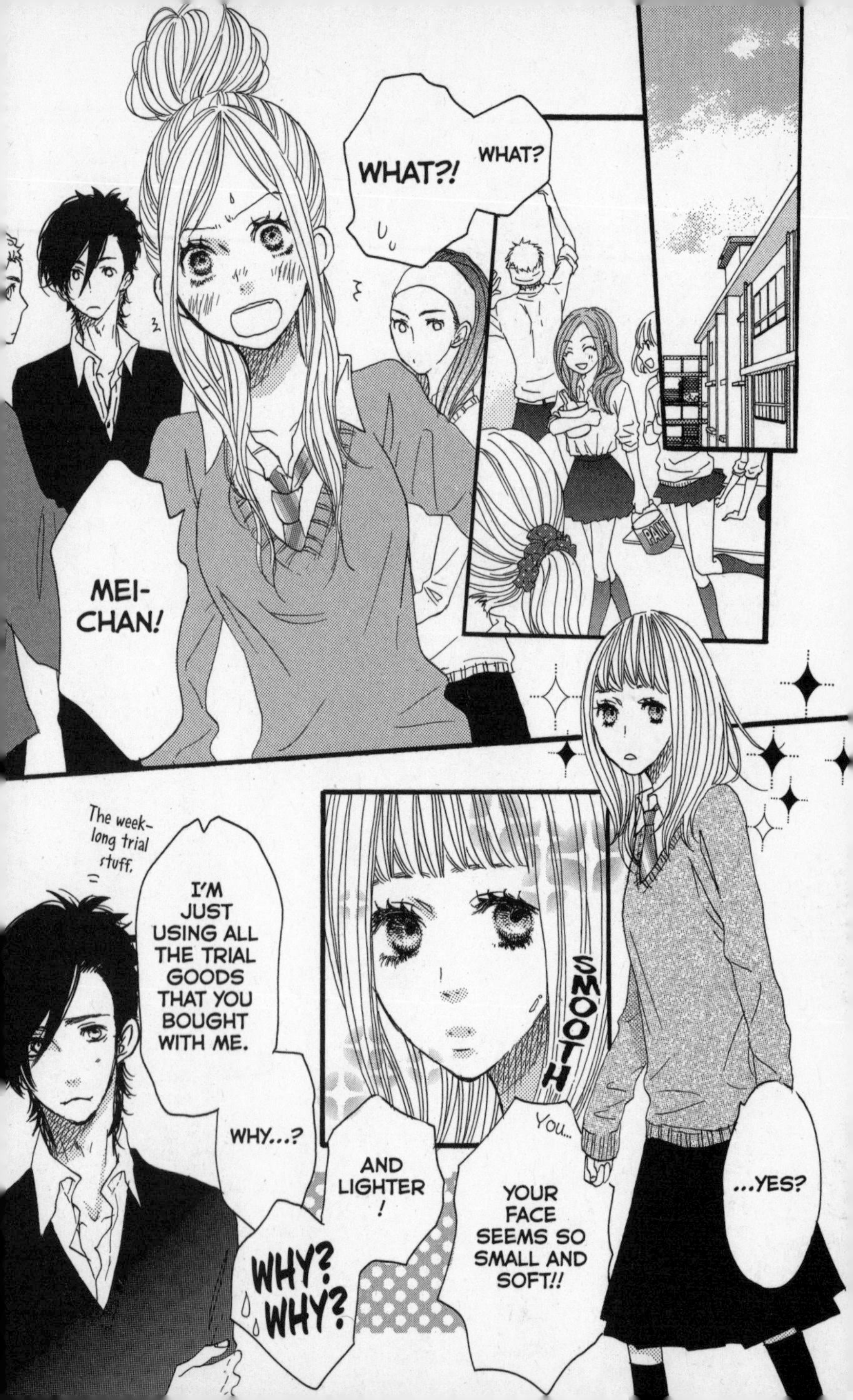

WHAT?
WHAT?!
MEI-CHAN!
...YES?
You...
YOUR FACE SEEMS SO SMALL AND SOFT!!
SMOOTH
AND LIGHTER!
WHY? WHY?
WHY...?
I'M JUST USING ALL THE TRIAL GOODS THAT YOU BOUGHT WITH ME.
The week-long trial stuff.

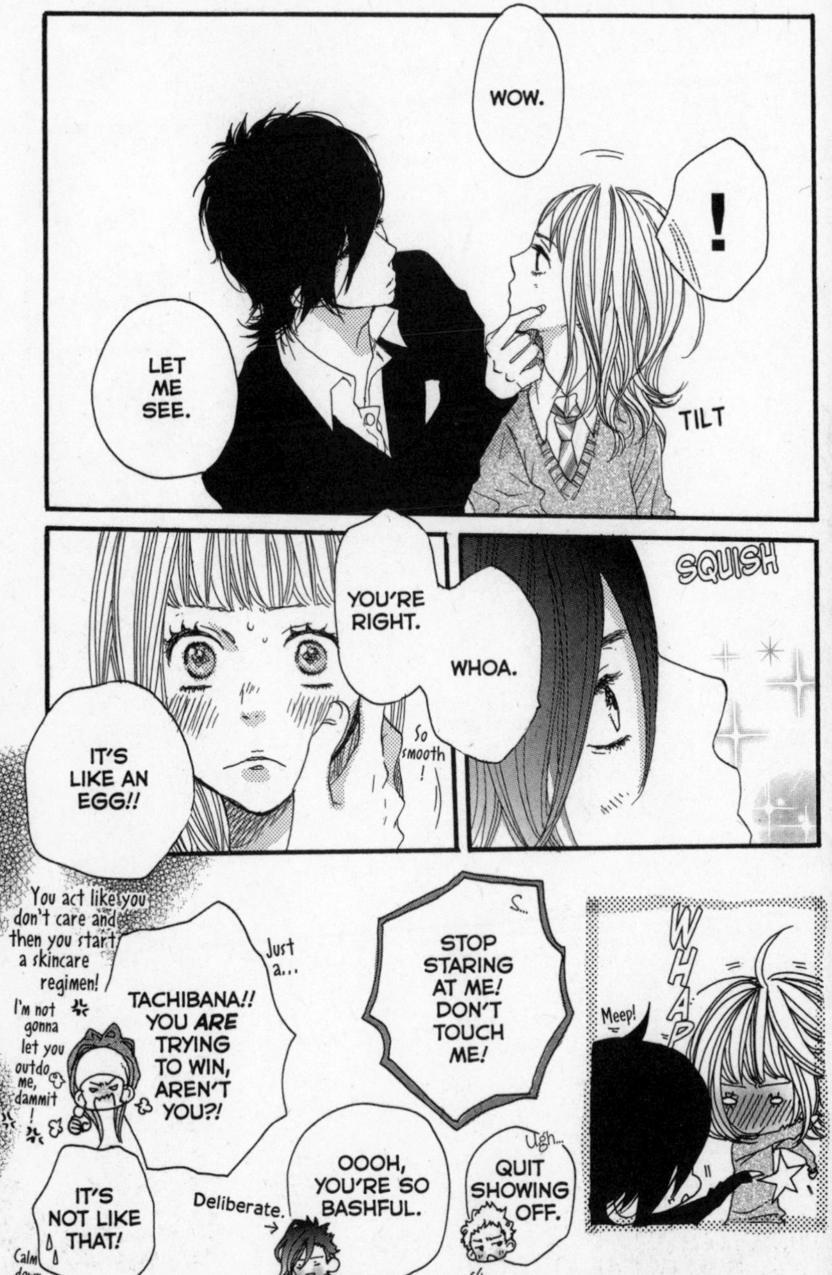
WOW.
!
TILT
LET ME SEE.
SQUISH
YOU'RE RIGHT.
WHOA.
So smooth!
IT'S LIKE AN EGG!!
WHAP
Meep!
S...
STOP STARING AT ME! DON'T TOUCH ME!
Just a...
TACHIBANA!! YOU *ARE* TRYING TO WIN, AREN'T YOU?!
You act like you don't care and then you start a skincare regimen!
I'm not gonna let you outdo me, dammit!
Ugh...
QUIT SHOWING OFF.
OOOH, YOU'RE SO BASHFUL.
Deliberate.
IT'S NOT LIKE THAT!
Calm down.

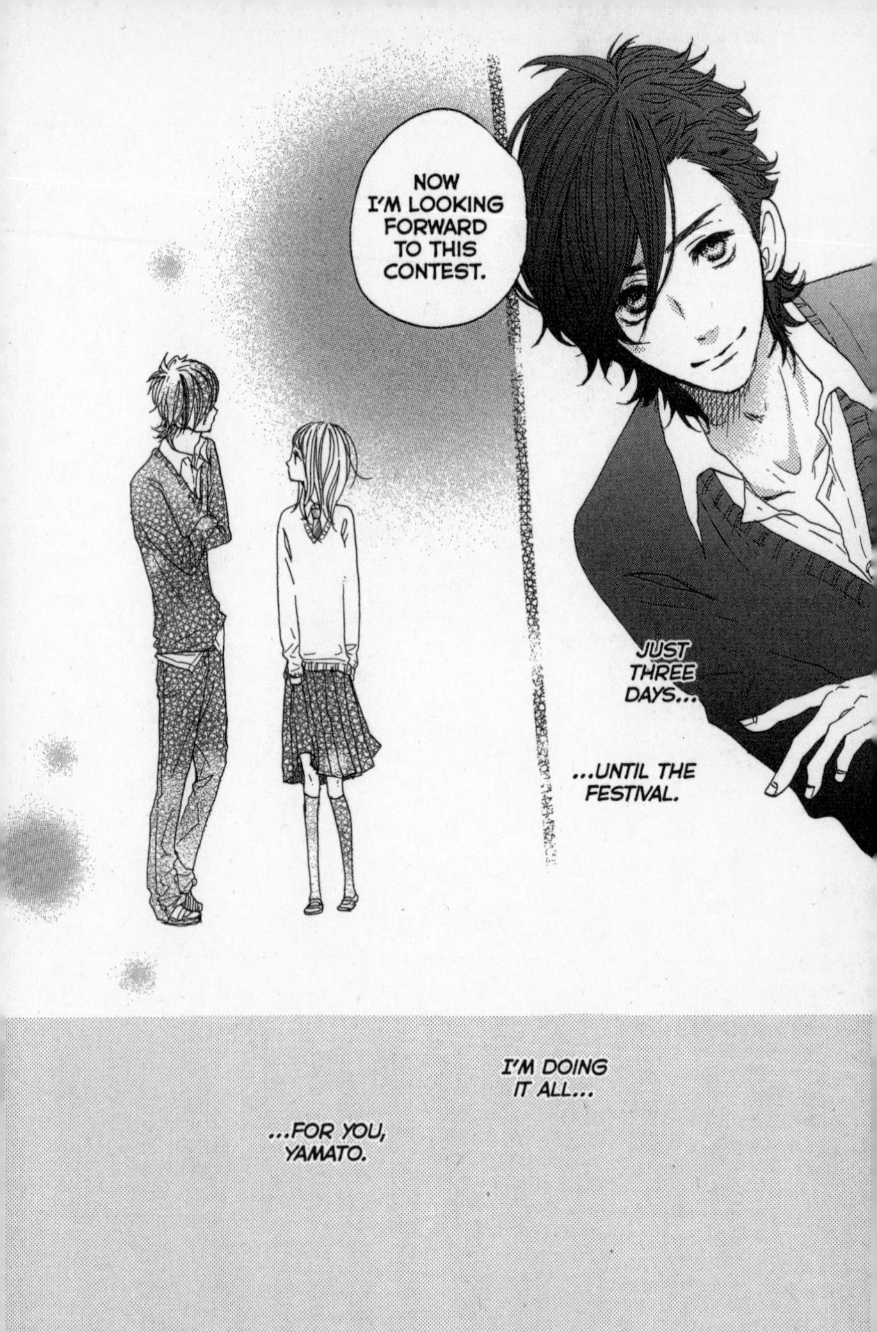
NOW I'M LOOKING FORWARD TO THIS CONTEST.
JUST THREE DAYS...
...UNTIL THE FESTIVAL.
I'M DOING IT ALL...
...FOR YOU, YAMATO.

Chapter 30 — End

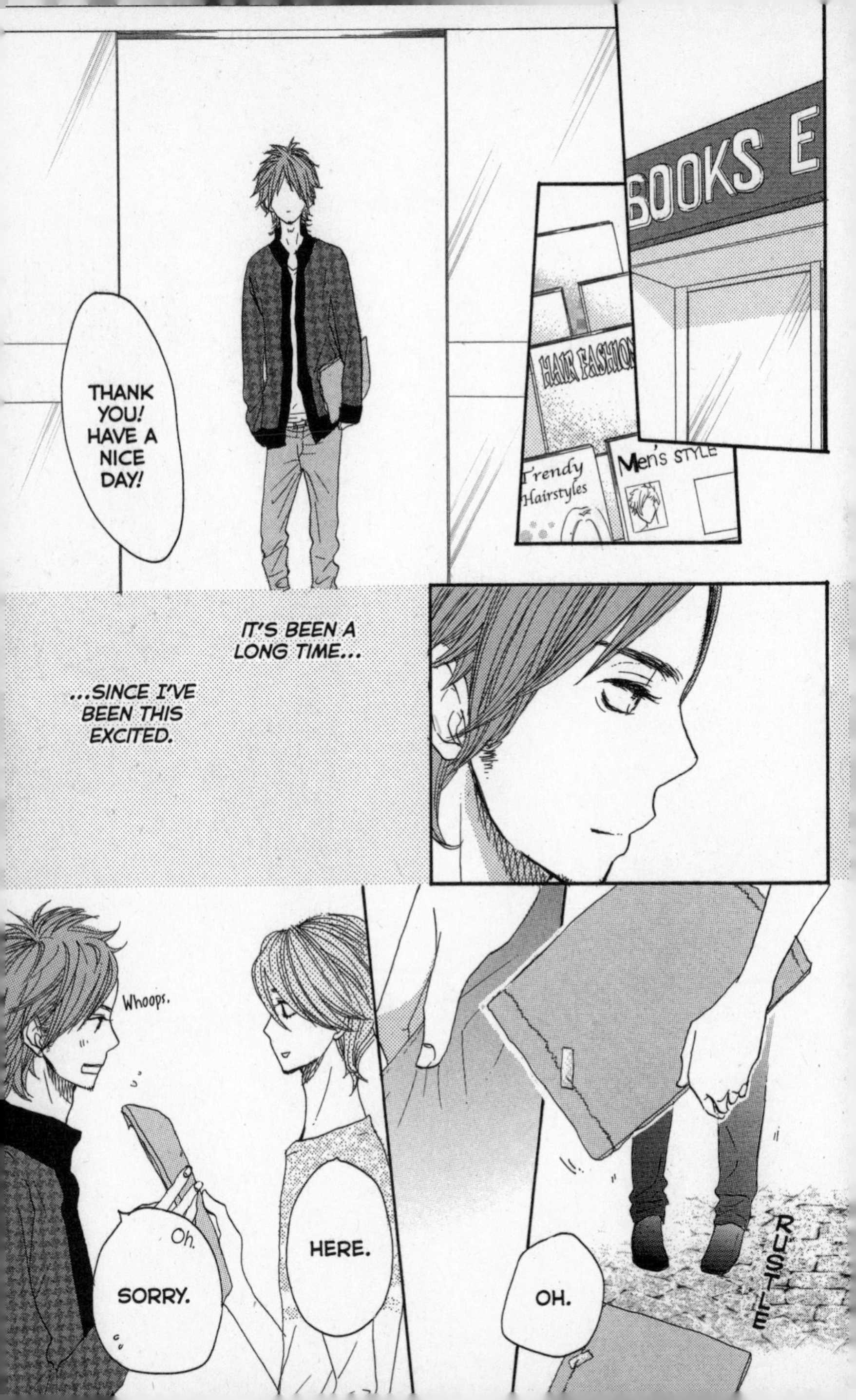
BOOKS E
HAIR FASHION
Men's STYLE
Trendy Hairstyles
THANK YOU! HAVE A NICE DAY!
IT'S BEEN A LONG TIME...
...SINCE I'VE BEEN THIS EXCITED.
RUSTLE
OH.
Whoops.
HERE.
Oh.
SORRY.

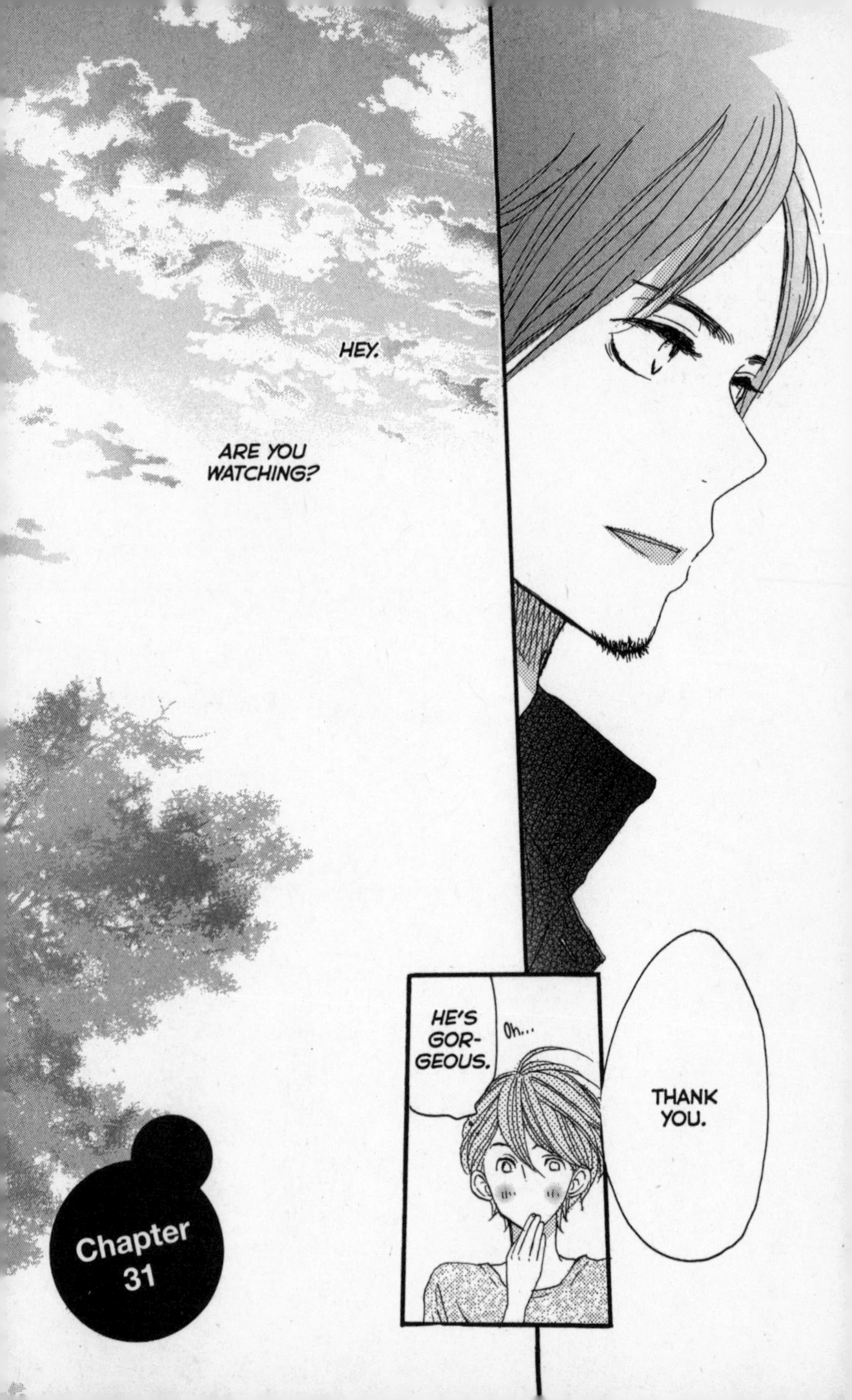
THANK YOU.
Oh...
HE'S GORGEOUS.
HEY.
ARE YOU WATCHING?
Chapter 31

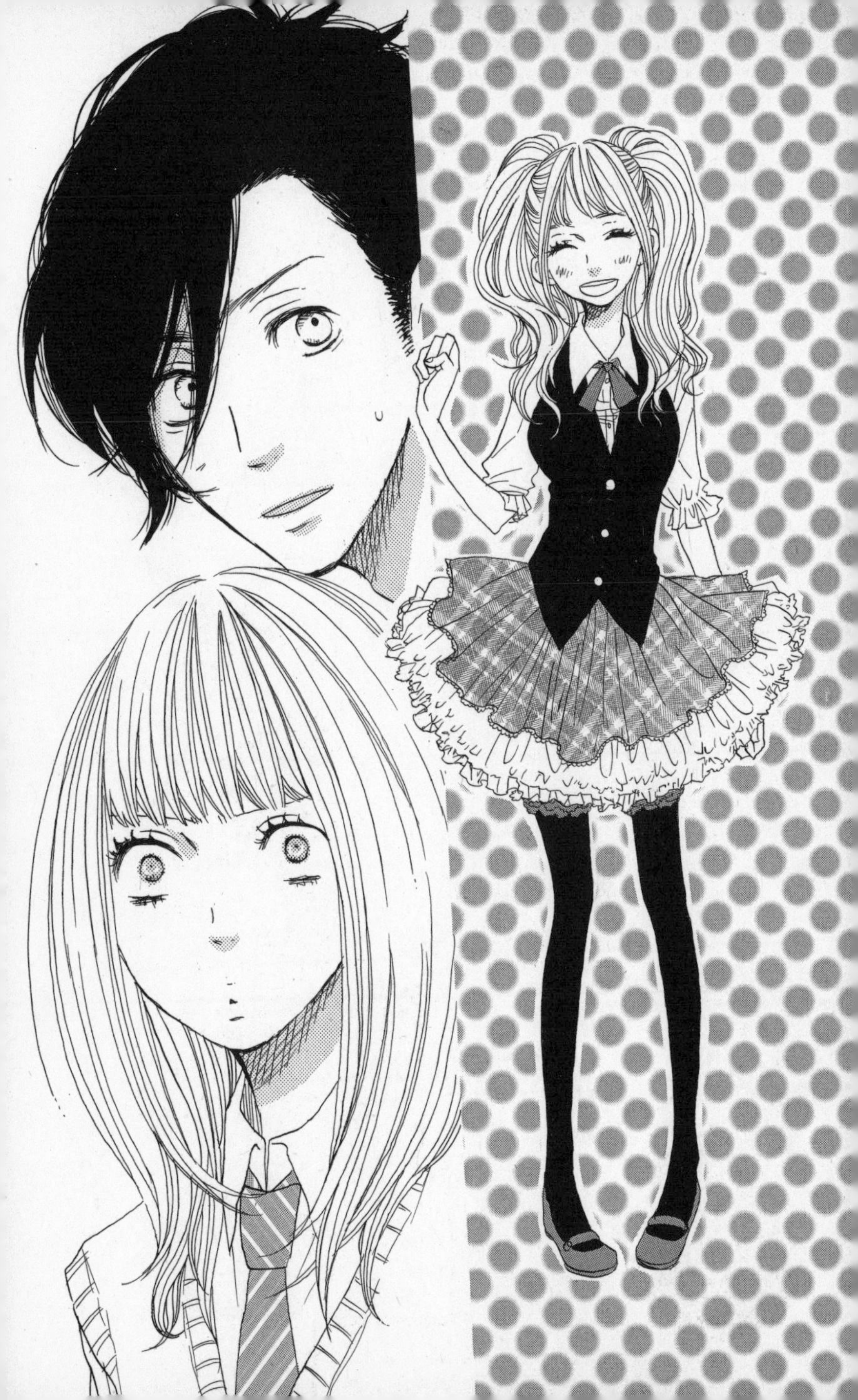

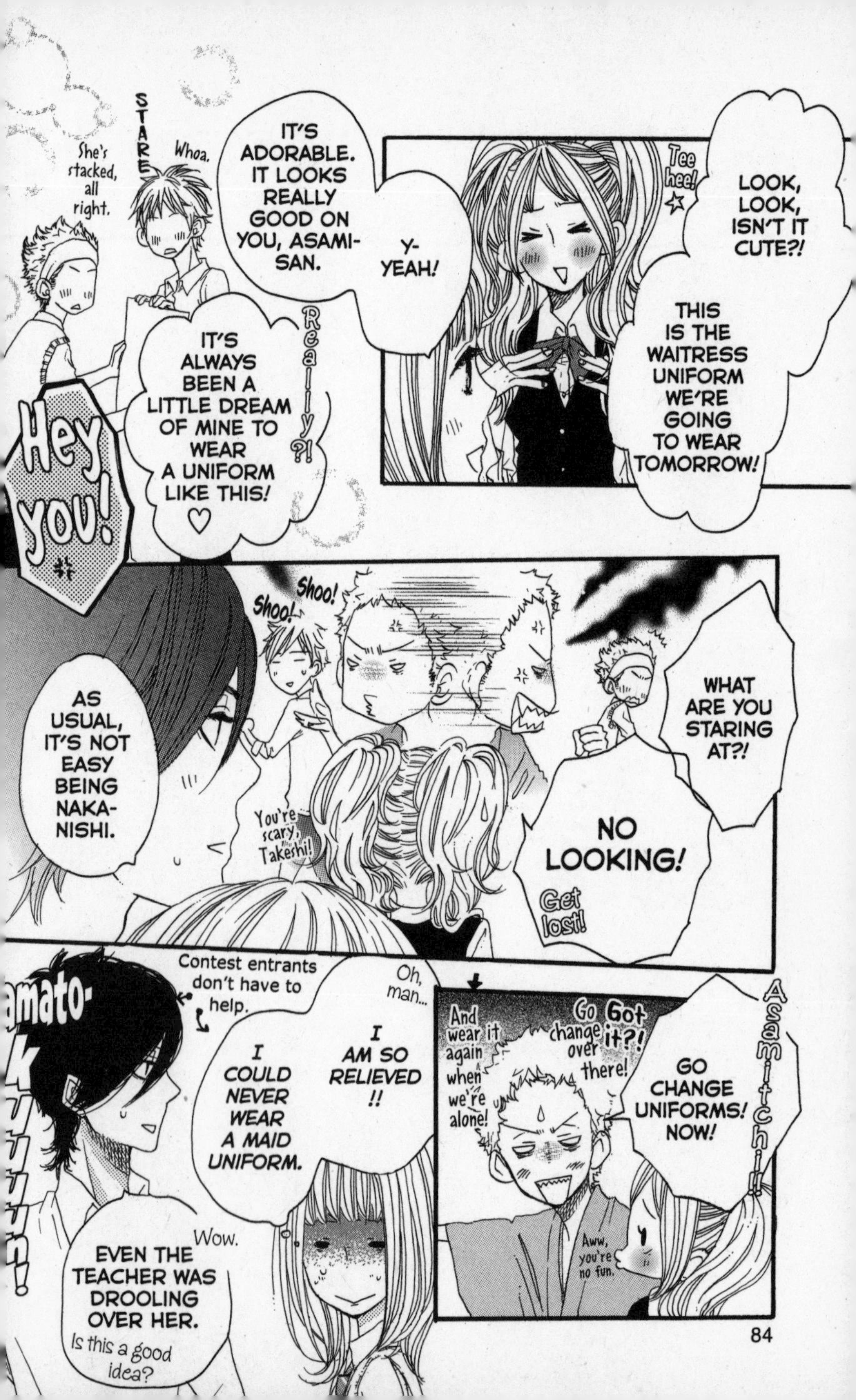

Tee hee! ☆
LOOK, LOOK, ISN'T IT CUTE?!
THIS IS THE WAITRESS UNIFORM WE'RE GOING TO WEAR TOMORROW!
IT'S ADORABLE. IT LOOKS REALLY GOOD ON YOU, ASAMI-SAN.
Y-YEAH!
Whoa.
STARE
She's stacked, all right.
IT'S ALWAYS BEEN A LITTLE DREAM OF MINE TO WEAR A UNIFORM LIKE THIS! ♡
Really?!
Hey you!
WHAT ARE YOU STARING AT?!
NO LOOKING!
Get lost!
Shoo!
Shoo!
You're scary, Takeshi!
AS USUAL, IT'S NOT EASY BEING NAKANISHI.
Asamitchi!
GO CHANGE UNIFORMS! NOW!
Got it?!
Go change over there!
And wear it again when we're alone!
Aww, you're no fun.
Oh, man...
I AM SO RELIEVED!!
I COULD NEVER WEAR A MAID UNIFORM.
Contest entrants don't have to help.
amato-kuuuuun!
Wow.
EVEN THE TEACHER WAS DROOLING OVER HER.
Is this a good idea?

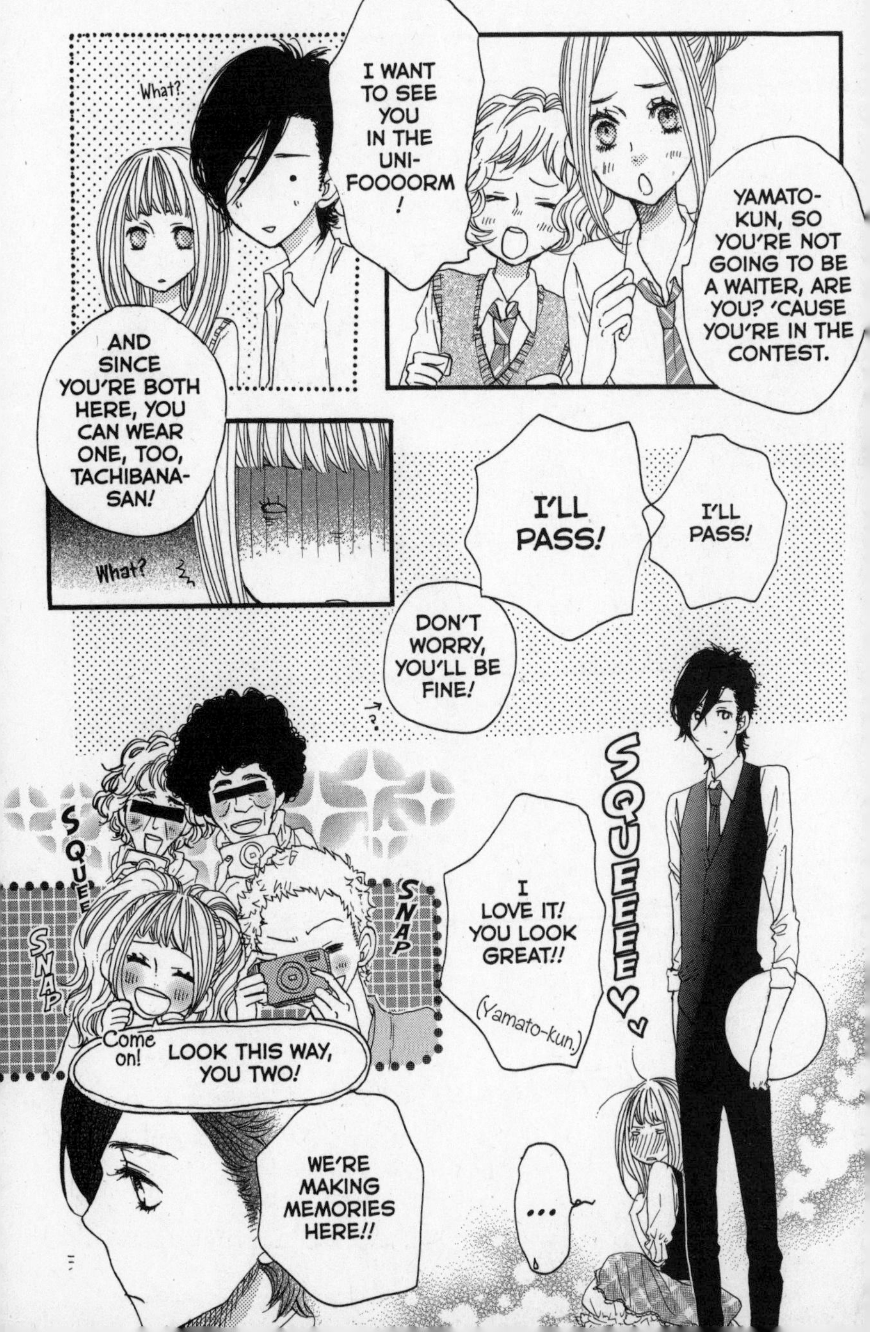
YAMATO-KUN, SO YOU'RE NOT GOING TO BE A WAITER, ARE YOU? 'CAUSE YOU'RE IN THE CONTEST.
I WANT TO SEE YOU IN THE UNI-FOOOORM!
What?
AND SINCE YOU'RE BOTH HERE, YOU CAN WEAR ONE, TOO, TACHIBANA-SAN!
What?
I'LL PASS!
I'LL PASS!
DON'T WORRY, YOU'LL BE FINE!
?
SQUEEEEE♥
I LOVE IT! YOU LOOK GREAT!!
(Yamato-kun.)
SQUEE
SNAP
SNAP
Come on!
LOOK THIS WAY, YOU TWO!
...
WE'RE MAKING MEMORIES HERE!!

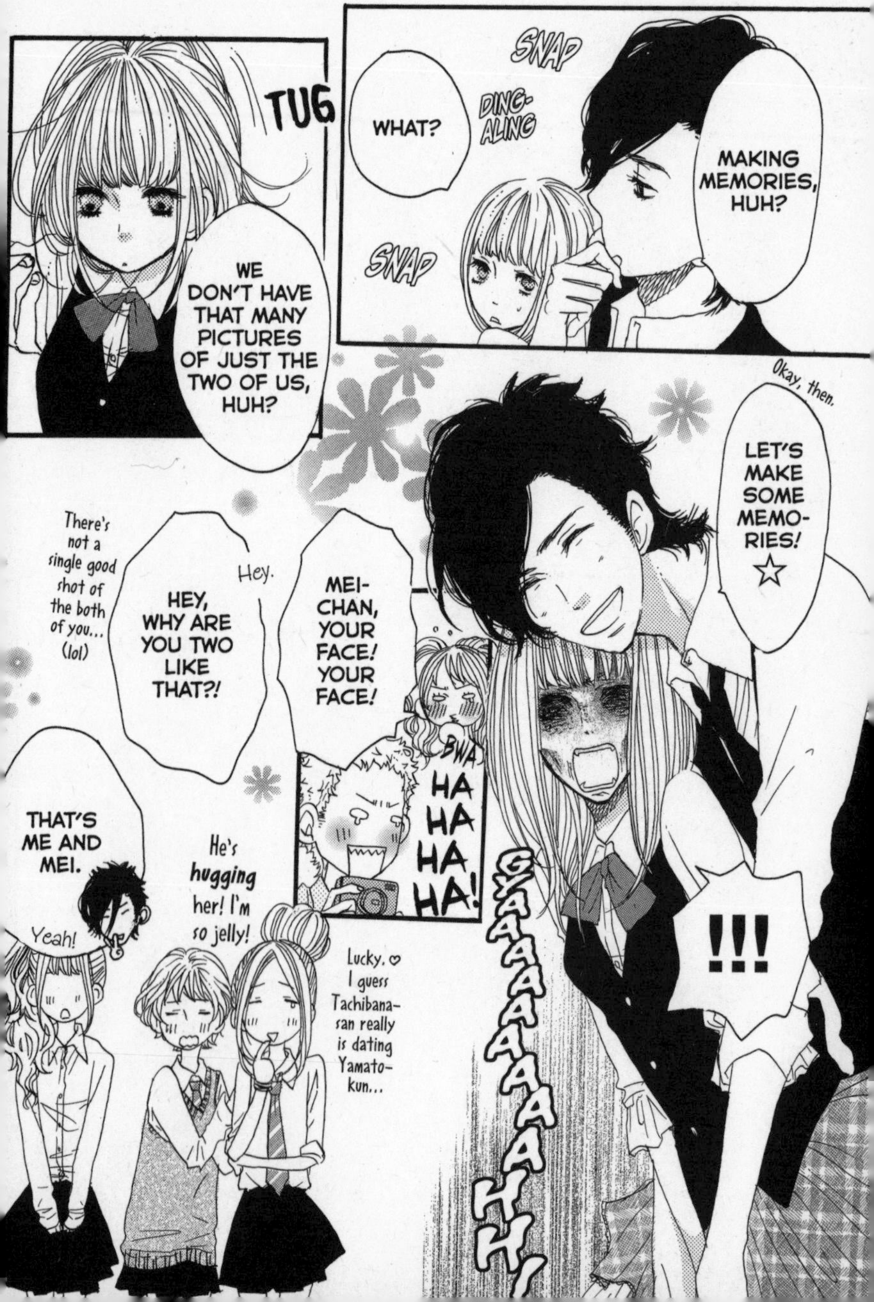
SNAP
DING-ALING
SNAP
MAKING MEMORIES, HUH?
WHAT?
TUG
WE DON'T HAVE THAT MANY PICTURES OF JUST THE TWO OF US, HUH?
Okay, then.
LET'S MAKE SOME MEMO-RIES! ☆
!!!
GYAAAAAAAAAH!
MEI-CHAN, YOUR FACE! YOUR FACE!
BWA HA HA HA HA!
Hey.
HEY, WHY ARE YOU TWO LIKE THAT?!
There's not a single good shot of the both of you... (lol)
THAT'S ME AND MEI.
Yeah!
He's hugging her! I'm so jelly!
Lucky. ♡ I guess Tachibana-san really is dating Yamato-kun...

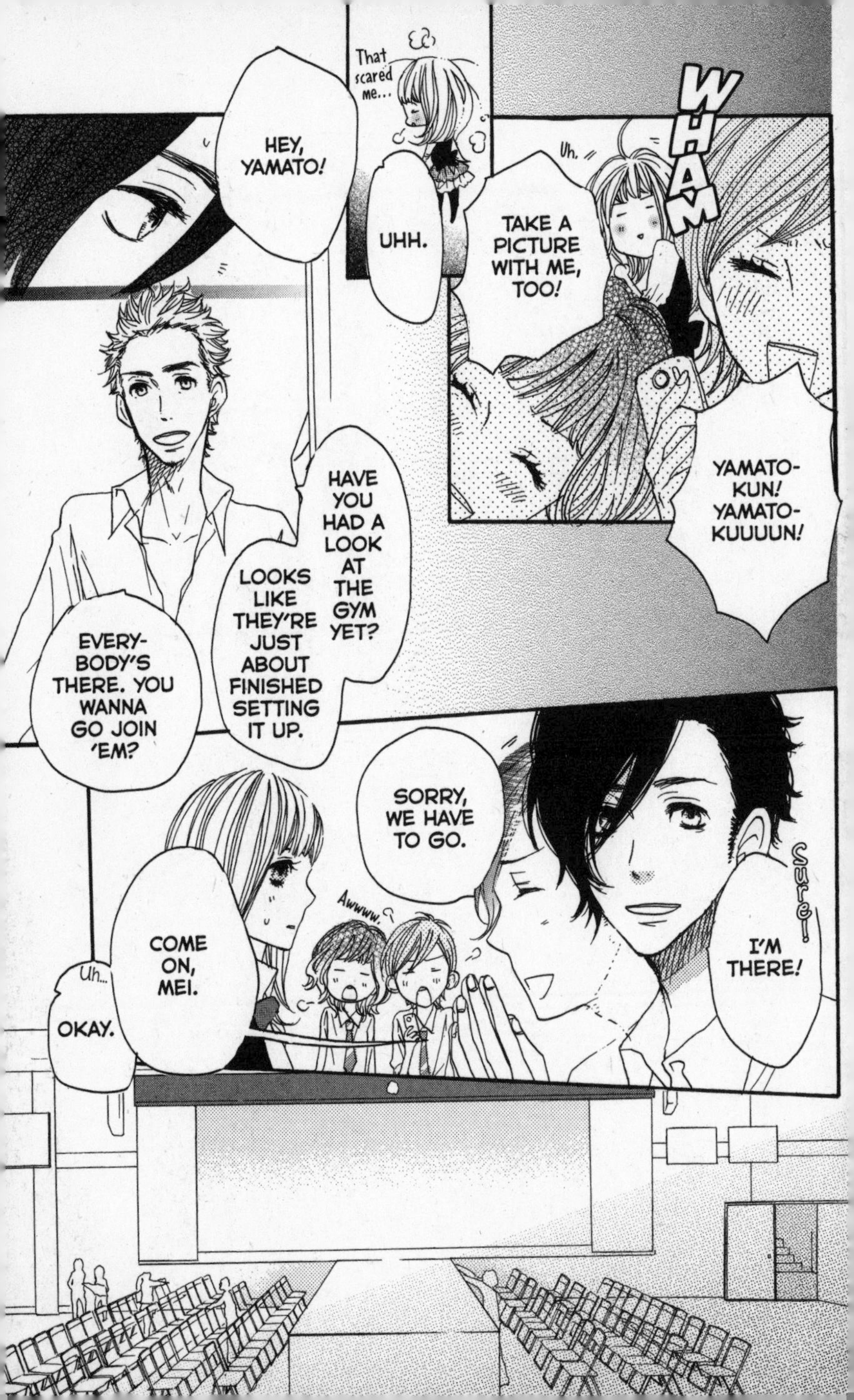
WHAM
Uh.
TAKE A PICTURE WITH ME, TOO!
YAMATO-KUN! YAMATO-KUUUUN!
That scared me...
UHH.
HEY, YAMATO!
HAVE YOU HAD A LOOK AT THE GYM YET?
LOOKS LIKE THEY'RE JUST ABOUT FINISHED SETTING IT UP.
EVERYBODY'S THERE. YOU WANNA GO JOIN 'EM?
Sure!
I'M THERE!
SORRY, WE HAVE TO GO.
Awwww.
COME ON, MEI.
Uh...
OKAY.

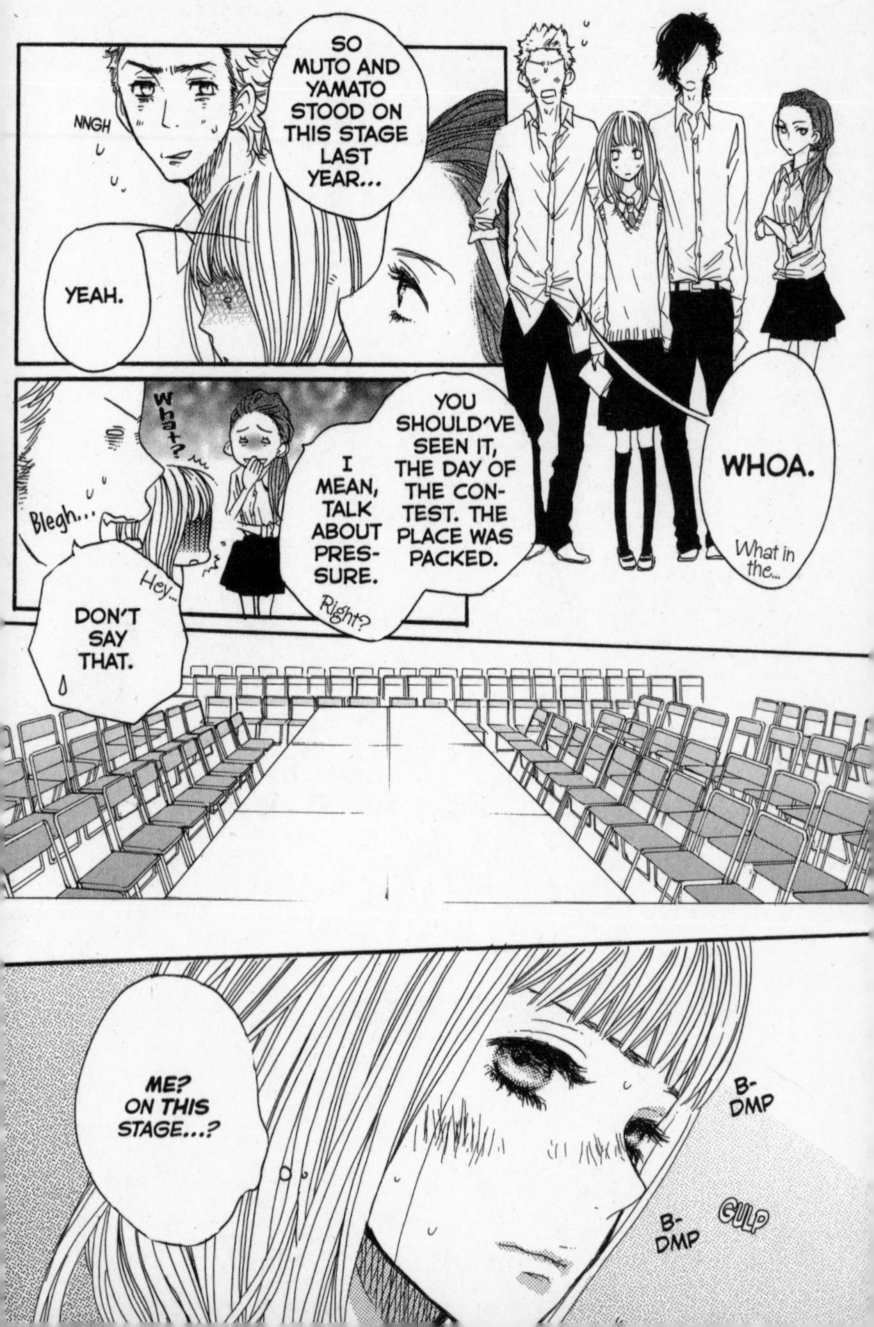
WHOA.
What in the...
SO MUTO AND YAMATO STOOD ON THIS STAGE LAST YEAR...
NNGH
YEAH.
YOU SHOULD'VE SEEN IT, THE DAY OF THE CON-TEST. THE PLACE WAS PACKED.
I MEAN, TALK ABOUT PRES-SURE.
Right?
What?
Blegh...
Hey...
DON'T SAY THAT.
ME? ON THIS STAGE...?
B-DMP
B-DMP
GULP

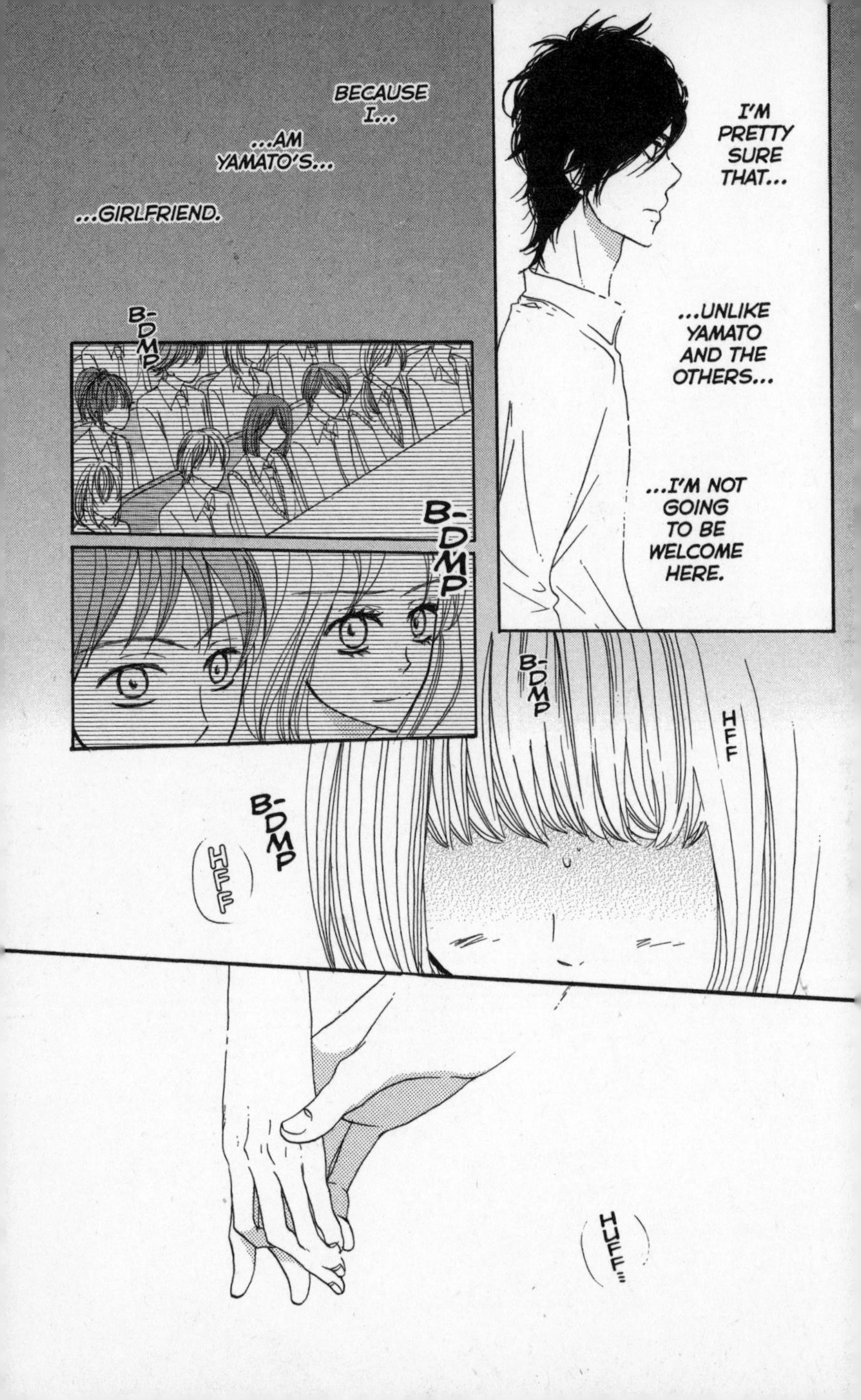
I'M PRETTY SURE THAT...
...UNLIKE YAMATO AND THE OTHERS...
...I'M NOT GOING TO BE WELCOME HERE.
BECAUSE I...
...AM YAMATO'S...
...GIRLFRIEND.
B-DMP
B-DMP
B-DMP
HFF
B-DMP
HFF
HUFF...

YOU WANNA GO DOWNSTAIRS AND TAKE A BREAK?

ARE YOU OKAY?

MEI...

■ Contest Outline
Participants will line up...
then they will walk down the...
stage right. The masters of ceremony...
a speech, and the entrants will exit stage...

Once the first part of the contest has en...
audience members on their way out...
...er the entrants will be ask...
...and prize winners. We w...
...nts are not allowed t...

...time.
...heme of this year's c...
...heme is a first date wh...
we ask that all entrants...
...the day of the event, the ma...
Please have your answers ready in time...
...re, you are allowed to show off tale...
...hope you all have fun.

A LITTLE.

ME TOO.

NERVOUS?

...SO MANY PEOPLE WANTED TO GET YOU OUT IN FRONT OF EVERYONE.

YEAH...

I KNOW HOW MUCH YOU HATE STANDING IN FRONT OF PEOPLE, MEI.

BUT MAYBE THAT'S WHY...

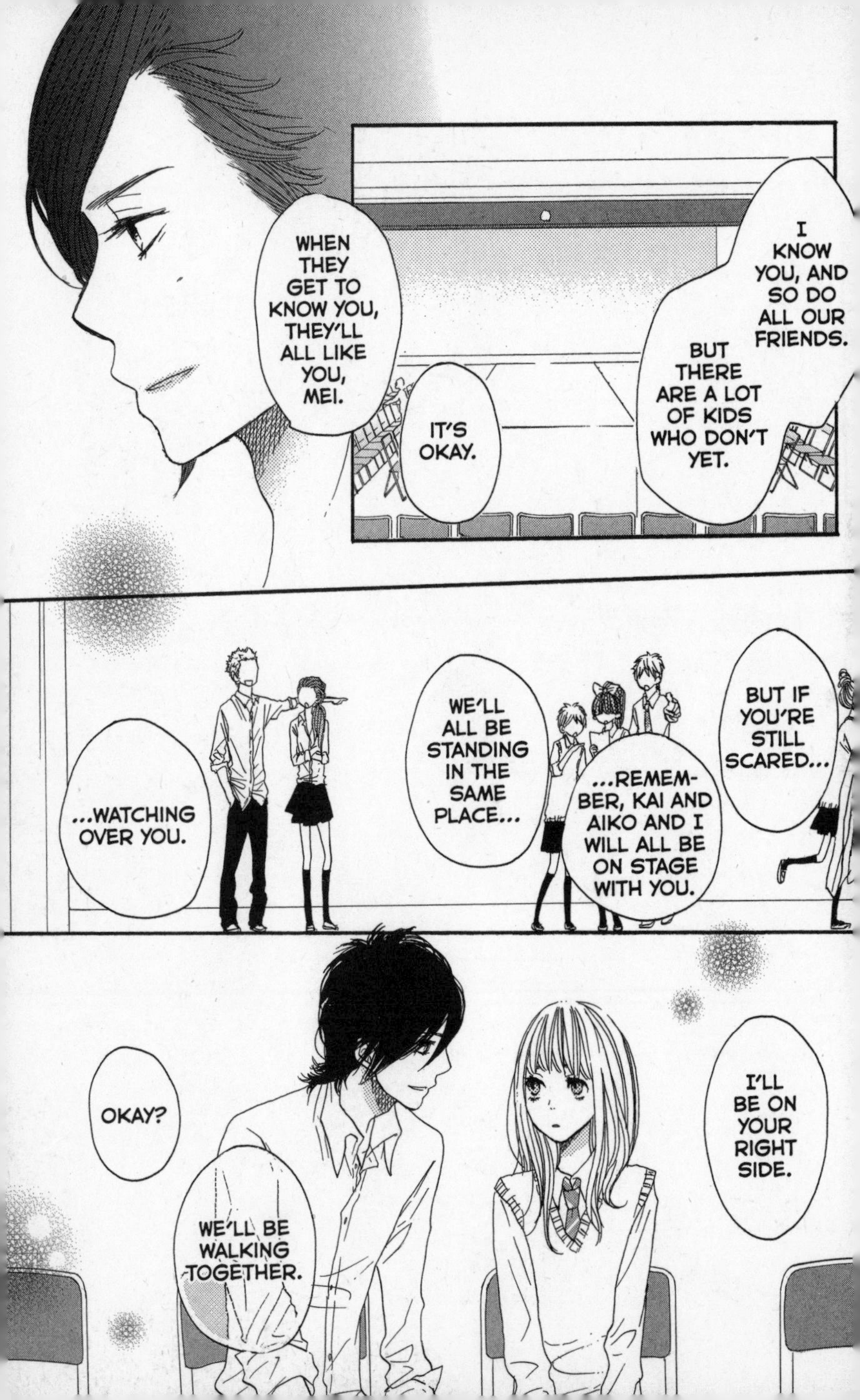
I KNOW YOU, AND SO DO ALL OUR FRIENDS.
BUT THERE ARE A LOT OF KIDS WHO DON'T YET.
IT'S OKAY.
WHEN THEY GET TO KNOW YOU, THEY'LL ALL LIKE YOU, MEI.
BUT IF YOU'RE STILL SCARED...
...REMEMBER, KAI AND AIKO AND I WILL ALL BE ON STAGE WITH YOU.
WE'LL ALL BE STANDING IN THE SAME PLACE...
...WATCHING OVER YOU.
I'LL BE ON YOUR RIGHT SIDE.
OKAY?
WE'LL BE WALKING TOGETHER.

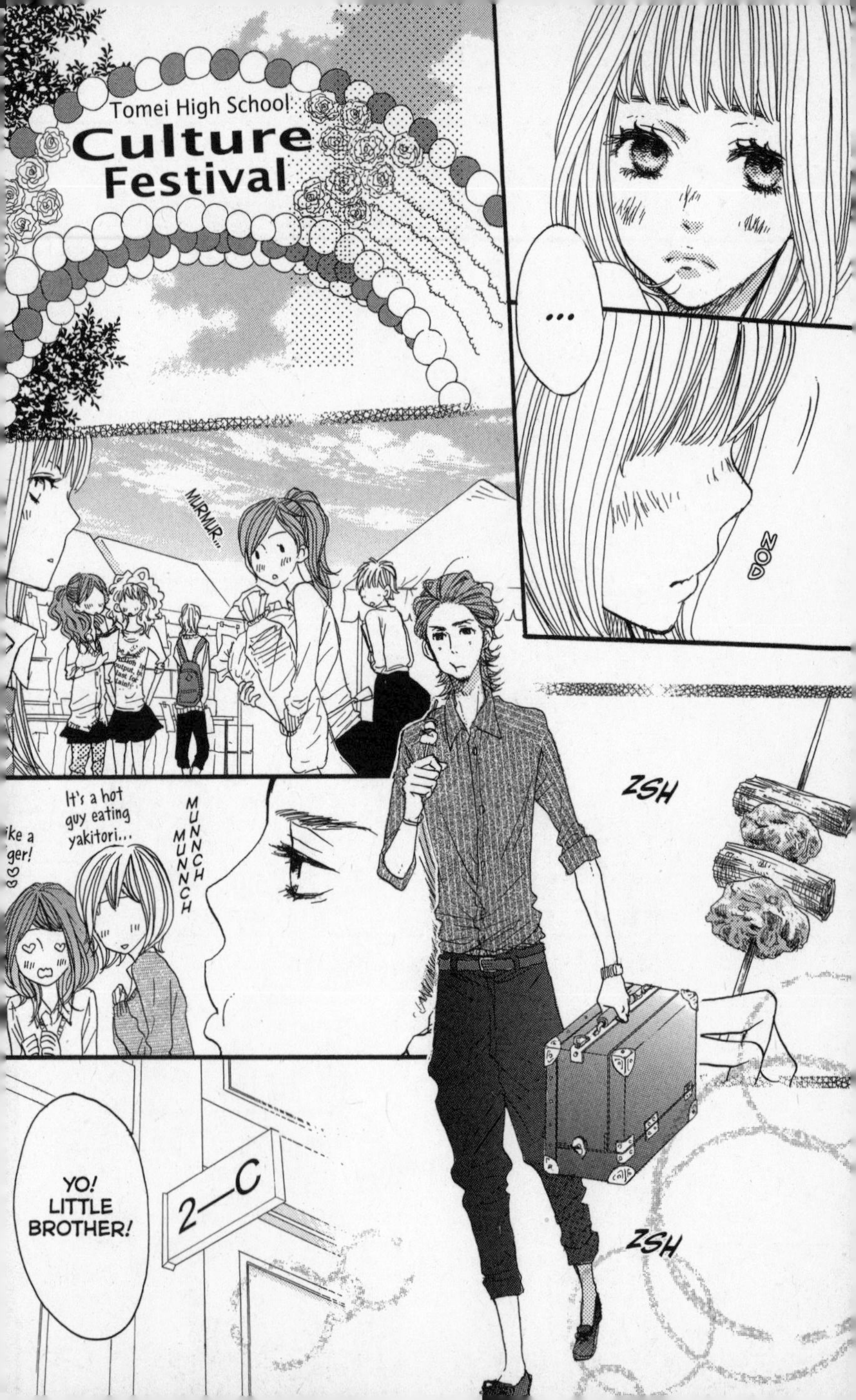
...
NOD
Tomei High School
Culture Festival
MURMUR...
ZSH
ZSH
MUNCH MUNCH
It's a hot guy eating yakitori...
2—C
YO! LITTLE BROTHER!

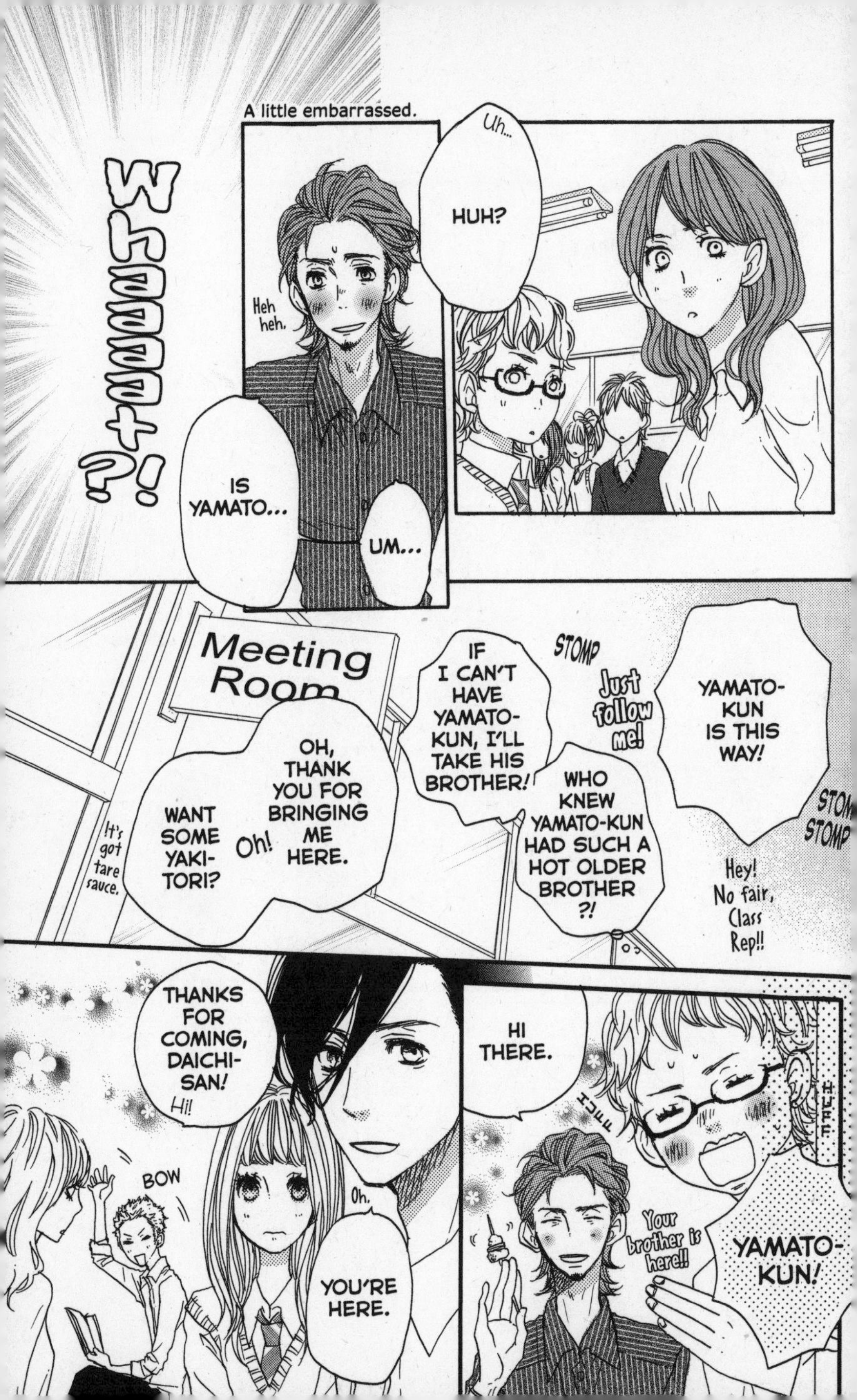
Uh...
HUH?
A little embarrassed.
Heh heh.
IS YAMATO...
UM...
Whaaaat?!
STOMP STOMP
YAMATO-KUN IS THIS WAY!
Hey! No fair, Class Rep!!
Just follow me!
STOMP
WHO KNEW YAMATO-KUN HAD SUCH A HOT OLDER BROTHER?!
IF I CAN'T HAVE YAMATO-KUN, I'LL TAKE HIS BROTHER!
Meeting Room
OH, THANK YOU FOR BRINGING ME HERE.
Oh!
WANT SOME YAKI-TORI?
It's got tare sauce.
HUFF
YAMATO-KUN!
HUFF
Your brother is here!!
HI THERE.
THANKS FOR COMING, DAICHI-SAN!
Hi!
Oh.
YOU'RE HERE.
BOW

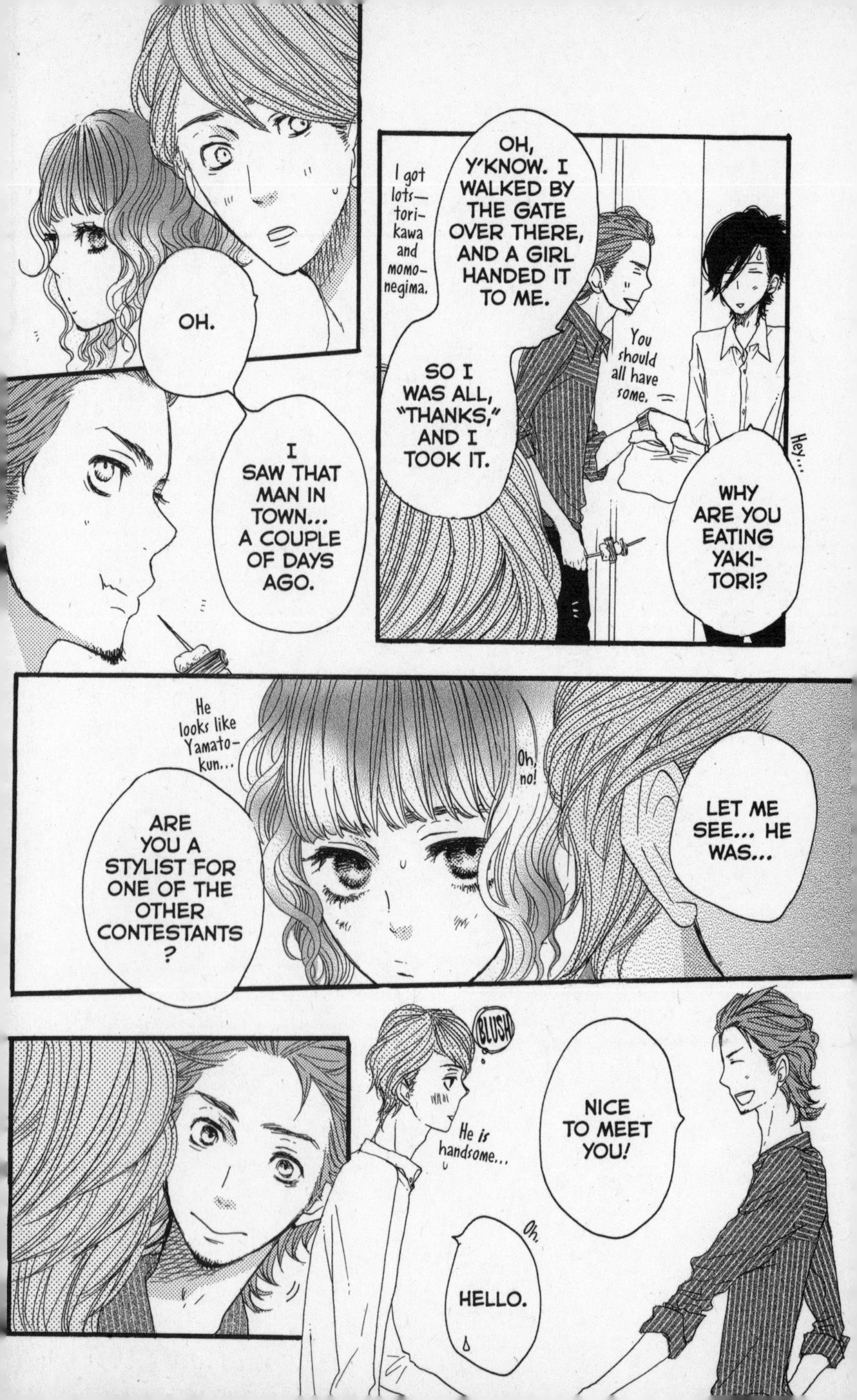
Hey...
WHY ARE YOU EATING YAKITORI?
You should all have some.
OH, Y'KNOW. I WALKED BY THE GATE OVER THERE, AND A GIRL HANDED IT TO ME.
I got lots—tori-kawa and momo-negima.
SO I WAS ALL, "THANKS," AND I TOOK IT.
OH.
I SAW THAT MAN IN TOWN... A COUPLE OF DAYS AGO.
LET ME SEE... HE WAS...
Oh, no!
He looks like Yamato-kun...
ARE YOU A STYLIST FOR ONE OF THE OTHER CONTESTANTS?
NICE TO MEET YOU!
BLUSH
He is handsome...
Oh.
HELLO.

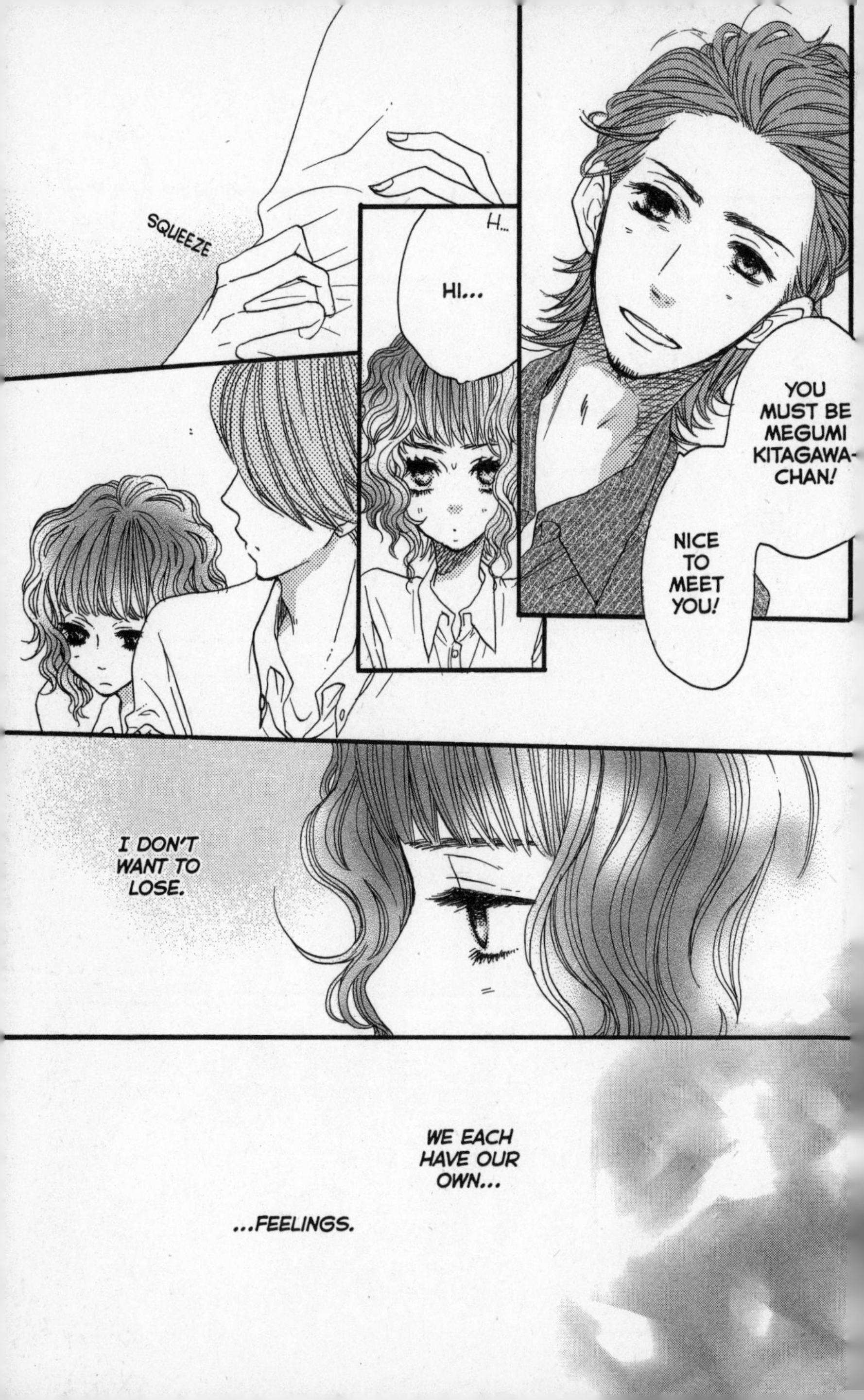
YOU MUST BE MEGUMI KITAGAWA-CHAN!
NICE TO MEET YOU!
H...
HI...
SQUEEZE
I DON'T WANT TO LOSE.
WE EACH HAVE OUR OWN...
...FEELINGS.

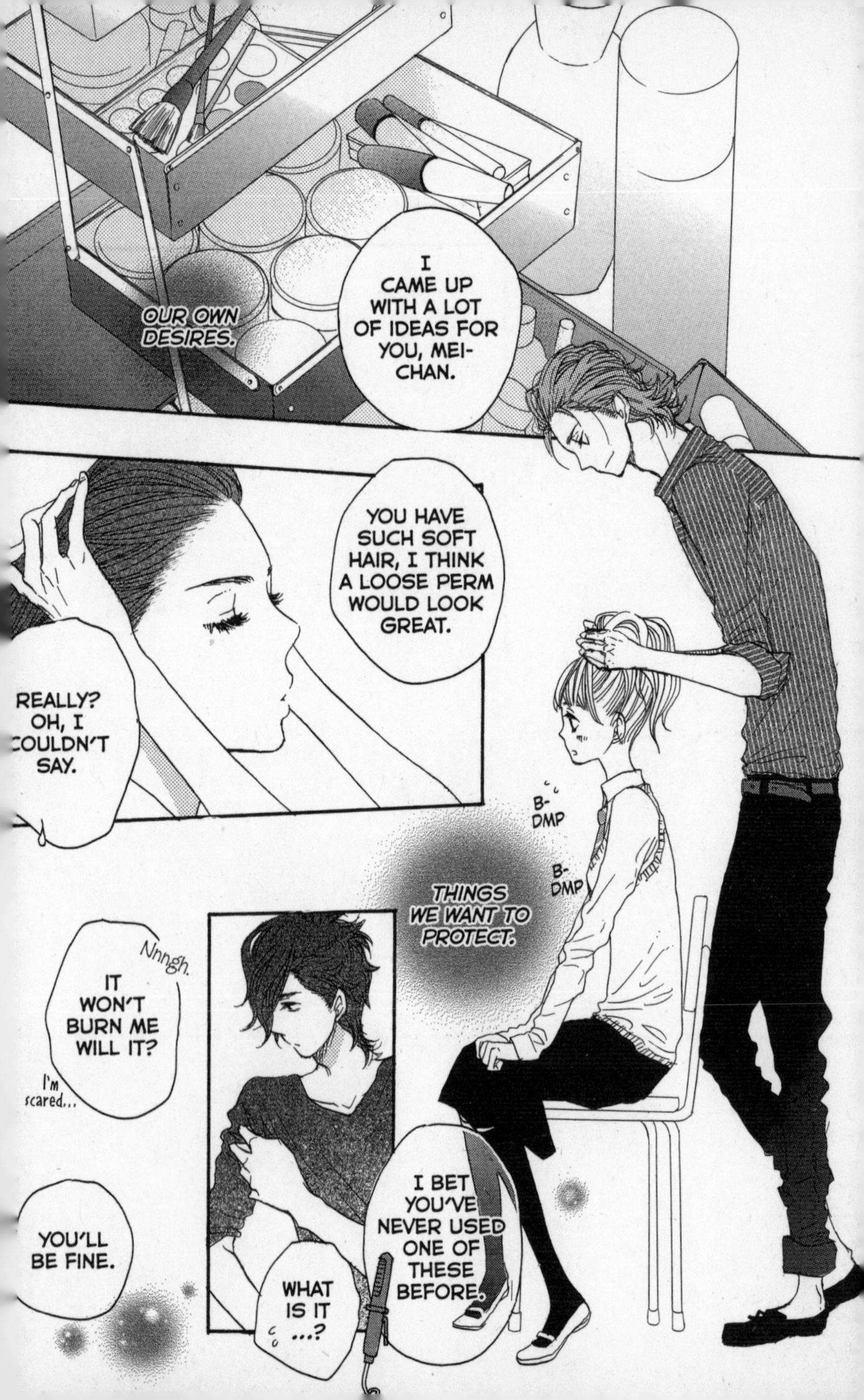
I CAME UP WITH A LOT OF IDEAS FOR YOU, MEI-CHAN.
OUR OWN DESIRES.
B-DMP
B-DMP
THINGS WE WANT TO PROTECT.
YOU HAVE SUCH SOFT HAIR, I THINK A LOOSE PERM WOULD LOOK GREAT.
REALLY? OH, I COULDN'T SAY.
I BET YOU'VE NEVER USED ONE OF THESE BEFORE.
WHAT IS IT ...?
Nnngh.
IT WON'T BURN ME WILL IT?
I'm scared...
YOU'LL BE FINE.

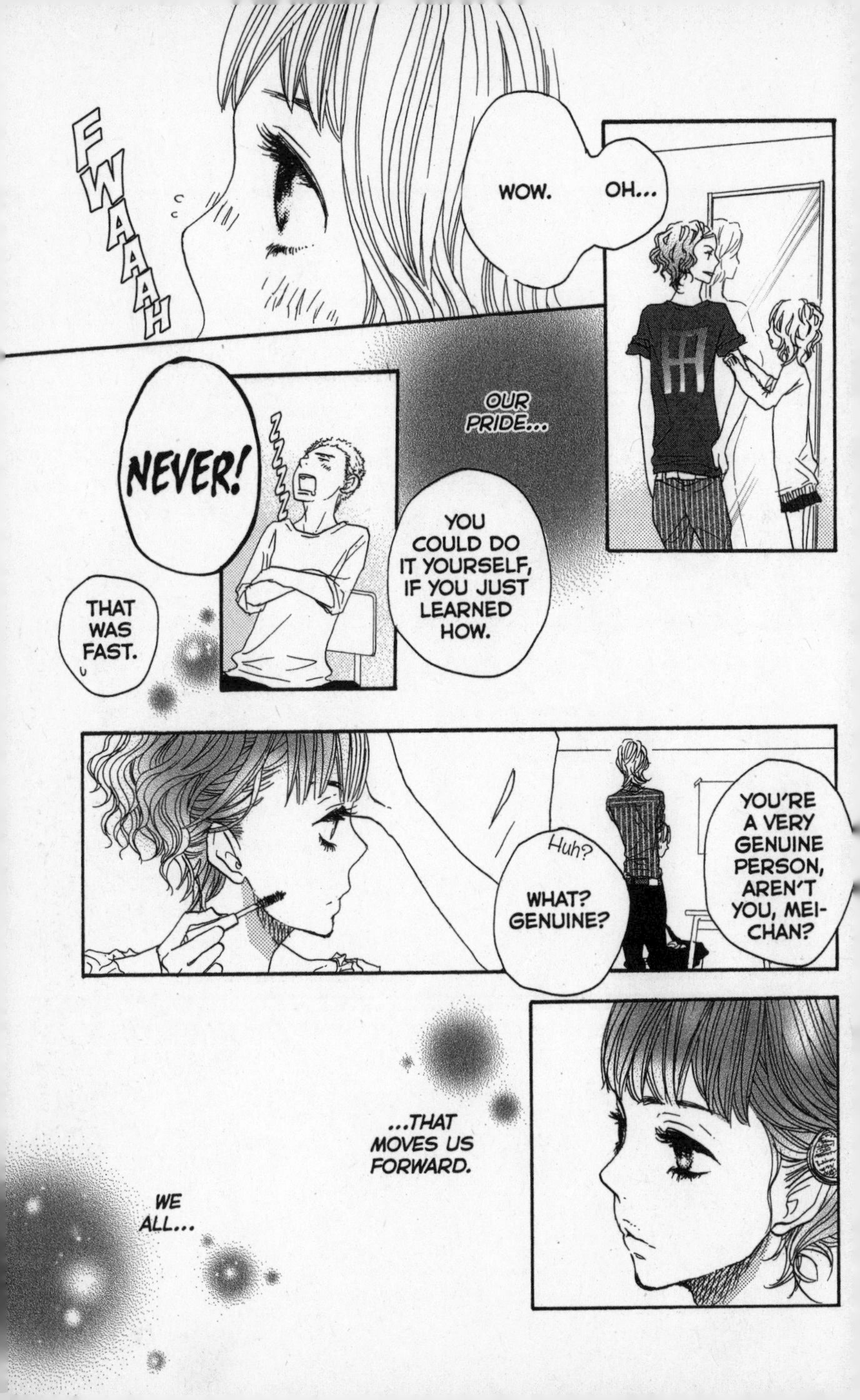
WOW. OH...
FWAAAAH
OUR PRIDE...
YOU COULD DO IT YOURSELF, IF YOU JUST LEARNED HOW.
NEVER!
ZZZZ
THAT WAS FAST.
YOU'RE A VERY GENUINE PERSON, AREN'T YOU, MEI-CHAN?
Huh?
WHAT? GENUINE?
...THAT MOVES US FORWARD.
WE ALL...

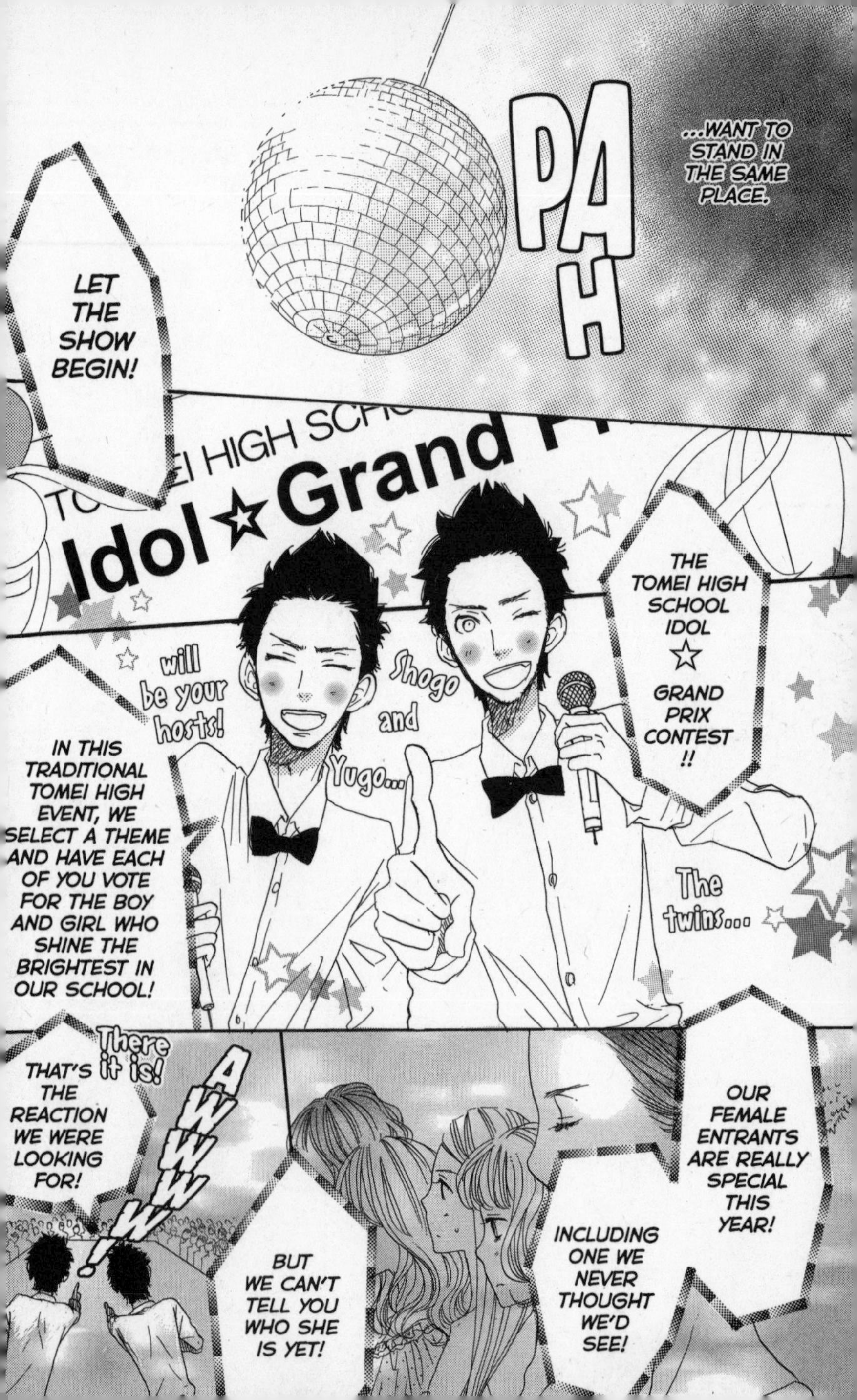
...WANT TO STAND IN THE SAME PLACE.
PAH
LET THE SHOW BEGIN!
HIGH SCH
Idol☆Grand
THE TOMEI HIGH SCHOOL IDOL ☆ GRAND PRIX CONTEST!!
The twins...
Shogo and Yugo...
will be your hosts!
IN THIS TRADITIONAL TOMEI HIGH EVENT, WE SELECT A THEME AND HAVE EACH OF YOU VOTE FOR THE BOY AND GIRL WHO SHINE THE BRIGHTEST IN OUR SCHOOL!
OUR FEMALE ENTRANTS ARE REALLY SPECIAL THIS YEAR!
INCLUDING ONE WE NEVER THOUGHT WE'D SEE!
BUT WE CAN'T TELL YOU WHO SHE IS YET!
AWWWWW!
There it is!
THAT'S THE REACTION WE WERE LOOKING FOR!

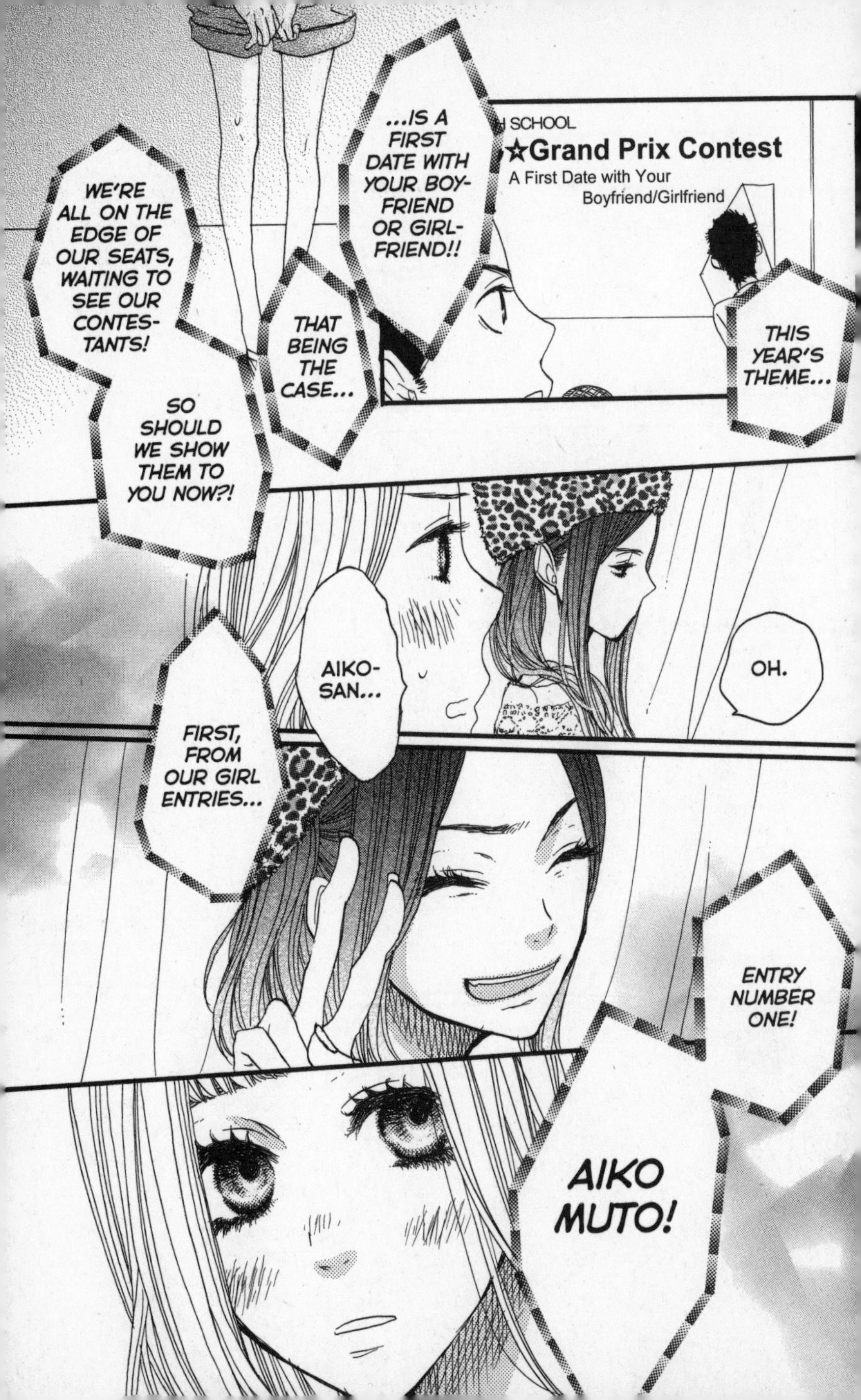
THIS YEAR'S THEME...
H SCHOOL
☆Grand Prix Contest
A First Date with Your Boyfriend/Girlfriend
...IS A FIRST DATE WITH YOUR BOY-FRIEND OR GIRL-FRIEND!!
THAT BEING THE CASE...
WE'RE ALL ON THE EDGE OF OUR SEATS, WAITING TO SEE OUR CONTES-TANTS!
SO SHOULD WE SHOW THEM TO YOU NOW?!
OH.
AIKO-SAN...
FIRST, FROM OUR GIRL ENTRIES...
ENTRY NUMBER ONE!
AIKO MUTO!

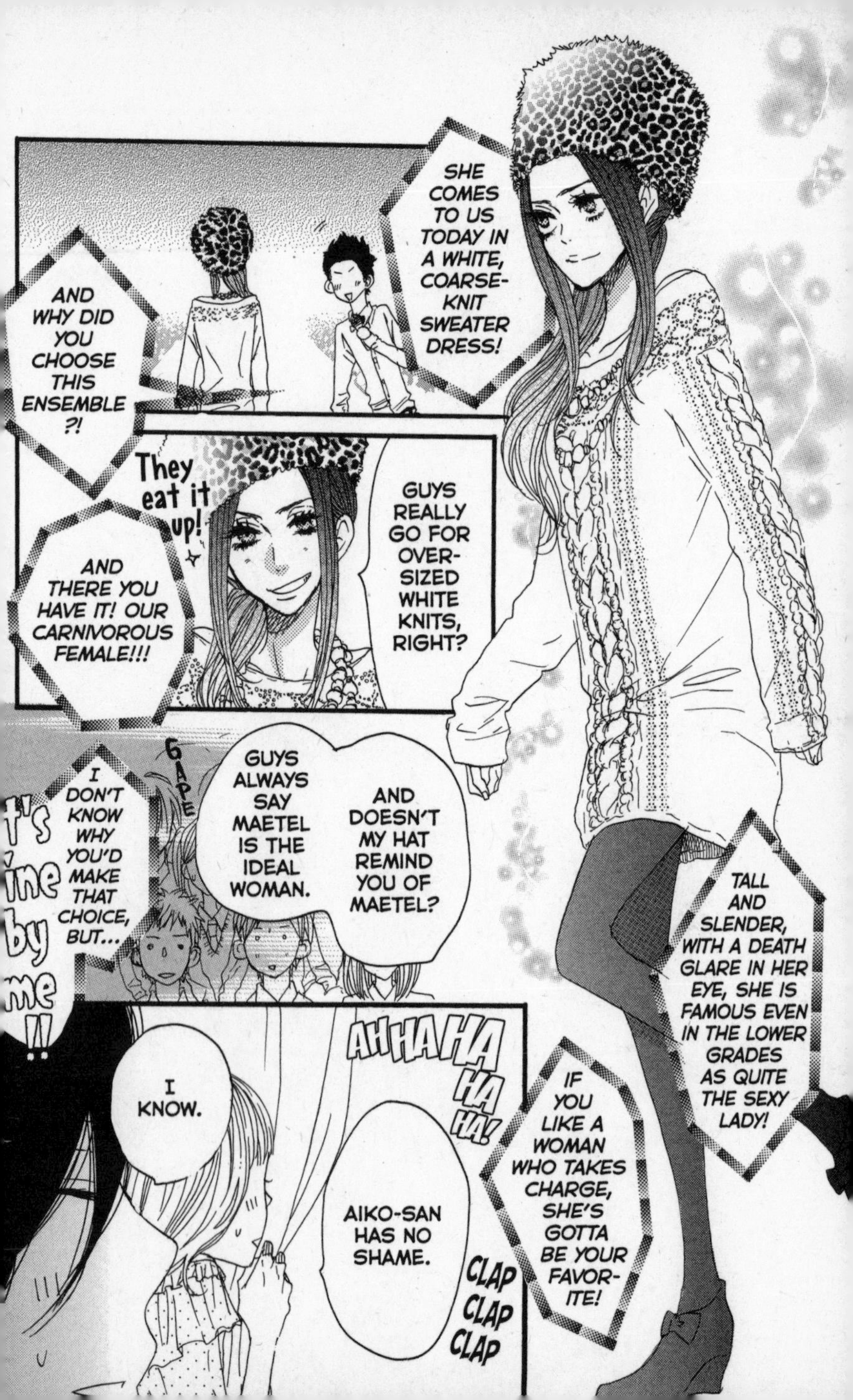
SHE COMES TO US TODAY IN A WHITE, COARSE-KNIT SWEATER DRESS!
AND WHY DID YOU CHOOSE THIS ENSEMBLE ?!
TALL AND SLENDER, WITH A DEATH GLARE IN HER EYE, SHE IS FAMOUS EVEN IN THE LOWER GRADES AS QUITE THE SEXY LADY!
IF YOU LIKE A WOMAN WHO TAKES CHARGE, SHE'S GOTTA BE YOUR FAVOR-ITE!
GUYS REALLY GO FOR OVER-SIZED WHITE KNITS, RIGHT?
They eat it up!
AND THERE YOU HAVE IT! OUR CARNIVOROUS FEMALE!!!
AND DOESN'T MY HAT REMIND YOU OF MAETEL?
GUYS ALWAYS SAY MAETEL IS THE IDEAL WOMAN.
GAPE
I DON'T KNOW WHY YOU'D MAKE THAT CHOICE, BUT...
AHHAHAHA HAHA HA!
CLAP CLAP CLAP
AIKO-SAN HAS NO SHAME.
I KNOW.

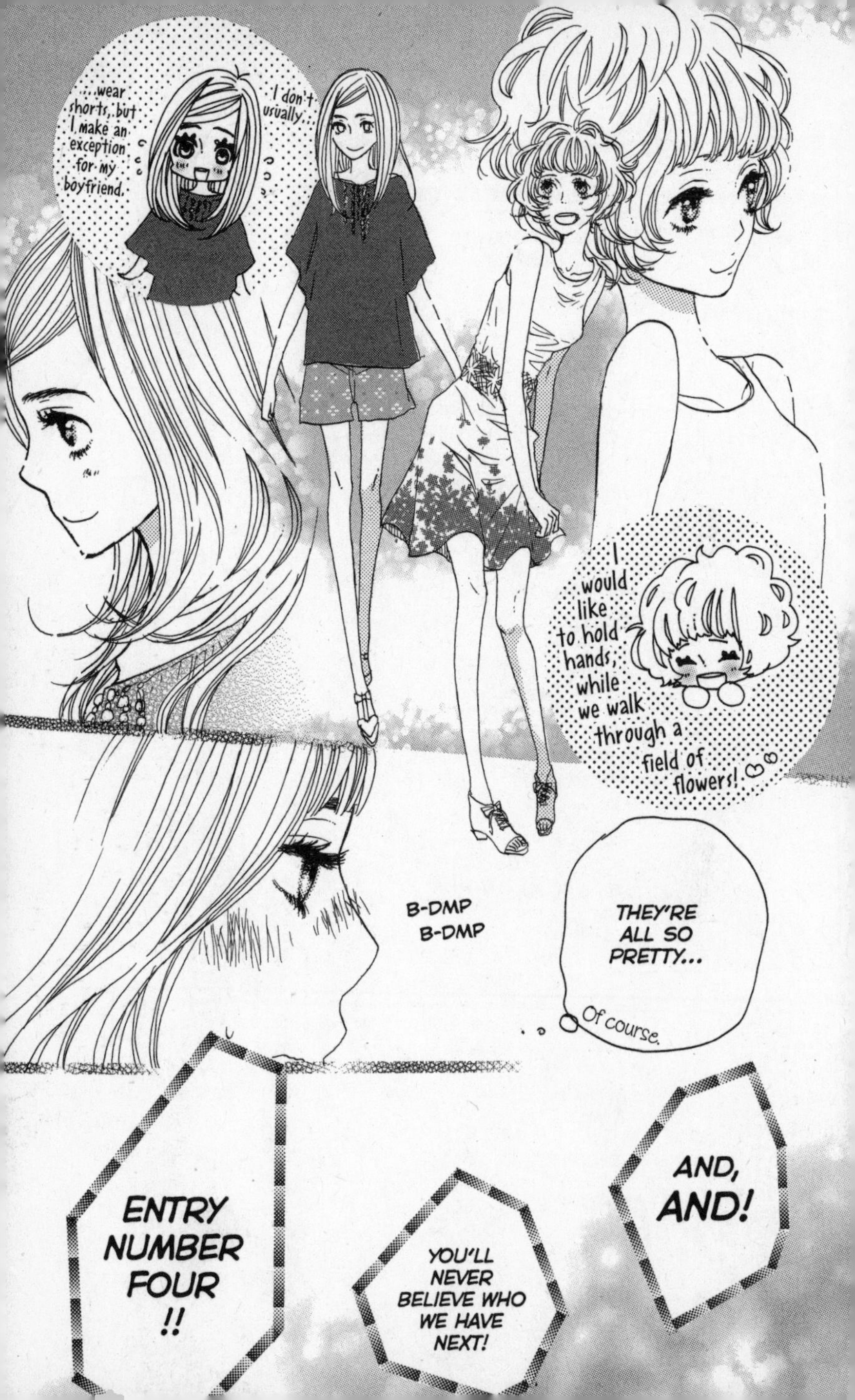

I would like to hold hands, while we walk through a field of flowers!
I don't usually...
...wear shorts, but I make an exception for my boyfriend.
THEY'RE ALL SO PRETTY...
Of course.
B-DMP B-DMP
AND, AND!
YOU'LL NEVER BELIEVE WHO WE HAVE NEXT!
ENTRY NUMBER FOUR !!

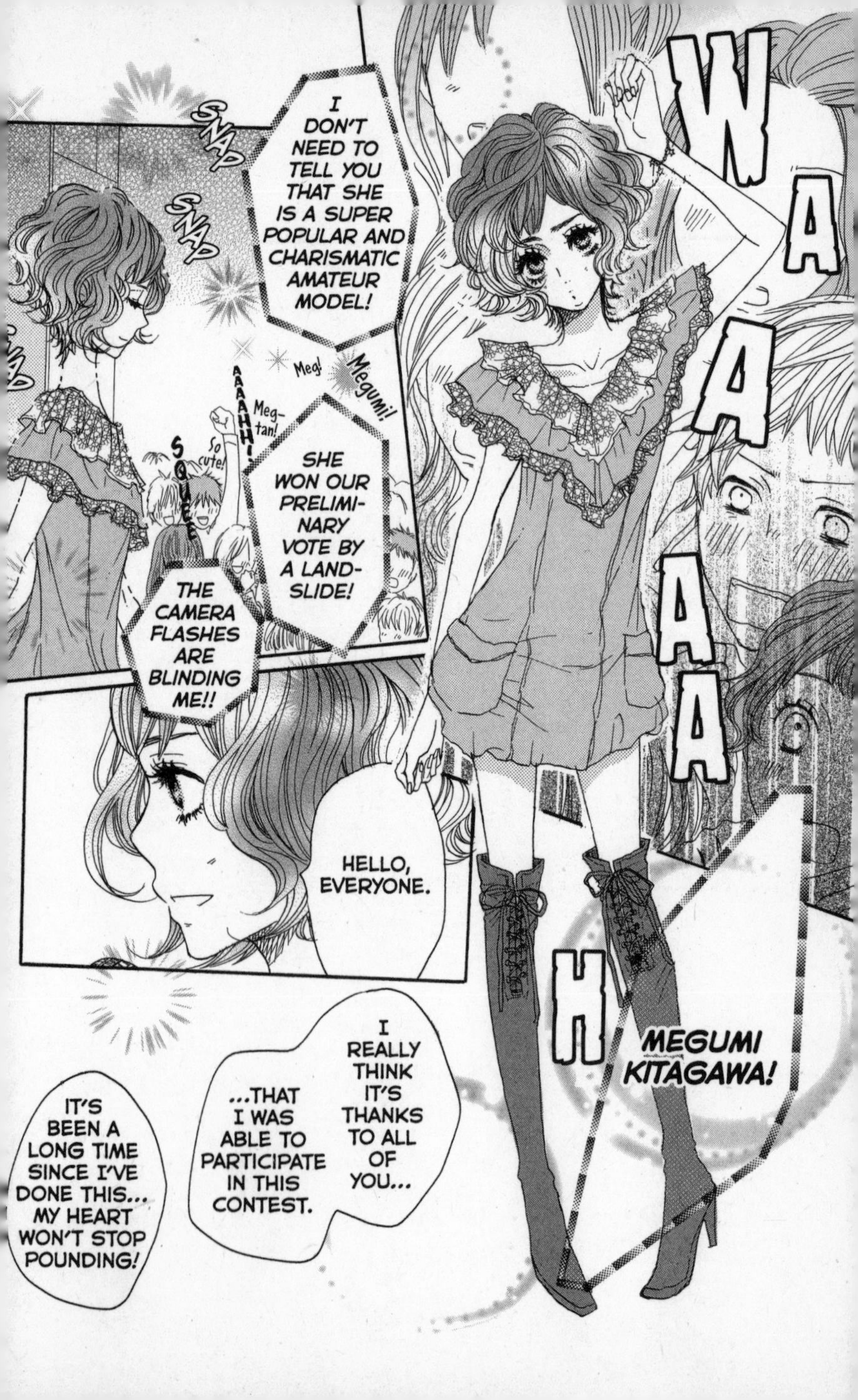
WAAAAAH
MEGUMI KITAGAWA!
I DON'T NEED TO TELL YOU THAT SHE IS A SUPER POPULAR AND CHARISMATIC AMATEUR MODEL!
SHE WON OUR PRELIMINARY VOTE BY A LANDSLIDE!
SNAP
SNAP
Megumi!
Meg!
AAAAHH!
Meg-tan!
So cute!
SQUEE
THE CAMERA FLASHES ARE BLINDING ME!!
HELLO, EVERYONE.
I REALLY THINK IT'S THANKS TO ALL OF YOU...
...THAT I WAS ABLE TO PARTICIPATE IN THIS CONTEST.
IT'S BEEN A LONG TIME SINCE I'VE DONE THIS... MY HEART WON'T STOP POUNDING!

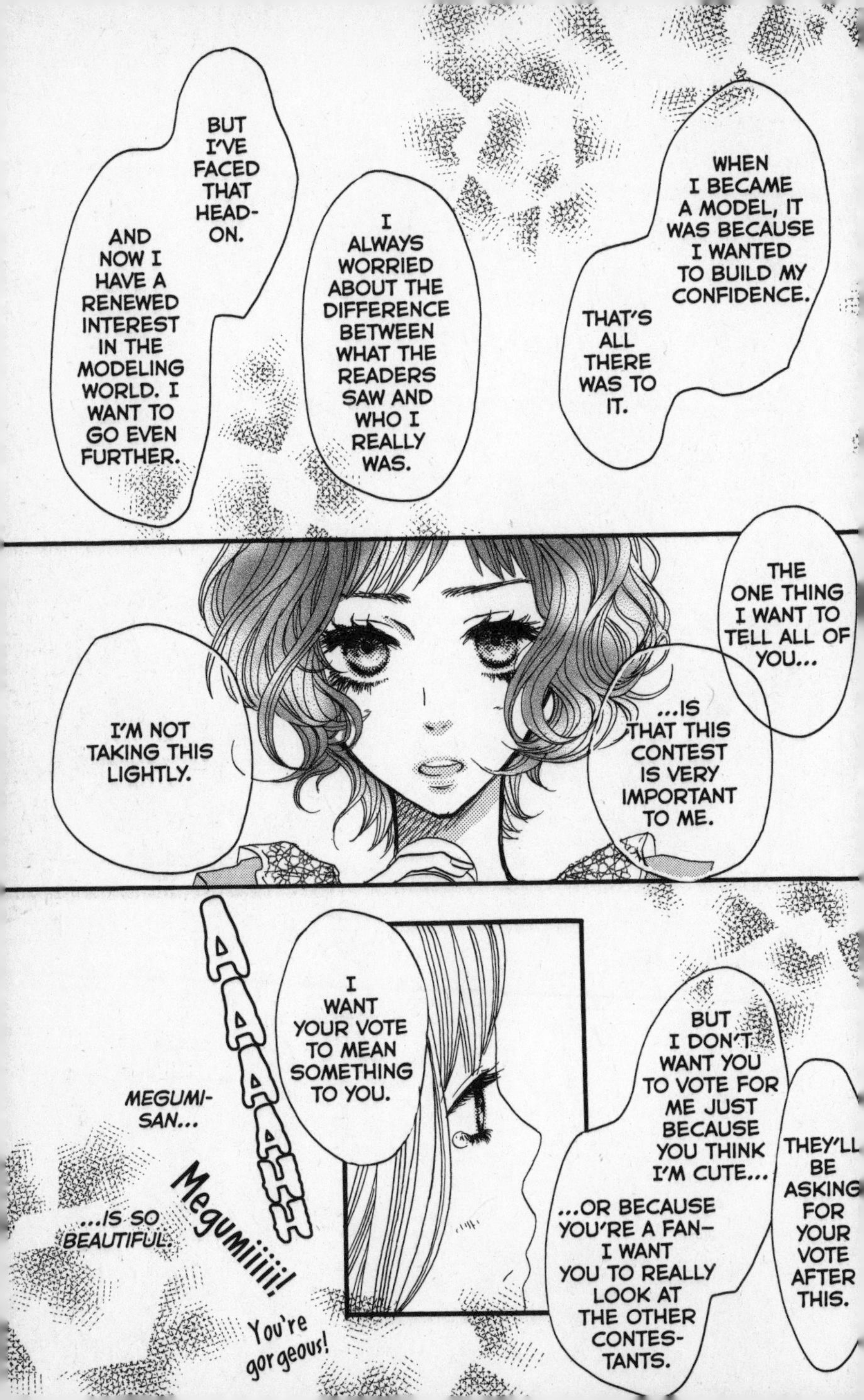

WHEN I BECAME A MODEL, IT WAS BECAUSE I WANTED TO BUILD MY CONFIDENCE.
THAT'S ALL THERE WAS TO IT.
I ALWAYS WORRIED ABOUT THE DIFFERENCE BETWEEN WHAT THE READERS SAW AND WHO I REALLY WAS.
BUT I'VE FACED THAT HEAD-ON.
AND NOW I HAVE A RENEWED INTEREST IN THE MODELING WORLD. I WANT TO GO EVEN FURTHER.
THE ONE THING I WANT TO TELL ALL OF YOU...
...IS THAT THIS CONTEST IS VERY IMPORTANT TO ME.
I'M NOT TAKING THIS LIGHTLY.
THEY'LL BE ASKING FOR YOUR VOTE AFTER THIS.
BUT I DON'T WANT YOU TO VOTE FOR ME JUST BECAUSE YOU THINK I'M CUTE...
...OR BECAUSE YOU'RE A FAN— I WANT YOU TO REALLY LOOK AT THE OTHER CONTESTANTS.
I WANT YOUR VOTE TO MEAN SOMETHING TO YOU.
AAAAAH
MEGUMI-SAN...
Megumiiiiii!
You're gorgeous!
...IS SO BEAUTIFUL.

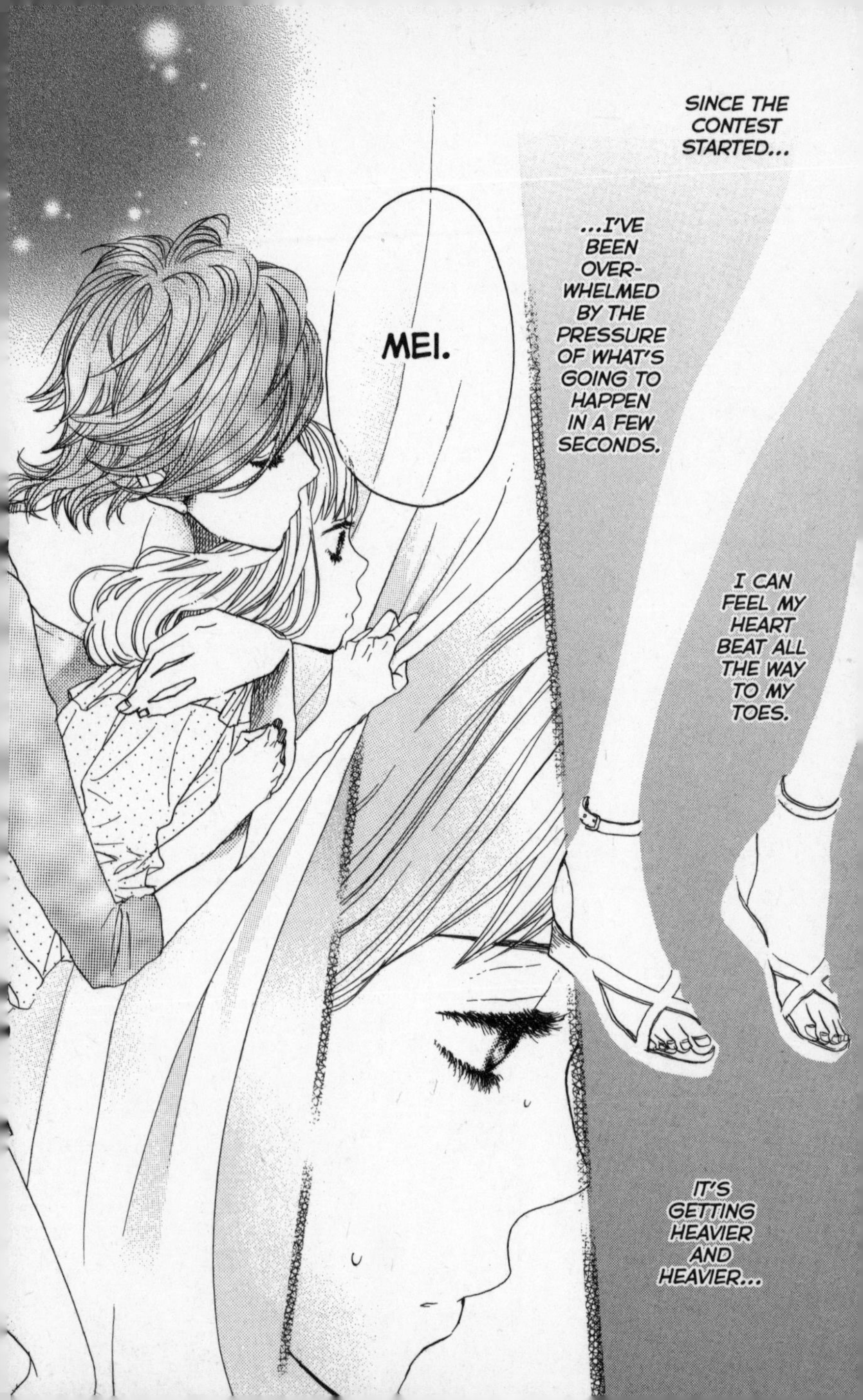
SINCE THE CONTEST STARTED...
...I'VE BEEN OVER-WHELMED BY THE PRESSURE OF WHAT'S GOING TO HAPPEN IN A FEW SECONDS.
MEI.
I CAN FEEL MY HEART BEAT ALL THE WAY TO MY TOES.
IT'S GETTING HEAVIER AND HEAVIER...

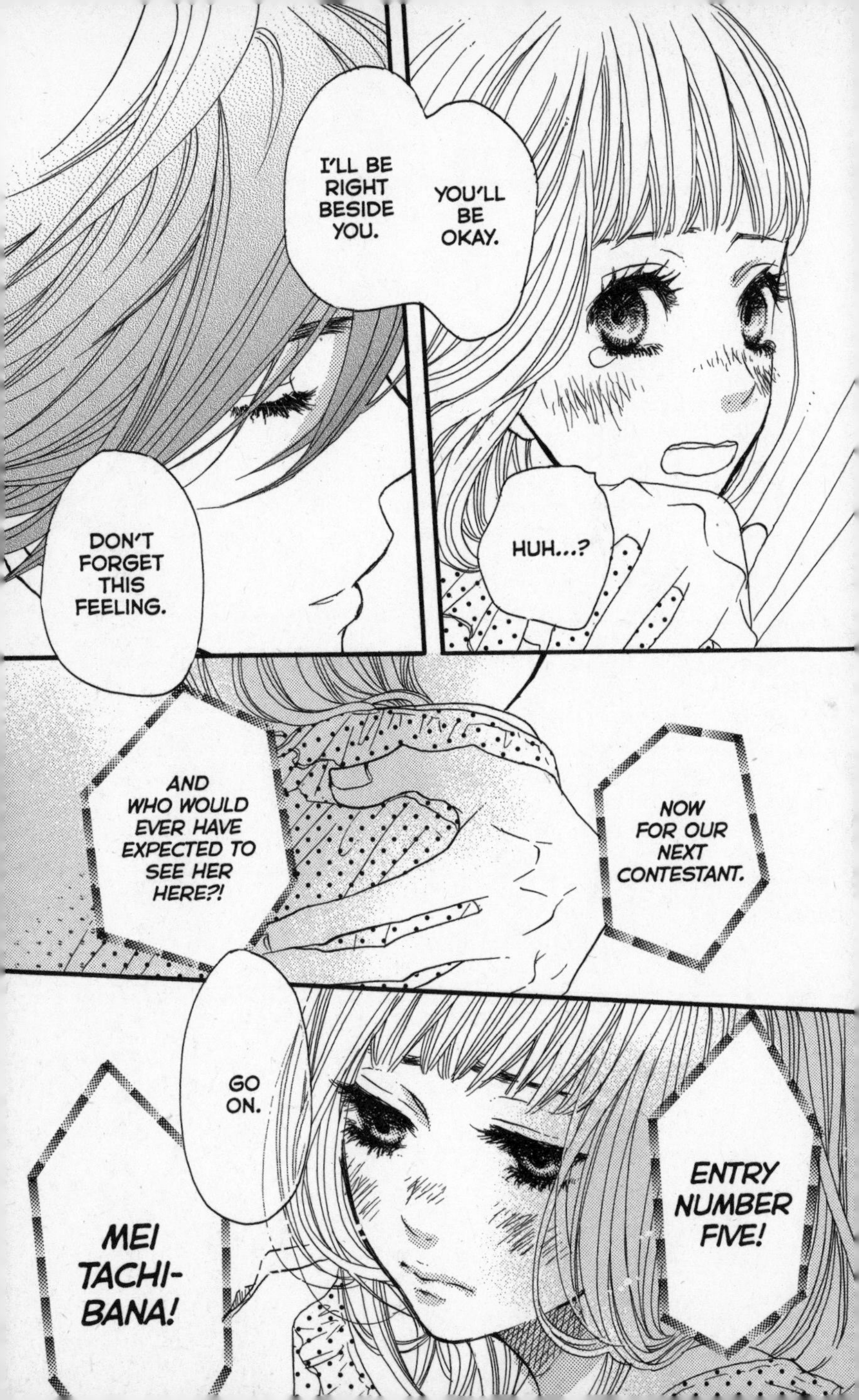
YOU'LL BE OKAY.
I'LL BE RIGHT BESIDE YOU.
HUH...?
DON'T FORGET THIS FEELING.
NOW FOR OUR NEXT CONTESTANT.
AND WHO WOULD EVER HAVE EXPECTED TO SEE HER HERE?!
ENTRY NUMBER FIVE!
GO ON.
MEI TACHIBANA!

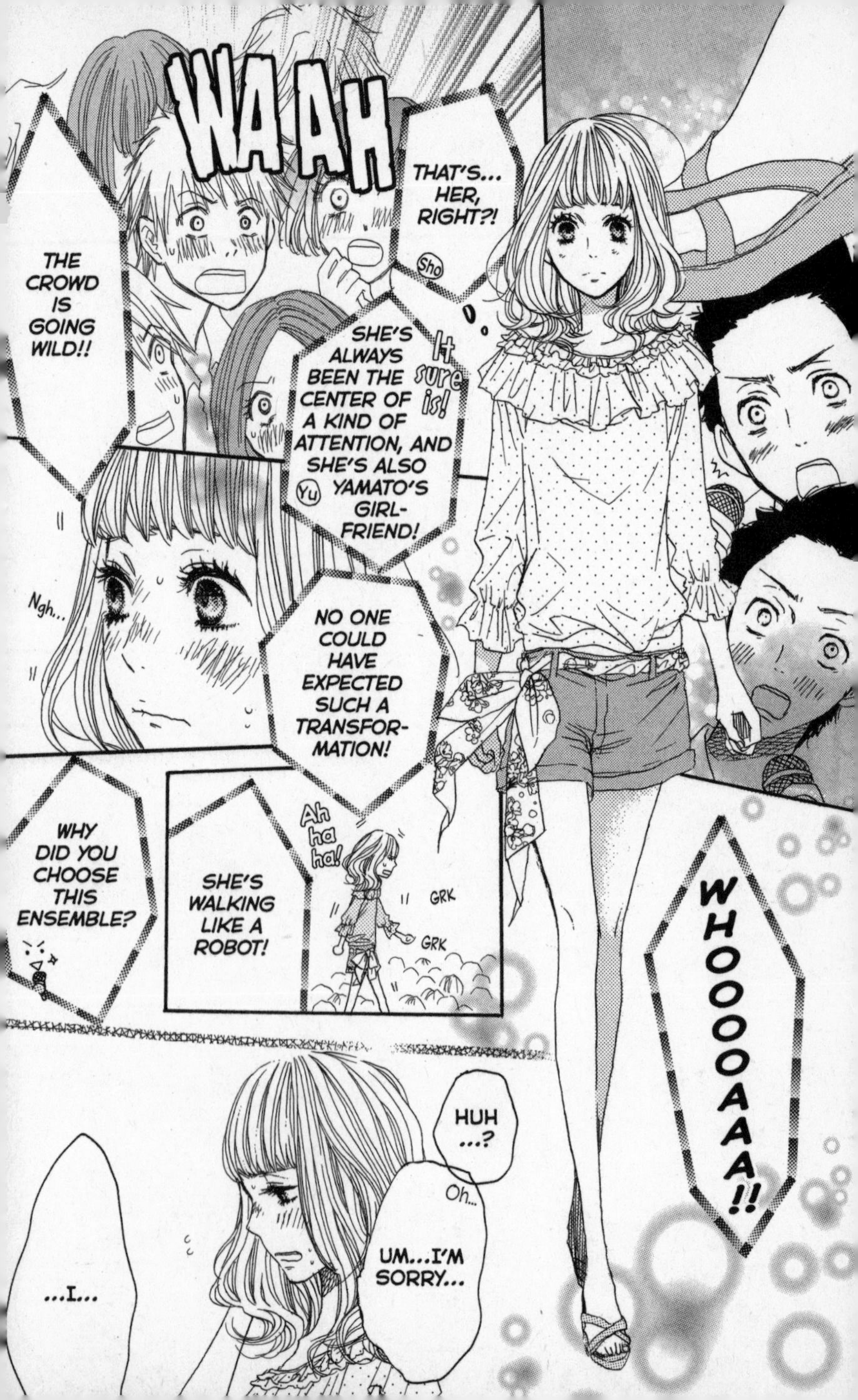
WHOOOOOAAA!!
WAAH
THAT'S... HER, RIGHT?!
Sho
SHE'S ALWAYS BEEN THE CENTER OF A KIND OF ATTENTION, AND SHE'S ALSO YAMATO'S GIRLFRIEND!
Yu
It sure is!
THE CROWD IS GOING WILD!!
NO ONE COULD HAVE EXPECTED SUCH A TRANSFORMATION!
Ngh...
SHE'S WALKING LIKE A ROBOT!
Ah ha ha!
GRK
GRK
WHY DID YOU CHOOSE THIS ENSEMBLE?
HUH ...?
Oh...
UM...I'M SORRY...
...I...

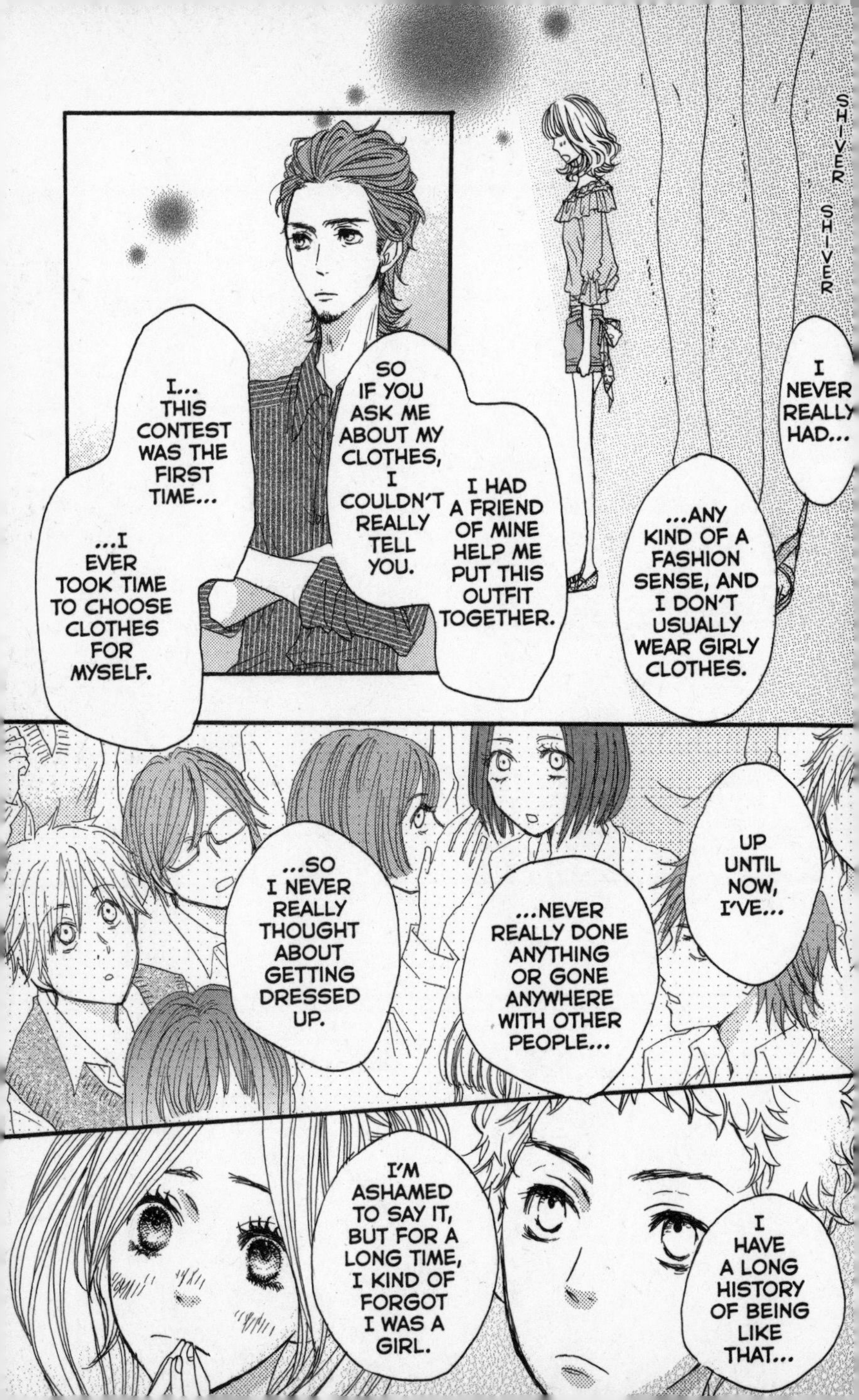
SHIVER SHIVER
I NEVER REALLY HAD...
...ANY KIND OF A FASHION SENSE, AND I DON'T USUALLY WEAR GIRLY CLOTHES.
I HAD A FRIEND OF MINE HELP ME PUT THIS OUTFIT TOGETHER.
SO IF YOU ASK ME ABOUT MY CLOTHES, I COULDN'T REALLY TELL YOU.
I... THIS CONTEST WAS THE FIRST TIME...
...I EVER TOOK TIME TO CHOOSE CLOTHES FOR MYSELF.
UP UNTIL NOW, I'VE...
...NEVER REALLY DONE ANYTHING OR GONE ANYWHERE WITH OTHER PEOPLE...
...SO I NEVER REALLY THOUGHT ABOUT GETTING DRESSED UP.
I HAVE A LONG HISTORY OF BEING LIKE THAT...
I'M ASHAMED TO SAY IT, BUT FOR A LONG TIME, I KIND OF FORGOT I WAS A GIRL.

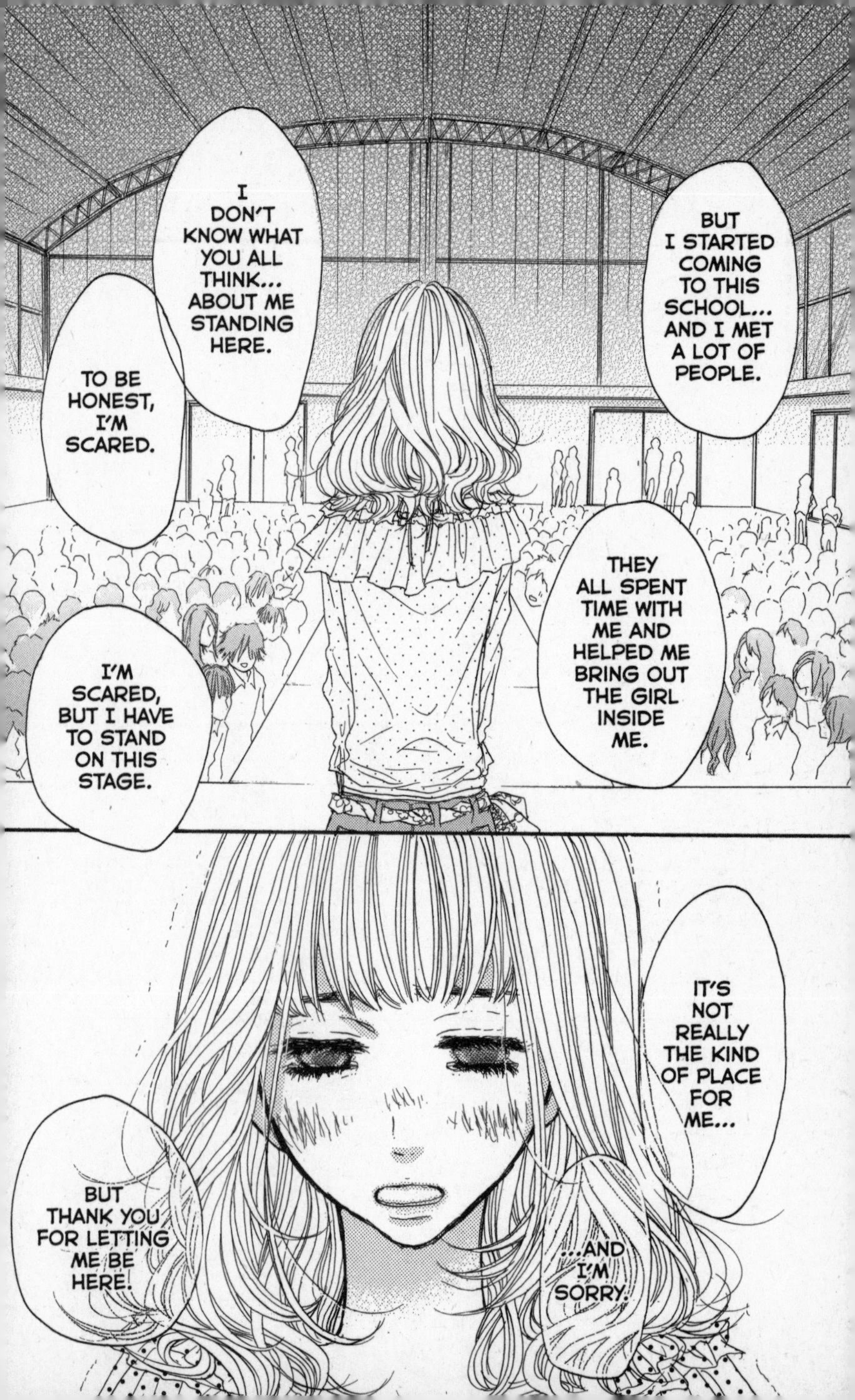
I DON'T KNOW WHAT YOU ALL THINK... ABOUT ME STANDING HERE.
TO BE HONEST, I'M SCARED.
I'M SCARED, BUT I HAVE TO STAND ON THIS STAGE.
BUT I STARTED COMING TO THIS SCHOOL... AND I MET A LOT OF PEOPLE.
THEY ALL SPENT TIME WITH ME AND HELPED ME BRING OUT THE GIRL INSIDE ME.
IT'S NOT REALLY THE KIND OF PLACE FOR ME...
BUT THANK YOU FOR LETTING ME BE HERE.
...AND I'M SORRY.

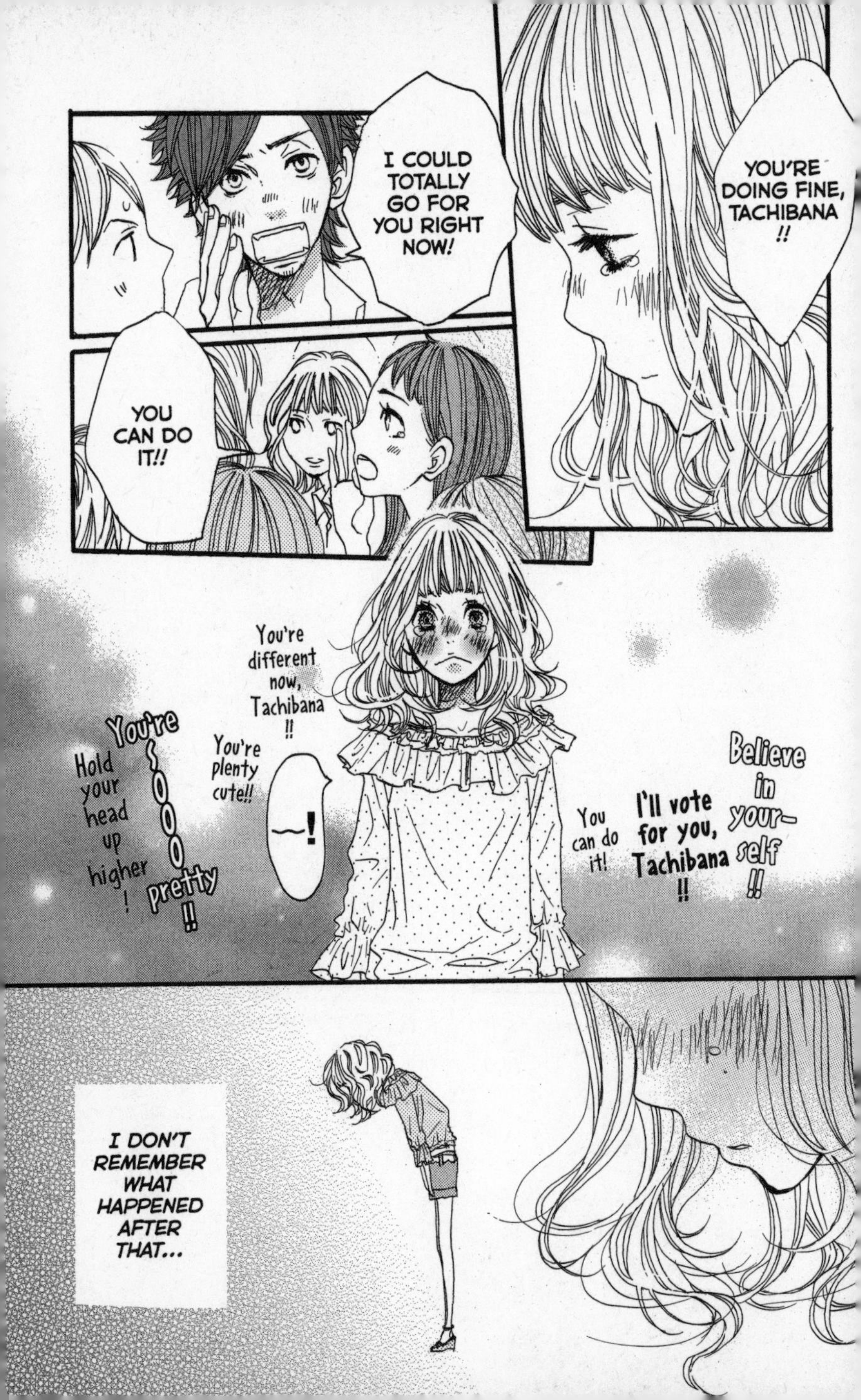
YOU'RE DOING FINE, TACHIBANA!!
I COULD TOTALLY GO FOR YOU RIGHT NOW!
YOU CAN DO IT!!
Believe in your-self!!
I'll vote for you, Tachibana!!
You can do it!
You're different now, Tachibana!!
~!
You're plenty cute!!
You're sooo pretty!!
Hold your head up higher!
I DON'T REMEMBER WHAT HAPPENED AFTER THAT...

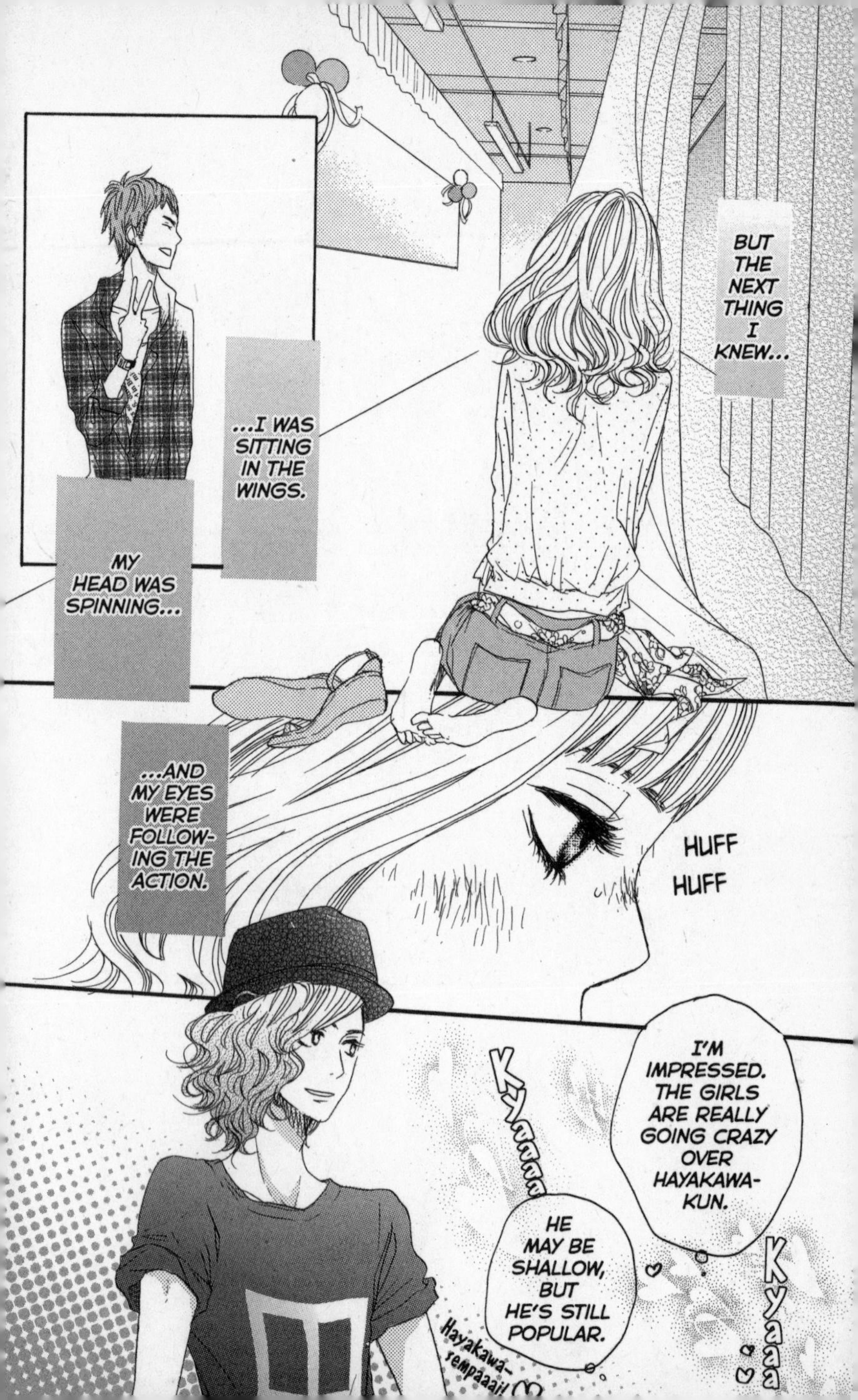
BUT THE NEXT THING I KNEW...
...I WAS SITTING IN THE WINGS.
MY HEAD WAS SPINNING...
...AND MY EYES WERE FOLLOWING THE ACTION.
HUFF
HUFF
Kyaaa
I'M IMPRESSED. THE GIRLS ARE REALLY GOING CRAZY OVER HAYAKAWA-KUN.
HE MAY BE SHALLOW, BUT HE'S STILL POPULAR.
Kyaaaaa
Hayakawa-sempaaai!

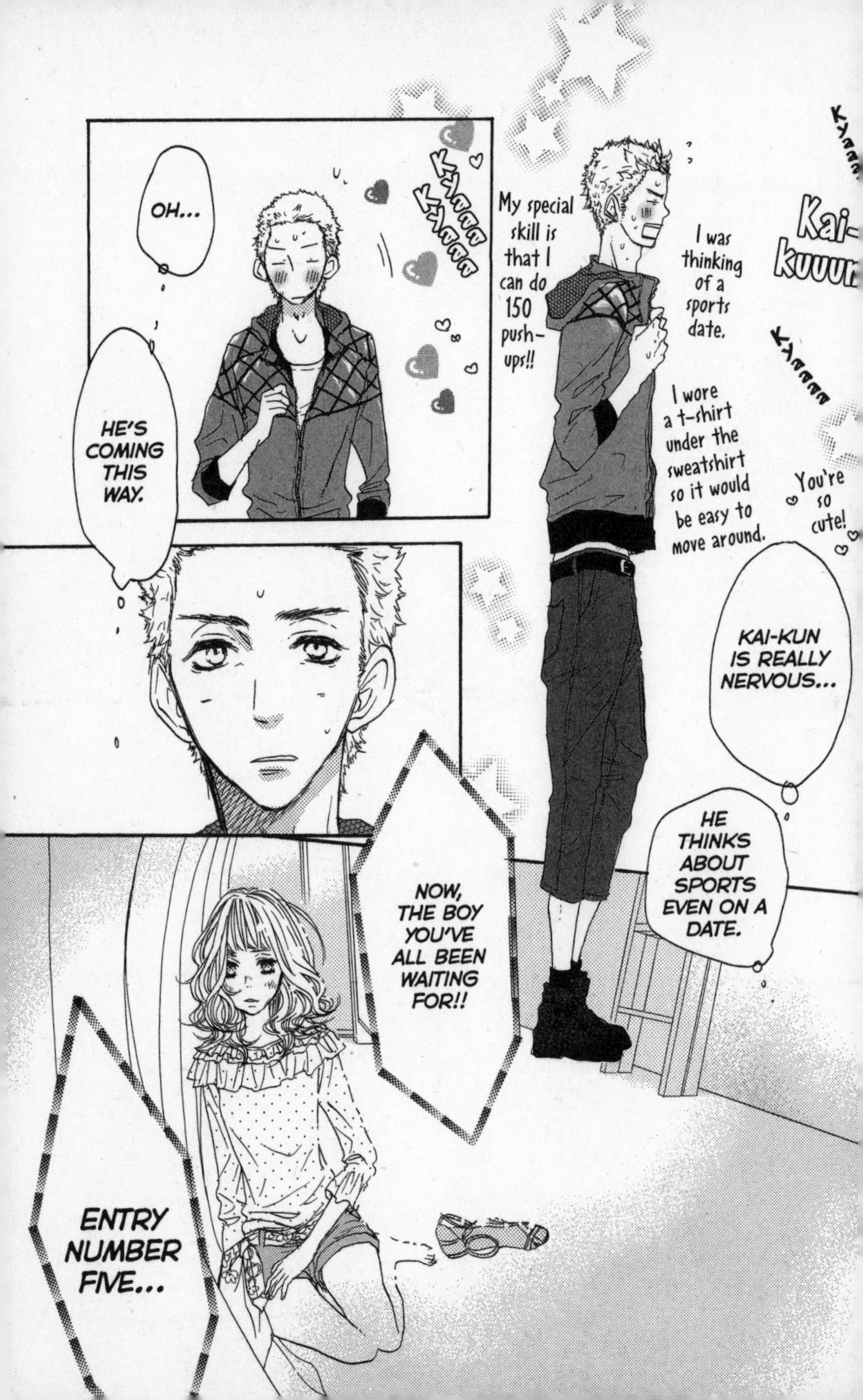
Kai-kuuun
I was thinking of a sports date.
My special skill is that I can do 150 push-ups!!
I wore a t-shirt under the sweatshirt so it would be easy to move around.
You're so cute!
KAI-KUN IS REALLY NERVOUS...
HE THINKS ABOUT SPORTS EVEN ON A DATE.
OH...
HE'S COMING THIS WAY.
NOW, THE BOY YOU'VE ALL BEEN WAITING FOR!!
ENTRY NUMBER FIVE...

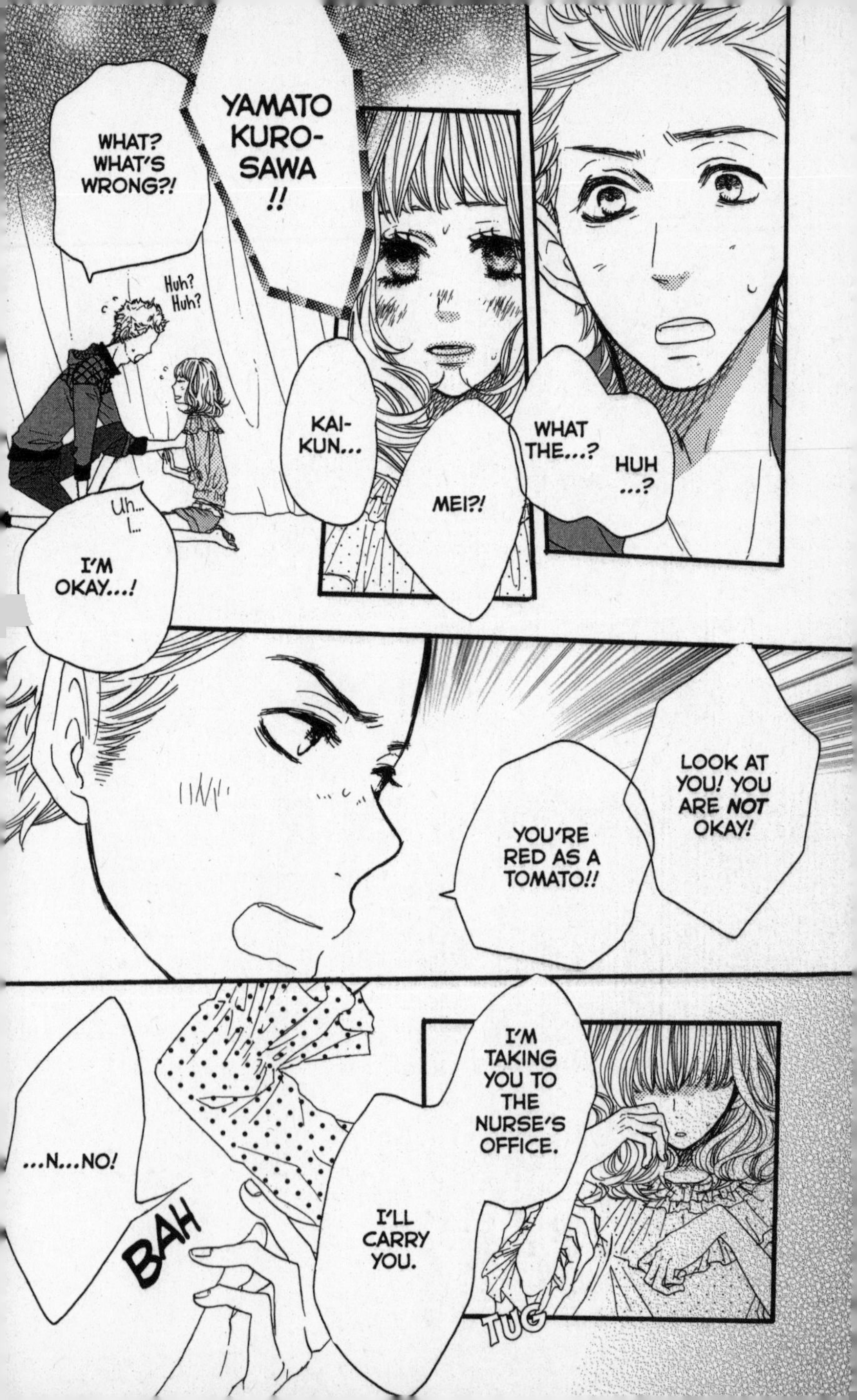
HUH ...?
WHAT THE...?
MEI?!
YAMATO KUROSAWA!!
KAI-KUN...
WHAT? WHAT'S WRONG?!
Huh? Huh?
Uh... I...
I'M OKAY...!
LOOK AT YOU! YOU ARE NOT OKAY!
YOU'RE RED AS A TOMATO!!
I'M TAKING YOU TO THE NURSE'S OFFICE.
TUG
I'LL CARRY YOU.
BAH
...N...NO!

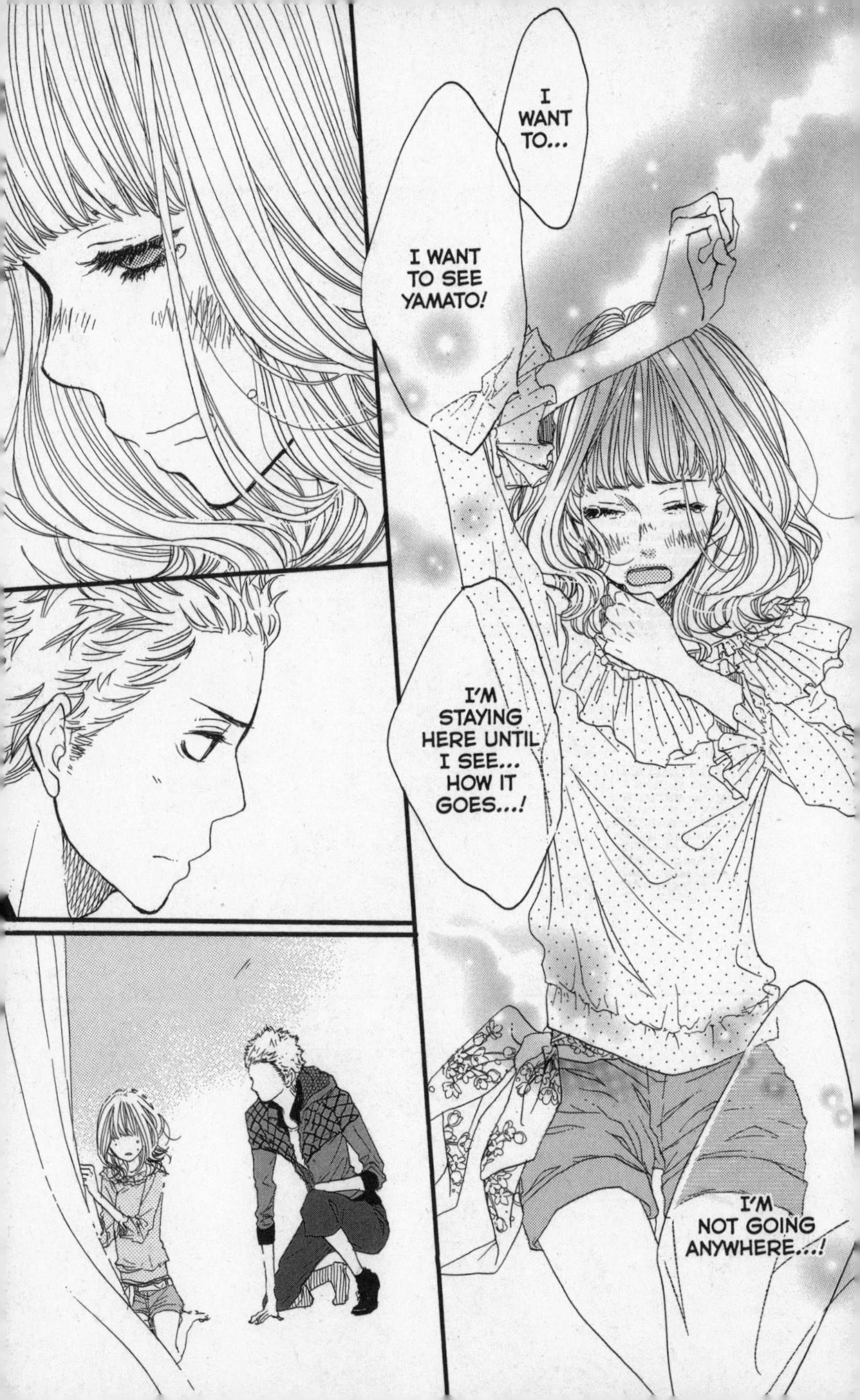
I WANT TO...
I WANT TO SEE YAMATO!
I'M STAYING HERE UNTIL I SEE... HOW IT GOES...!
I'M NOT GOING ANYWHERE...!

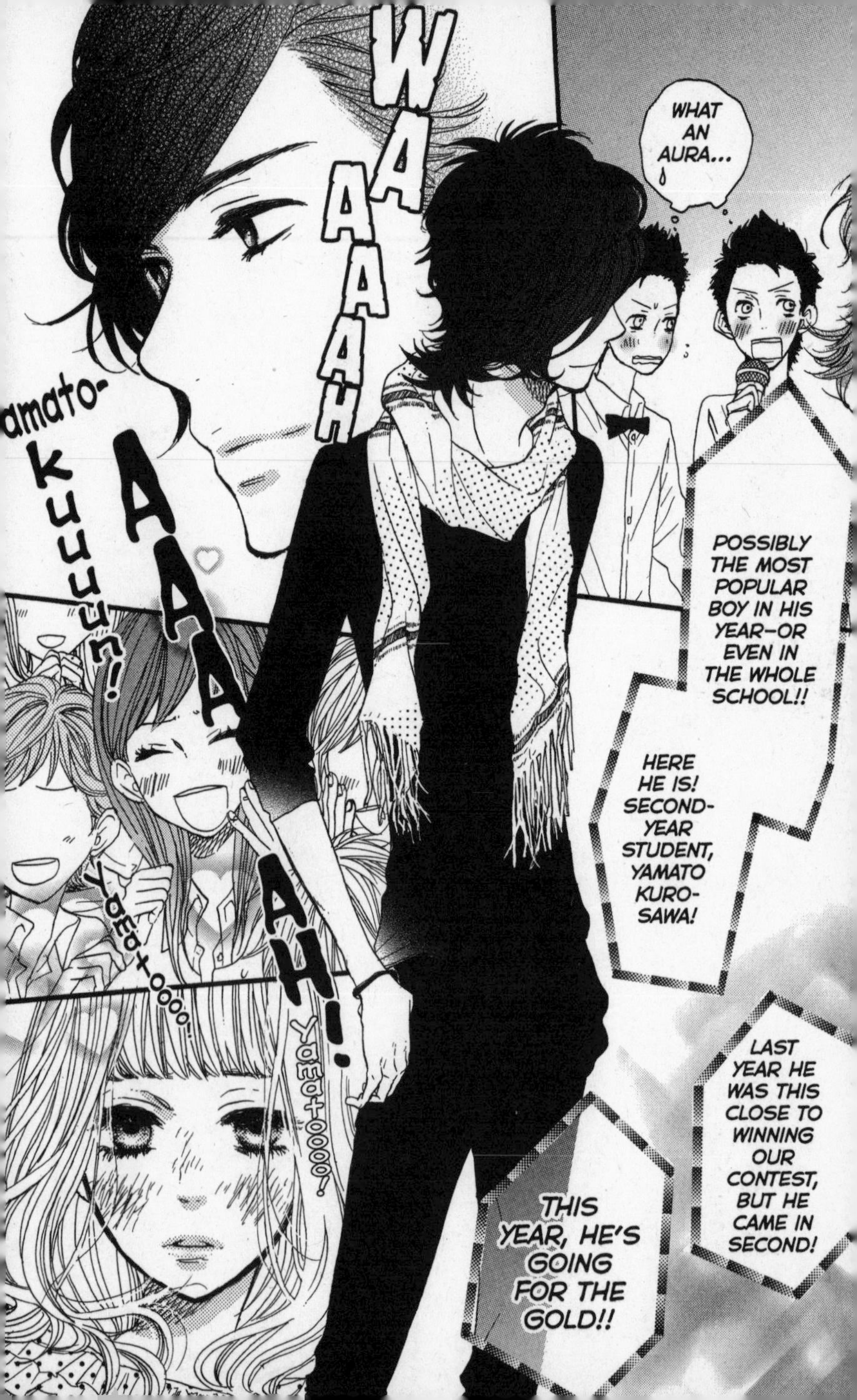
WHAT AN AURA...
POSSIBLY THE MOST POPULAR BOY IN HIS YEAR—OR EVEN IN THE WHOLE SCHOOL!!
HERE HE IS! SECOND-YEAR STUDENT, YAMATO KURO-SAWA!
LAST YEAR HE WAS THIS CLOSE TO WINNING OUR CONTEST, BUT HE CAME IN SECOND!
THIS YEAR, HE'S GOING FOR THE GOLD!!
WAAAAAH
AAAAAH!
amato-kuuuun!
Yamato-oooo!!
Yamatoooo!

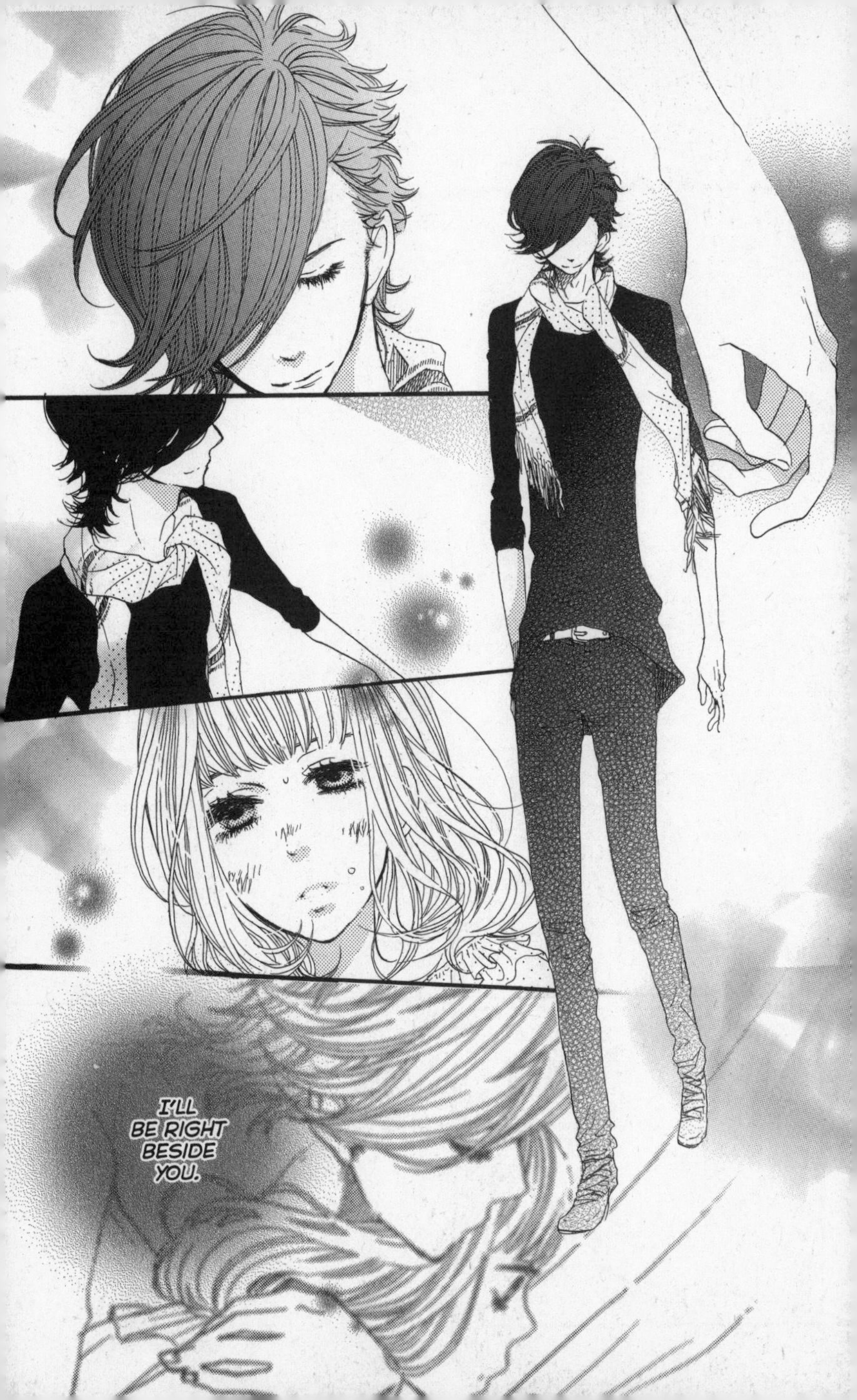
I'LL BE RIGHT BESIDE YOU.

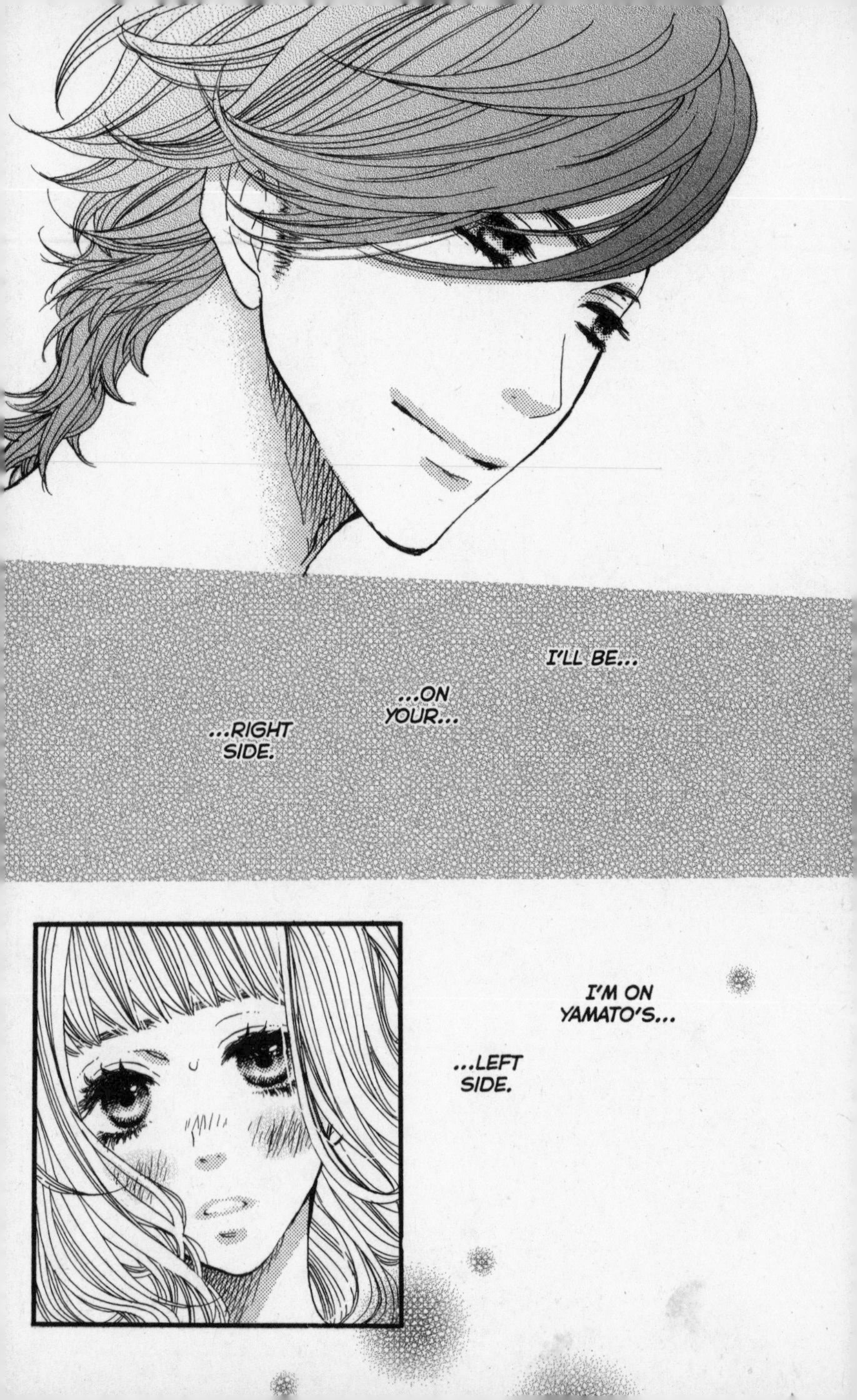
I'LL BE...
...ON YOUR...
...RIGHT SIDE.
I'M ON YAMATO'S...
...LEFT SIDE.

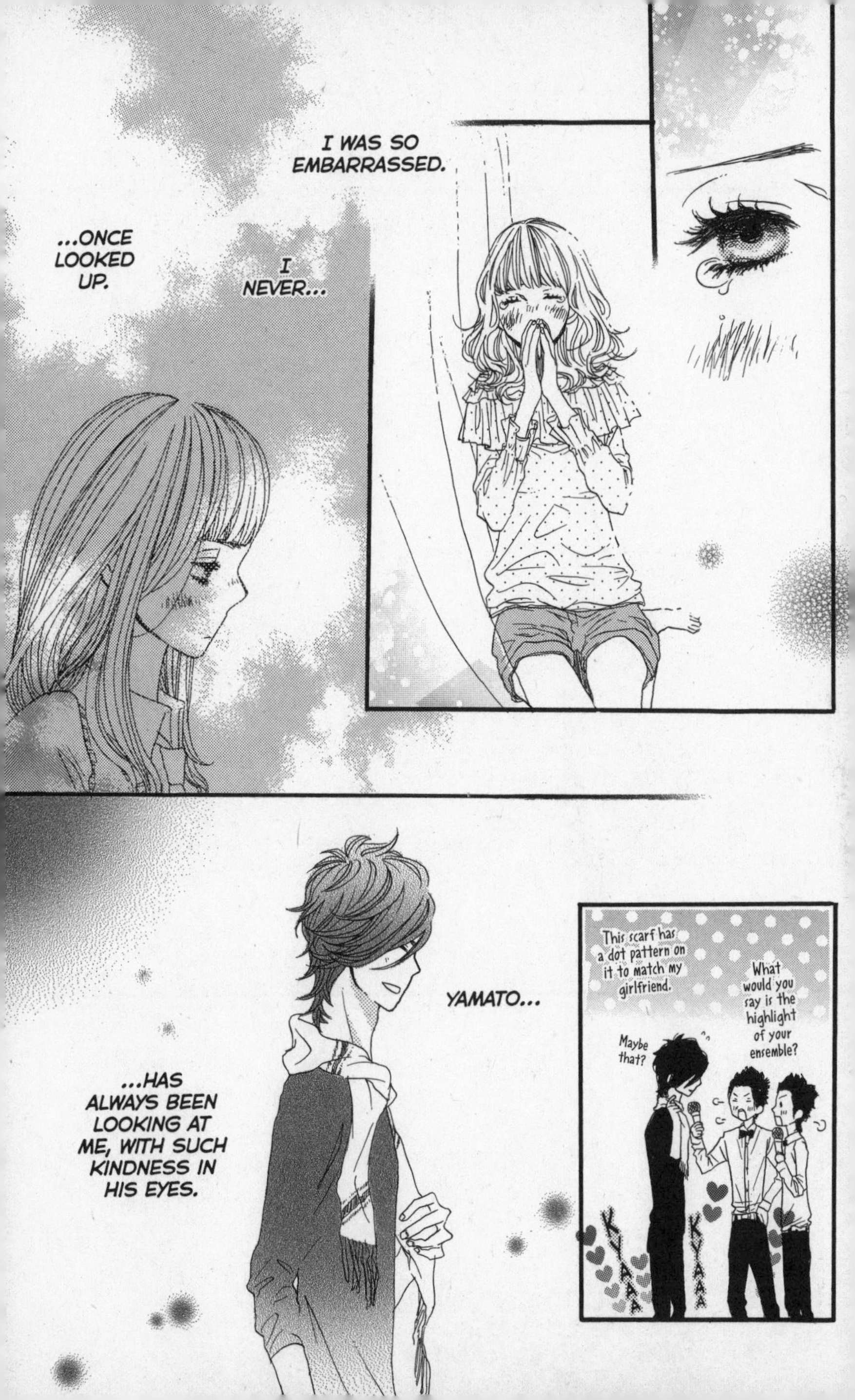
I WAS SO EMBARRASSED.
I NEVER...
...ONCE LOOKED UP.
What would you say is the highlight of your ensemble?
This scarf has a dot pattern on it to match my girlfriend.
Maybe that?
KYAAA
KYAAA
YAMATO...
...HAS ALWAYS BEEN LOOKING AT ME, WITH SUCH KINDNESS IN HIS EYES.

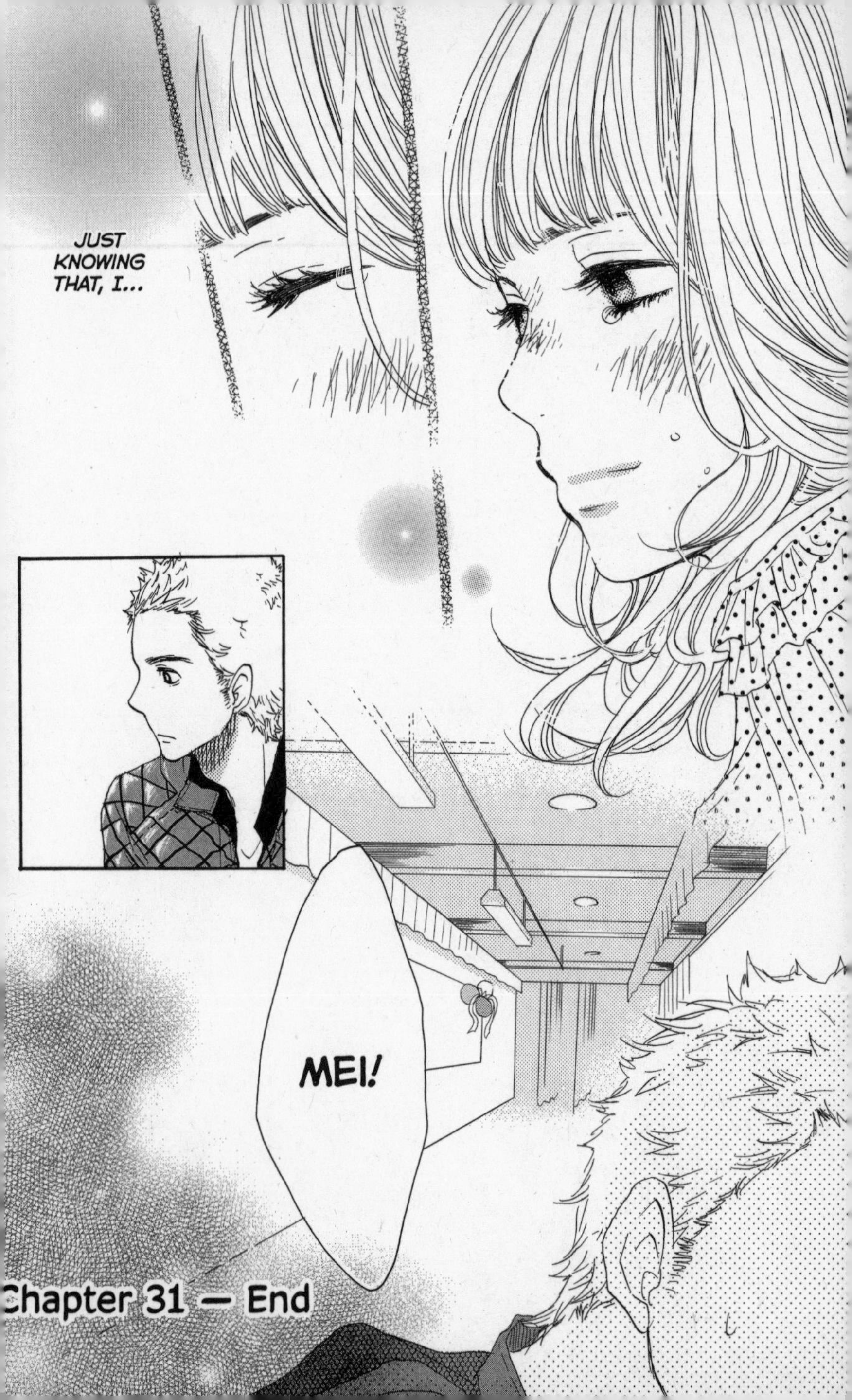
JUST KNOWING THAT, I...
MEI!

Chapter 31 — End

Say "I love you".

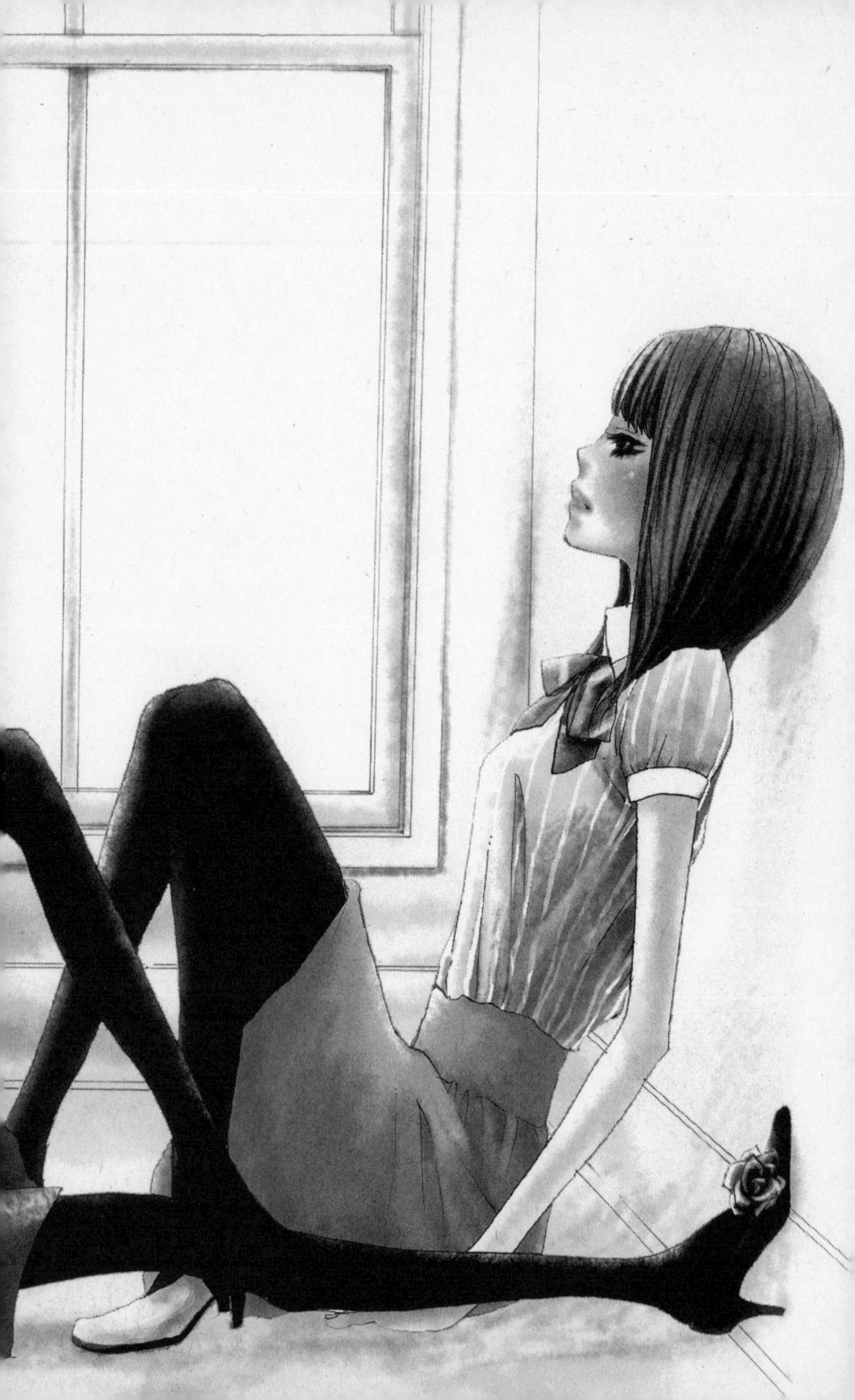

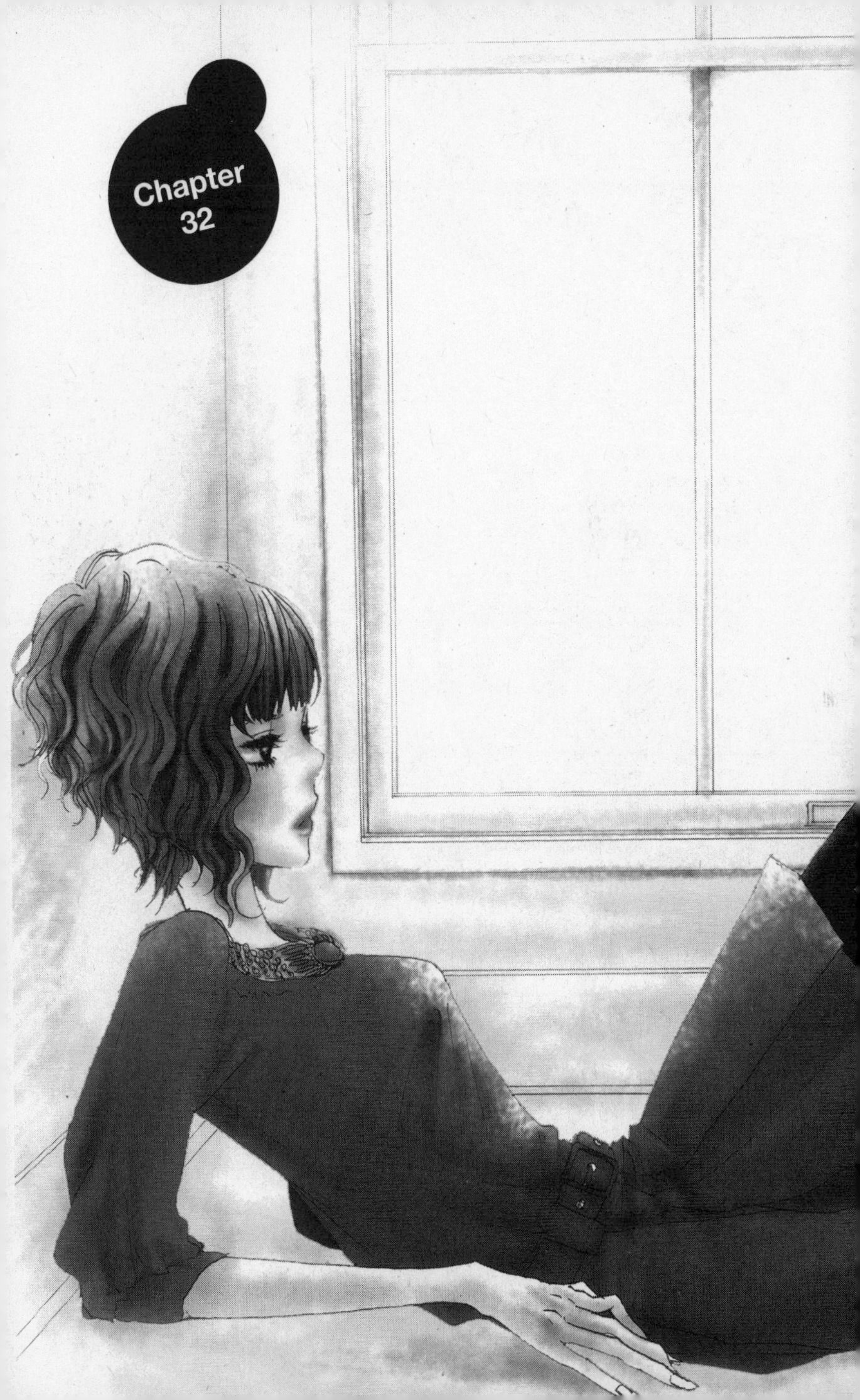
Chapter
32

In fact...

There was one more costume idea for the ***contest***...

Personally, I love the matching couple look.

But the theme of the contest was "first date"...

So I thought about them walking around town like that... and it was like, "Ooooh, yikes," so...

denied!!

Mei would wear tartan overalls, and Yamato would wear a matching tie.☆

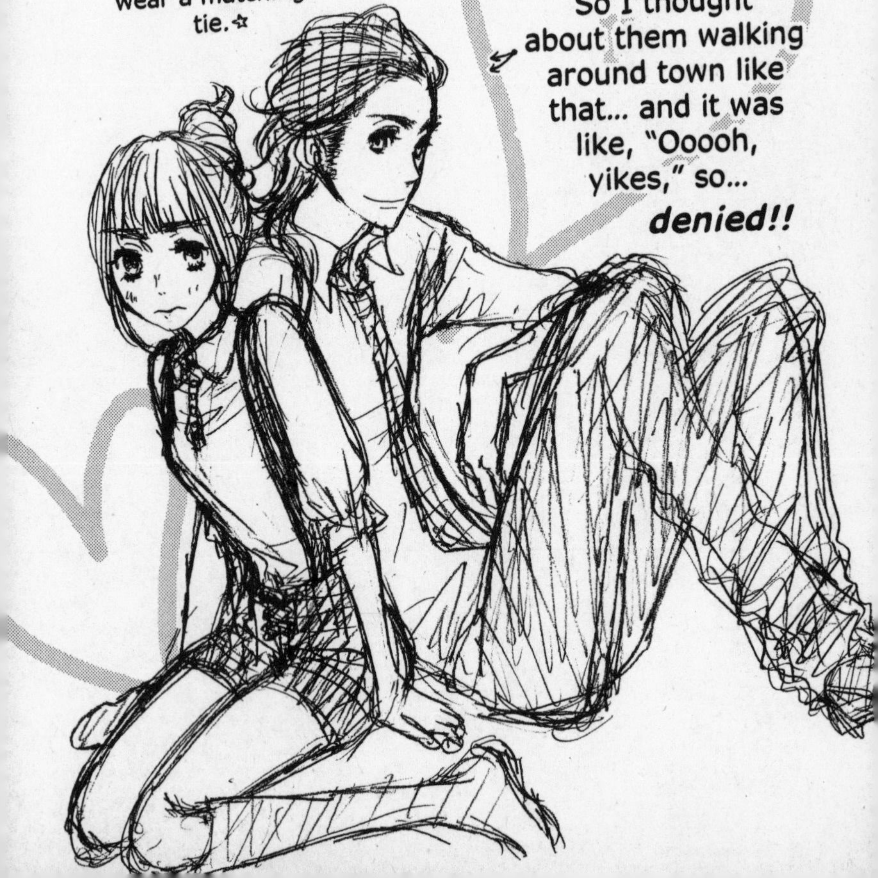

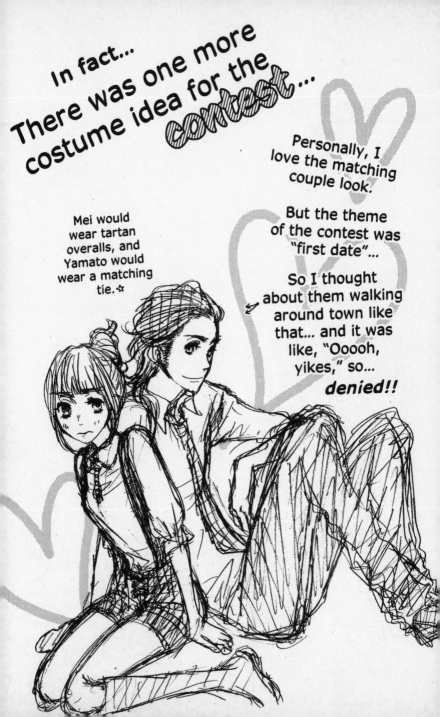

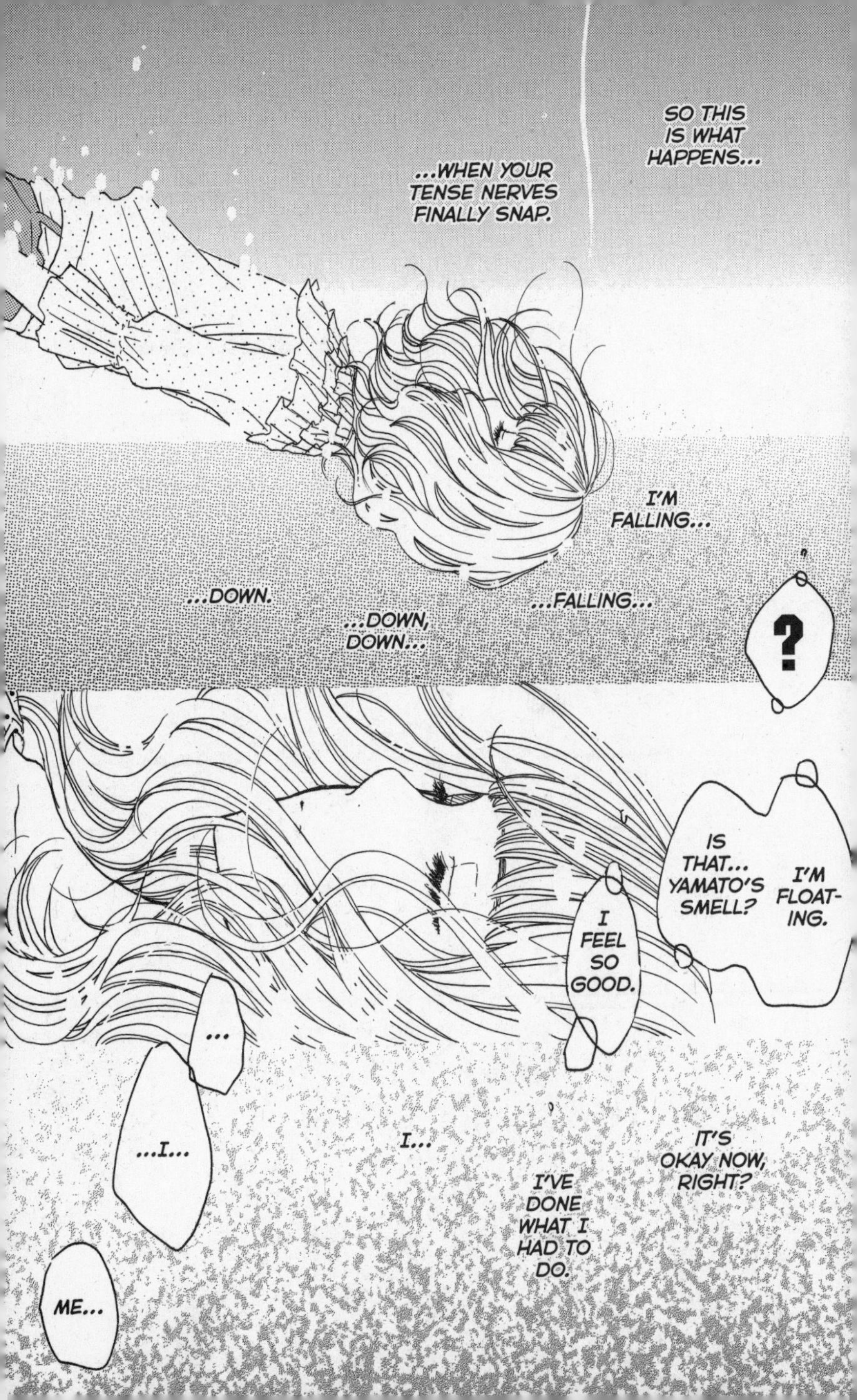
SO THIS IS WHAT HAPPENS...
...WHEN YOUR TENSE NERVES FINALLY SNAP.
I'M FALLING...
?
...FALLING...
...DOWN, DOWN...
...DOWN.
I'M FLOAT-ING.
IS THAT... YAMATO'S SMELL?
I FEEL SO GOOD.
...
IT'S OKAY NOW, RIGHT?
I'VE DONE WHAT I HAD TO DO.
I...
...I...
ME...

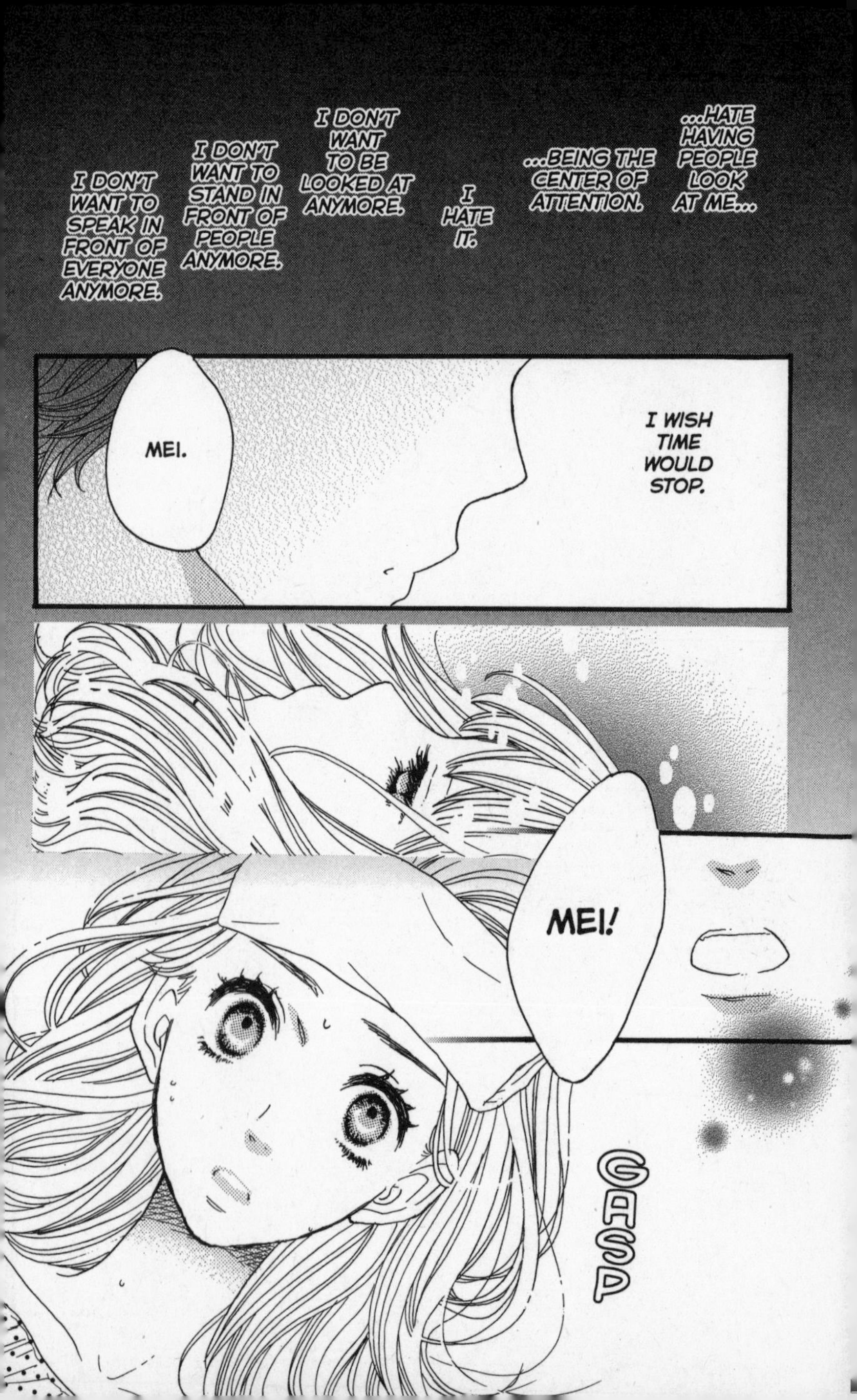
...HATE HAVING PEOPLE LOOK AT ME...
...BEING THE CENTER OF ATTENTION.
I HATE IT.
I DON'T WANT TO BE LOOKED AT ANYMORE.
I DON'T WANT TO STAND IN FRONT OF PEOPLE ANYMORE.
I DON'T WANT TO SPEAK IN FRONT OF EVERYONE ANYMORE.
I WISH TIME WOULD STOP.
MEI.
MEI!
GASP

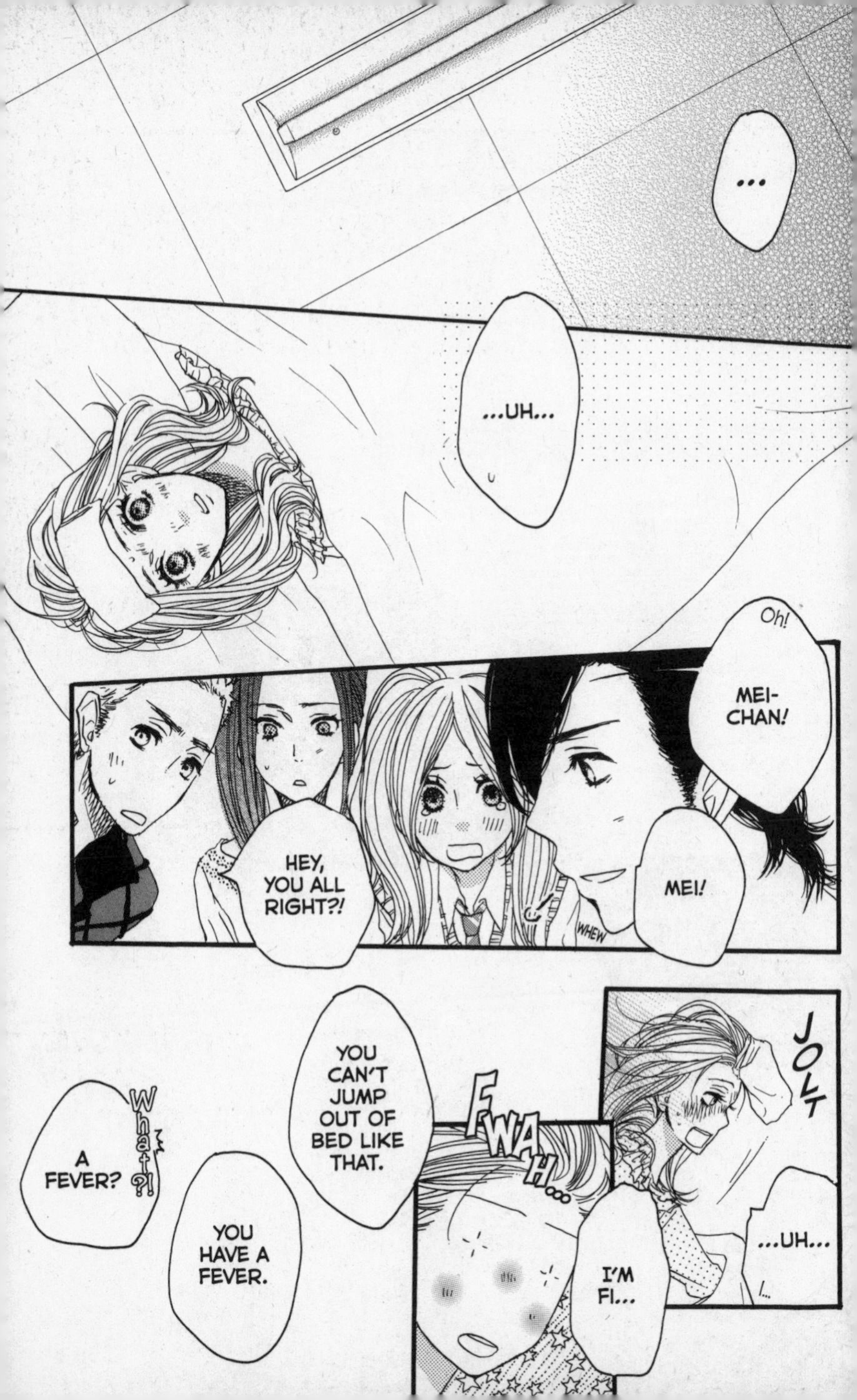
...
...UH...
Oh! MEI-CHAN!
MEI!
WHEW
HEY, YOU ALL RIGHT?!
JOLT
...UH... I...
FWAH...
I'M FI...
YOU CAN'T JUMP OUT OF BED LIKE THAT.
YOU HAVE A FEVER.
A FEVER?
What?!

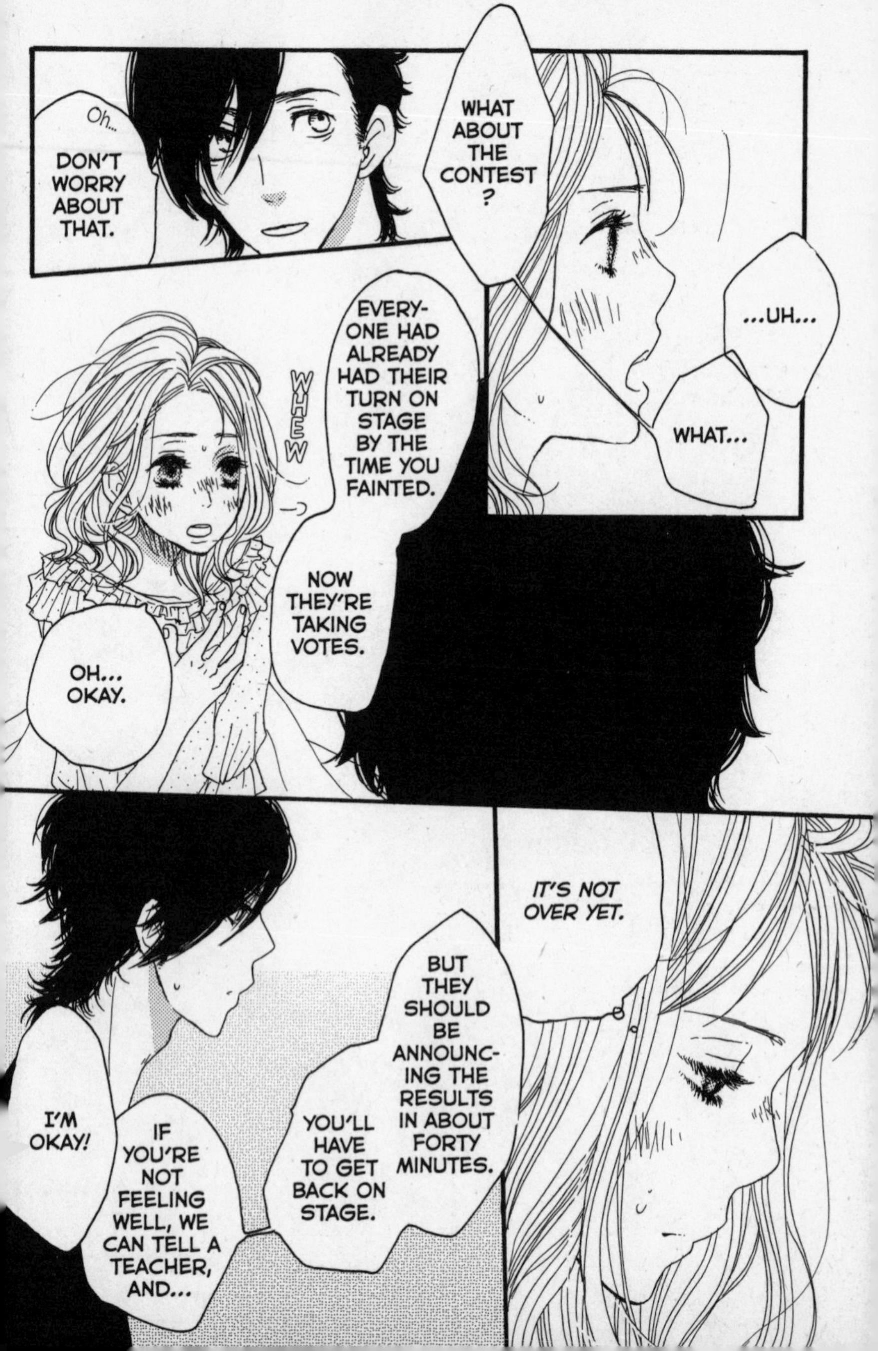

...UH...
WHAT...
WHAT ABOUT THE CONTEST?
Oh...
DON'T WORRY ABOUT THAT.
EVERYONE HAD ALREADY HAD THEIR TURN ON STAGE BY THE TIME YOU FAINTED.
WHEW
NOW THEY'RE TAKING VOTES.
OH... OKAY.
IT'S NOT OVER YET.
BUT THEY SHOULD BE ANNOUNCING THE RESULTS IN ABOUT FORTY MINUTES.
YOU'LL HAVE TO GET BACK ON STAGE.
IF YOU'RE NOT FEELING WELL, WE CAN TELL A TEACHER, AND...
I'M OKAY!

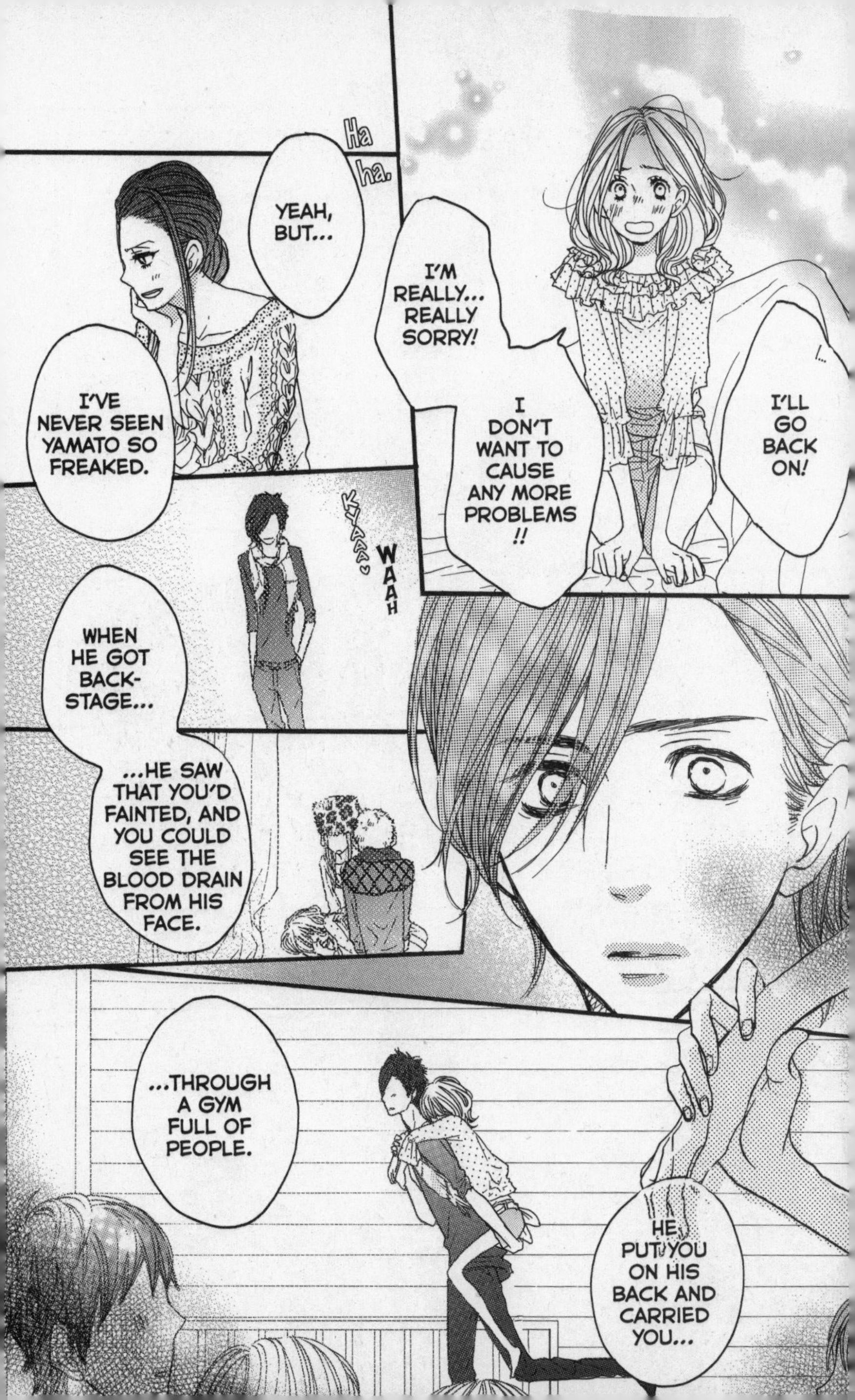
I'M REALLY... REALLY SORRY!
I DON'T WANT TO CAUSE ANY MORE PROBLEMS!!
I'LL GO BACK ON!
Ha ha.
YEAH, BUT...
I'VE NEVER SEEN YAMATO SO FREAKED.
KYAAA♡
WAAH
WHEN HE GOT BACK-STAGE...
...HE SAW THAT YOU'D FAINTED, AND YOU COULD SEE THE BLOOD DRAIN FROM HIS FACE.
HE PUT YOU ON HIS BACK AND CARRIED YOU...
...THROUGH A GYM FULL OF PEOPLE.

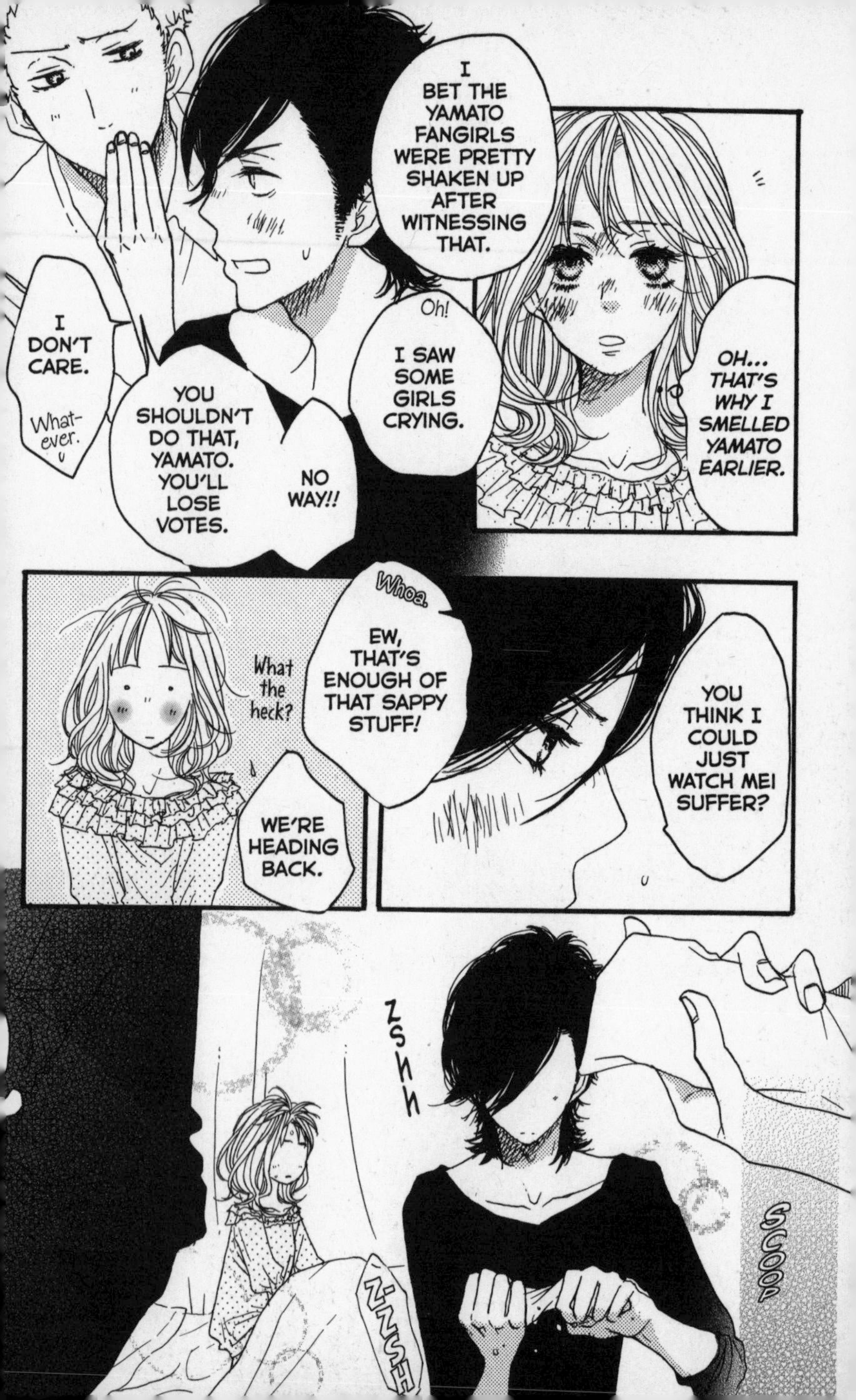
I BET THE YAMATO FANGIRLS WERE PRETTY SHAKEN UP AFTER WITNESSING THAT.
OH... THAT'S WHY I SMELLED YAMATO EARLIER.
Oh!
I SAW SOME GIRLS CRYING.
NO WAY!!
YOU SHOULDN'T DO THAT, YAMATO. YOU'LL LOSE VOTES.
I DON'T CARE.
What-ever.
YOU THINK I COULD JUST WATCH MEI SUFFER?
Whoa.
EW, THAT'S ENOUGH OF THAT SAPPY STUFF!
What the heck?
WE'RE HEADING BACK.
SCOOP
ZSHH
SHNN

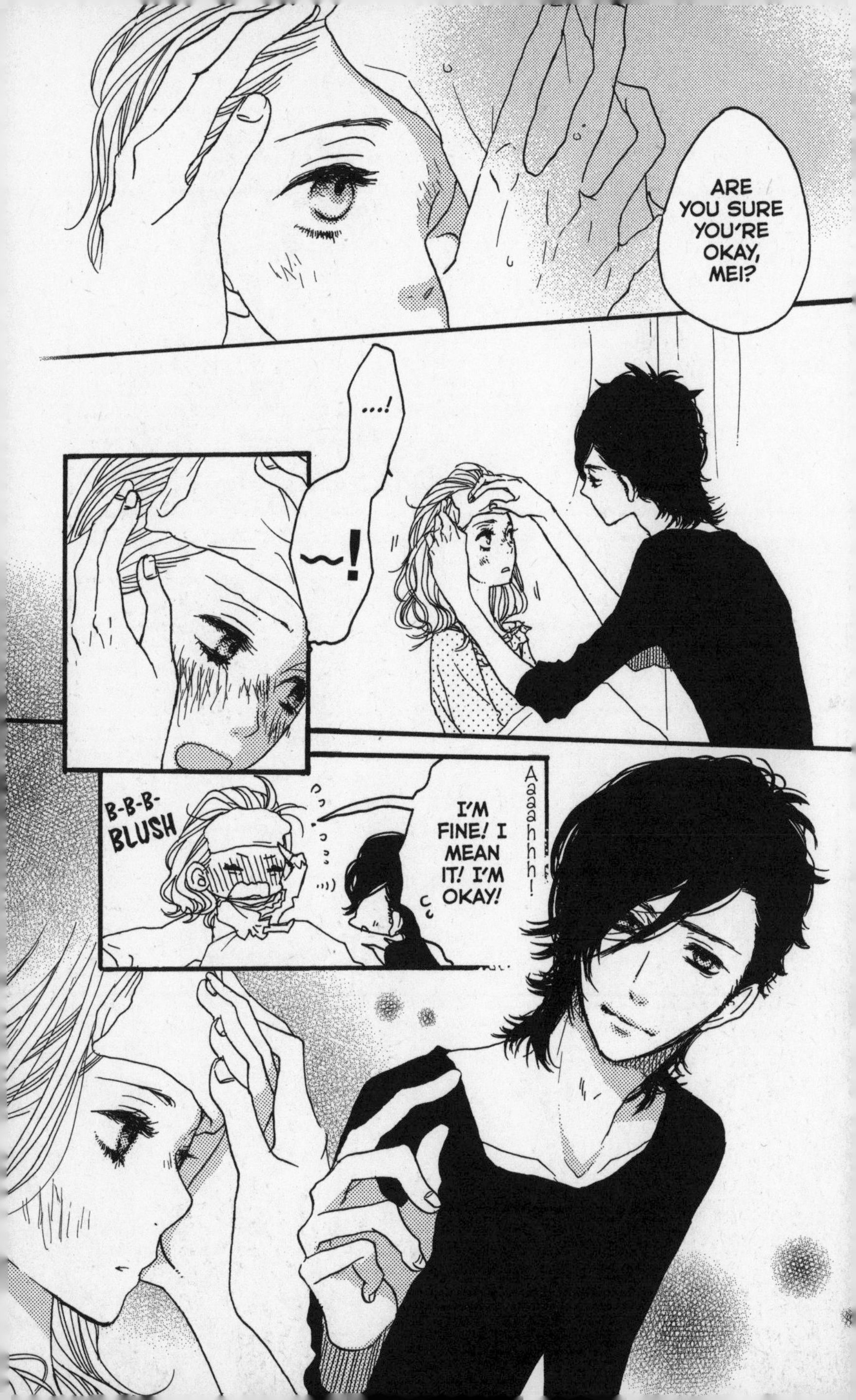
ARE YOU SURE YOU'RE OKAY, MEI?
...!
~!
Aaaahhh!
I'M FINE! I MEAN IT! I'M OKAY!
B-B-B-BLUSH

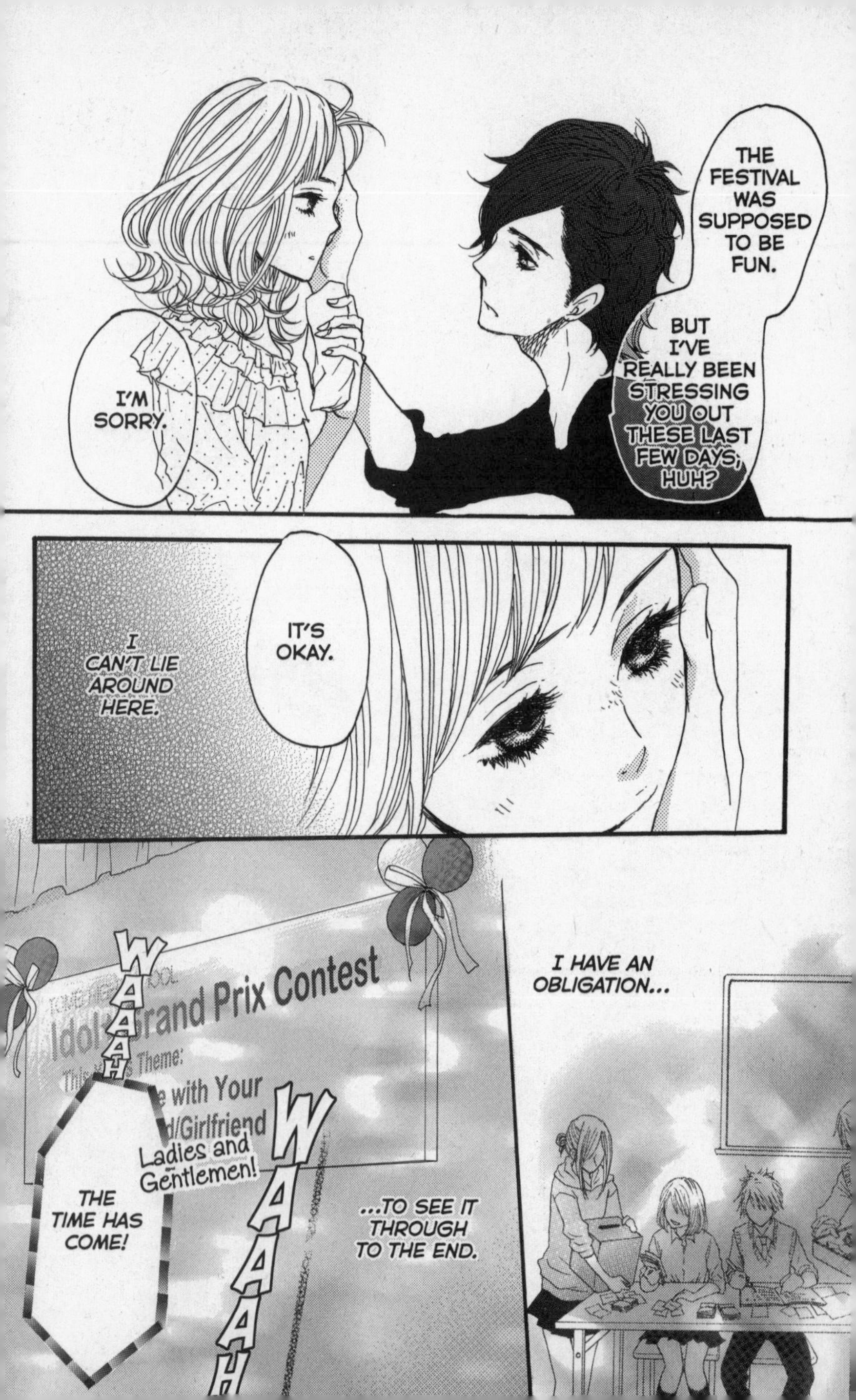
THE FESTIVAL WAS SUPPOSED TO BE FUN.
BUT I'VE REALLY BEEN STRESSING YOU OUT THESE LAST FEW DAYS, HUH?
I'M SORRY.
IT'S OKAY.
I CAN'T LIE AROUND HERE.
I HAVE AN OBLIGATION...
...TO SEE IT THROUGH TO THE END.
Grand Prix Contest
Ladies and Gentlemen!
THE TIME HAS COME!
WAAAAH
WAAAAAH

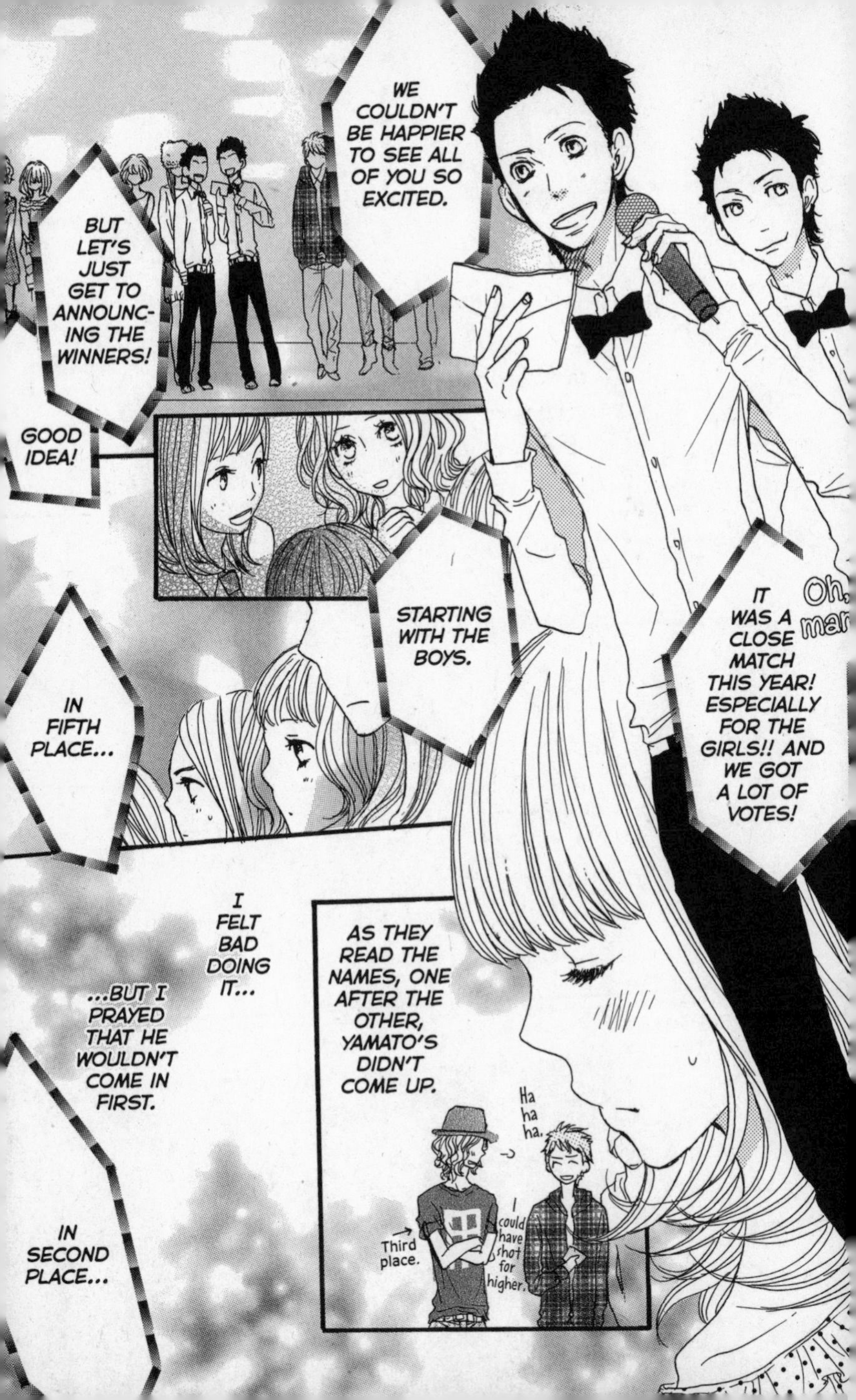
WE COULDN'T BE HAPPIER TO SEE ALL OF YOU SO EXCITED.
BUT LET'S JUST GET TO ANNOUNC-ING THE WINNERS!
GOOD IDEA!
IT WAS A CLOSE MATCH THIS YEAR! ESPECIALLY FOR THE GIRLS!! AND WE GOT A LOT OF VOTES!
STARTING WITH THE BOYS.
IN FIFTH PLACE...
AS THEY READ THE NAMES, ONE AFTER THE OTHER, YAMATO'S DIDN'T COME UP.
Ha ha ha.
I could have shot for higher.
Third place.
I FELT BAD DOING IT...
...BUT I PRAYED THAT HE WOULDN'T COME IN FIRST.
IN SECOND PLACE...

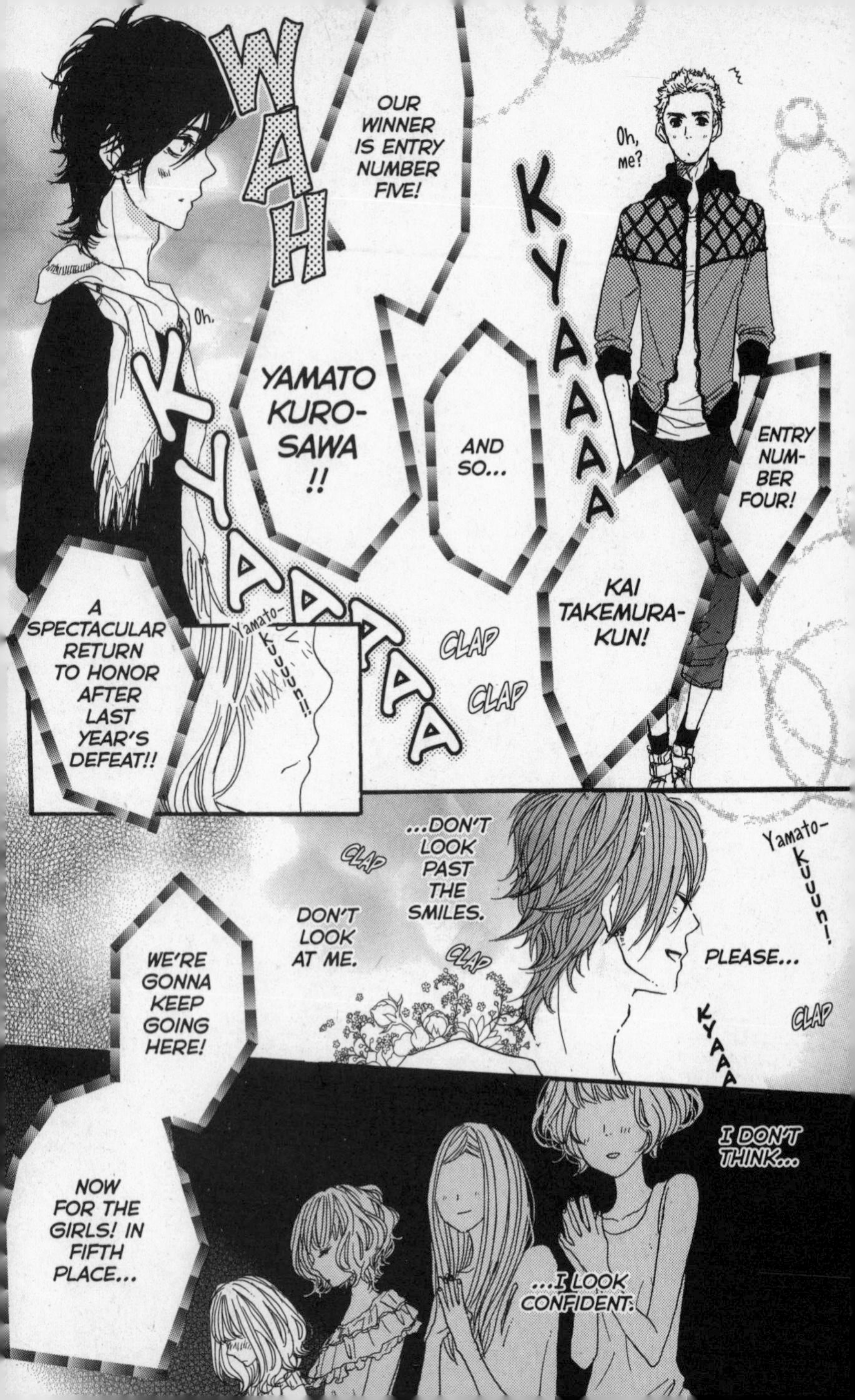
ENTRY NUMBER FOUR!
KAI TAKEMURA-KUN!
KYAAAA
Oh, me?
AND SO...
OUR WINNER IS ENTRY NUMBER FIVE!
YAMATO KURO-SAWA!!
WAH
KYAAAAAA
Oh.
CLAP
CLAP
Yamato-KUUUUN!!
A SPECTACULAR RETURN TO HONOR AFTER LAST YEAR'S DEFEAT!!
Yamato-KUUUN!
PLEASE...
CLAP
KYAAA
...DON'T LOOK PAST THE SMILES.
DON'T LOOK AT ME.
CLAP
CLAP
WE'RE GONNA KEEP GOING HERE!
I DON'T THINK...
...I LOOK CONFIDENT.
NOW FOR THE GIRLS! IN FIFTH PLACE...

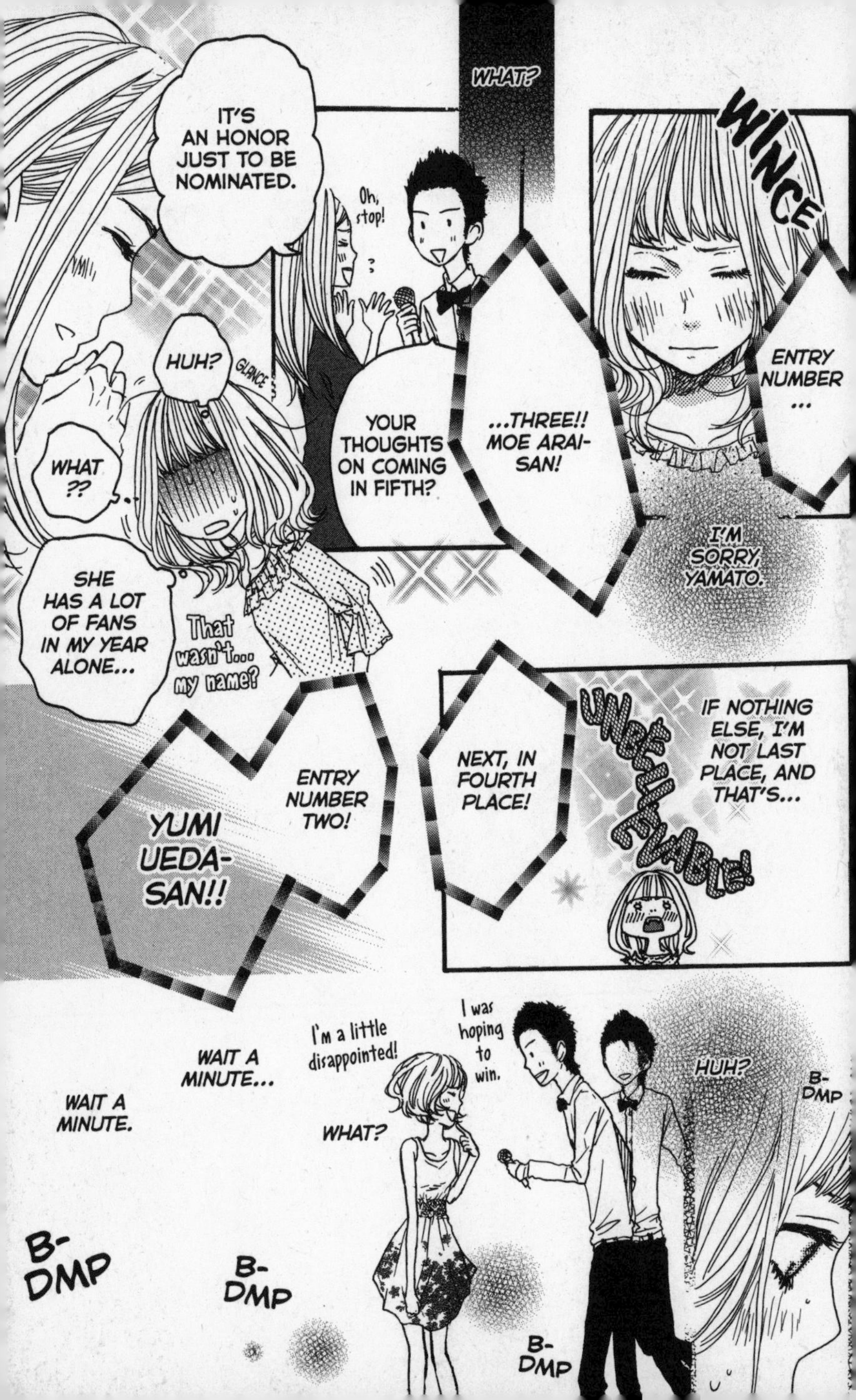
WINCE
ENTRY NUMBER ...
...THREE!! MOE ARAI-SAN!
I'M SORRY, YAMATO.
WHAT?
YOUR THOUGHTS ON COMING IN FIFTH?
Oh, stop!
?
IT'S AN HONOR JUST TO BE NOMINATED.
HUH?
GLANCE
WHAT ??
SHE HAS A LOT OF FANS IN MY YEAR ALONE...
That wasn't... my name?
IF NOTHING ELSE, I'M NOT LAST PLACE, AND THAT'S...
UNBELIEVABLE!
NEXT, IN FOURTH PLACE!
ENTRY NUMBER TWO!
YUMI UEDA-SAN!!
B-DMP
HUH?
I was hoping to win.
I'm a little disappointed!
WHAT?
B-DMP
WAIT A MINUTE...
B-DMP
WAIT A MINUTE.
B-DMP

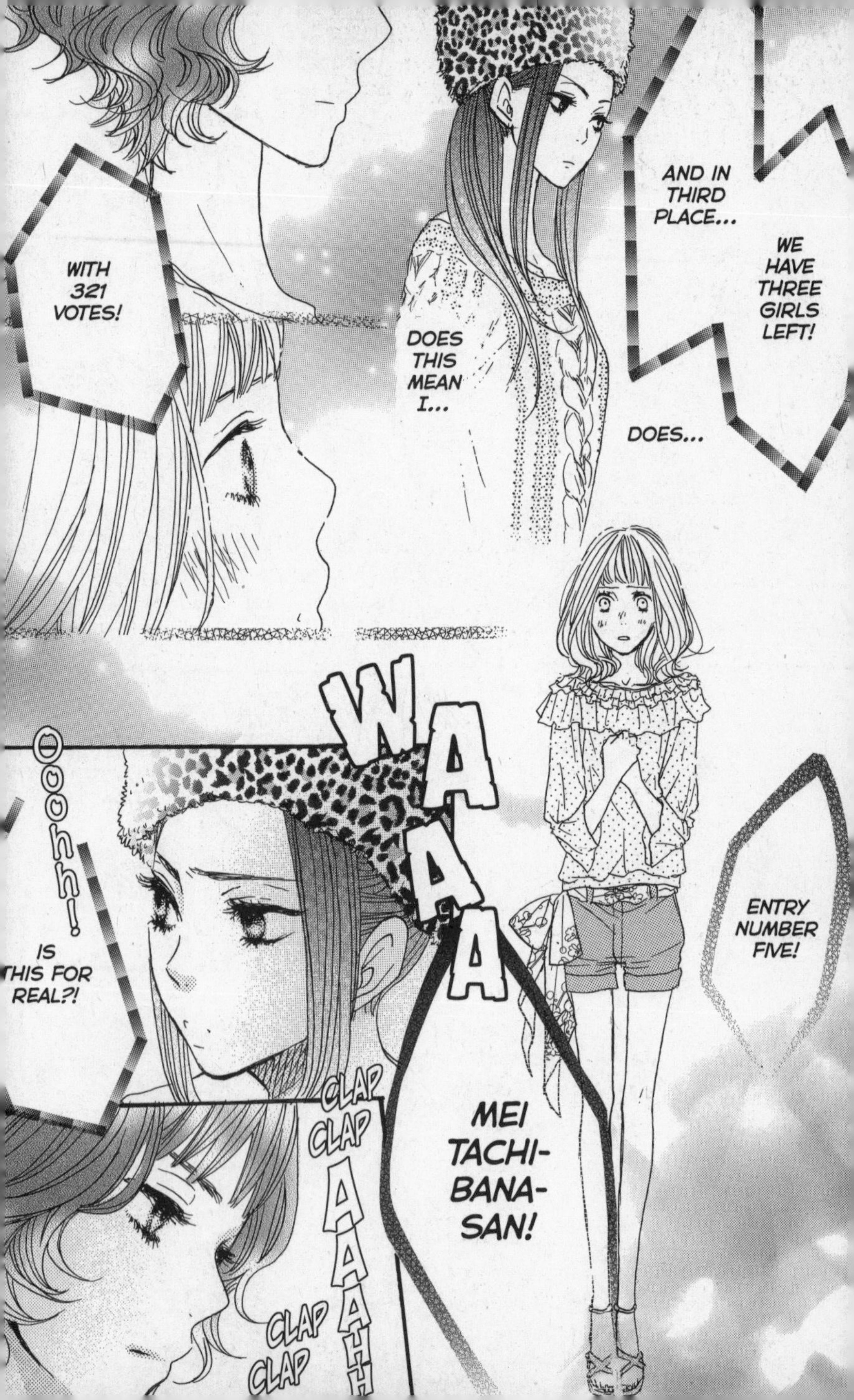
WE HAVE THREE GIRLS LEFT!
AND IN THIRD PLACE...
DOES...
DOES THIS MEAN I...
WITH 321 VOTES!
ENTRY NUMBER FIVE!
MEI TACHIBANA-SAN!
WAAA
IS THIS FOR REAL?!
Ooohh!
CLAP CLAP
AAAAAHH
CLAP CLAP

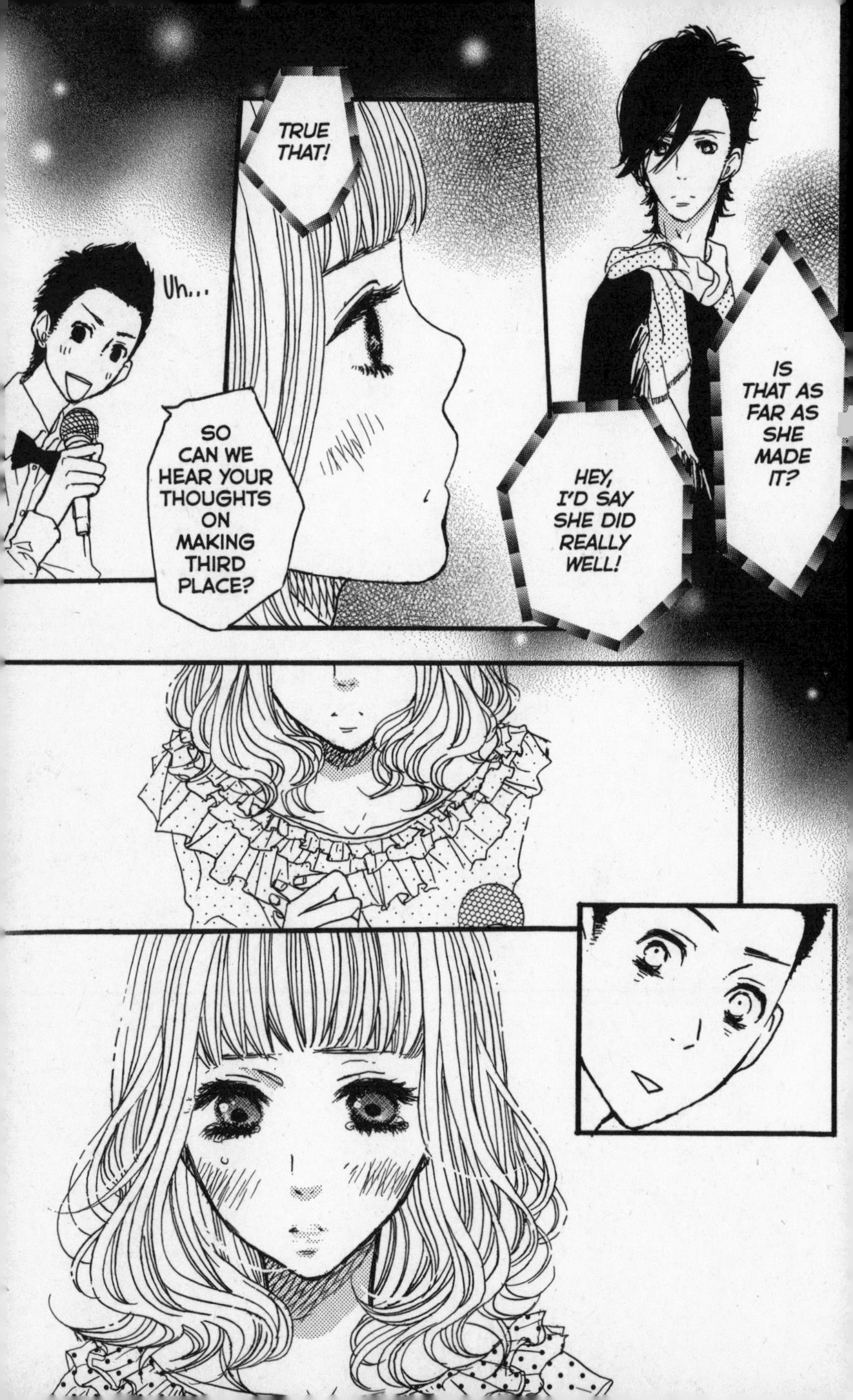
IS THAT AS FAR AS SHE MADE IT?
HEY, I'D SAY SHE DID REALLY WELL!
TRUE THAT!
Uh...
SO CAN WE HEAR YOUR THOUGHTS ON MAKING THIRD PLACE?

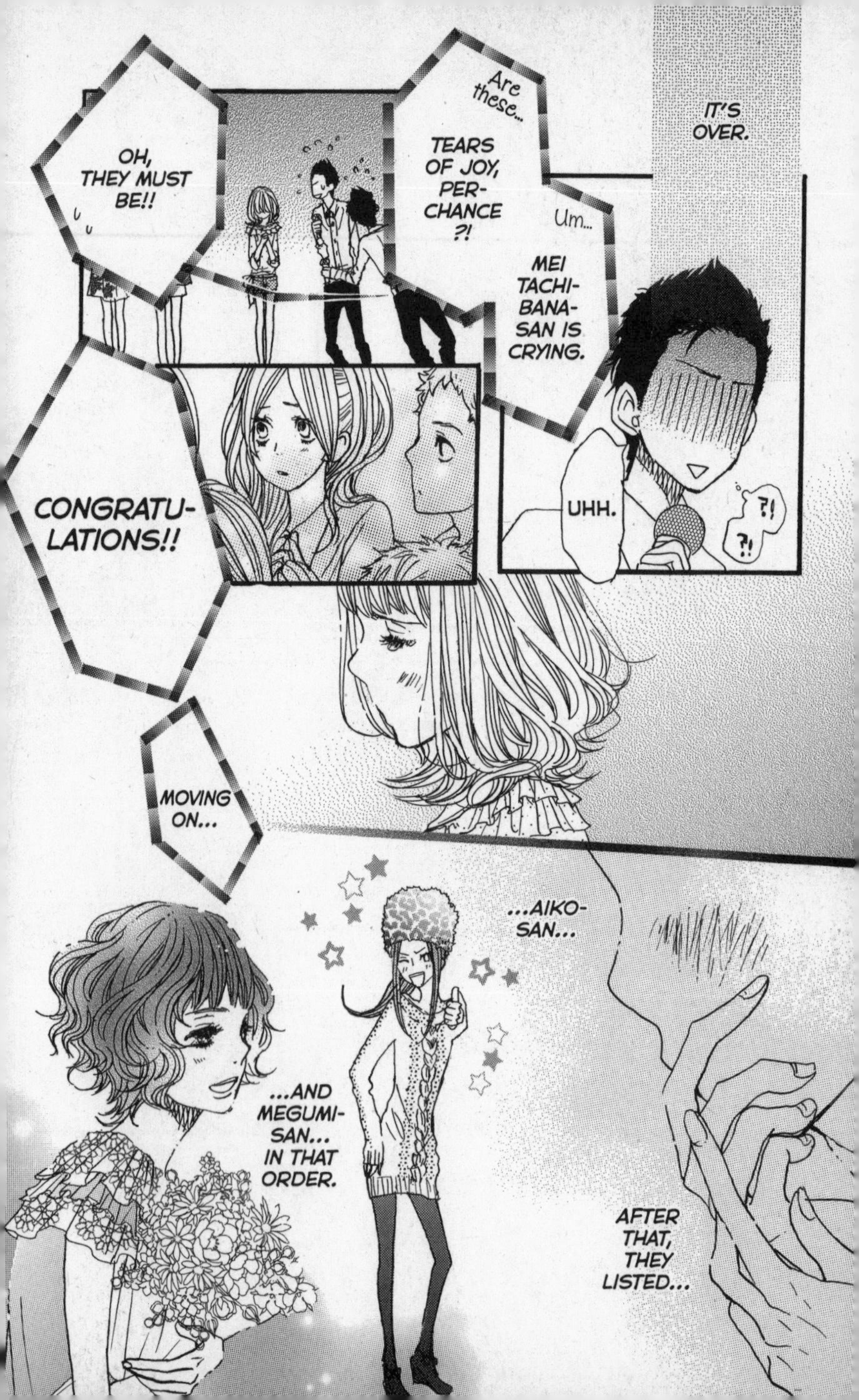

IT'S OVER.
Um...
MEI TACHIBANA-SAN IS CRYING.
UHH.
?!
?!
Are these...
TEARS OF JOY, PERCHANCE?!
OH, THEY MUST BE!!
CONGRATULATIONS!!
MOVING ON...
AFTER THAT, THEY LISTED...
...AIKO-SAN...
...AND MEGUMI-SAN... IN THAT ORDER.

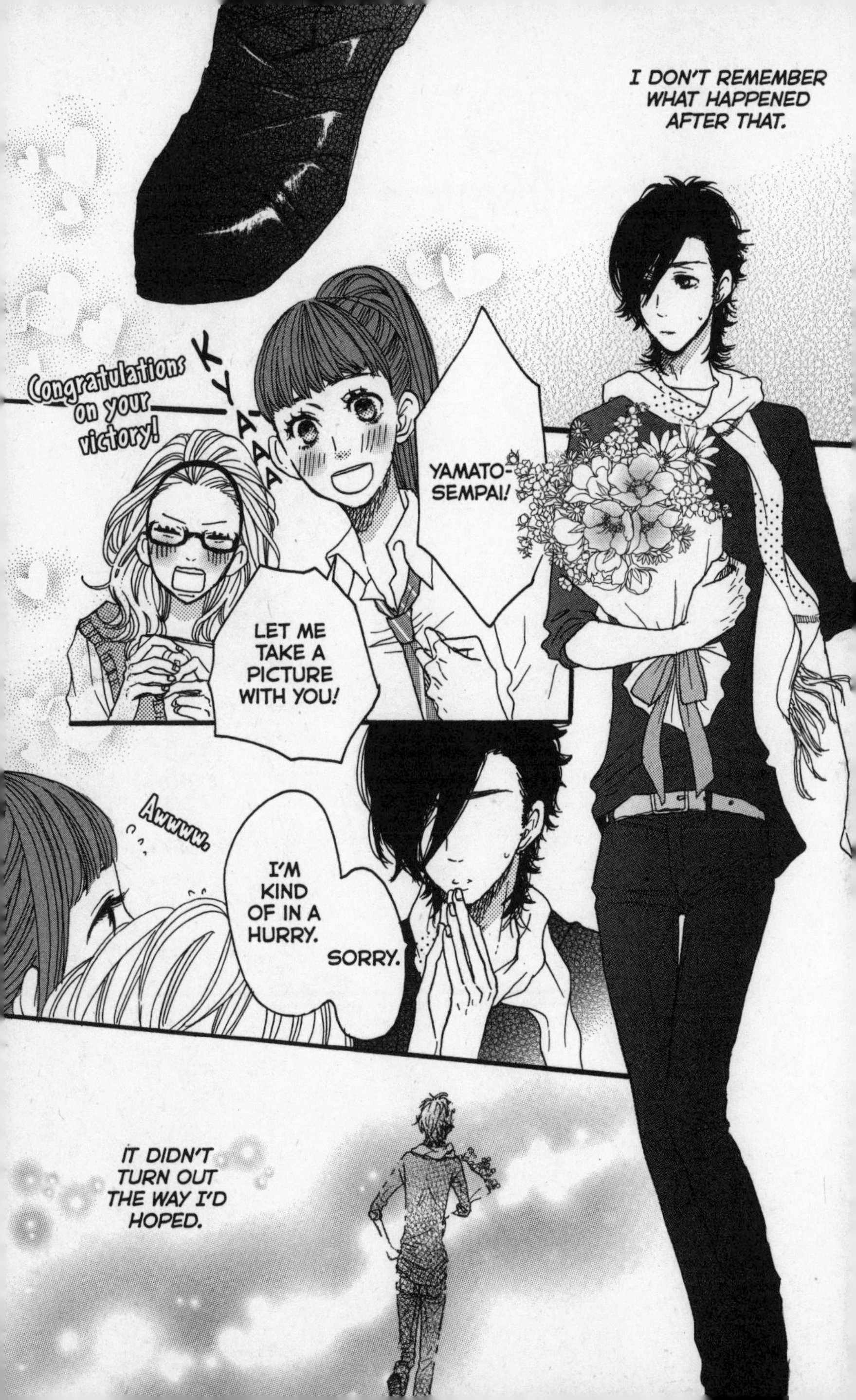
I DON'T REMEMBER WHAT HAPPENED AFTER THAT.
YAMATO-SEMPAI!
KYAAAA
Congratulations on your victory!
LET ME TAKE A PICTURE WITH YOU!
I'M KIND OF IN A HURRY.
SORRY.
Awwww.
IT DIDN'T TURN OUT THE WAY I'D HOPED.

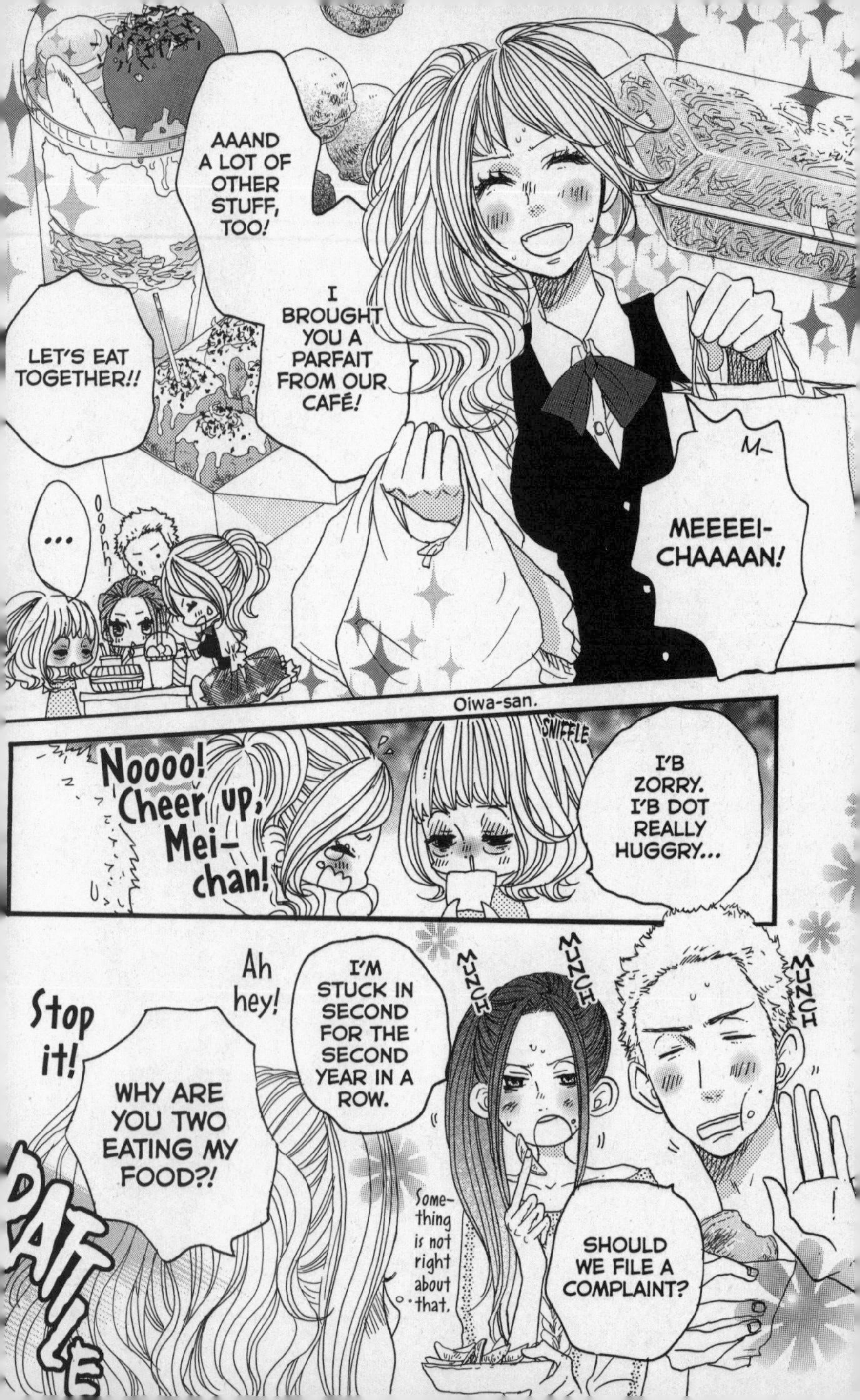
M–
MEEEEI-CHAAAAN!
I BROUGHT YOU A PARFAIT FROM OUR CAFÉ!
AAAND A LOT OF OTHER STUFF, TOO!
LET'S EAT TOGETHER!!
...
Ooohh!
Oiwa-san.
SNIFFLE
I'B ZORRY. I'B DOT REALLY HUGGRY...
Noooo! Cheer up, Mei-chan!
MUNCH
SHOULD WE FILE A COMPLAINT?
MUNCH
MUNCH
I'M STUCK IN SECOND FOR THE SECOND YEAR IN A ROW.
Something is not right about that.
Ah hey!
Stop it!
WHY ARE YOU TWO EATING MY FOOD?!

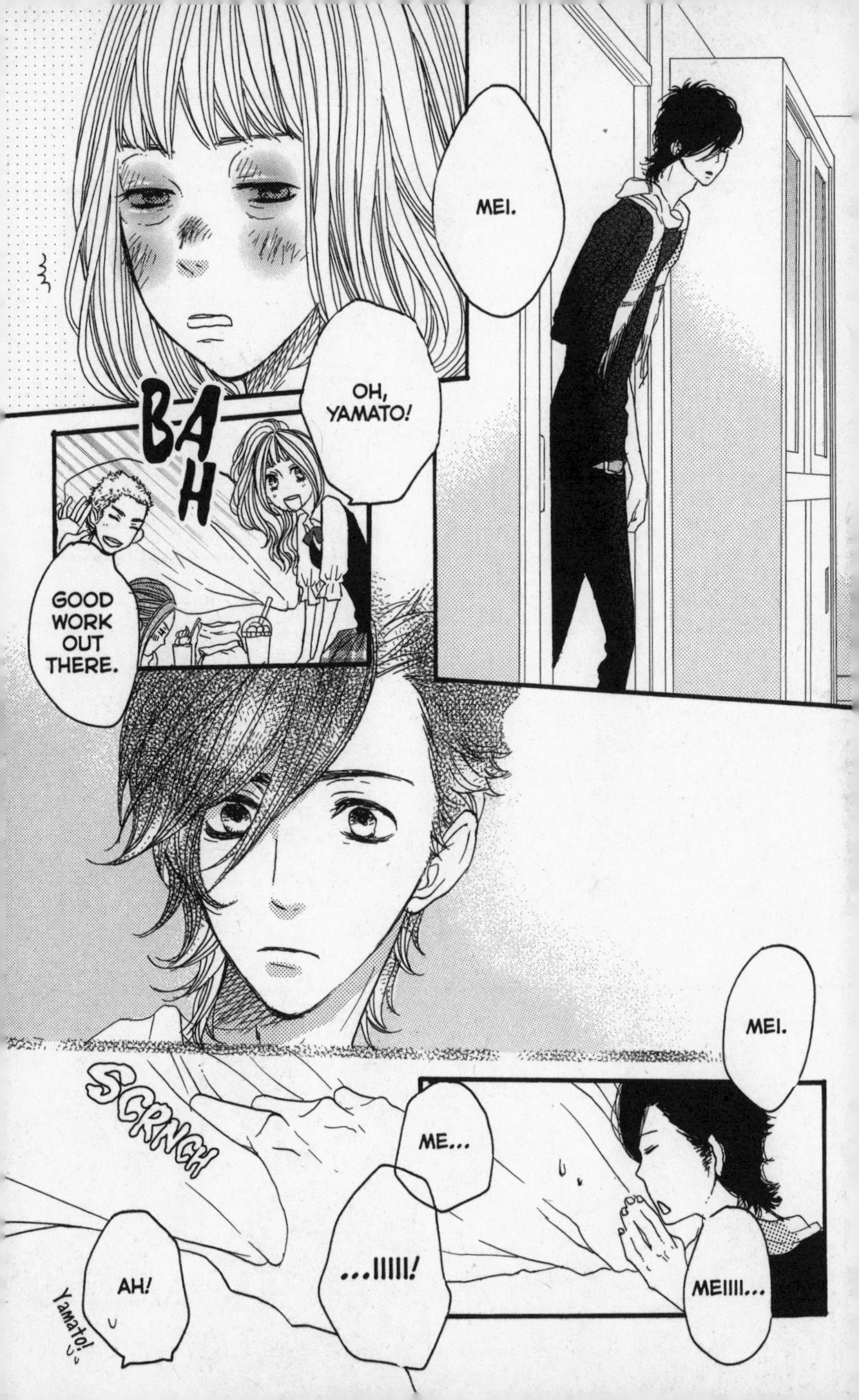
MEI.
OH, YAMATO!
BAH
GOOD WORK OUT THERE.
MEI.
MEIIII...
ME...
...IIIII!
SCRNCH
AH!
Yamato!

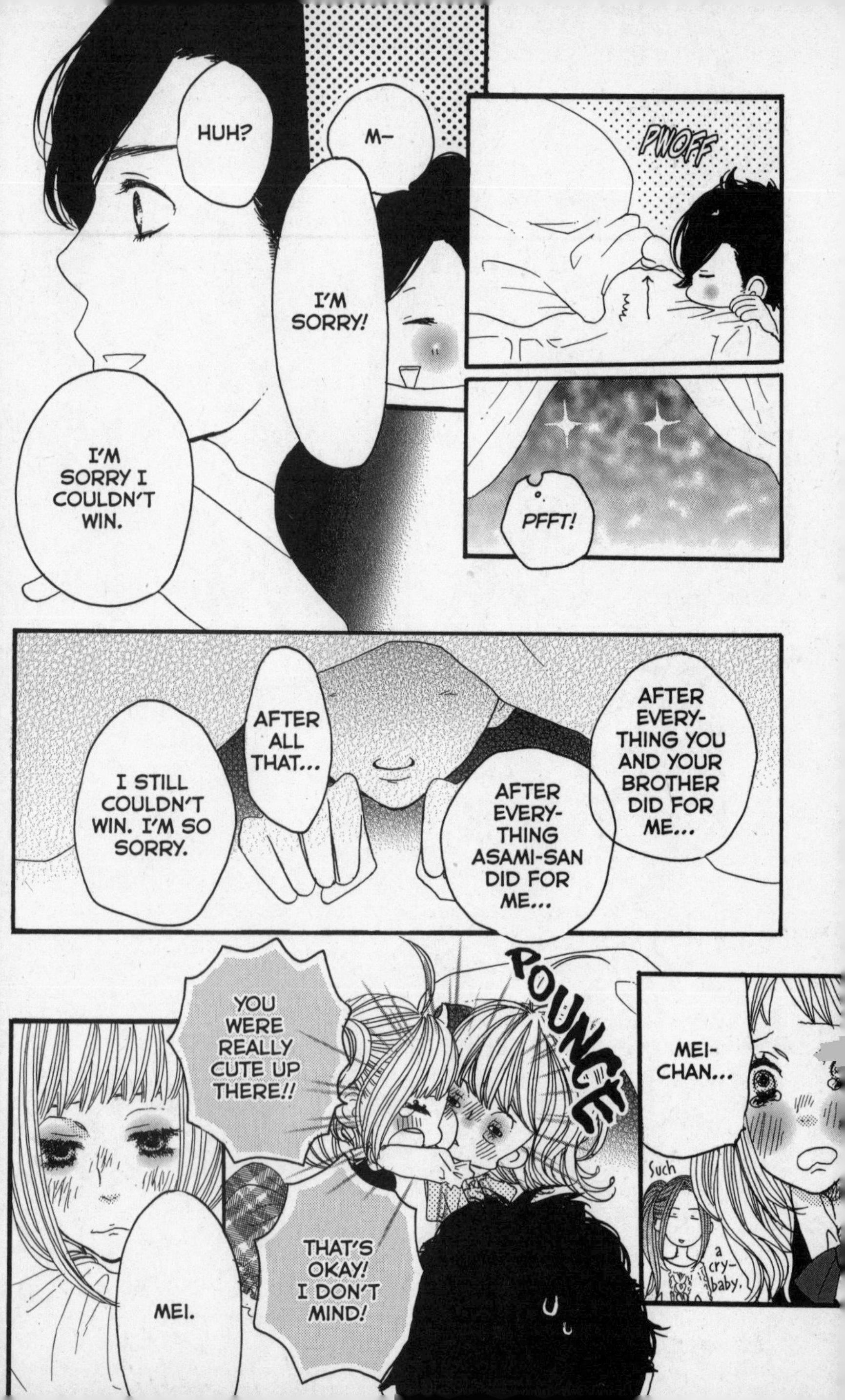
PWOFF
PFFT!
M-
I'M SORRY!
HUH?
I'M SORRY I COULDN'T WIN.
AFTER EVERYTHING YOU AND YOUR BROTHER DID FOR ME...
AFTER EVERYTHING ASAMI-SAN DID FOR ME...
AFTER ALL THAT...
I STILL COULDN'T WIN. I'M SO SORRY.
MEI-CHAN...
Such a cry-baby.
POUNCE
YOU WERE REALLY CUTE UP THERE!!
THAT'S OKAY! I DON'T MIND!
MEI.

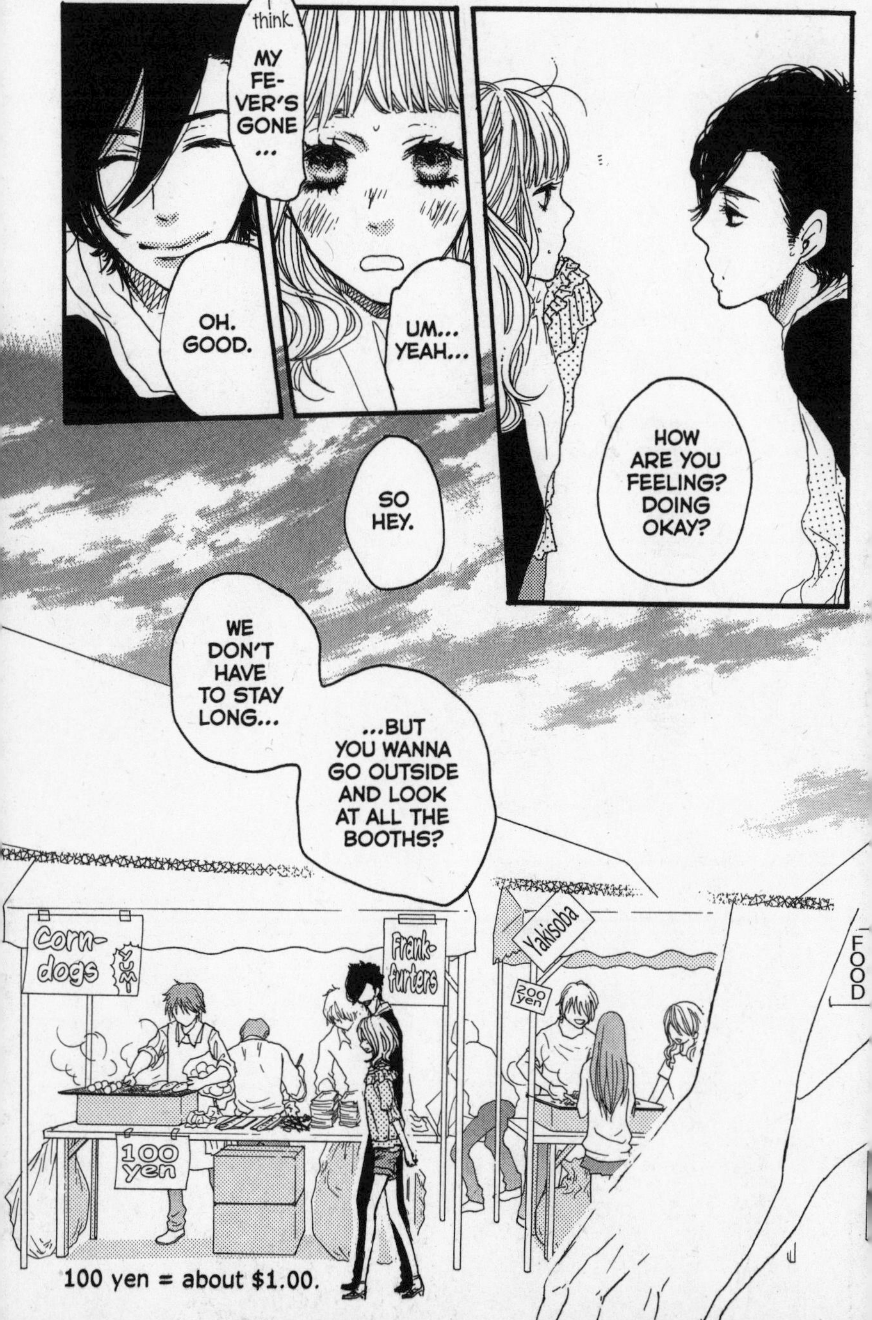
HOW ARE YOU FEELING? DOING OKAY?
UM... YEAH...
MY FE-VER'S GONE ... I think.
OH. GOOD.
SO HEY.
WE DON'T HAVE TO STAY LONG...
...BUT YOU WANNA GO OUTSIDE AND LOOK AT ALL THE BOOTHS?
FOOD
Yakisoba
200 yen
Frank-furters
Corn-dogs
YUM!
100 yen
100 yen = about $1.00.

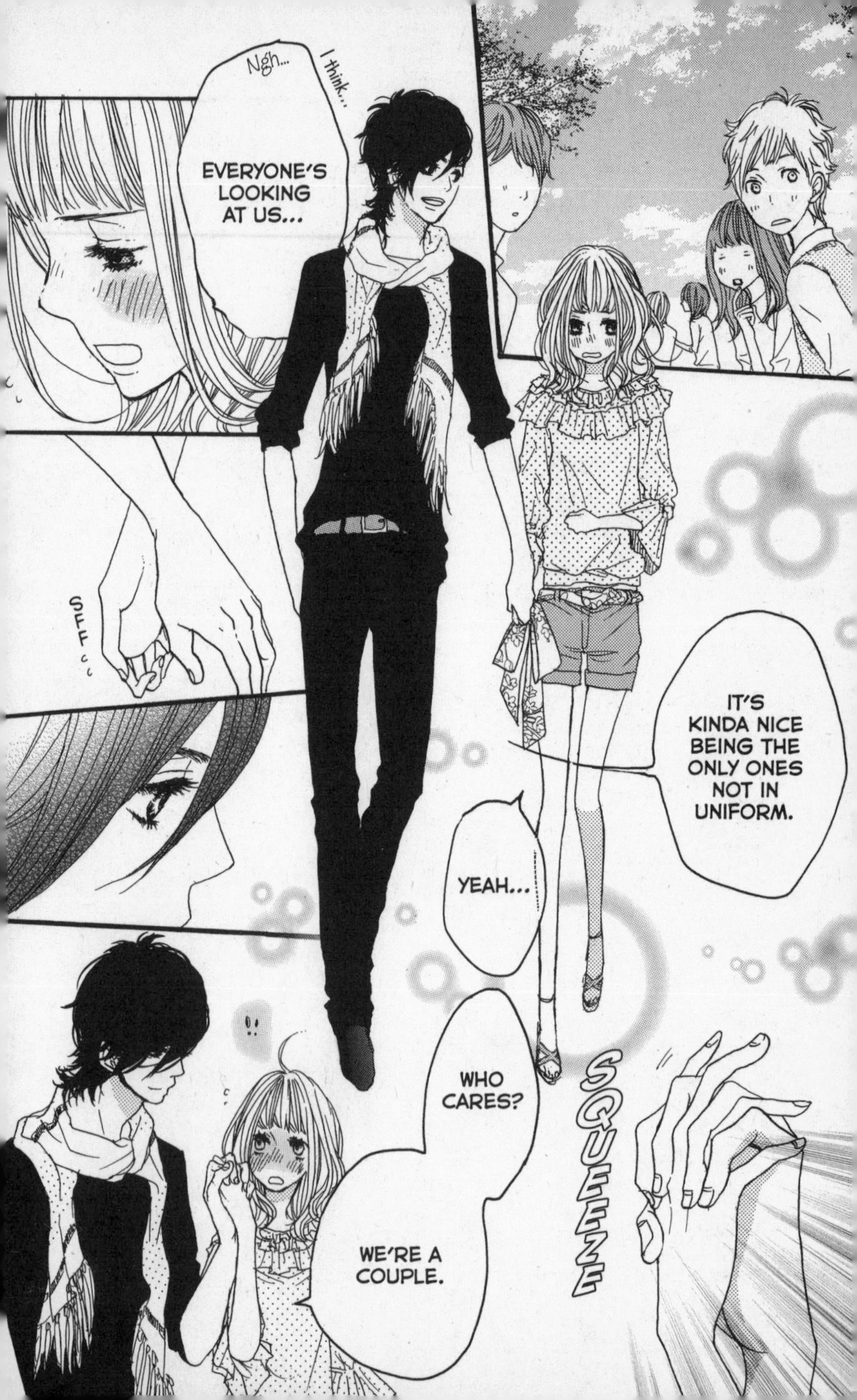

Ngh...
I think...
EVERYONE'S LOOKING AT US...
IT'S KINDA NICE BEING THE ONLY ONES NOT IN UNIFORM.
YEAH...
SFF
SQUEEZE
WHO CARES?
WE'RE A COUPLE.
!!

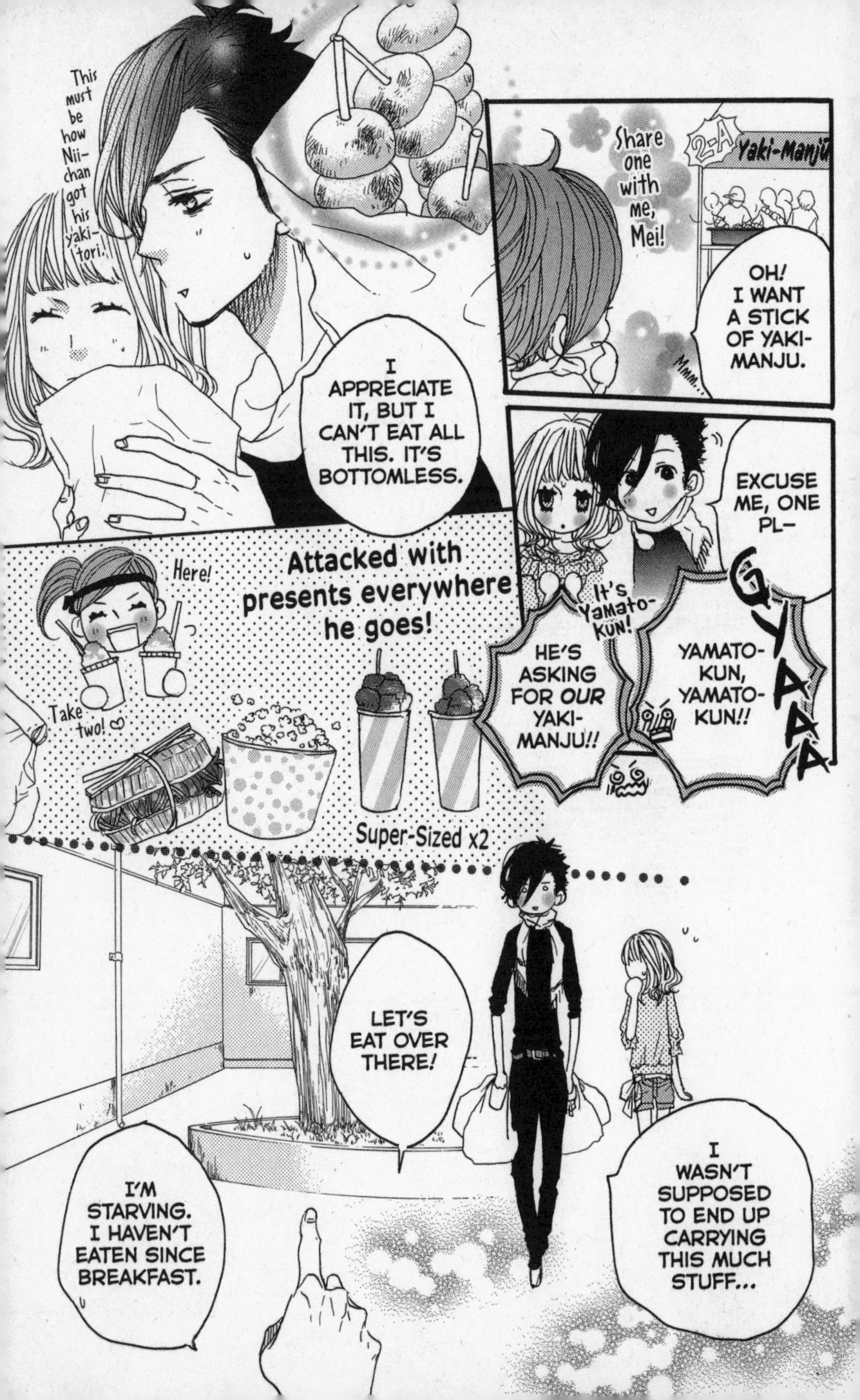
2-A
Yaki-Manjū
Share one with me, Mei!
OH! I WANT A STICK OF YAKI-MANJU.
Mmm...
EXCUSE ME, ONE PL—
GYAAA
YAMATO-KUN, YAMATO-KUN!!
It's Yamato-kun!
HE'S ASKING FOR *OUR* YAKI-MANJU!!
This must be how Nii-chan got his yaki-tori.
I APPRECIATE IT, BUT I CAN'T EAT ALL THIS. IT'S BOTTOMLESS.
Attacked with presents everywhere he goes!
Here!
Take two!
Super-Sized x2
....
LET'S EAT OVER THERE!
I WASN'T SUPPOSED TO END UP CARRYING THIS MUCH STUFF...
I'M STARVING. I HAVEN'T EATEN SINCE BREAKFAST.

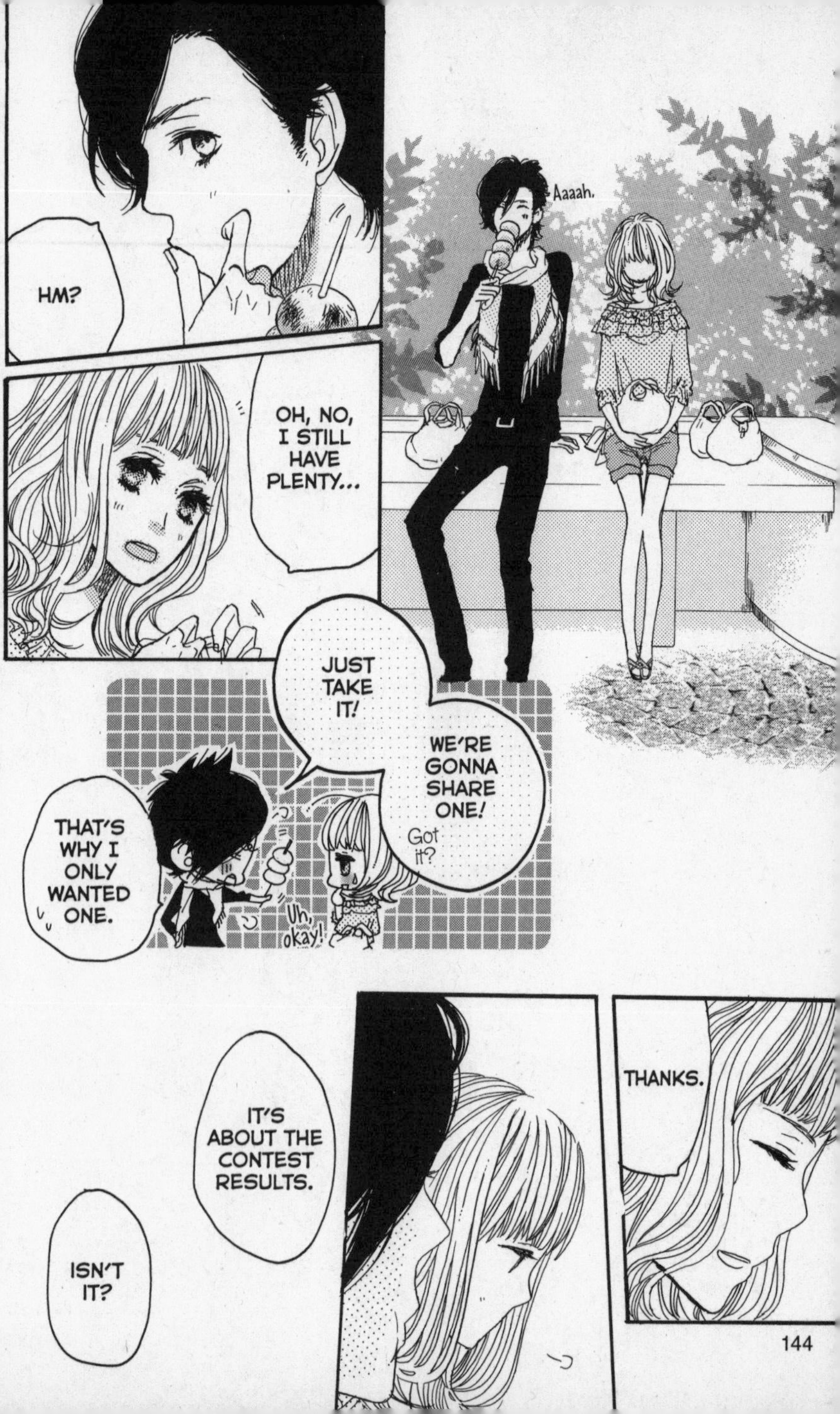
Aaaah.
HM?
OH, NO, I STILL HAVE PLENTY...
JUST TAKE IT!
WE'RE GONNA SHARE ONE!
Got it?
THAT'S WHY I ONLY WANTED ONE.
Uh, okay!
THANKS.
IT'S ABOUT THE CONTEST RESULTS.
ISN'T IT?

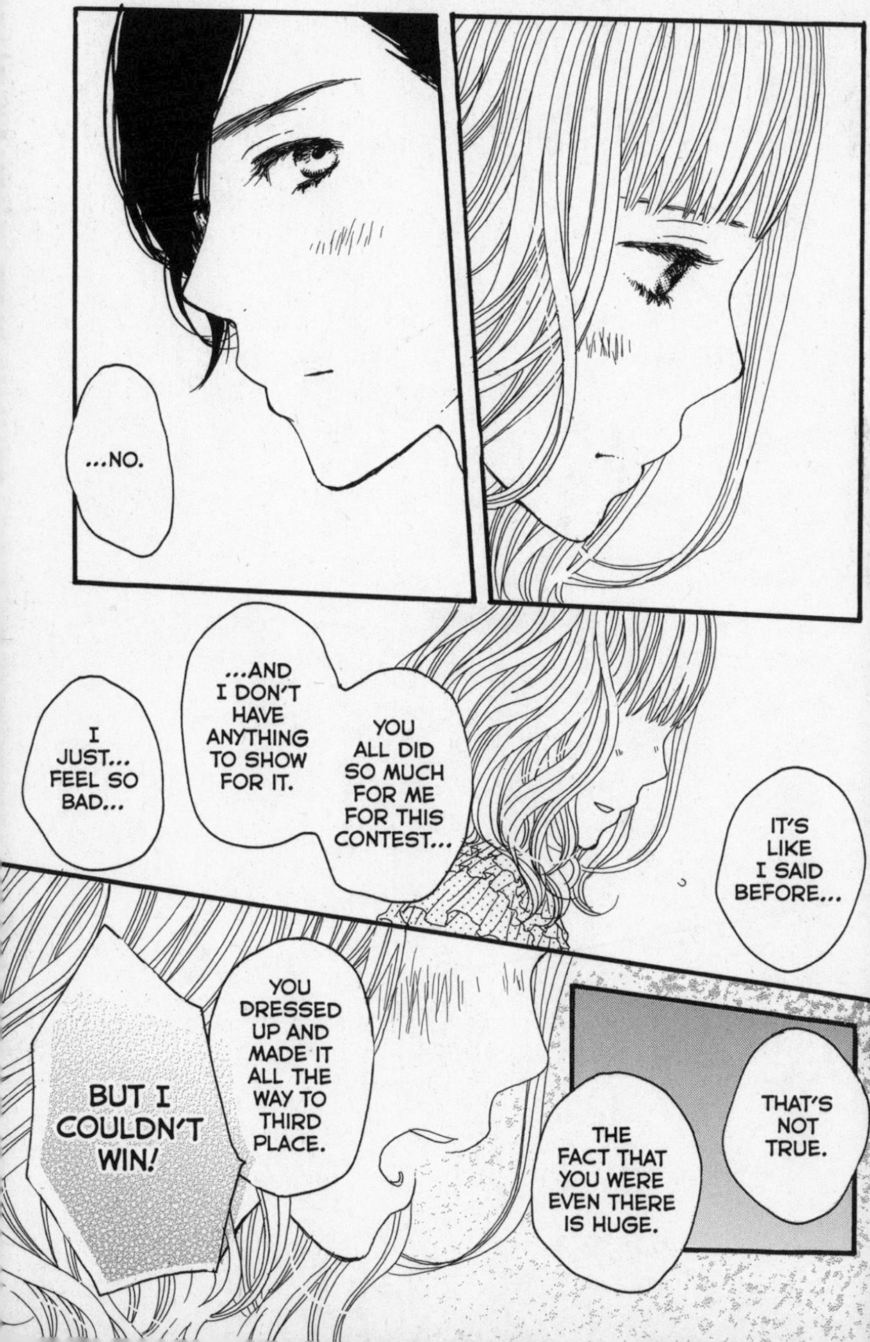
...NO.
IT'S LIKE I SAID BEFORE...
YOU ALL DID SO MUCH FOR ME FOR THIS CONTEST...
...AND I DON'T HAVE ANYTHING TO SHOW FOR IT.
I JUST... FEEL SO BAD...
THAT'S NOT TRUE.
THE FACT THAT YOU WERE EVEN THERE IS HUGE.
YOU DRESSED UP AND MADE IT ALL THE WAY TO THIRD PLACE.
BUT I COULDN'T WIN!

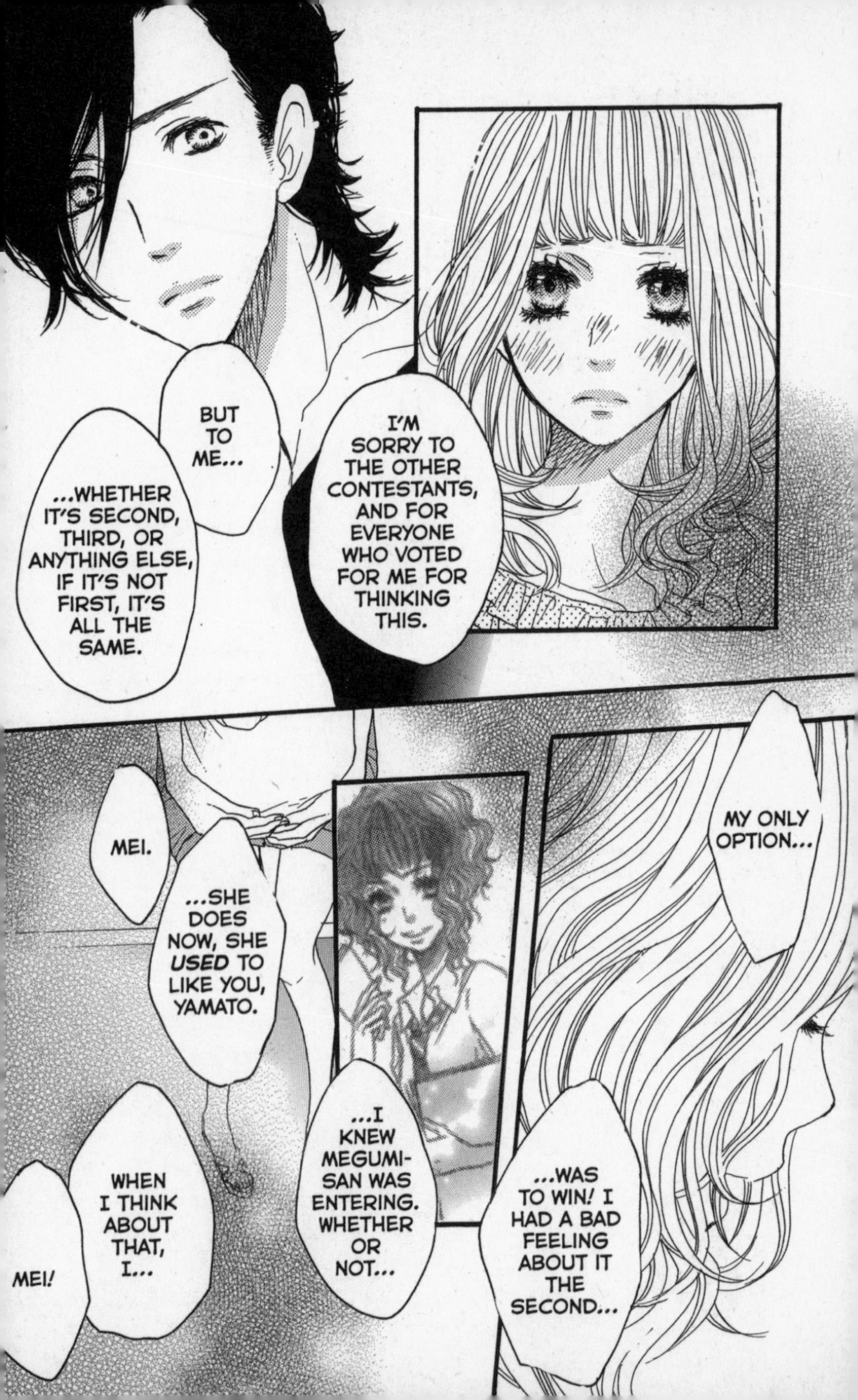
I'M SORRY TO THE OTHER CONTESTANTS, AND FOR EVERYONE WHO VOTED FOR ME FOR THINKING THIS.
BUT TO ME...
...WHETHER IT'S SECOND, THIRD, OR ANYTHING ELSE, IF IT'S NOT FIRST, IT'S ALL THE SAME.
MY ONLY OPTION...
...WAS TO WIN! I HAD A BAD FEELING ABOUT IT THE SECOND...
...I KNEW MEGUMI-SAN WAS ENTERING. WHETHER OR NOT...
...SHE DOES NOW, SHE *USED* TO LIKE YOU, YAMATO.
MEI.
WHEN I THINK ABOUT THAT, I...
MEI!

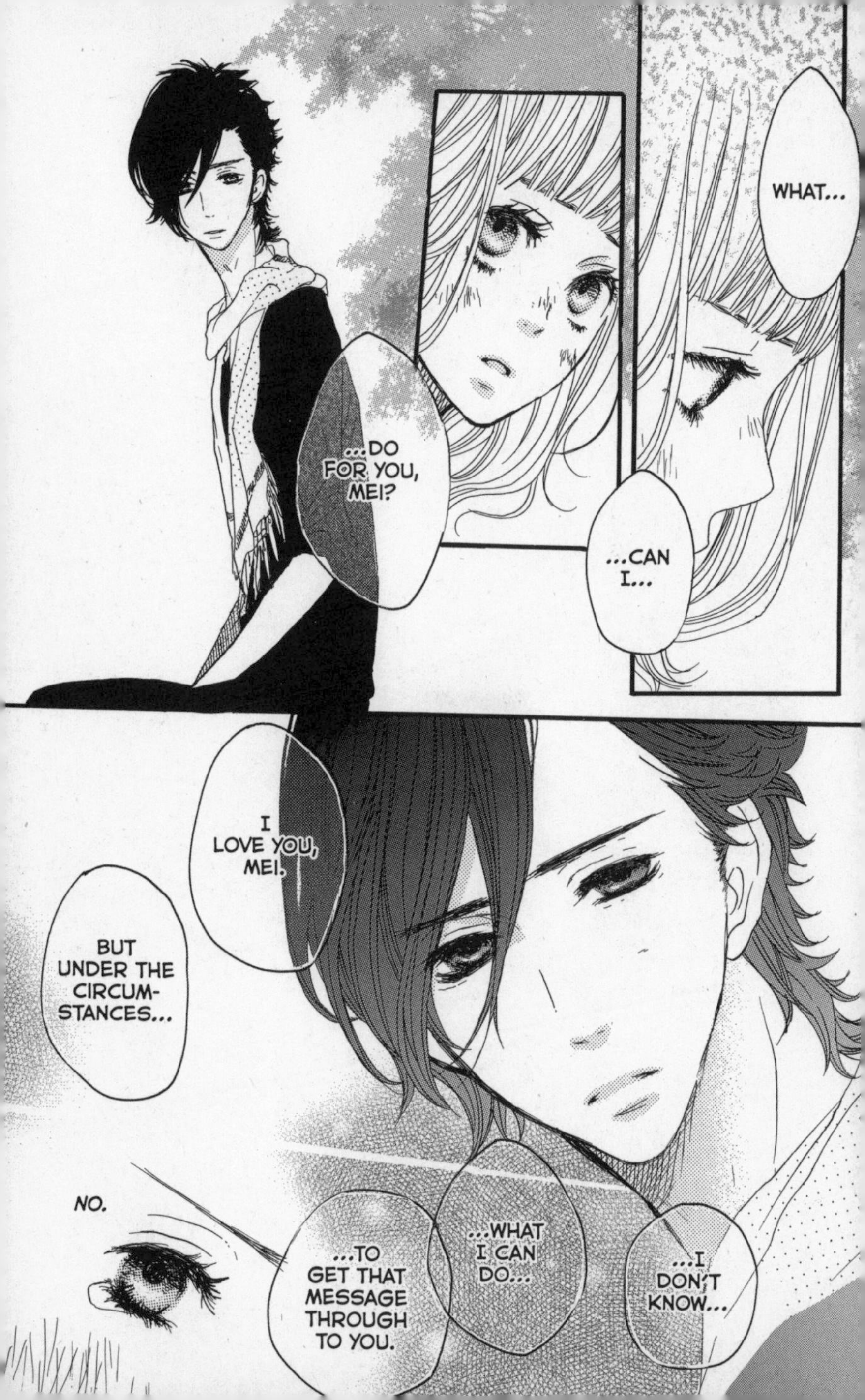
WHAT...
...CAN I...
...DO FOR YOU, MEI?
I LOVE YOU, MEI.
BUT UNDER THE CIRCUM-STANCES...
...I DON'T KNOW...
...WHAT I CAN DO...
...TO GET THAT MESSAGE THROUGH TO YOU.
NO.

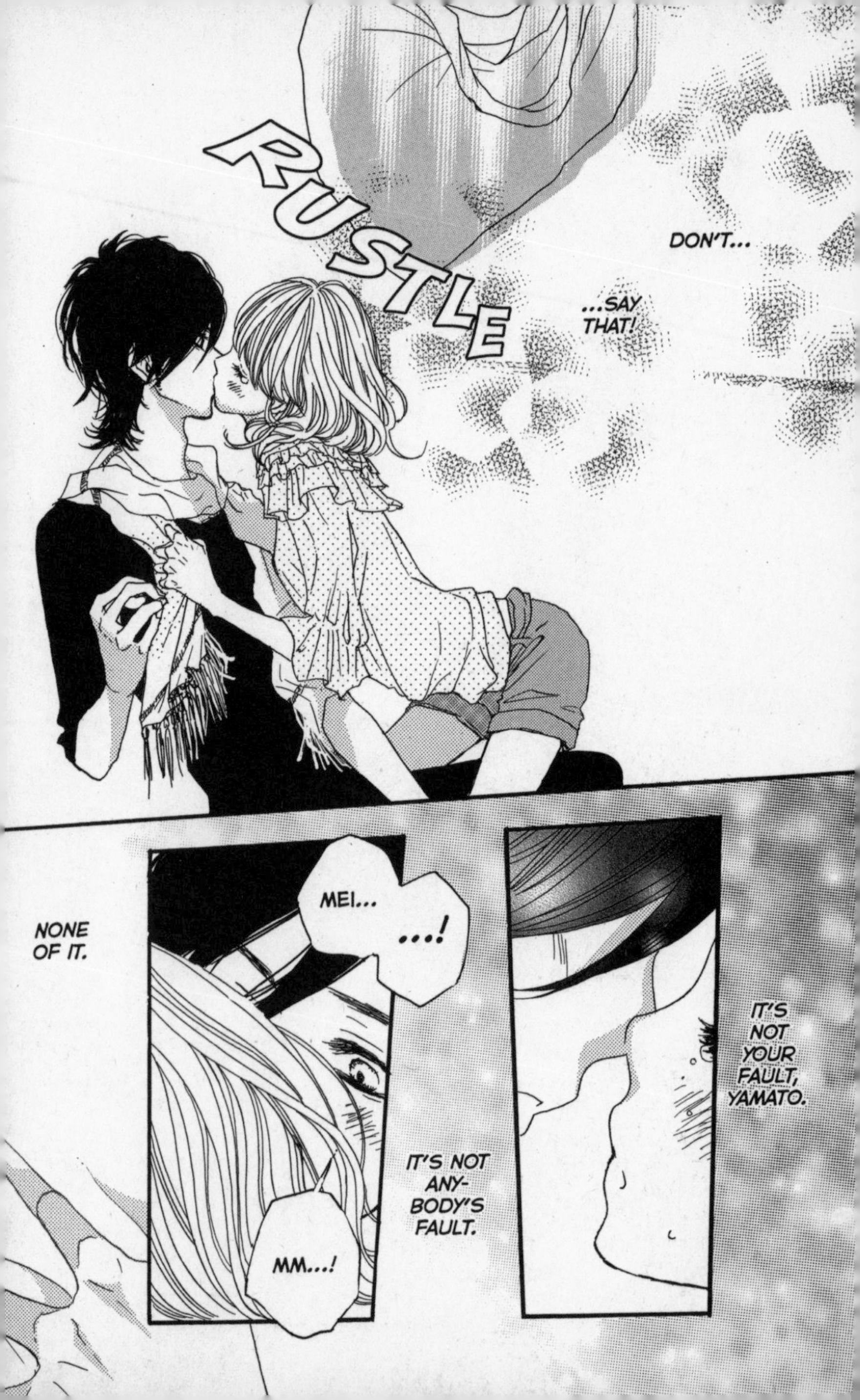
RUSTLE
DON'T...
...SAY THAT!
IT'S NOT YOUR FAULT, YAMATO.
IT'S NOT ANY-BODY'S FAULT.
MEI...
...!
MM...!
NONE OF IT.

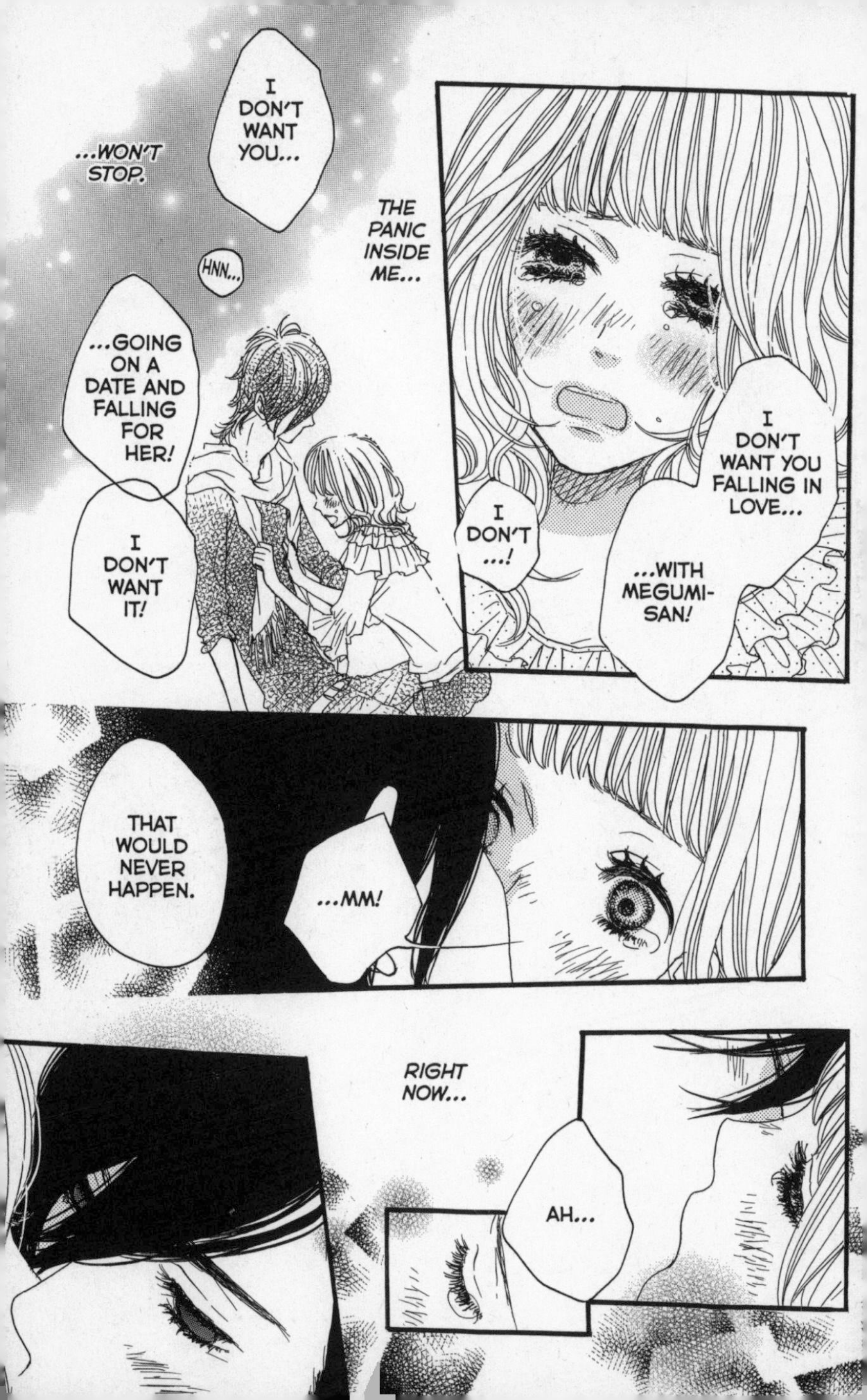
I DON'T WANT YOU FALLING IN LOVE...
...WITH MEGUMI-SAN!
I DON'T ...!
THE PANIC INSIDE ME...
...WON'T STOP.
I DON'T WANT YOU...
HNN...
...GOING ON A DATE AND FALLING FOR HER!
I DON'T WANT IT!
...MM!
THAT WOULD NEVER HAPPEN.
RIGHT NOW...
AH...

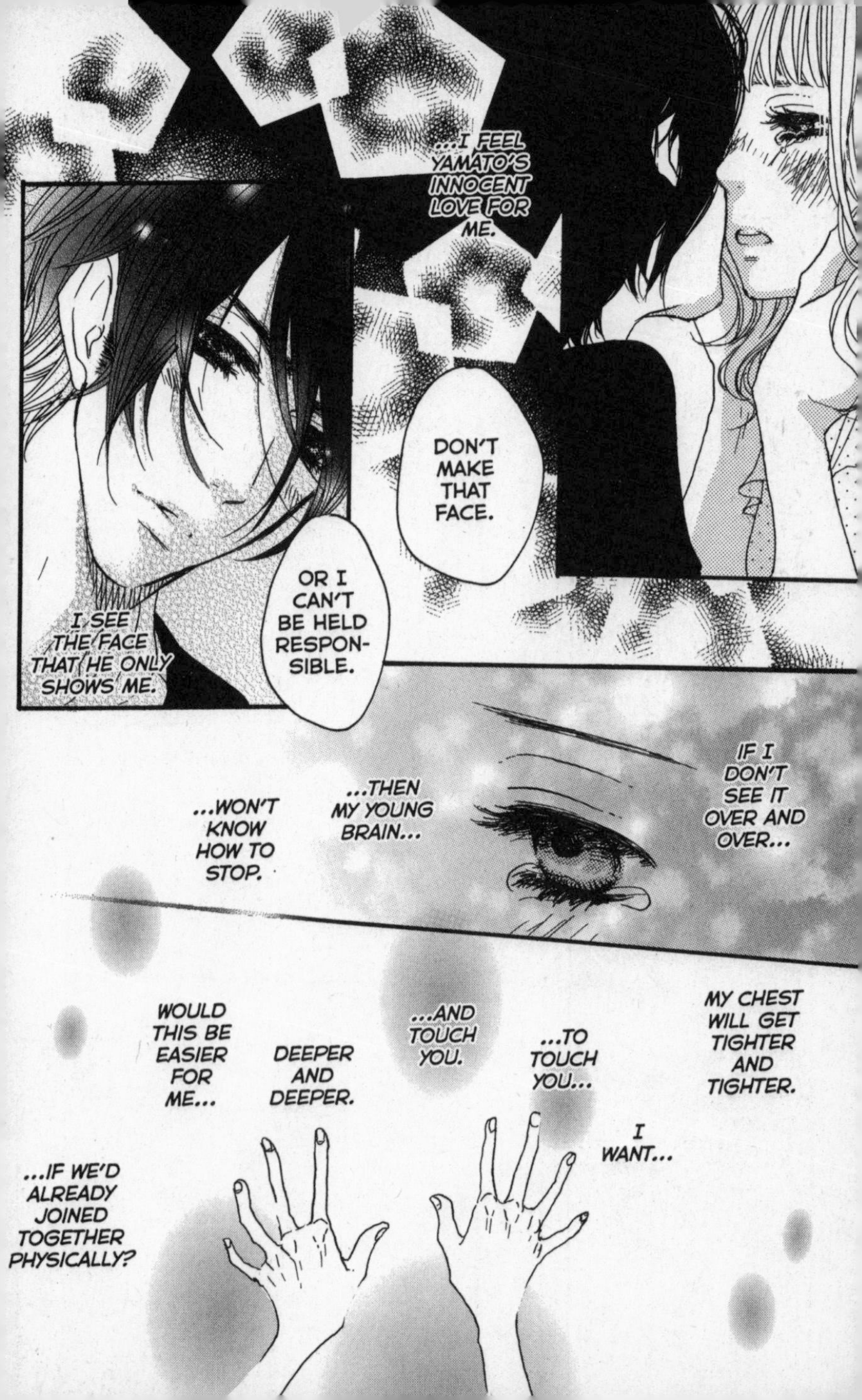
...I FEEL YAMATO'S INNOCENT LOVE FOR ME.
DON'T MAKE THAT FACE.
OR I CAN'T BE HELD RESPONSIBLE.
I SEE THE FACE THAT HE ONLY SHOWS ME.
IF I DON'T SEE IT OVER AND OVER...
...THEN MY YOUNG BRAIN...
...WON'T KNOW HOW TO STOP.
MY CHEST WILL GET TIGHTER AND TIGHTER.
I WANT...
...TO TOUCH YOU...
...AND TOUCH YOU.
DEEPER AND DEEPER.
WOULD THIS BE EASIER FOR ME...
...IF WE'D ALREADY JOINED TOGETHER PHYSICALLY?

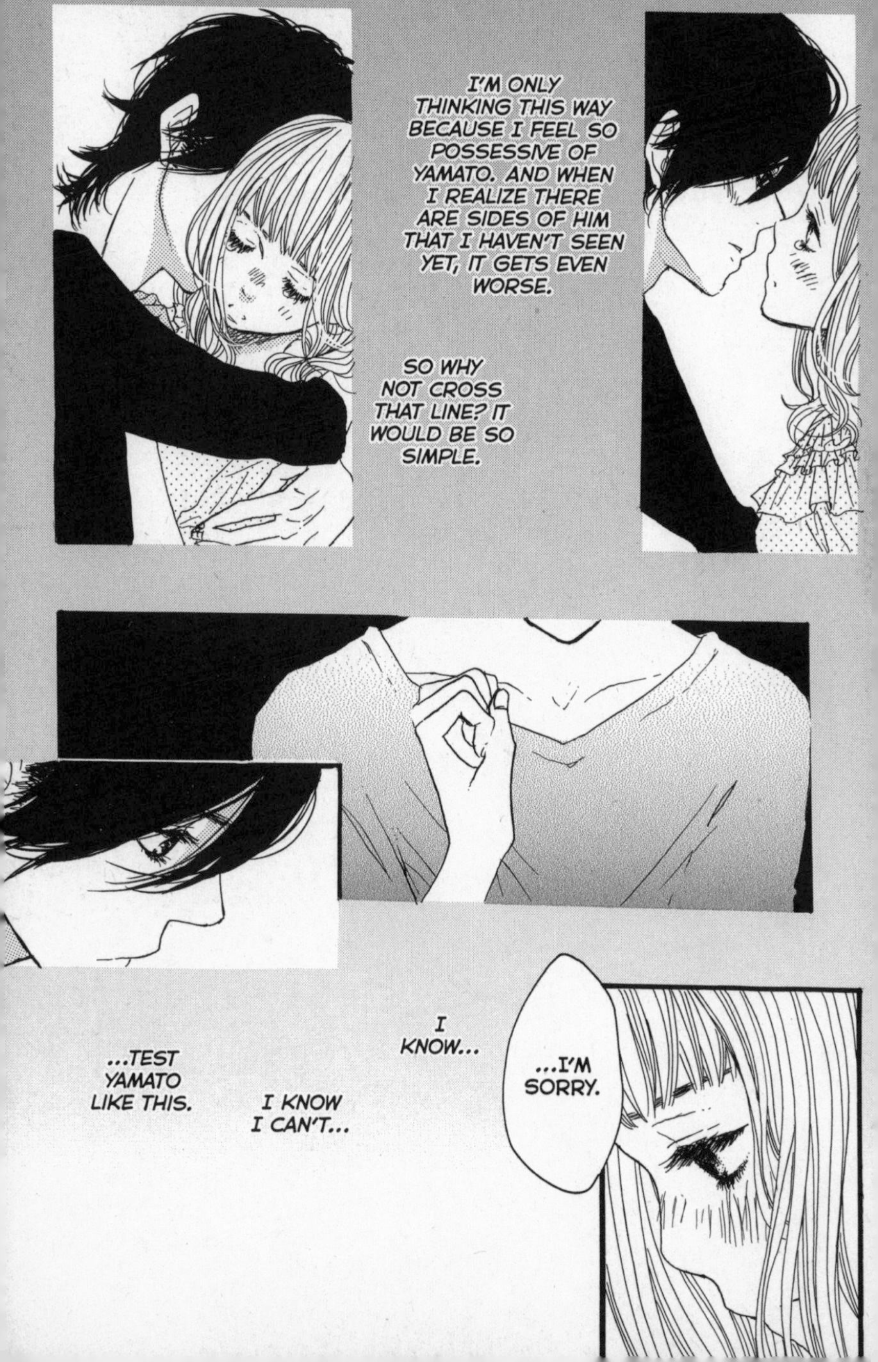
I'M ONLY THINKING THIS WAY BECAUSE I FEEL SO POSSESSIVE OF YAMATO. AND WHEN I REALIZE THERE ARE SIDES OF HIM THAT I HAVEN'T SEEN YET, IT GETS EVEN WORSE.
SO WHY NOT CROSS THAT LINE? IT WOULD BE SO SIMPLE.
...I'M SORRY.
I KNOW...
I KNOW I CAN'T...
...TEST YAMATO LIKE THIS.

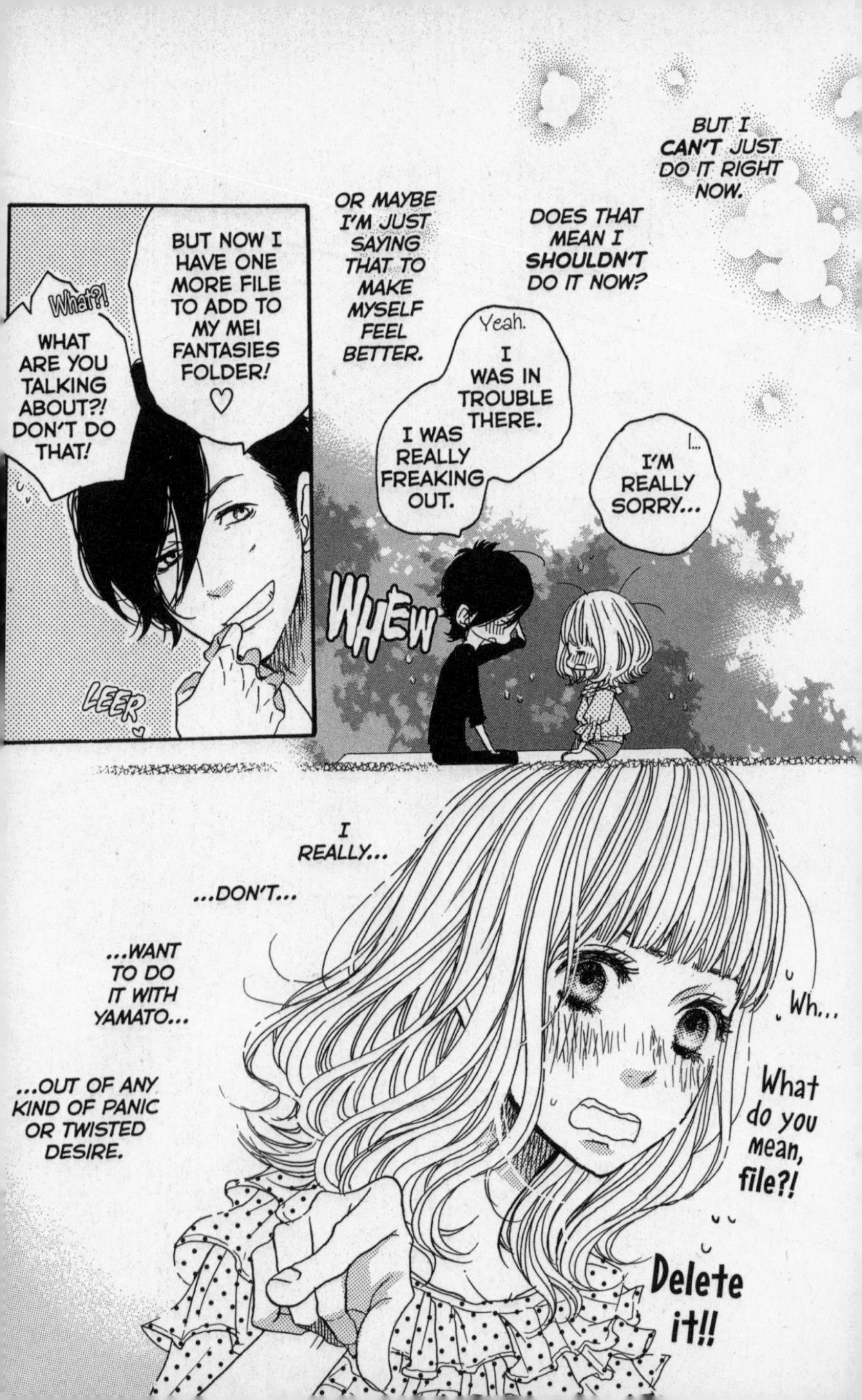
BUT I CAN'T JUST DO IT RIGHT NOW.
DOES THAT MEAN I SHOULDN'T DO IT NOW?
OR MAYBE I'M JUST SAYING THAT TO MAKE MYSELF FEEL BETTER.
I... I'M REALLY SORRY...
Yeah. I WAS IN TROUBLE THERE.
I WAS REALLY FREAKING OUT.
WHEW
BUT NOW I HAVE ONE MORE FILE TO ADD TO MY MEI FANTASIES FOLDER! ♡
LEER
What?!
WHAT ARE YOU TALKING ABOUT?! DON'T DO THAT!
Wh... What do you mean, file?!
Delete it!!
I REALLY...
...DON'T...
...WANT TO DO IT WITH YAMATO...
...OUT OF ANY KIND OF PANIC OR TWISTED DESIRE.

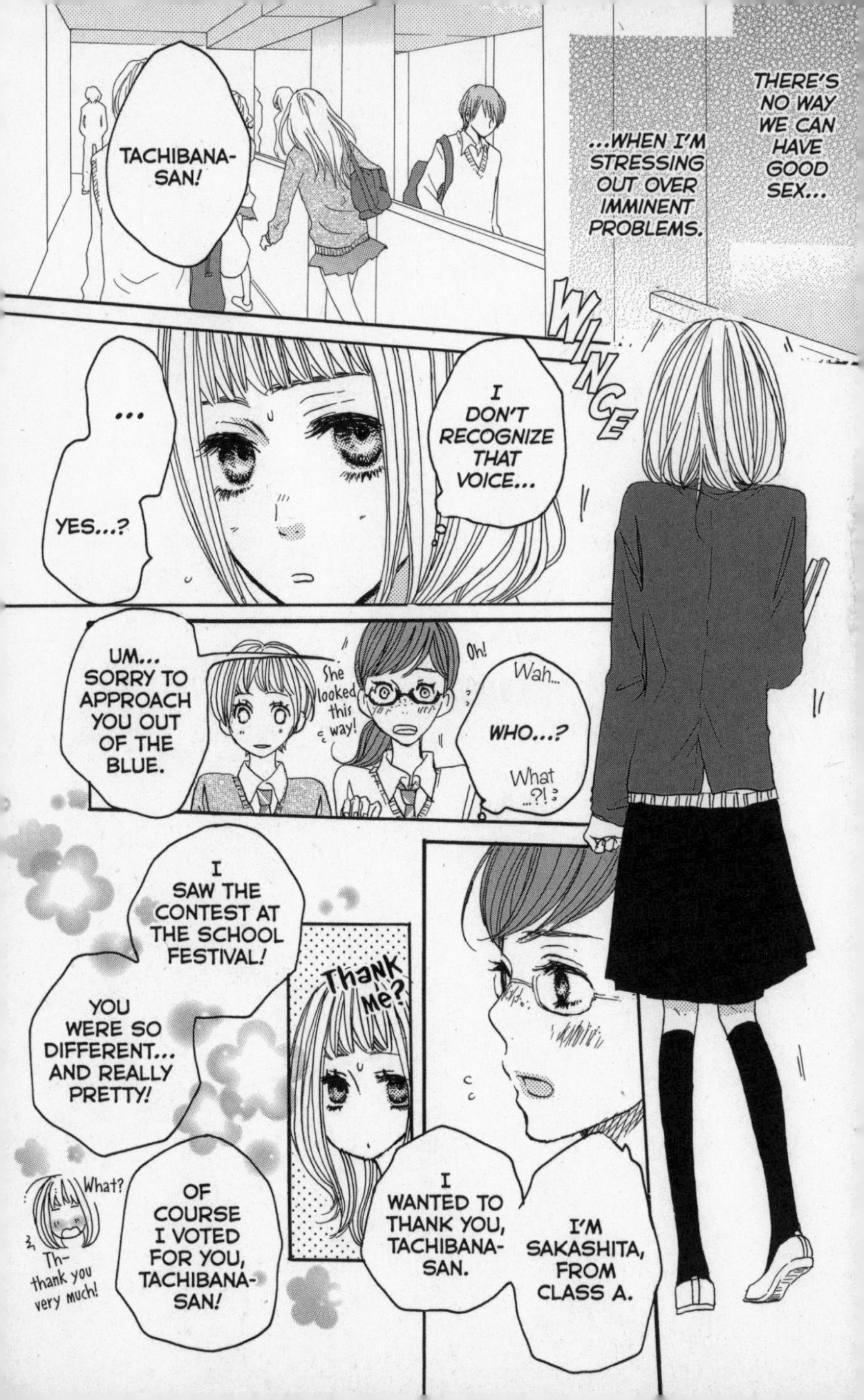

THERE'S NO WAY WE CAN HAVE GOOD SEX...
...WHEN I'M STRESSING OUT OVER IMMINENT PROBLEMS.
TACHIBANA-SAN!
WINCE
I DON'T RECOGNIZE THAT VOICE...
...
YES...?
Wah...
WHO...?
What ...?!
Oh!
She looked this way!
UM... SORRY TO APPROACH YOU OUT OF THE BLUE.
I'M SAKASHITA, FROM CLASS A.
I WANTED TO THANK YOU, TACHIBANA-SAN.
Thank me?
I SAW THE CONTEST AT THE SCHOOL FESTIVAL!
YOU WERE SO DIFFERENT... AND REALLY PRETTY!
OF COURSE I VOTED FOR YOU, TACHIBANA-SAN!
What?
Th-thank you very much!

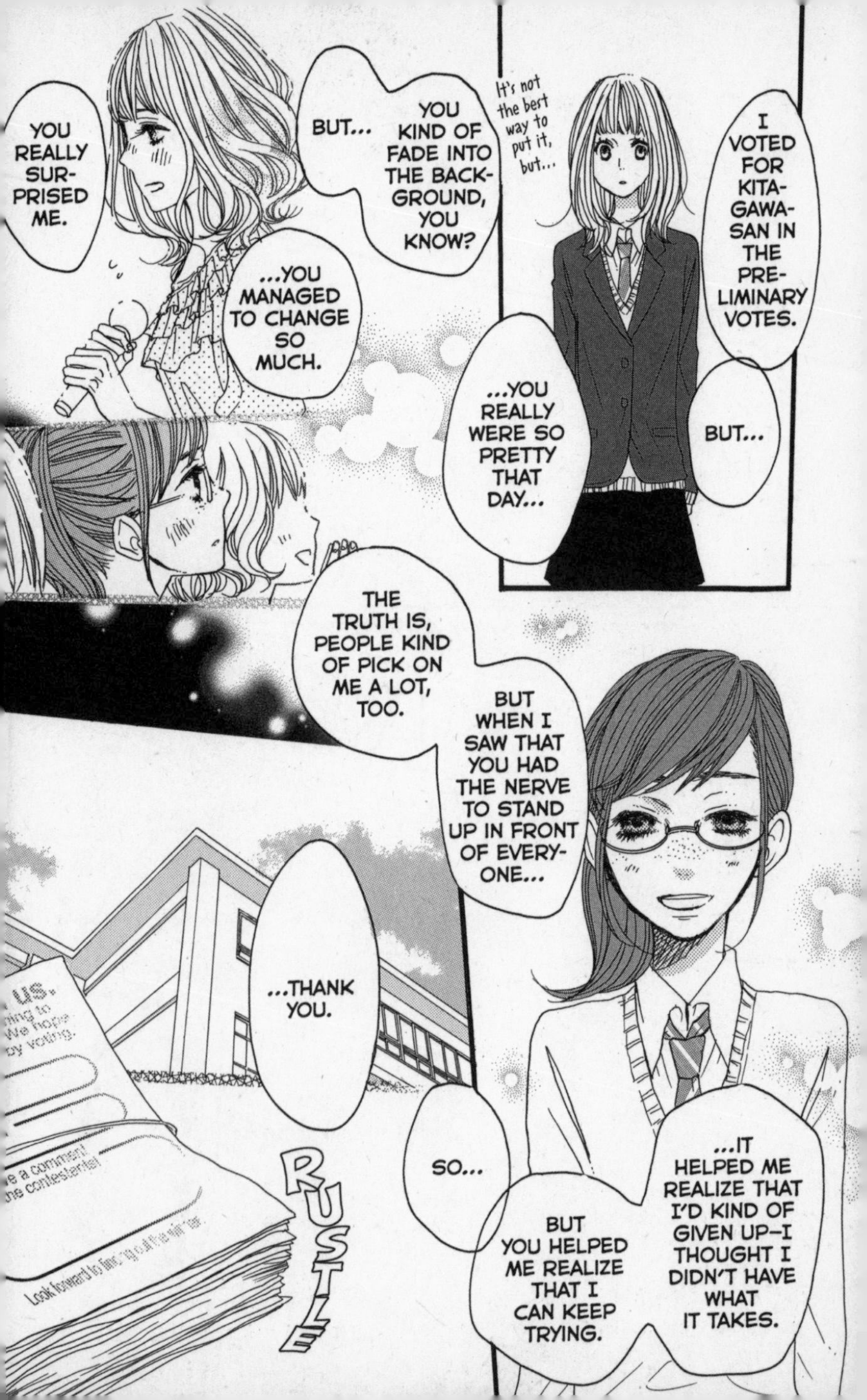
I VOTED FOR KITA-GAWA-SAN IN THE PRE-LIMINARY VOTES.
BUT...
...YOU REALLY WERE SO PRETTY THAT DAY...
It's not the best way to put it, but...
YOU KIND OF FADE INTO THE BACK-GROUND, YOU KNOW?
BUT...
YOU REALLY SUR-PRISED ME.
...YOU MANAGED TO CHANGE SO MUCH.
THE TRUTH IS, PEOPLE KIND OF PICK ON ME A LOT, TOO.
BUT WHEN I SAW THAT YOU HAD THE NERVE TO STAND UP IN FRONT OF EVERY-ONE...
...IT HELPED ME REALIZE THAT I'D KIND OF GIVEN UP—I THOUGHT I DIDN'T HAVE WHAT IT TAKES.
SO...
BUT YOU HELPED ME REALIZE THAT I CAN KEEP TRYING.
...THANK YOU.
RUSTLE

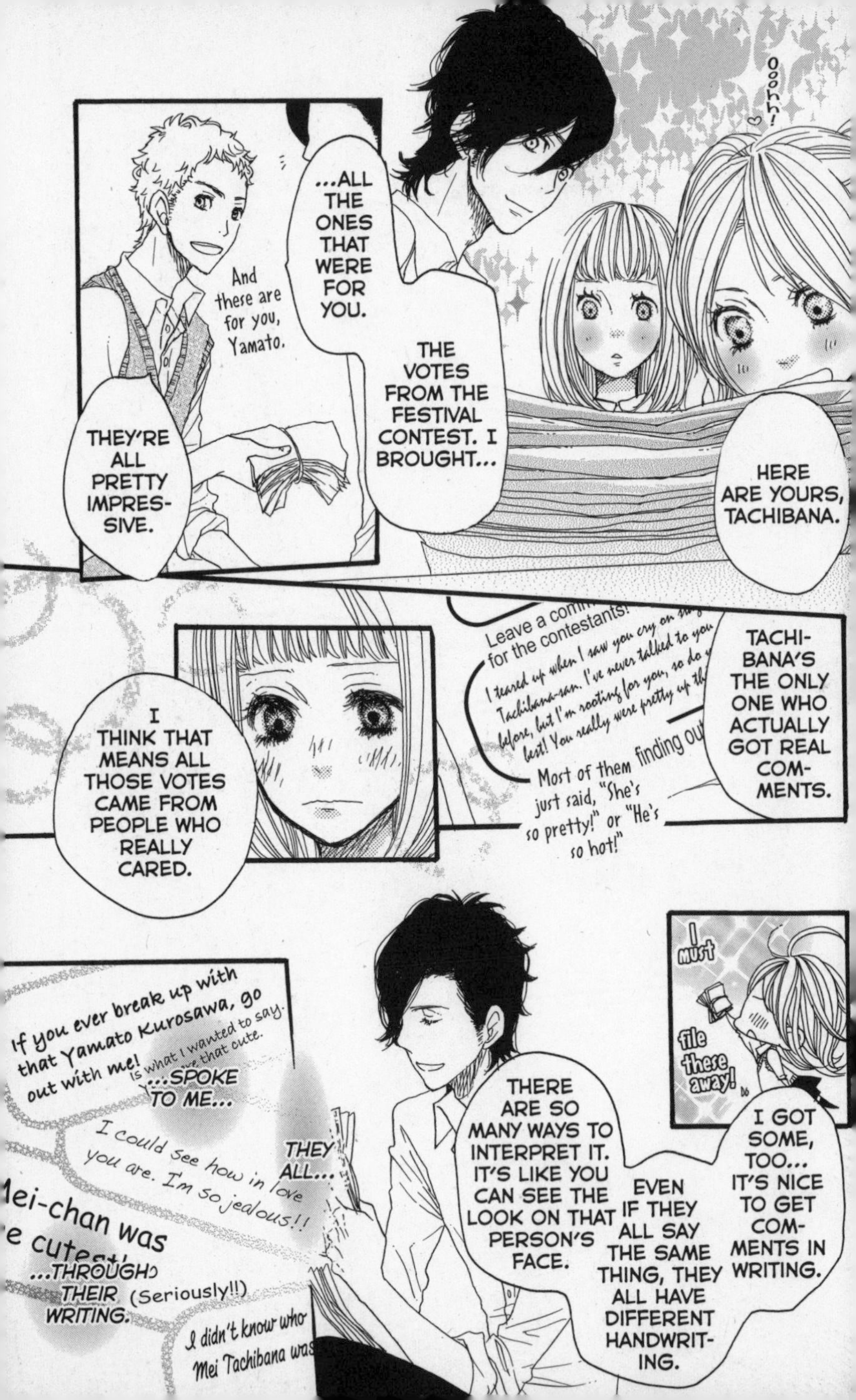
Ooohh!
HERE ARE YOURS, TACHIBANA.
THE VOTES FROM THE FESTIVAL CONTEST. I BROUGHT...
...ALL THE ONES THAT WERE FOR YOU.
And these are for you, Yamato.
THEY'RE ALL PRETTY IMPRESSIVE.
TACHIBANA'S THE ONLY ONE WHO ACTUALLY GOT REAL COMMENTS.
Leave a comm
for the contestants!
I teared up when I saw you cry on
Tachibana-san. I've never talked to you
before, but I'm rooting for you, so do
best! You really were pretty up th
Most of them just said, "She's so pretty!" or "He's so hot!"
I THINK THAT MEANS ALL THOSE VOTES CAME FROM PEOPLE WHO REALLY CARED.
I must file these away!
I GOT SOME, TOO... IT'S NICE TO GET COMMENTS IN WRITING.
EVEN IF THEY ALL SAY THE SAME THING, THEY ALL HAVE DIFFERENT HANDWRITING.
THERE ARE SO MANY WAYS TO INTERPRET IT. IT'S LIKE YOU CAN SEE THE LOOK ON THAT PERSON'S FACE.
THEY ALL...
If you ever break up with that Yamato Kurosawa, go out with me!
is what I wanted to say.
...SPOKE TO ME...
I could see how in love you are. I'm so jealous!!
Mei-chan was
...THROUGH THEIR WRITING.
(Seriously!!)
I didn't know who Mei Tachibana was

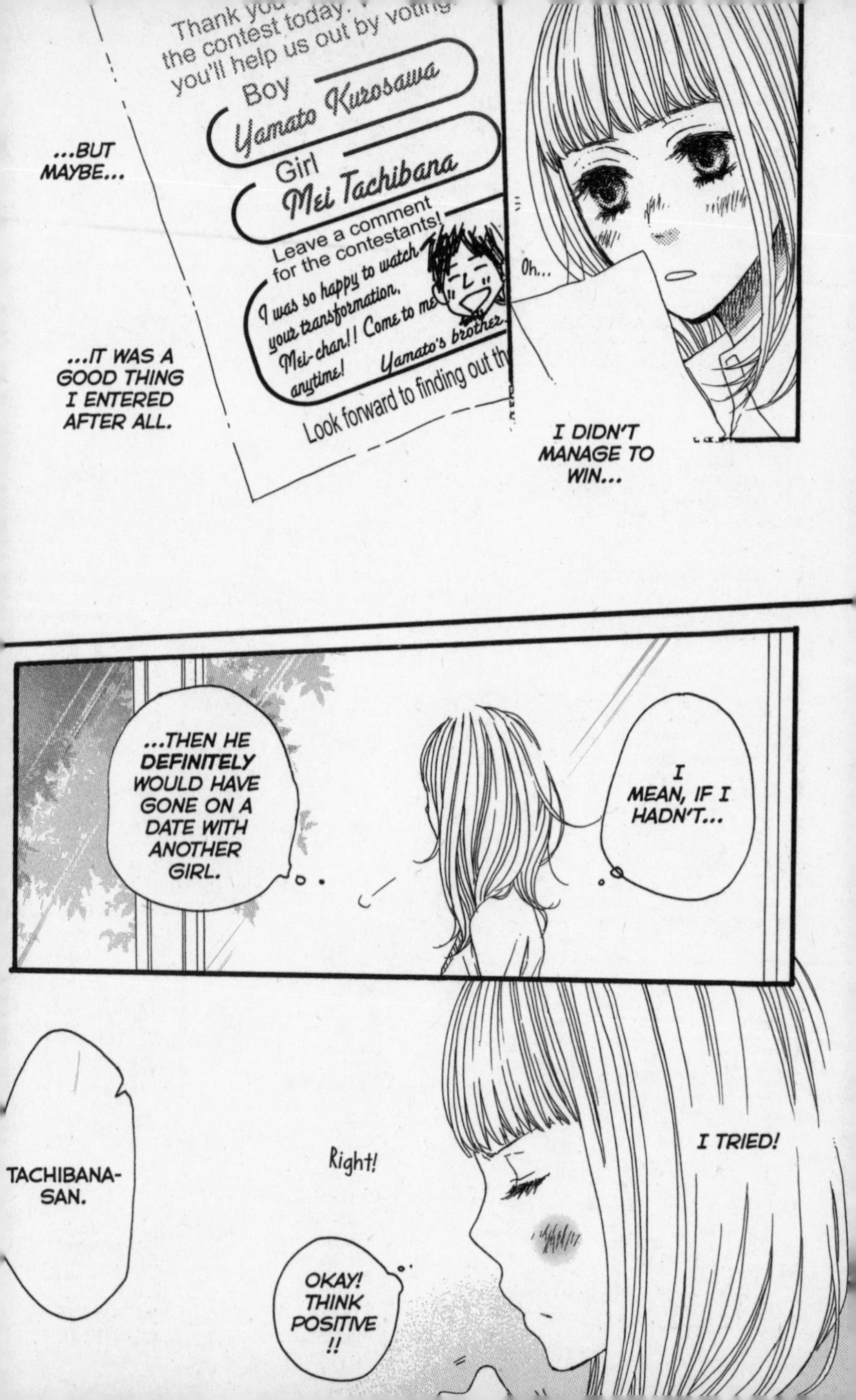

Oh...
I DIDN'T MANAGE TO WIN...
Thank you
the contest today.
you'll help us out by voting.
Boy
Yamato Kurosawa
Girl
Mei Tachibana
Leave a comment for the contestants!
I was so happy to watch your transformation, Mei-chan!! Come to me anytime!
Yamato's brother
Look forward to finding out th
...BUT MAYBE...
...IT WAS A GOOD THING I ENTERED AFTER ALL.
I MEAN, IF I HADN'T...
...THEN HE DEFINITELY WOULD HAVE GONE ON A DATE WITH ANOTHER GIRL.
I TRIED!
OKAY! THINK POSITIVE!!
Right!
TACHIBANA-SAN.

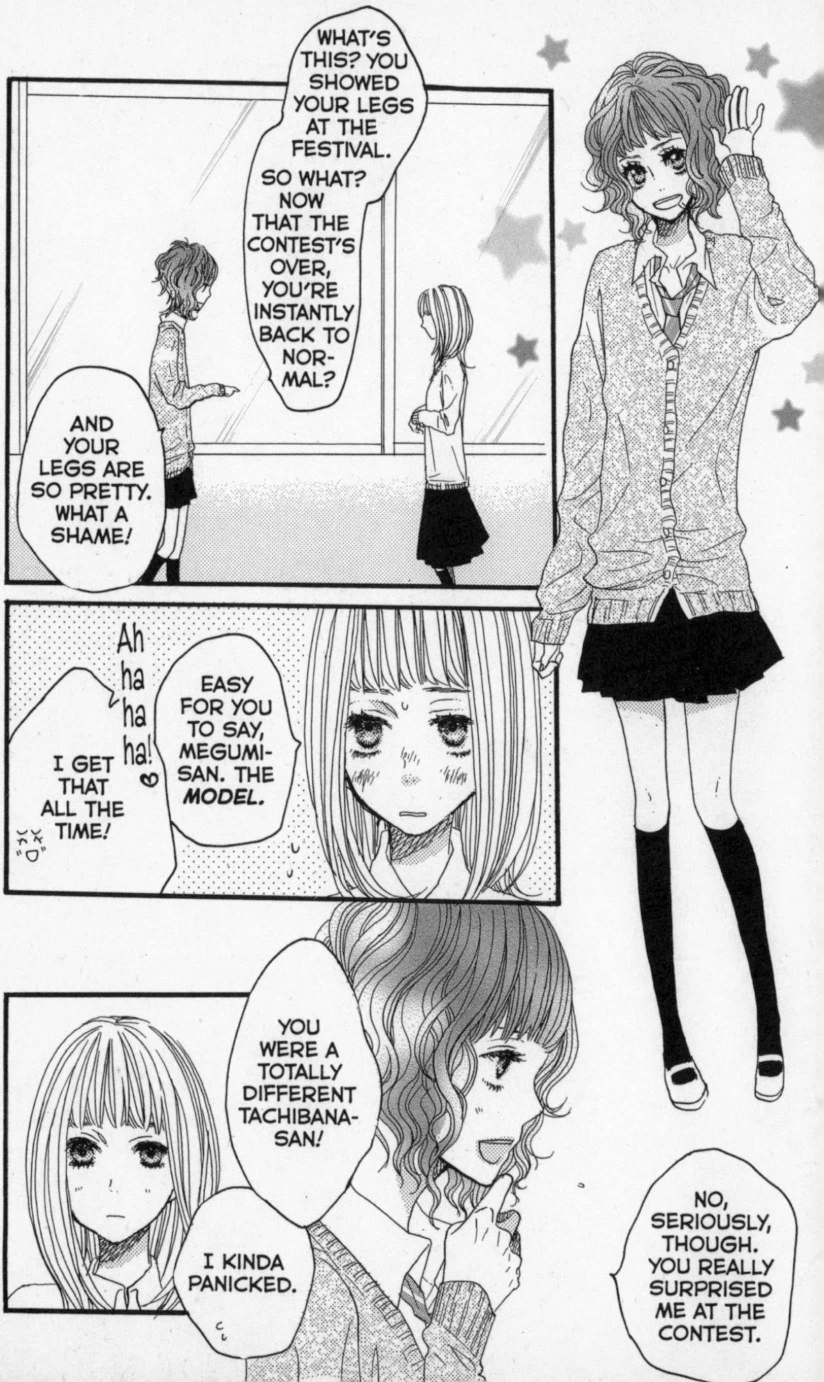
WHAT'S THIS? YOU SHOWED YOUR LEGS AT THE FESTIVAL.
SO WHAT? NOW THAT THE CONTEST'S OVER, YOU'RE INSTANTLY BACK TO NOR-MAL?
AND YOUR LEGS ARE SO PRETTY. WHAT A SHAME!
EASY FOR YOU TO SAY, MEGUMI-SAN. THE *MODEL.*
Ah ha ha ha!
I GET THAT ALL THE TIME!
NO, SERIOUSLY, THOUGH. YOU REALLY SURPRISED ME AT THE CONTEST.
YOU WERE A TOTALLY DIFFERENT TACHIBANA-SAN!
I KINDA PANICKED.

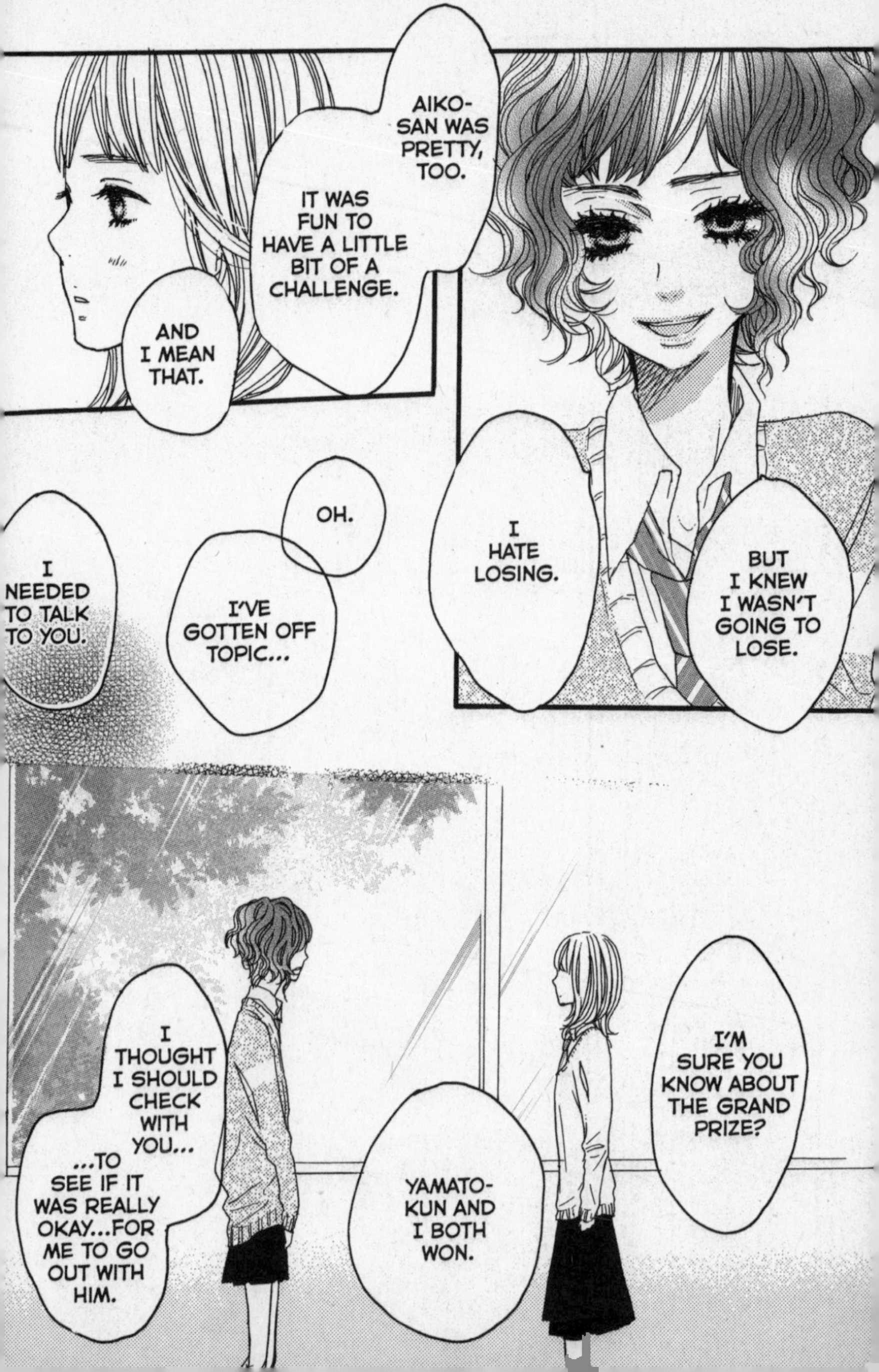
AIKO-SAN WAS PRETTY, TOO.
IT WAS FUN TO HAVE A LITTLE BIT OF A CHALLENGE.
AND I MEAN THAT.
I HATE LOSING.
BUT I KNEW I WASN'T GOING TO LOSE.
OH.
I'VE GOTTEN OFF TOPIC...
I NEEDED TO TALK TO YOU.
I'M SURE YOU KNOW ABOUT THE GRAND PRIZE?
YAMATO-KUN AND I BOTH WON.
I THOUGHT I SHOULD CHECK WITH YOU...
...TO SEE IF IT WAS REALLY OKAY...FOR ME TO GO OUT WITH HIM.

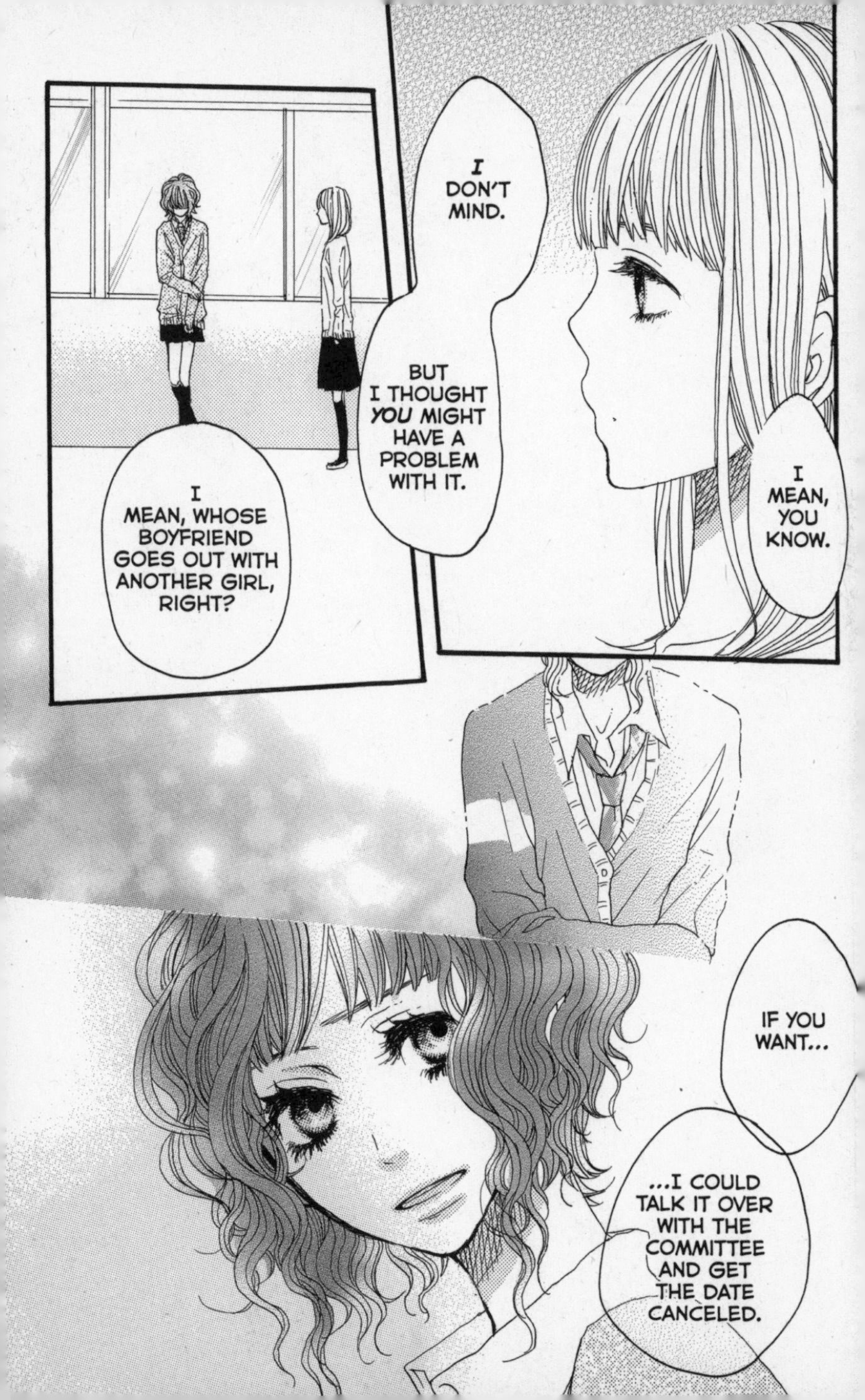
I DON'T MIND.
BUT I THOUGHT *YOU* MIGHT HAVE A PROBLEM WITH IT.
I MEAN, YOU KNOW.
I MEAN, WHOSE BOYFRIEND GOES OUT WITH ANOTHER GIRL, RIGHT?
IF YOU WANT...
...I COULD TALK IT OVER WITH THE COMMITTEE AND GET THE DATE CANCELED.

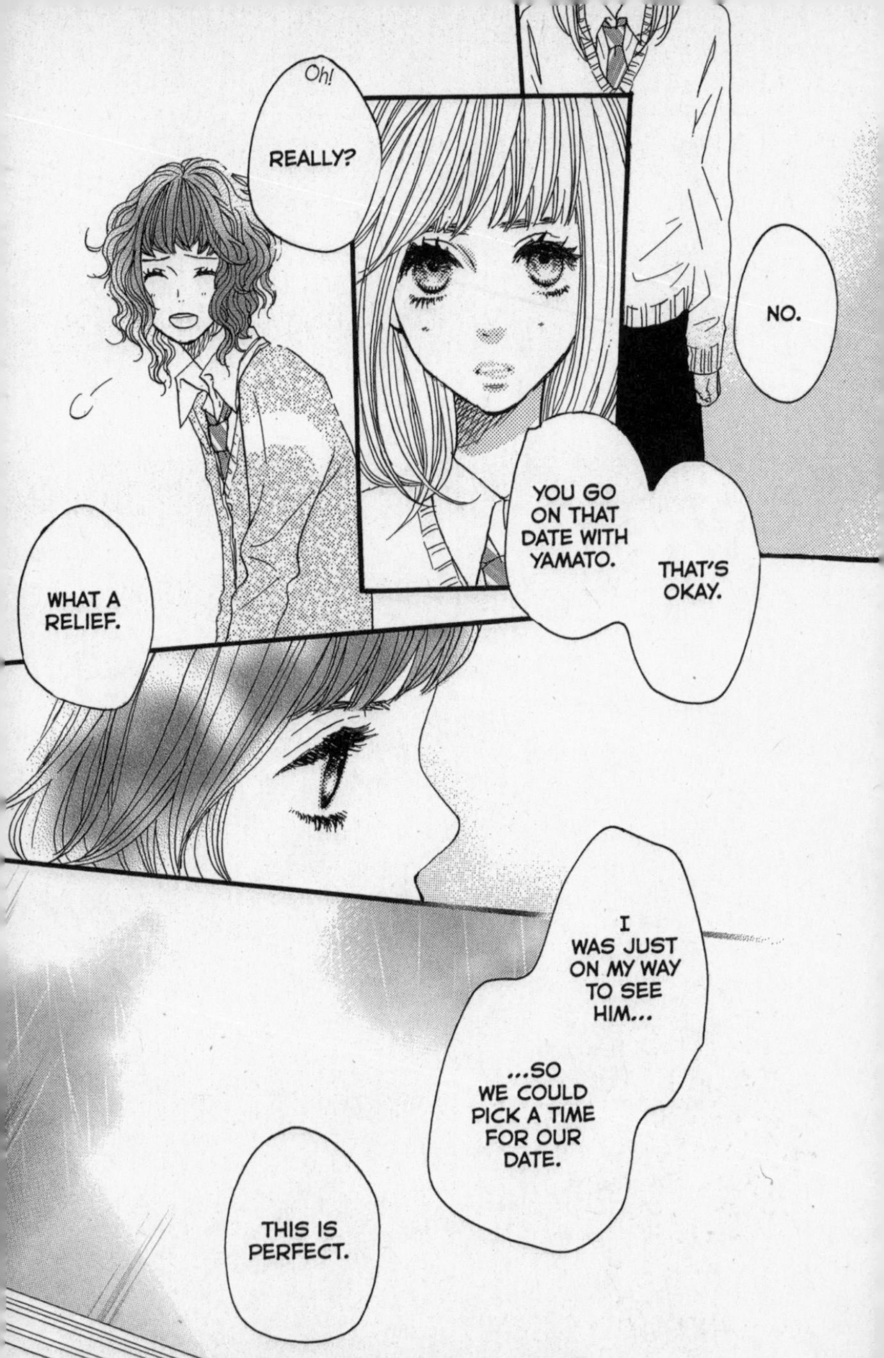
NO.
Oh!
REALLY?
WHAT A RELIEF.
THAT'S OKAY.
YOU GO ON THAT DATE WITH YAMATO.
I WAS JUST ON MY WAY TO SEE HIM...
...SO WE COULD PICK A TIME FOR OUR DATE.
THIS IS PERFECT.

Chapter 32 — End

I hate
losing!!

Hello, Kanae Hazuki here. This is volume eight. Time flies.

Every night, I line up volumes one through eight and smile to myself. When I started the series, I figured it would end pretty quickly, so I didn't put a whole lot of depth into the characters. Now that we're at volume eight, of course, I love each and every one of them so dearly I can hardly stand it. And I love them more every time I draw them. Sorry for being such a doting parent. I'd like to do little spinoff stories for each character, so I really look forward to drawing them even more. I would love for you all to join us.

Now, about what's been going on with me. It's about time, I guess, but after a really long time, I've finally completed my mother's grave! (Sorry to start out with grave stories. I think I've written about my mother in an afterword before, so I thought I'd give a report.) I'd been looking off and on for a grave for some time, but I wanted her to stay with me in my new place for a while, so it took longer than expected.

When my mother was alive, she would say, "When I die, I want to be put in my mother and father's tomb," and at first I thought it would be impossible, but I managed to make her wish come true. I never did anything for her when she was alive, so I'm really sorry that it wasn't until after she was gone, but right now I'm relieved that I was able to do something to honor my mother.

I look back at my life, and I really think that humans are tragic creatures. When someone's alive, we don't appreciate what a blessing it is to have them. We don't realize until after they're gone. I feel it more and more strongly as I get older. I think there are more than a few people who write stuff like this. And, at first, when I read it, I would roll my eyes.

I never really listened to my mother. I was always rebellious. I said lots of terrible things to her, and I caused her a lot of grief. But she never abandoned me. Even as a single mother, she wasn't perfect, but she made sure I had everything I needed. Growing up, I never saw anything but strength from my mother.

And so, when she ended up in the hospital, I thought, "My mom can't get sick; that doesn't happen." I couldn't believe it, and I couldn't bring myself to look her in the face. I didn't want to see my mother weak. But however strong a person is, he or she is still a human being. It's just a matter of strength of mind.

I guess my mom went through a lot when she was alive (a relative told me some stories after her death, and they all shocked me), but everyone said she was kind and caring. These days, I think she was able to be so kind because she went through so much.

Back then, I didn't know any of that. Now I think about how awful I was to her. From now on, I don't want to make that mistake again. I want to develop a heart that can be thoughtful of others. That's one of the last things my mother taught me.

These days, when I meet someone, they all say, "You must really love people, Hazuki-san!" A lot happens when you spend time with different kinds of people, but maybe that's life. Maybe it's because I go through so much that I can enjoy life and be glad I'm alive. As for people... yes, I love them. That's all I can say.

Again, I want to say thank you to all my friends and acquaintances, and everyone who shares their feelings with me through my manga.

—Kanae Hazuki, December 2011

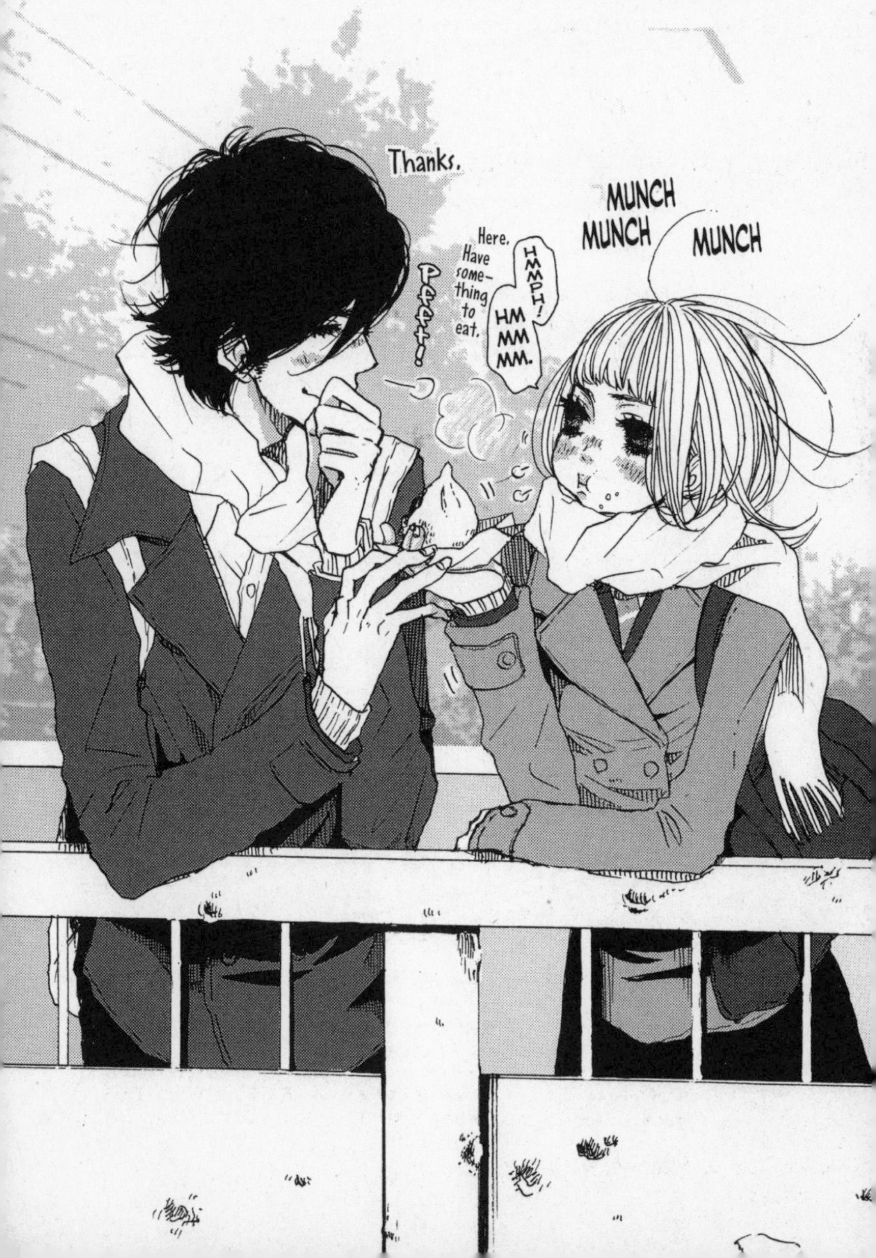
MUNCH
MUNCH
MUNCH
HMMPH! HM MM MM.
Here. Have something to eat.
Thanks.
Pfft!

TRANSLATION NOTES

Page 14: Make an example

The word this girl used was *sarashi-kubi,* which literally means "exposed head." This is a reference to the Edo practice of cutting off a criminal's head and putting it on display as a warning to any other potential lawbreakers. In other words, this twisted young woman plans to publicly humiliate Mei, to teach her, and any other girl who has the gall to take Yamato off the market, what sort of consequences may await them.

HERE
YOU
GO.

CLUNK

Natade Coco

Dietary Fiber

Page 16: Natade coco

Nata de coco is Spanish for "cream of coconut." It is a jelly-like substance made from fermented coconut water, traditionally eaten as a dessert in the Philippines. What Mei is getting now is probably a beverage version.

Page 92: Like a tiger

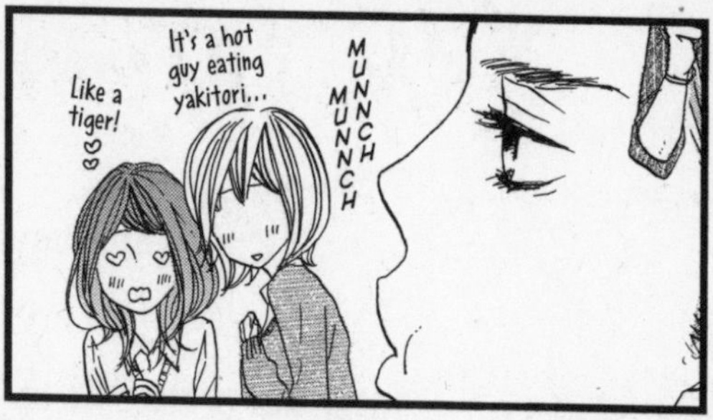
MUNNCH MUNNCH
It's a hot guy eating yakitori...
Like a tiger!

More literally, this girl called Daichi a carnivore—a very accurate description for someone eating meat. But it also has a double meaning. In Japanese dating culture, men and women are sometimes divided into carnivores and herbivores. Carnivores are more aggressive in their pursuit of the opposite sex, which might make for more passionate romance.

Page 94: Daichi's yakitori

Apparently Daichi got two kinds of yakitori—torikawa, or chicken skin, and momo-negima, which is chicken thighs with spring onions.

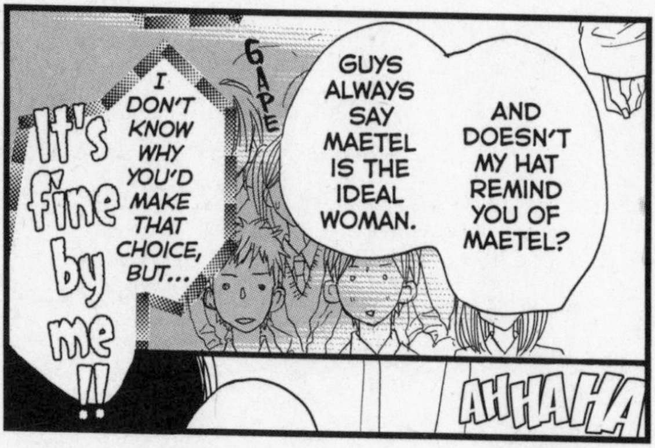
GUYS ALWAYS SAY MAETEL IS THE IDEAL WOMAN.
AND DOESN'T MY HAT REMIND YOU OF MAETEL?
GAPE
I DON'T KNOW WHY YOU'D MAKE THAT CHOICE, BUT...
It's fine by me!!
AHHAHA

Page 100: Maetel

In her choice of headwear, Aiko is trying to look like a character from the manga *Galaxy Express 999.* She is a mysterious and beautiful woman, who was so popular that she starred in more than one spinoff story.

Page 138: Oiwa-san

Oiwa is the heroine of the famous Japanese ghost story "Yotsuya Kaidan." She was given a poison that scarred her face, and caused her hair to fall out. Most depictions of her include at least one drooping eye, so when someone has eyes as puffy as Mei's, people may be reminded of Oiwa.

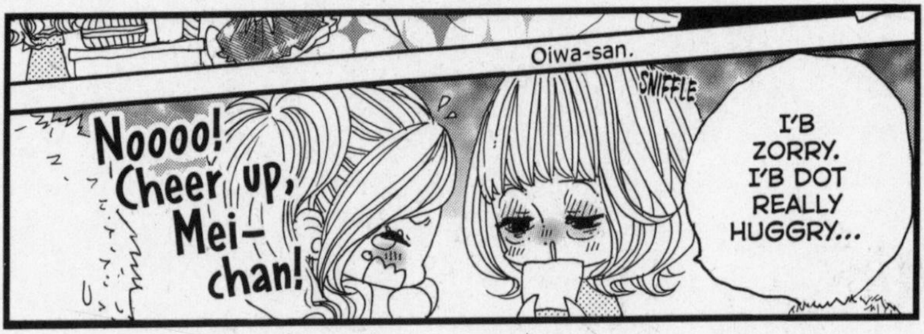
Oiwa-san.
SNIFFLE
I'B ZORRY. I'B DOT REALLY HUGGRY...
Noooo! Cheer up, Mei-chan!

My Little Monster

OPPOSITES ATTRACT...MAYBE?

Haru Yoshida is feared as an unstable and violent "monster." Mizutani Shizuku is a grade-obsessed student with no friends. Fate brings these two together to form the most unlikely pair. Haru firmly believes he's in love with Mizutani and she firmly believes he's insane.

KC
KODANSHA
COMICS

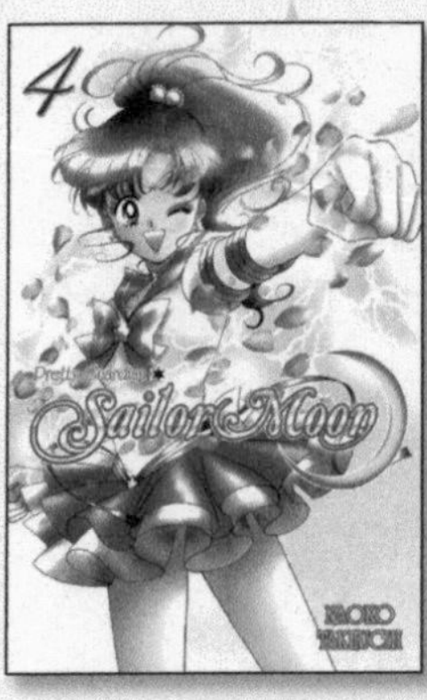
4
Pretty Guardian
Sailor Moon
NAOKO TAKEUCHI

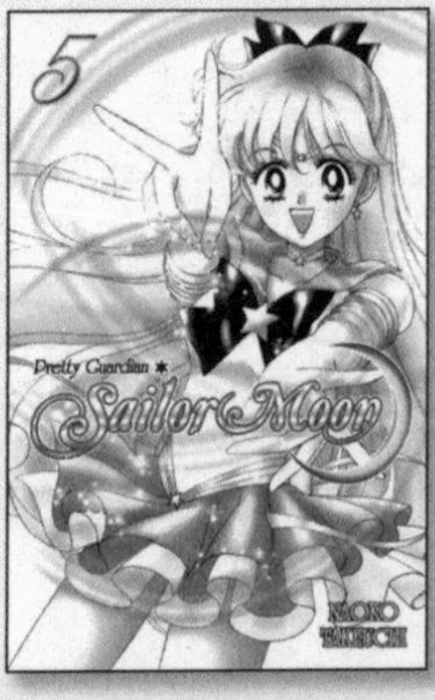
5
Pretty Guardian
Sailor Moon
NAOKO TAKEUCHI

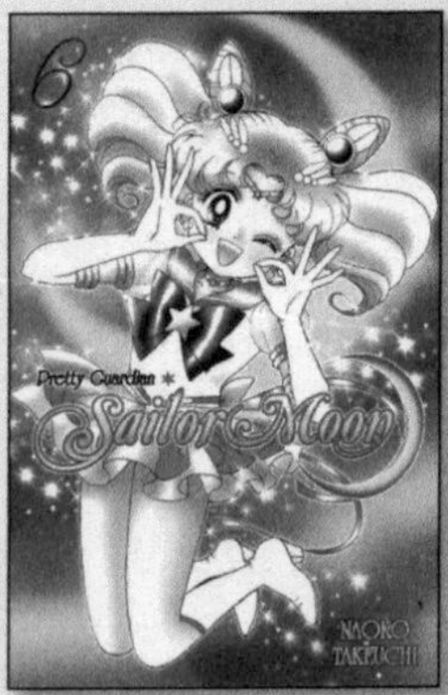
6
Pretty Guardian
Sailor Moon
NAOKO TAKEUCHI

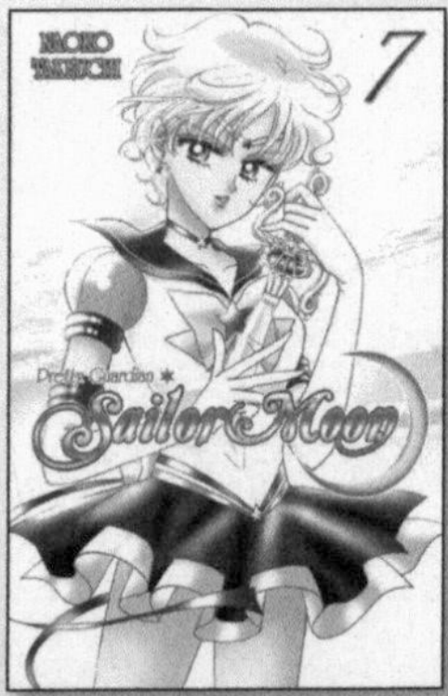
NAOKO TAKEUCHI
7
Sailor Moon

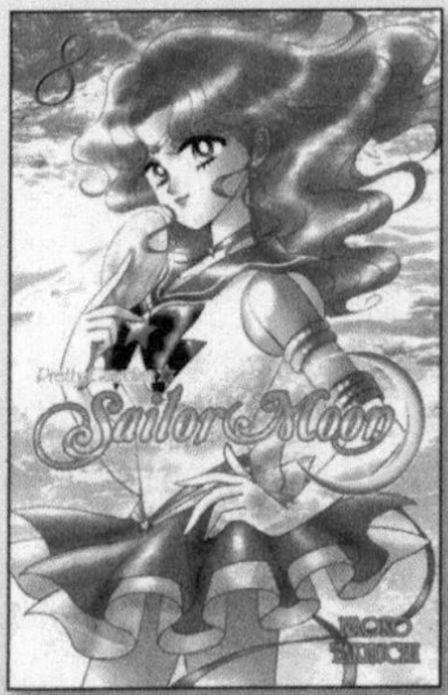
8
Sailor Moon
NAOKO TAKEUCHI

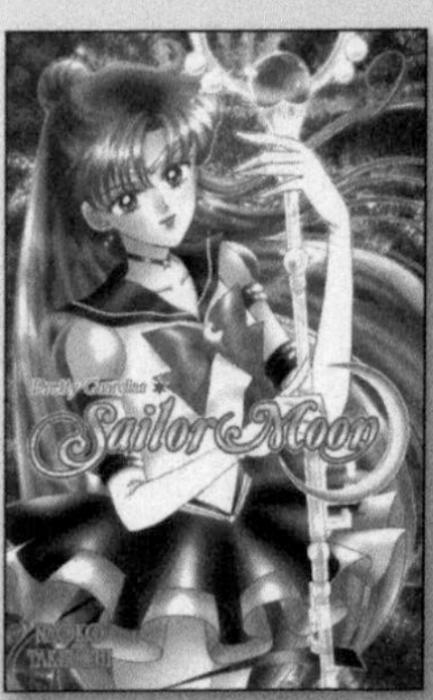
Pretty Guardian
Sailor Moon
NAOKO TAKEUCHI

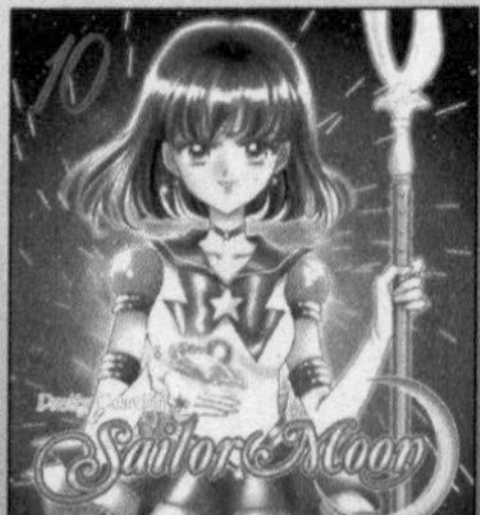
10
Sailor Moon
NAOKO TAKEUCHI

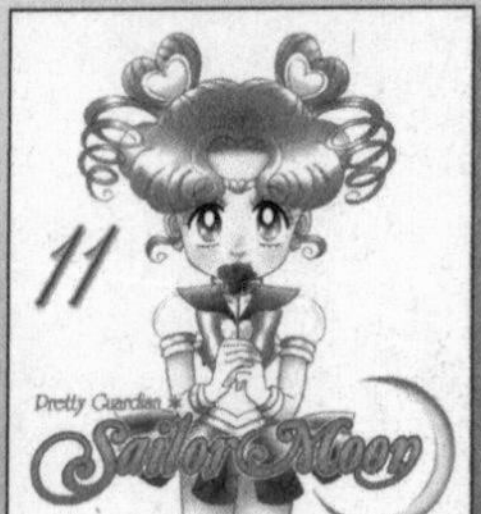
11
Pretty Guardian
Sailor Moon
NAOKO TAKEUCHI

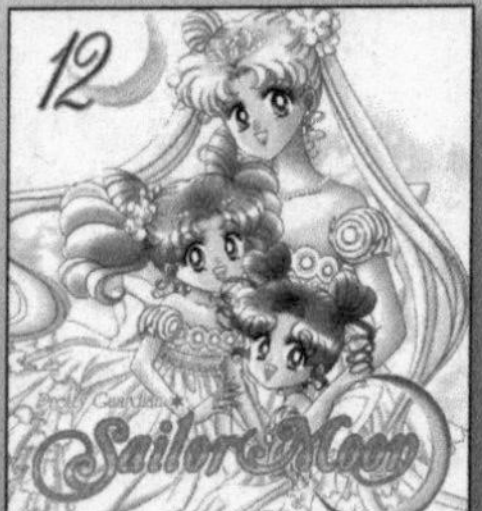
12
Sailor Moon
NAOKO TAKEUCHI

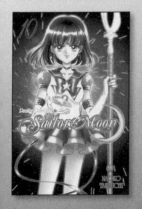

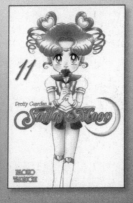

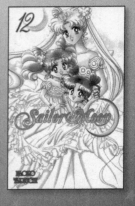

KC
KODANSHA COMICS

The Pretty Guardians
are back!

✴

Kodansha Comics is proud to present
Sailor Moon with all new translations.

For more information, go to **www.kodanshacomics.com**

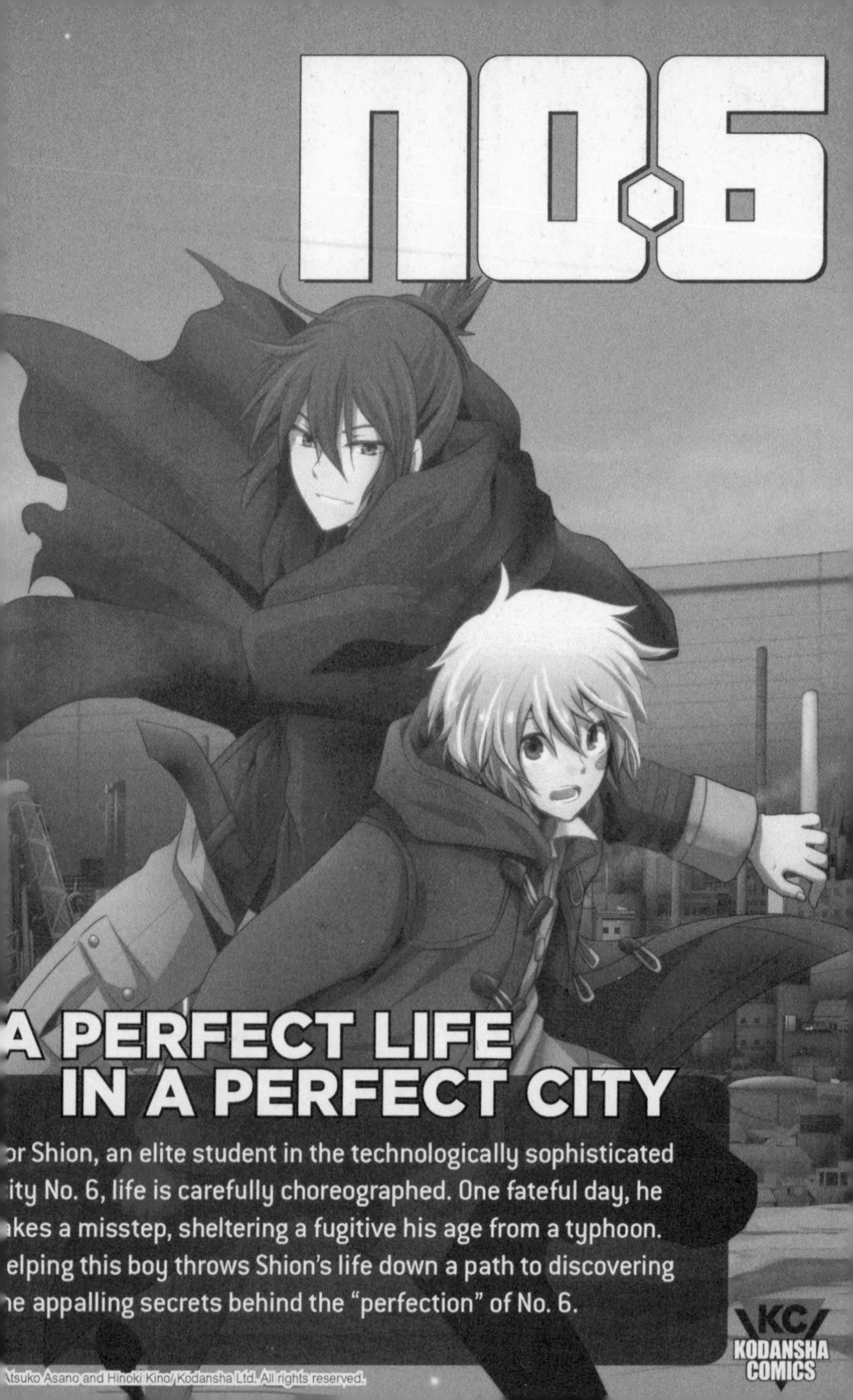
NO.6
A PERFECT LIFE
IN A PERFECT CITY
or Shion, an elite student in the technologically sophisticated
ity No. 6, life is carefully choreographed. One fateful day, he
kes a misstep, sheltering a fugitive his age from a typhoon.
elping this boy throws Shion's life down a path to discovering
e appalling secrets behind the "perfection" of No. 6.
KC
KODANSHA COMICS
Atsuko Asano and Hinoki Kino/Kodansha Ltd. All rights reserved.

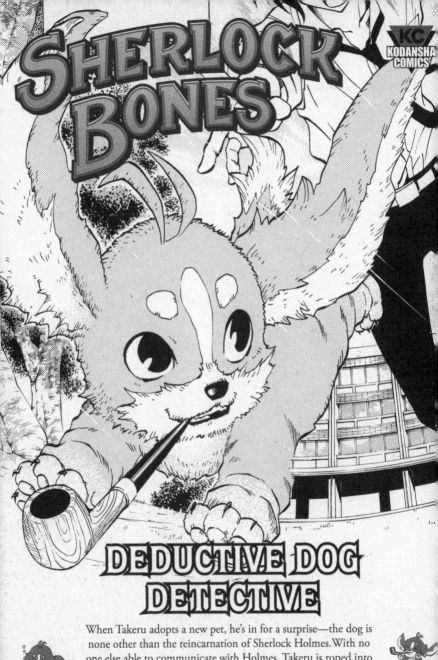

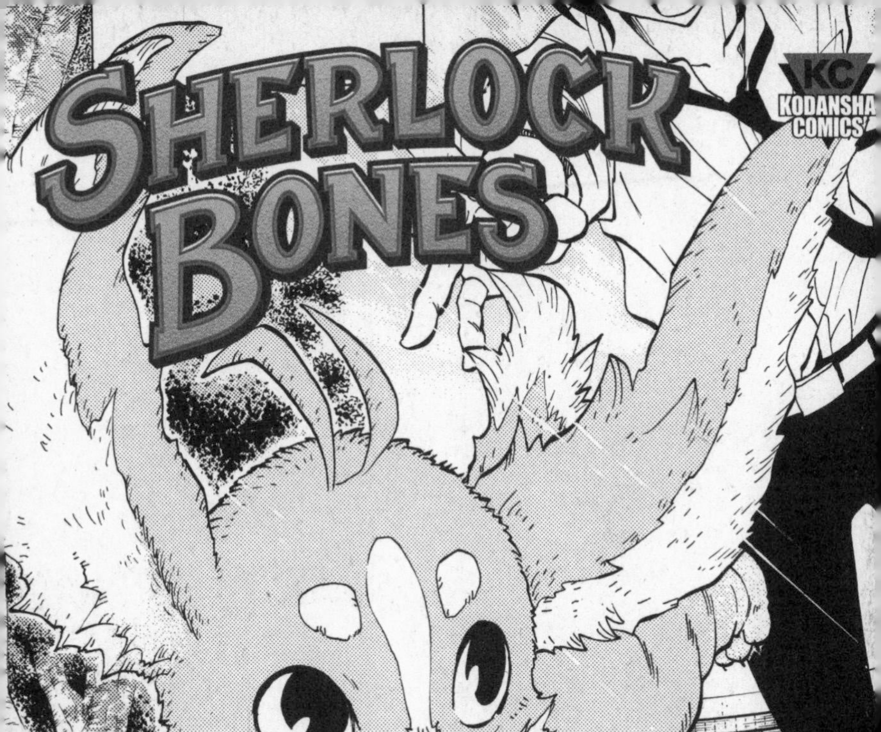
KC
KODANSHA COMICS
SHERLOCK BONES

DEDUCTIVE DOG DETECTIVE

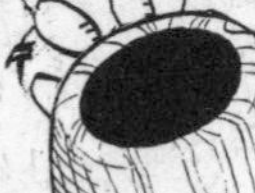

When Takeru adopts a new pet, he's in for a surprise—the dog is none other than the reincarnation of Sherlock Holmes. With no one else able to communicate with Holmes, Takeru is roped into becoming Sherdog's assistant, John Watson. Using his sleuthing skills, Holmes uncovers clues to solve the trickiest crimes.

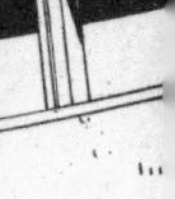

SANKAREA

undying love

"I ONLY LIKE ZOMBIE GIRLS."

Chihiro has an unusual connection to zombie movies. He doesn't feel bad for the survivors – he wants to comfort the undead girls they slaughter! When his pet passes away, he brews a resurrection potion. He's discovered by local heiress Sanka Rea, and she serves as his first test subject!

A Kodansha Comics Trade Paperback Original
Say I Love You. volume 8 copyright © 2012 Kanae Hazuki
English translation copyright © 2015 Kanae Hazuki

Published in the United States by Kodansha Comics, an imprint of Kodansha USA Publishing, LLC, New York.

Publication rights for this English edition arranged through Kodansha Ltd, Tokyo.

First published in Japan in 2012 by Kodansha Ltd., Tokyo as *Sukitte iinayo.* volume 8.

ISBN 978-1-61262-673-4

Printed in the United States of America.

www.kodanshacomics.com

9 8 7 6 5 4 3 2 1
Translation: Alethea and Athena Nibley
Lettering: John Clark
Editing: Ben Applegate
Kodansha Comics edition cover design by Phil Balsman

TOMARE!
STOP

You're going the wrong way!

Manga is a completely different type of reading experience.

To start at the beginning, Go to the end!

That's right! Authentic manga is read the traditional Japanese way—from right to left, exactly the opposite of how American books are read. It's easy to follow: Just go to the other end of the book and read each page—and each panel—from right side to left side, starting at the top right. Now you're experiencing manga as it was meant to be!